Bertolt Brecht's *Furcht und Elend des Dritten Reiches*

Studies in German Literature, Linguistics, and Culture

Bertolt Brecht's *Furcht und Elend des Dritten Reiches*

A German Exile Drama in the Struggle against Fascism

John J. White and Ann White

CAMDEN HOUSE

Rochester, New York

First published 2010
by Camden House

Camden House is an imprint of Boydell & Brewer Inc.
668 Mt. Hope Avenue, Rochester, NY 14620, USA
www.camden-house.com
and of Boydell & Brewer Limited
PO Box 9, Woodbridge, Suffolk IP12 3DF, UK
www.boydellandbrewer.com

ISBN-13: 978-1-57113-373-1
ISBN-10: 1-57113-373-9

Library of Congress Cataloging-in-Publication Data

White, John J., 1940–
    Bertolt Brecht's Furcht und elend des dritten reiches: a German exile
drama in the struggle against fascism / John J. White and Ann White.
        p. cm. — (Studies in German literature, linguistics, and culture)
Includes bibliographical references and index.
ISBN-13: 978-1-57113-373-1 (acid-free paper)
ISBN-10: 1-57113-373-9 (acid-free paper)
    1. Brecht, Bertolt, 1898–1956. Furcht und Elend des III. Reiches.
I. White, Ann. II. Title. III. Series.

PT2603.R397F839 2010
832'.912—dc22
                                                                2010004401

A catalogue record for this title is available from the British Library.

This publication is printed on acid-free paper.
Printed in the United States of America.

Contents

Acknowledgments

SOME PARTS OF THE ARGUMENT in Chapters Four, Five, and Six of the present study are based on readings that have been published elsewhere in an earlier form. We are grateful to the Modern Humanities Research Association for permission to re-use material from "Bertolt Brecht's *Furcht und Elend des III. Reiches* and the Moscow 'Realism' Controversy," first published in *The Modern Language Review* in 2005. A draft of Chapter Five was presented as a paper at the international conference "Bertolt Brecht: A Reassessment of His Work and Legacy," held at the Institute of Germanic and Romance Studies, School of Advanced Studies (University of London), in February 2006. We should like to thank Gerd Labroisse, editor of the Rodopi series *Amsterdamer Beiträge zur Neueren Germanistik*, for permission to use some sections of our London paper in the present volume. We also want to express our thanks to the following friends and colleagues for commenting on various versions of the present study and for other forms of help given during our work on the project: Robert Gillett (London), Michael Minden (Cambridge), Hamish Ritchie (Sheffield), Ritchie Robertson (Oxford), Ronald Speirs (Birmingham), Martin Swales (London), Alfred Trupat (Berlin), and Godela Weiss-Sussex (London). We owe a special debt of gratitude to William Abbey, former librarian of the erstwhile Institute of Germanic Studies in the School of Advanced Studies, University of London. Bill, a scholar-librarian of the old school, was of inestimable help to us in our search for early versions of *Furcht und Elend* and material relating to Brecht's exile antifascist work. He is the embodiment of the academic ethos of a specialist research library. We should also like to thank Camden House's two expert readers, Stephen Brockmann (Carnegie Mellon University, Pittsburgh) and Stephen Parker (University of Manchester), for their challenging queries, comments, and suggestions. We are much indebted to Edward Batchelder for his scrupulous copy editing, valuable observations, and assistance with presentation. Particular thanks go, as always, to Jim Walker at Camden House for encouraging the present project and for the tireless patience with which he helped us nurse it through to completion.

This book is dedicated to Jonathan White (London School of Economics) and Lea Ypi (Nuffield College, Oxford) for all the support and encouragement they gave us over the years.

J. J. W. and A. W.
March 2010

Textual Note

IN THE FOLLOWING STUDY, quotations in German from *Furcht und Elend des Dritten Reiches* and references to individual parts of the play are to the version in the *Große kommentierte Berliner und Frankfurter Ausgabe* (*BFA* 4:339–453). This standard thirty-volume scholarly edition is also our source when other material by Brecht is cited in the German original. The *BFA* text of the play, published in 1988 as *Furcht und Elend des III. Reiches*, is that of a surviving Prague galley proof dating from 1938. The *BFA* corpus comprises twenty-seven scenes arranged in the sequence approved by Brecht for publication in Volume 3 of the aborted Malik-Verlag edition of his *Gesammelte Werke*. (Two further scenes, "Der Gefühlsersatz" and "Moorsoldaten," are contained in an appendix to the main corpus.) Our decision to work with this source is, however, not unproblematic. Some scenes subsequently added to the ever-changing corpus do not appear here, nor does the expository information about the setting and date of each episode that was printed at the beginning of each scene in later versions. Some scenes that formed part of the *Malik Ur*-version were dropped or replaced in subsequent editions. Those relegated to the *BFA* appendix are, unfortunately, made to appear less important, even though one of them was eventually integrated into the *Aurora* edition (New York, 1945) that superseded the planned *Malik* sequence. The *Aurora* edition became the textual basis for virtually all subsequent versions of *Furcht und Elend*, including those in the East and West German Suhrkamp editions of Brecht's *Gesammelte Stücke*, upon which the Methuen translation (*Fear and Misery of the Third Reich*) is based. The order of scenes in the *Aurora* edition differs significantly from that in prior publications. It represents the final text approved for publication by the playwright: the "Ausgabe letzter Hand."

Nonetheless, in the chapters of our study that follow, pagination and indications of a scene's position within the sequence refer to the version in *BFA* 4, which is now the standard edition of Brecht's collected works, so far as Brecht scholarship is concerned. The notes to this edition, details of variants, and copious documentation of the work's genesis and reception make it indispensable for anyone working on Brecht. Major differences in the order of scenes in other editions of *Furcht und Elend* have, where appropriate, been taken into account in our analyses. Substantial reference will also be made to *The Private Life of the Master Race*, the first

English translation of some of the work's principal scenes. Although never reprinted after 1944, this version remains crucial to an understanding of the complex evolution of Brecht's *Furcht und Elend* project.

In responding to our publisher's request to supply, where we felt it was appropriate, English translations for passages from Brecht's writings quoted in German, we have, whenever possible, cited the standard published English translations, using the abbreviations given in the list that follows. Where published translations are not available, we offer our own. For reasons of space, we have not normally offered English translations in our footnotes, nor have we translated passages from secondary literature, historical sources, or the writings of other German exile literature cited in footnotes, unless we felt that these were vital to our readings.

Note

Titles of individual published works by Brecht that were not given, or approved, by him follow the *BFA* convention of indicating this by the use of square brackets.

Abbreviations of Works Frequently Cited

Aurora Bertolt Brecht, *Furcht und Elend des III. Reiches: 24 Szenen* (New York: Aurora, 1945).

BAP *Brecht on Art and Politics*, ed. Tom Kuhn and Steve Giles, trans. Laura Bradley, Steve Giles, and Tom Kuhn (London: Methuen, 2003).

BBB *Die Bibliothek Bertolt Brechts: Ein kommentiertes Verzeichnis.* Bearbeitet von Erdmut Wizisla, Helgrid Streidt, and Heidrun Loeper (Frankfurt am Main: Suhrkamp, 2007). Items by published catalogue number.

BBJ Bertolt Brecht, *Journals, 1934–1955*, ed. John Willett, trans. Hugh Rorrison (London: Methuen, 1993).

BBL Bertolt Brecht, *Letters, 1913–1956*, ed. with commentary and notes by John Willett, trans. Ralph Manheim (London: Methuen, 1990).

BBP Bertolt Brecht, *Poems, 1913–1956*, ed. John Willett and Ralph Manheim, with the co-operation of Erich Fried (London: Eyre Methuen, 1978).

BFA Bertolt Brecht, *Große kommentierte Berliner und Frankfurter Ausgabe*, ed. Werner Hecht, Jan Knopf, Werner Mittenzwei, and Klaus-Detlef Müller, 30 vols. + *Registerband* (Berlin, Weimar: Aufbau and Frankfurt am Main: Suhrkamp, 1988–2000). By volume and page number.

BHB *Brecht-Handbuch in fünf Bänden*, ed. Jan Knopf (Stuttgart, Weimar: Metzler, 2001–3). By volume and page number.

BMD Bertolt Brecht, *The Messingkauf Dialogues*, ed. and trans. John Willett (London: Methuen, 1965).

BT *Brecht on Theatre*, ed. and trans. John Willett (London: Methuen, 1964).

FM Bertolt Brecht, *Fear and Misery of the Third Reich*, ed. and introduced by John Willett and Tom Kuhn, trans. John Willett (London: Methuen, 2002).

GW   Bertolt Brecht, *Gesammelte Werke: Werkausgabe*, ed. Suhrkamp Verlag in collaboration with Elisabeth Hauptmann, 20 vols. (Frankfurt am Main: Suhrkamp, 1967). By volume and page number.

Malik   Bertolt Brecht, *Furcht und Elend des III. Reiches*, galley-proof version (Prague: Malik-Verlag, 1938). First published in 1988 in *BFA* 4:339–455.

MEW   Karl Marx and Friedrich Engels, *Werke*, ed. Institut für Marxismus-Leninismus beim ZK der SED (Berlin: Dietz, 1956–90). By volume and page number.

The Private Life Bertolt Brecht, *The Private Life of the Master Race: A Documentary Play*, trans. Eric Russell Bentley, assisted by Elisabeth Hauptmann (New York: New Directions, 1944).

1: The Historical Context of the *Furcht und Elend* Project

WRITING IN MARCH 1938 to Wieland Herzfelde of the Malik-Verlag, an influential left-wing German publisher by then in exile in Prague, Bertolt Brecht made the first of a series of pleas for expediting the publication of his *Gedichte im Exil* (Poems Written in Exile) and a new play with the working-title *Deutschland — Ein Greuelmärchen* (Germany — an Atrocity Story). It was not by chance that one of these two literary exposés of the ugly reality of Hitler's Third Reich was a cycle of mainly satirical poems and the other a series of dramatized illustrations of life during the first five years of National Socialist rule. Satirical poetry and political drama were by this time the two genres Brecht tended to favor for his orchestrated campaign of attacks on the ruthless dictatorial regime that had driven numerous German writers and intellectuals into exile and was now threatening many of the country's European neighbors. What made Brecht's new antifascist play[1] exceptional was the fact that the method of attack had now changed. *Deutschland — Ein Greuelmärchen* (later to bear the title *Furcht und Elend des Dritten Reiches*) was neither an austerely didactic play (*Lehrstück*) in the manner of Brecht's early political theater nor was it a piece of Epic Theater making its propaganda points via a series of often contrived "anti-illusionistic" illustrations. In generic terms, it occupied a unique position among Brecht's antifascist works by virtue of its subtle combination of documented source material, a series of fictive, yet plausibly realistic, incidents, and a framework designed to embrace both Epic and Aristotelian elements. Brecht's letter to Slatan Dudow of 24 April 1938 modestly describes the entire project as "technically interesting" (*BFA* 29:90), which in many respects it most emphatically is. More importantly, however, *Furcht und Elend*'s unforgettable pictures of harsh life in Third Reich Germany and the play's theatrical contribution to our

---

[1] Brecht had already published two antifascist dramas in the 1930s: the parable play *Die Rundköpfe und die Spitzköpfe* (1932) and the Spanish Civil War play *Die Gewehre der Frau Carrar* (1937). After *Furcht und Elend*, he went on to write further antifascist works, including the first version of *Leben des Galilei* (1939), *Der Aufstieg des Arturo Ui* (1941) and *Schweyk* (1943). He also collaborated on Fritz Lang's film about the assassination of Reinhard Heydrich: *Hangmen Also Die* (1943).

understanding of what is nowadays called "Alltagsfaschismus" (everyday fascism) are a rare achievement among exile literature's continuously proliferating depictions of the Hitler regime's impact on Germany's seventy million citizens, a population soon to rise to around eighty million as a result of various territorial plebiscites and annexations.

Although optimistically conceived with theater performance foremost in mind, *Furcht und Elend* more often than not tended to make its way into the public arena via the prepublication of a string of seemingly autonomous individual scenes. While initial dissemination of extracts from plays via literary journals and the substitution of *Buchdrama* for live performance were common enough phenomena during the exile years, this unavoidable feature of *Furcht und Elend*'s reception persisted well into postwar decades.[2] Brecht's friend Walter Benjamin tried to make a virtue of the predicament, claiming that the play's ingenious montage of powerful scenes could appeal to a reading public as much as to theater audiences,[3] an assertion at odds with Brecht's own position. "Das *Lesen* der Stücke, die doch eigentlich immer Soufflierbücher sind," Brecht once confessed to the painter George Grosz, "ist ungemein schwer" (*BFA* 28:484; It's exceedingly difficult to *read* the plays, which are actually nothing more than prompt books: *BBL* 198). That is to say, he felt that the dialogue demanded more contextual support, visual detail, and stage presence than the printed page could usually offer.[4] As early as May 1933, Brecht had taken exception to his theater agent's assumption that none of his plays was likely to be staged in the foreseeable future (*BFA* 28:358). Despite such a bleak prospect, his tireless devotion to the practicalities of staging *Furcht und Elend* and his other antifascist plays is well documented. For example, he suggests in 1938, the year of *Furcht und Elend*'s premiere, that a series of short plays ("eine Reihe kleiner Stücke (zu zehn Minuten)") could, together with *Die Gewehre der Frau Carrar* (Señora Carrar's Rifles) make a full evening (*BFA* 29:36). Such a claim seems to have ignored the fact that one of the play's main challenges was its overall length.[5] By 1938, the work was already becoming, on

---

[2] After attending a seminar for proletarian students at Leipzig University in January 1949, Brecht complained that young people only knew the book edition of *Furcht und Elend* (*BFA* 27:299). This was hardly surprising, given that both the Soviet Zone of Occupation and the later GDR authorities had little time for literary attempts at coming to terms with what they claimed was an exclusively West German problem.

[3] "Das Land, in dem das Proletariat nicht genannt werden darf: Zur Uraufführung von acht Einaktern Brechts" (*Die Neue Weltbühne*, 30 June 1938).

[4] In his letter to Herzfelde of March 1938, Brecht compromises by suggesting that the play was "ein großes Stück [und] eigentlich auch ein Lesestück" (*BFA* 29:79).

[5] According to James K. Lyon, *Bertolt Brecht in America* (Princeton: Princeton UP, 1980), 138, "virtually every reviewer of the American stage-adaptation faulted

Brecht's admission, a project of enormous dimensions (*BFA* 29:88). Very few of the play's scenes would take a mere ten minutes to perform. Not that the problem of burgeoning length ever deterred Brecht from continuing his energetic crusade on behalf of the project! His correspondence for the first half of 1938 repeatedly displays a paternalistic concern with ensuring that Dudow, the Bulgarian director of the Paris production, got the German casting for the principal parts and other details right (*BFA* 29:86–87). Even throughout the darkest years of Scandinavian and American exile, Brecht's journal entries and correspondence remain full of suggestions about ways in which *Furcht und Elend* might be staged, how the material could be bulked out or, if necessary, pruned. He unstintingly gave advice on which actors, music, and stage sets should be used, and how such an essentially "German" work might be repackaged to reach as large an audience and in as palatable a form as was possible under current exile conditions.

The Predicament of German Antifascist Writers: Agendas and Setbacks

The following two passages from "Bericht über die Stellung der Deutschen im Exil" (*BFA* 23:32–33; Report on the situation of Germans in exile), written when Brecht was contemplating staging and ultimately publishing *The Private Life of the Master Race*, sum up some of the feelings and the pressures under which such a work had been written, staged, and eventually brought to press:

> Die Deutschen im Exil sind wohl einstimmig in diesem Krieg für die Niederlage Deutschlands. Sie bedauern jeden Sieg der deutschen Waffen, sie begrüßen jeden Fehlschlag. Sie wissen, daß jeder Fehlschlag tausend deutscher Soldaten das Leben kostet, aber auch jeder Sieg kostet Tausenden deutscher Soldaten das Leben. [. . .] Ein Sieg würde die ganze bewohnte Welt in solchem Elend sehen, Deutschland natürlich eingeschlossen. Dieses System blutiger Unterdrückung, hemmungsloser Profitiererei, völliger Unfreiheit würde wie eine einzige ungeheure Dreckwelle alles verschlingen, was von den Völkern in Hunderten von Jahren mit solchen Opfern errungen wurde. Die endgültige Niederlage Deutschlands hingegen wird nicht nur die andern Völker von der ständigen Bedrohung befreien, sondern auch das deutsche Volk. (*BFA* 23:32)

> [Germans in exile are, it is fair to say, unanimously in favour of Germany's defeat in this war. They regret every victory won by German

---

[*The Private Life*] for its length and its slow gait," even though it consisted of only nine of the original twenty-seven *Furcht und Elend* scenes.

weapons, they welcome every failure. They know that each failure costs the lives of thousands of German soldiers, but equally that every German victory costs the lives of thousands of German soldiers. The inevitable final defeat of Hitler's Germany will see our country in inconceivable misery. A victory would see the entire inhabited world in such misery, naturally including Germany. This system of bloody oppression, unbridled profiteering and complete lack of freedom would, like a single tidal wave of mud, swallow up everything that the people of different nations had achieved through centuries of sacrifice. The final defeat of Germany, on the other hand, will liberate not only the people of other nations from constant threat, but also the German people. (*BAP* 292)]

Having summed up the ambiguous predicament and feelings of Germans in exile, Brecht moves on to the role of their antifascist program and the hopes they had that Germans in the homeland would play a major part in the Third Reich's downfall:

Wir hoffen, wir sagen, was das deutsche Volk selber sagen würde, könnte es reden. Wir sagen, daß Hitler und seine Hintermänner nicht Deutschland sind, was immer sie behaupten mögen. Daß sie Deutschland sind, das ist die erste ihrer unverschämten Lügen. In Wahrheit haben sie die Deutschen unterworfen, wie sie die Tschechen oder die Franzosen unterworfen haben. Sie haben das deutsche Volk unterworfen mit Polizeigewalt und Propaganda, wie sie die fremden Völker mit Militärgewalt und falschen Versprechungen unterworfen haben. Sie haben Franzosen und Engländer und Tschechen eingefangen mit Propaganda, wie sie Deutsche eingefangen haben. Diese Eingefangenen werden aufwachen. Sie werden aufwachen oder untergehen. Sie werden überzeugt werden können oder beseitigt werden müssen. An dem endgültigen Sieg über Hitler und seine Hintermänner in Militär, Diplomatie und Finanz wird das deutsche Volk einen gewaltigen Anteil haben. (*BFA* 23:33)

[We trust that we are saying what the German people itself would say, if it could talk. We say that Hitler and his backers are not Germany, whatever they may claim. Their claim to represent Germany is the first of their barefaced lies. The truth is that they have subjugated the Germans, like they subjugated the Czechs or the French. They have subjugated the German people with the violent authority of the police and with propaganda, just as they have subjugated foreign peoples with the violence of the military and with false promises. They have captured French, English and Czech people with their propaganda, just as they have captured Germans. But these captives will awake. Either they will awake, or they will perish. Either they will allow themselves to be convinced, or they will have to be removed. The German people will have an immense role in the final victory over Hitler and his backers in the military, diplomatic service and the world of finance. (*BAP* 293)]

Brecht may have nurtured misplaced hopes about the German people's role in bringing about the defeat of Third Reich Germany, but the above passages give some sense of the thinking that lay behind the *Furcht und Elend* project, both during the build up to hostilities (the context of the original *Furcht und Elend des III. Reiches*) and during the Second World War itself, when *The Private Life* came into being.

Originally scheduled to appear in Volume 3 of the *Malik* edition of his *Gesammelte Werke*,[6] the work that would become known as *Furcht und Elend des Dritten Reiches* was, Brecht suggested to Herzfelde, "wahrscheinlich das repräsentativste, was ich, seit wir aus Deutschland heraußen sind, veröffentlichen kann" (*BFA* 29:79; probably the most representative work that I am able to publish since we left Germany). *Gedichte im Exil* and *Deutschland — Ein Greuelmärchen*, he insisted, "*müßten*, vor allem aus politischen Gründen, noch dieses Jahr herauskommen" (ibid.; *have* to appear this year, above all for political reasons).[7] As late as July 1941, Brecht, now in the United States, still expressed the opinion that, of all his antifascist works, "beinahe die meisten Chancen scheint [. . .] *Furcht und Elend des Dritten Reiches* zu haben" (*BFA* 29:208; It now seems to me that *Fear and Misery of the Third Reich* might almost have the best chances: *BBL* 336). Due in no small part to his tireless campaigning on its behalf, the work would become the first to date of Brecht's major plays to be put on in the United States, although unfortunately represented by a modest handful of scenes at that time.

Brecht's main political reasons for placing *Deutschland — Ein Greuelmärchen* and *Gedichte im Exil* at the top of his publication agenda back in 1938 were self-evident under the circumstances. The Hitler regime's aggressive expansionist policy had by then begun systemati-

---

[6] Volume 3 of Brecht's collected works had been scheduled to include a representative cross-section of plays from the Weimar Republic years: *Baal*, *Leben König Eduards des Zweiten von England*, *Im Dickicht der Städte*, and *Trommeln in der Nacht*. Brecht later toyed with the idea of a miscellany that would place *Furcht und Elend* in more meaningful antifascist combinations alongside *Die Gewehre der Frau Carrar*, *Leben des Galilei*, *Deutsche Kriegsfibel 1937*, and "Fünf Schwierigkeiten beim Schreiben der Wahrheit." A further project was at one stage considered, to be called "Neunzehnhundertachtunddreißig." This would have combined *Furcht und Elend* with *Gedichte im Exil* and three essays (*BFA* 29:98). Which essays the playwright had in mind is not specified.

[7] Herzfelde's original plan had been to publish *Die Gewehre der Frau Carrar* and *Deutschland — Ein Greuelmärchen* as freestanding volumes before bringing them out in the *Gesammelte Werke* edition together with other items. By the end of May 1938, Brecht was becoming impatient: "nach allem, was ich über die Pariser Aufnahme [. . .] höre, scheint es mir ganz unumgänglich, daß man dieses Stück [*Furcht und Elend*] *sofort* veröffentlicht. Herbst ist viel zu spät" (*BFA* 29:95).

cally to target much of continental Europe, including a number of territories confiscated from a defeated Germany by the Versailles Treaty of 1919. With the 1935 Saar Plebiscite deciding in Germany's favor[8] and the French-occupied Rhineland region having been audaciously repossessed by the German military in 1936, Hitler's territorial intentions towards Czechoslovakia, the Polish Corridor, Memelland, and — despite repeated disclaimers on his part — Alsace-Lorraine had become too saber-rattling to ignore. Virtually half of Europe now found itself facing the threat of an unprovoked attack from the Third Reich, invariably to be followed by punitive occupation and systematic economic exploitation, as the Versailles Treaty's conditions were deliberately flouted alongside the requirements of the League of Nations, from which Third Reich Germany had withdrawn for tactical reasons in October 1933. In the wake of Germany's annexation of Austria in March 1938, the Nazi majority among Czechoslovakia's Sudeten Germans promptly ratcheted up their campaign to be integrated into the new Greater Germany (*Großdeutschland*). The infamous Munich Agreement responded that same year by handing over the entire Sudetenland region to Nazi Germany in fulfillment of Neville Chamberlain's misguided appeasement policy, soon predictably interpreted by its beneficiaries as giving the Third Reich a green light for the invasion of the Czech provinces of Bohemia and Moravia and their incorporation into Hitler's newly created *Reichsprotektorat*. These territorial achievements, coupled with the fact that Germany was still successfully continuing its covert involvement in the Spanish Civil War on General Franco's Nationalist side, gave Hitler sufficient leeway to set his sights on further irredentist goals in western Poland and Upper Silesia. The widespread threat to European peace that these developments collectively represented, together with the intolerably oppressive conditions within Third Reich Germany itself, account for the urgency of Brecht's claim that *Deutschland — Ein Greuelmärchen* needed to be published before the year was out. The truth about Nazi Germany needed to be known by the outside world. "Kein deutscher Wissenschaftler, kein deutscher Künstler, kein deutscher Politiker," he declared in "[Nicht Deutschlands Interessen]" (Not in Germany's Interests), in all probability as a result of his frustration with the outcome of the Munich Agreement,

> hält heute Deutschland für von irgendeiner Macht bedroht oder für berechtigt, der Tschechoslowakei ihre innere oder äußere Politik zu diktieren. Niemand glaubt Herrn Hitler, daß er lediglich die deutsch-sprechenden Menschen der Tschechoslowakei "befreien" will, was

---

[8] In his poem on the plebiscite's political significance, "Das Saarlied: Der 13. Januar" (*BFA* 14:219–20), Brecht refers to the event as "für längere Zeit das letzte Bollwerk," i.e., a final bulwark against the threat of NS territorial expansionism (*BFA* 28:450).

sie der Gestapo ausliefern hieße; jedermann weiß, daß er die Tsche-
choslowakei als Ganzes zertrümmern, gleichschalten, besetzen will,
um sich damit ein Sprungbrett nach Osten zu schaffen [. . .]. (*BFA*
22:471)

[These days no German scientist, no German artist and no German
politician believes that Germany is threatened by any power or justified in dictating Czechoslovakia's internal or external policies. No one
believes Mr. Hitler when he says he simply wants to "liberate" the
German-speaking people, meaning that they would be handed over
to the Gestapo; everyone knows that he wants to destroy the whole of
Czechoslovakia, to coordinate and occupy it, and in so doing to give
himself a springboard towards the East [. . .].]

The *Reich* is expanding, Brecht noted in March 1939 (*BFA* 26:332).
Within months, he would be warning about the danger of imminent war
(*BFA* 22:587). But by this time his plans for an adequate antifascist literary
response had already been overtaken by events.

Brecht's publisher, the Malik-Verlag, soon to decamp to London, was
no longer safe from the hostile attentions of Czech anticommunists and ex-
Freikorps wreckers. By the time German troops rolled into Prague in March
1939, extreme right-wingers had broken into its premises, destroying the
plates for the print run of *Furcht und Elend* along with all but one set of
page proofs.[9] "Wielands Prager Satz ist (zusammen mit dem von *Furcht und
Elend* und den *Gesammelten Gedichten*) verloren," Brecht's journal entry for
23 April records (*BFA* 26:337; Wieland's Prague type-formes are lost (along
with those for *Fear and Misery* and the *Collected Poems*): BBJ 29). In his
application for a financial subvention in September 1938, Brecht explained
to the American Guild for German Cultural Freedom: "Die augenblickli-
che Verschärfung der politischen Lage macht das Herauskommen der neuen
Bände [der Malikschen Gesamtausgabe], in die viel Arbeit investiert ist, sehr
zweifelhaft" (*BFA* 29:111; The present worsening of the political situation
makes it very doubtful whether the new volumes, in which a great deal of
work has been invested, will ever appear: BBL 292). In fact, it would be
1945 before Herzfelde's New York–based Aurora publishing house, the suc-
cessor to the Malik-Verlag in exile, was able to publish the full German text[10]
of what to this day remains Brecht's most impressive antifascist work, one he
had judged to be virtually complete back in April 1938 (*BFA* 29:90).

As his petition to the American Guild suggests, Brecht's reasons for
exerting maximum pressure on Herzfelde were at the time not primarily
motivated by any personal need to enhance a once-famous exile writer's
literary standing, although that had originally been one of the *Malik* edi-

---

[9] "Furcht und Elend des III. Reiches" (the surviving galley proof).
[10] *Furcht und Elend des III. Reiches: 24 Szenen* (New York: Aurora, 1945).

tion's tasks.[11] Now, however, the subsequent campaign for accelerated publication was driven first and foremost by Brecht's determination to ensure optimal dissemination of a play that in his judgment still had the capability (even in the late 1930s) to become an effective weapon in the ideological struggle against fascism. *Furcht und Elend* was, Brecht felt, precisely the kind of counter-propagandistic work that needed to get through to sympathetic audiences — or if all attempts to get it staged failed, then at least to a politically receptive clandestine readership. His confidence on this score was echoed in Eric Bentley's essay "Bertolt Brecht and His Work," published in 1944 as a postscript to the American adaptation: "No single work of Brecht's is more important than *Fears and Miseries of the Third Reich* [*sic*], of which *The Private Life of the Master Race* is the stage version" (*The Private Life*, 132).

Of all his exile plays, the *Furcht und Elend* project alone had the potential, Brecht remained convinced, to serve a range of vital political functions:

(i) by presenting an unsparing picture of the brutal conditions currently prevailing in Nazi Germany, it could give the lie to the heroic propaganda image still being peddled by the NS media, above all by press, radio, and cinema newsreels

(ii) by offering a spectrum of images of a discontented, often politically disenchanted society, it could give renewed political and moral impetus to the resistance cause within the country, as well as to Nazi Germany's critics in the outside world

(iii) by undermining drastically the regime's repeated claims to have forged a new classless Germany (a national community, *Volksgemeinschaft*, which offered its followers the rewards of socialism after releasing the country from the harsh constraints imposed on it by the Versailles Treaty), it would bring out the contrast between the Third Reich's façade of socialism and what Brecht took to be the exemplary socialism of the USSR

(iv) by giving expression to the idea that in the Third Reich a "good Germany" still existed alongside the "bad" one, such a work would offer a crucial rebuttal of the crude wartime Vansittartist position[12] according to which Germany was axiomatically an empire of evil whose citizens shared in a collective guilt for the crimes committed in the country's name

---

[11] In his letter to Herzfelde of 31 May 1938 (*BFA* 29:96), Brecht sets out his personal reasons for needing *Gesammelte Werke* to be a success.

[12] The reference is to Sir Robert Vansittart's *Black Record: Germans Past and Present* (London: Hamish, 1941), based on an extremist thesis that Brecht frequently contested. See "The *Other* Germany: 1943" (*BFA* 23:24–30), "Bericht über die Stellung der Deutschen im Exil" (*BFA* 23:32–33), and "[Komplizierte Lage]" (*BFA* 23:33–34).

However, each of these overlapping agendas faced enormous challenges. Some of the principal practical ones are identified in Brecht's landmark Popular Front essay "Fünf Schwierigkeiten beim Schreiben der Wahrheit" (Five Difficulties in Writing the Truth), written in the first year after the NSDAP (Nationalsozialistische Deutsche Arbeiterpartei) had come to power in 1933. As Brecht saw it in that essay:

> Wer heute die Lüge und Unwissenheit bekämpfen und die Wahrheit schreiben will, hat zumindest fünf Schwierigkeiten zu überwinden. Er muß den *Mut* haben, die Wahrheit zu schreiben, obwohl sie allenthalben unterdrückt wird; die *Klugheit*, sie zu erkennen, obwohl sie allenthalben verhüllt wird; die *Kunst*, sie handhabbar zu machen als eine Waffe; das *Urteil*, jene auszuwählen, in deren Händen sie wirksam wird; die *List*, sie unter diesen zu verbreiten. (*BFA* 22:74)
>
> [Today anyone who wants to fight lies and ignorance and to write the truth has to overcome at least five difficulties. He must have the *courage* to write the truth, even though it is suppressed everywhere; the *cleverness* to recognise it, even though it is disguised everywhere; the *skill* to make it fit for use as a weapon; the *judgement* to select those in whose hands it will become effective; the *cunning* to spread it amongst them. (*BAP* 141–42)]

During his long years of Scandinavian exile, Brecht did on the whole manage to display the requisite attributes for a writer intent on uncovering the true ugly face of National Socialism. As Chapter Two of the present study will show, he clearly felt confident that he possessed the *cleverness* to recognize the truth ("die *Klugheit*, [die Wahrheit] zu erkennen"), inasmuch as he unerringly based his antifascist campaign on a rigorously class-oriented Marxist-Leninist analysis of the characterizing features of European fascism, as well as its specifically German manifestation. What is more, his 1934 essay "Über die Wiederherstellung der Wahrheit" (*BFA* 22:89–90; On Restoring the Truth) and his crusading "Rede über die Widerstandskraft der Vernunft" (*BFA* 22:333–36; Speech on the Power of Resistance of Reason) of 1937 are eloquent testimony to the fact that Brecht for a long time subscribed to the belief that truth and reason, and not just the power of military might, would in the long term prevail over fascist propaganda, mindlessly brutal oppression, and, most important of all, ideological bankruptcy.

Brecht's conception of *Furcht und Elend* as a work predicated on accurate, well-researched evidence of what life was like in the Third Reich is very much of a piece with his trust in the powers of logical reasoning and convincingly presented contemporary source material. As Chapters Three and Four of our study are designed to show, Brecht worked, from the very onset of the NSDAP's coming to power, with a dialectical conception of the relationship between fear and misery, on the one hand, and resistance, on the other — a conception ideologically reinforced where it was most successful by a Marxist-Leninist underpinning. There is little doubt either, as subsequent chapters of the present study will demonstrate, that by the late 1930s Brecht had become a master in the art of transforming his ideological and socio-historical insights into a program of literary-political interventionist activity; or, put another way, that he possessed the *skill* to make the truth fit for use as a weapon ("die *Kunst*, [die Wahrheit] handhabbar zu machen"). Nevertheless, with Brecht becoming progressively deprived of adequate outlets for the effective dissemination of the true nature of Third Reich Germany, even the ambitious *Furcht und Elend* project ran the risk of foundering. The numerous obstacles and challenges arising from an ever-fluctuating, volatile exile predicament ultimately meant that the two most imperative requisites of "Fünf Schwierigkeiten" — the *judgment* to select in whose hands the truth would become effective, and the *cunning* to spread the truth amongst them ("das *Urteil*, jene auszuwählen, in deren Händen [die Wahrheit] wirksam wird" and "die *List*, sie unter diesen zu verbreiten") — at times eluded Brecht's grasp or remained beyond his personal control. This was especially true in the case of such a complex play as *Furcht und Elend*, an uncompromising work of counter-propaganda that frequently had to be launched from within various host communities that either failed to understand, or could not accept, the playwright's conception of German National Socialism, his broader materialist (anticapitalist) platform, or even his basic aesthetic assumptions about what made for effective contemporary political theater. Seldom had Brecht encountered so many difficulties when trying to access the most effective means of communication in order to target appropriate audiences and readers. And never before had he had to plead so forcefully to get one particularly promising documentary work positioned in what was left of the public domain before it was too late for it to have its intended impact.

"Meine Betätigungen, selbst die gegen Hitler, waren immer rein literarische, und sie waren von niemandem abhängig," Brecht claimed in the personal statement he was prevented from reading out to the House Committee on Un-American Activities in Washington ("Anrede an den Kongreßausschuß für unamerikanische Betätigungen in Washington 1947" [*BFA* 23:61; My activities, even those against Hitler, were always purely literary, and they were dependent on no one: *BAP* 300]). This may have been what Brecht wanted HUAC to believe, and on occasions he may himself have thought this to be the case. Yet far from being dependent on "no one," his literary antifascist campaign was precariously dependent on many others in the theater world, inasmuch as his creative activities were always the result of teamwork, but also because exile often made him very reliant on the underground for access to information about the terrible things currently happening within the Third Reich. The fact that by 1938 Brecht's various Scandinavian host countries (Denmark, Sweden, and Finland) sensed the threat of imminent Nazi invasion now hanging over them suggested that he would have a struggle getting *Furcht und Elend* staged anywhere in free Europe. He had probably already seen the writing on the wall in 1938 when a selection of scenes from *Furcht und Elend* premiered in Paris under the title "99%" because the French censorship authorities threatened to ban any work with "Third Reich" in its title (*BFA* 29:95). Self-censoring political caution vis-à-vis fascist neighbors was becoming virtually the norm in Europe by the late 1930s. It was to have a marked impact on the German exile community, especially in the case of left-wing writers and intellectuals who had been granted refugee status in Western democracies on the explicit understanding that they abstained from political activity. Despite the fact that Dudow's Paris production was about to be mounted, Brecht felt a need to inform Karl Korsch in April 1938 that few immediate outlets would soon remain available to the work, "da die Furcht jetzt ja auch Europa ergriffen hat" (*BFA* 29:92; because the fear has now gripped Europe: *BBL* 281).

In certain respects, *Furcht und Elend* was a doubly compromising work to be associated with in such dark times. While ostensibly confined to conditions in Nazi Germany during the period 1933–38, Brecht's play also had a prophetic dimension, given that the Third Reich's own "Furcht und Elend" was soon to be exported with a vengeance to most of German-occupied continental Europe, a development that the replacement frame used in *The Private Life of the Master Race* would go on to thematize in 1944. In the meantime, as an inevitable consequence of the disastrous Molotov-Ribbentrop Nonaggression Pact of August 1939, all forms of writing critical of Hitler's Third Reich were banned in the USSR — until, that is, the Wehrmacht's invasion of the country in June 1941. Like Stalin's recent disbanding of the Communist International (usually known as the Comintern), the USSR's pact with the Third Reich was inevitably a great disappointment to Brecht, as well as many others on the Left who thought that they were engaged alongside comrades in the Soviet Union in the great antifascist struggle. In Brecht's judgment, the consequences were dire:

Die [Sowjetunion] trägt vor dem Weltproletariat das fürchterliche Stigma einer Hilfeleistung an den Faschismus, den wildesten und arbeiterfeindlichsten Teil des Kapitalismus. Ich glaube nicht, daß mehr gesagt werden kann, als daß die Union sich eben rettete, um den Preis, das Weltproletariat ohne Losungen, Hoffnungen und Beistand zu lassen. (Journal entry for 9 September 1939 [*BFA* 26:344])

[The [Soviet Union] will in the eyes of the proletariat of the world bear the terrible stigma of aiding and abetting fascism, the wildest element in capitalism and the most hostile to the workers. I don't think more can be said than that the [Soviet Union] saved its skin at the cost of leaving the proletariat of the world without solutions, hopes or help. (*BBJ* 35)]

Yet not even this calamitous setback could diminish Brecht's belief in *Furcht und Elend*'s continuing propaganda value. His plans for the play had to be put on temporary hold, at least until he started to focus his hopes on the anti–Axis Alliance's newfound ally, the post–Pearl Harbor United States. America was both a logical resistance base and a safer haven for an exile German writer unwilling to risk his chances in post–Great Purge Stalinist Russia. "Ich bringe neue Stücke mit und vor allem viel Lust zur Arbeit," he informed Erwin Piscator shortly before leaving for America: "Ich glaube, die USA gehören jetzt zu den wenigen Ländern, in denen man noch frei literarisch arbeiten und Stücke wie *Furcht und Elend* vorzeigen kann" (*BFA* 29:172; I'll be bringing new plays with me and, most important, an enormous desire to work. The USA, I believe, is now one of the few countries where it's possible to do free literary work and to put on plays like *Fear and Misery*. BBL 326), a deliberately ambiguous formulation implying a contrast with the USSR as well as German-occupied Europe.

Even after the Prague setback of 1939, Brecht had assiduously continued to explore other channels of dissemination for his *Furcht und Elend* material. Mindful of having successfully placed a number of the play's showcase scenes in Soviet, French, English, Swiss and (exile) German literary journals, he asked Ruth Berlau to assemble the available translations and prepare them, where feasible, for republication (*BFA* 29:238). As has been pointed out,[13] the *Furcht und Elend* cycle's epic structure lent itself admirably to piecemeal recycling of this kind. Individual scenes were staged (often in translation) in towns and cities across a number of countries, including France, Britain, the United States, and the Soviet Union (for details, see *FM* viii). Brecht also renewed his efforts to ensure that the work would be discussed, whenever appropriate, within the context of antifascist drama in general, rather than being measured against his earlier Epic Theater. Following the German Wehrmacht's invasion of the Soviet Union in 1941, Brecht's play was no longer taboo in Stalinist Russia. Russian and English translations were prepared and rushed into print in the following months, and in 1942 a selection of scenes was reframed to create the script for a propaganda-film version made under the direction of Vsevolod Pudovkin: *Ubitsy vychodyat na dorogu* (The murderers are on their way). Not long afterwards, East and West Coast American productions of *The Private Life of the Master Race*, staged in the presence of invited actors and influential film and theater personalities (many of them German exiles), were also intended to re-kindle interest in the work, though with limited

---

[13] Tom Kuhn, "The Politics of the Changeable Text: *Furcht und Elend des III. Reiches* and the new Brecht edition," *Oxford German Studies*, 18–19 (1989–90), 132–49, and id., "Literary Form and Politics in German Exile Drama" (D.Phil. thesis, University of Oxford, 1985).

success.[14] The alternative solution might have been to continue publishing individual scenes from the play. Under the adverse exile circumstances, nothing could adequately compensate for the substantial impoverishment that *selective* presentation of a miscellany of *Furcht und Elend* scenes represented, whether on the stage or on the page. "Gedacht war das Ganze als Stück," Brecht stressed in a letter to Erwin Piscator of July 1941, "alles müßte hintereinanderweg gespielt werden" (*BFA* 29:209; The whole was conceived as a play, with the scenes played successively: *BBL* 337). He spells out to Hoffman Hays the main rationale behind this claim by drawing attention to the panoramic nature of the work's

> 27 Szenen aus den Jahren 33–38, welche das Leben unter der Diktatur der Nazis zeigen, und zwar das Leben der Arbeiter, Kleinbürger, Intellektuellen in Familie, Schule, Kaserne, Klinik, Gerichtshof usw. (*BFA* 29:208)
>
> [27 scenes from the years 1933 to 1939, showing life under the Nazi dictatorship, the life of the workers, petty bourgeoisie, and intellectuals, in family, school, barracks, hospital, courtroom, etc. (*BBL* 336)]

In further epistolary crusades on behalf of *Furcht und Elend*, Brecht again draws attention to the work's geographical sweep and the broad socio-political spectrum covered: "Das Stück gibt einen Querschnitt durch alle Schichten" (*BFA* 29:83; The play gives a cross-section of all German society: *BBL* 280), he told Piscator. More accurately, the words of his letter to the American Guild describe the play's montage of scenes as being structured as a

> Zyklus [. . .], der [. . .] nahezu alle Schichten des deutschen Volkes in ihrer Reaktion auf die nationalsozialistische Diktatur zu zeigen versucht. Ich versuchte, zwei mir für das Ausland besonders wichtig erscheinende Punkte herauszuholen: erstens die Versklavung, Entrechtung, Lähmung *aller* Schichten unter der nationalsozialistischen Diktatur (davon wissen die in Demokratien lebenden Menschen noch viel zuwenig Konkretes); zweitens die seelische Verfassung der Armee des totalitären Staates, die ja die ganze Bevölkerung umfaßt (so daß sich das Ausland ein Bild von der Brüchigkeit dieser Kriegsmaschine bilden kann). (*BFA* 29:110)
>
> [cycle, an attempt [. . .] to show the reaction of almost every section of the German people to the National Socialist dictatorship. I tried to bring out two points which I thought it vital to make known abroad:

---

[14] "In 1945 I helped prepare the New York production of his *Private Life of the Master Race*," Eric Bentley admits, "which is nothing to boast of: it was a disaster." (Eric Bentley, *The Brecht Commentaries, 1943–1980*, London: Eyre Methuen, 1981, 15) The redeeming fact that the problems were above all with the production can be seen from the account in Lyon, *Bertolt Brecht in America*, 132–41.

first, the enslavement, disfranchisement, paralysis of *all* sections of the population under the National Socialist dictatorship (people living in the democracies have far too little concrete knowledge of this); second, the state of mind prevailing in the army of the totalitarian state, which is a cross section of the population as a whole (to give people outside Germany an idea of the fragility of this war machine). (*BBL* 291–92)]

As the present study's analysis of the play's montage structure will try to show, only when encountered in its entirety does *Furcht und Elend* reveal itself to be a unique work of subtly arranged illustrative episodes. Too much of its thematic integrity risks being sacrificed when individual component scenes are published in isolation or producers cherry-pick which ones to include or omit. This problem continued to challenge the ingenuity of theater companies long after Brecht's return to Europe; indeed, it has remained associated with this particularly complicated example of Epic Theater right up to the present day. Understandably, therefore, *Furcht und Elend* has no more often been staged in its entirety than has Karl Kraus's mammoth play *Die letzten Tage der Menschheit*, one of Brecht's models for the work. As a consequence, its elaborate presentation of the resistance theme, developed incrementally from scene to scene (a feature discussed below in Chapter Four), and the many illustrations of the ways in which the NS regime systematically prepared the German people for war, tend to be deprived of their cumulative effect and didactic narrative continuity. The same holds true for the leitmotifs of "Furcht" and "Elend" that appear in numerous variations throughout the entire sequence.

Furcht und Elend as a Work of Literary Counter-Propaganda

In the fall of 1938, Brecht wrote an essay entitled "Furcht und Elend des Dritten Reiches,"[15] a piece possibly intended as retrospective contextualization of the work's Paris staging, although only published posthumously. The essay draws attention to a series of concrete details symptomatic of daily life in Nazi Germany, daunting factual information that Brecht assumed was not generally known to those living in Western democracies. The citizens of Third Reich Germany are presented as "ein Volk von 2 Millionen Spitzeln und 80 Millionen Bespitzelten. Sein Leben besteht in dem Prozeß, der ihm gemacht wird. Es besteht nur aus Schuldigen" (*BFA* 22:474; a people of 2 million spies and 80 million people being spied on. Life for these people

---

[15] This essay is available in English translation as "Fear and Misery of the Third Reich" (*FM* 93–96).

consists in the case being made against them. They are composed exclusively of the guilty: *FM* 94). Elaborating on the consequences of such intimidating close surveillance, Brecht vividly captures the resultant mood of fear and paranoia among the population, a dominant theme in the *Furcht und Elend* cycle that we will return to in later chapters of the present study:

> Der Priester blättert seine Bibel durch, Sätze zu finden, die er aussprechen kann, ohne verhaftet zu werden. Der Lehrer sucht für irgendeine Maßnahme Karls des Großen einen Beweggrund, den er lehren kann, ohne daß man ihn verhaftet. Den Totenschein unterzeichnend, wählt der Arzt die Todesursache, die nicht zu seiner Verhaftung führt. Der Dichter zerbricht sich den Kopf nach einem Reim, für den man ihn nicht verhaften kann. Und um der Verhaftung zu entgehen, beschließt der Bauer, seine Sau nicht zu füttern. Wie man sieht, sind die Ausnahmemittel erstaunlich, die der Staat ergreifen muß. (*BFA* 22:474)

> [The priest thumbs through his Bible to find sentences he can quote without being arrested. The teacher puzzles over some action of Charlemagne's, looking for motives that he can teach without somebody arresting him. The doctor who signs a death certificate chooses a cause of death that is not going to lead to his arrest. The poet racks his brains for a rhyme he won't be arrested for. And it is to escape arrest that the farmer decides not to feed his sow. As you can see, the measures which the State is driven to take are exceptional. (*FM* 94–95)]

As we will see in Chapter Three, *Furcht und Elend*, like its companion essay "Furcht und Elend des Dritten Reiches," presents a picture of widespread political gloom and individual fear in the face of repeated experiences of totalitarian repression, coupled with an overwhelming sense of the dire economic misery under which so many of the regime's subjects were forced to live. Although the essay reads at times like a résumé of the specifically angst-ridden nature of certain *Furcht und Elend* scenes, it concludes by positing a more promising causal relationship between fear and misery, on the one hand, and resistance, on the other, than some of the play's scenes might lead audiences to expect:

> Sollte es nötig sein, daß auch diese Schichten erst in jenen Zustand der äußersten Vertierung getrieben werden müssen, gegen den sich nach dem Wort der sozialistischen Klassiker das Proletariat in seinem Kampf um die Menschenwürde wehrt? Wird erst das Elend die Furcht besiegen? (*BFA* 22:477)

> [Might the sections in question have to be forced into the same condition of extreme dehumanisation that the proletariat, according to the Socialist classics, is resisting by its fight for the dignity of mankind? Will it be the misery that eventually defeats the fear? (*FM* 96)]

As the later parts of the *Furcht und Elend* montage sequence are clearly meant to show, the essay's concluding sentence was much more than a mere rhetorical question. Indeed, the longer the war continued, the more the theme of resistance began to change its complexion in Brecht's perception.

It was in the context of his move to the United States that Brecht made some of his most helpful comments concerning *Furcht und Elend*, remarks usually made in private correspondence. Writing in April 1938 to Erwin Piscator, who was himself about to move to America to take up a post at the Dramatic Workshop of the New School for Social Research in New York, Brecht signals that he is sending him a copy of *Furcht und Elend*, adding defensively in explanation:

> Ich könnte mir denken, daß es für Amerika etwas außerordentlich Passendes wäre. Alle Welt fragt sich, ob, wie, wie lang Hitler Krieg führen kann. Und die sogenannten Demokratien interessieren sich sehr für die Wirkungen, welche die Diktatur des Hakenkreuzes auf die verschiedenen Schichten hat. [. . .]. Terror und Widerstand in allen Schichten. Dazwischen könntest Du Dokumentarisches einfügen. [. . .] Ich denke sehr an *New York* und möchte alles versuchen, eine Aufführung dort zustande zu bringen. (*BFA* 29:82–83)

> [This would be just the thing for America I think. Everybody is wondering how long a war Hitler could fight. And the so-called democracies are very much interested in knowing how the Nazi dictatorship affects the various social groupings. [. . .]. Terror and resistance everywhere. You could project some documentary material in between. [. . .] I've been thinking a good deal about New York, I'm going to do all I can to swing a production there. (*BBL* 280)]

The idea of inserting supporting evidence — presumably in the form of projected historical documentation, still photographs, and film sequences — was no doubt initially intended to whet Piscator's appetite. (Brecht at one stage pinned his hopes on having the doyen of German political theater stage the play in America.) He did, of course, also approach Max Reinhardt and, after falling out with Piscator, was eventually to settle for Reinhardt's friend and associate Berthold Viertel. Arguably, this sudden cultivation of high-profile directors currently in exile was a further indication of the value Brecht attached to the *Furcht und Elend* project, even at a time when the Second World War was nearing its conclusion and the play, having lost some of its topicality, faced the possibility of being demoted to little more than an interesting theatrical experiment all too painfully reminiscent of a recent traumatic era in Europe's history.[16]

---

16 Some New York critics were quick to suggest that "Germany's recent capitulation had robbed the material of much of its timeliness," according to Lyon. He also quotes a letter of 14 February 1945 from Hallie Flanagan of the Federal Theater

Sources and Related Antifascist Projects

When New Directions published *The Private Life of the Master Race* in 1944, it was subtitled *A Documentary Play*.[17] In one sense, such a subtitle would seem to state the obvious, given that Brecht usually carried out extensive research prior to writing his anticapitalist and antifascist works. With the exception of a handful of his more contrived parables for the stage, Brecht's writing was as a rule preceded by an impressive body of (often collaborative) historical, socio-economic, and scientific research, albeit often less of the narrowly academic kind, and invariably in the service of an interventionist agenda. "Ich [plane] fortwährend Schläge gegen die Verbrecher, die im Süden hausen," Brecht wrote to Grosz in September 1934. "Ich höre jeden ihrer Vorträge im Radio, lese ihre Gesetzentwürfe und sammle ihre Fotografien" (*BFA* 28:436; I am constantly planning blows against the criminals who dwell in the south, [. . .]. I listen to all their speeches over the radio, read their draft laws and collect their photographs: *BBL* 184). In the case of the American stage-adaptation, Eric Bentley refers loosely to "the succession of historical documents which constitute the play" (*The Private Life*, 133). Likewise, and no doubt prompted to do so by Brecht, Hoffman Hays declared the documentary element to be the play's core (quoted in *BHB* 1:347). Such claims can, of course, be misleading. The Erwin Piscator of *Trotz alledem!* and the Karl Kraus of *Die letzten Tage der Menschheit* may have claimed with justification that their respective plays were composed exclusively of quoted documentary material.[18] But Brecht's own preparatory research, in contrast, seldom led to unadulterated documentary evidence being integrated verbatim into the text as a work's sole, or even predominant, ingredient. What is above all striking about the months of combined research and fieldwork undertaken

---

Project to James Laughlin of New Directions, who was at the time considering publishing *The Private Life*. Flanagan judged the work to be "of historical interest rather than of topical interest [. . .] five years ago it would have been very strong — ten years from now it would have great historical significance, but definitely the moment is not now" (Lyon, *Bertolt Brecht in America*, 139). Laughlin took the long view and published *The Private Life* in the same year.

[17] Given that the scenes used in *The Private Life* were all, with one exception, translated from *Furcht und Elend*, we assume that the term "A Documentary Play" applies retrospectively to the original *Malik* version of the work, as well as to *Aurora* and all subsequent German editions.

[18] "Die unwahrscheinlichsten Gespräche, die hier geführt werden, sind wörtlich gesprochen worden," according to Kraus's preface to *Die letzten Tage der Menschheit: Tragödie in fünf Akten mit Vorspiel und Epilog* (Vienna-Leipzig: Verlag "Die Fackel," 1919), 1. For a comparably totalizing claim on Piscator's part, see note 41 (below).

in the case of the *Furcht und Elend* project is the sheer range of sources that Brecht and his collaborators sifted for crucial information about daily life in the Third Reich. These included published documents, contemporary memoirs, quasi-autobiographical works of fiction, NS film, radio and press propaganda material, personal correspondence from fellow exiles and political comrades still inside Third Reich Germany, newspaper reports (in various languages), oral recollections of experiences, and information from the antifascist underground. Nevertheless, consideration of Brecht's plethora of sources has, for understandable reasons, tended to concentrate on the available written material to which the playwright was indebted. Before embarking on *Furcht und Elend*, for example, Brecht had studied Hitler's published speeches and, inevitably, *Mein Kampf* in some detail, as well as acquainting himself, inter alia, with the Hitler biographies of Rudolf Olden and Konrad Heiden, Joseph Goebbels's autobiography *Vom Kaiserhof zur Reichskanzlei*, the histories of National Socialism by Heiden and Fritz Sternberg, and Hanns Heinz Ewers's biography of the Nazi "martyr" Horst Wessel.[19] I'm hard at work, Brecht boasted of his strenuous program of preparatory reading (*BFA* 28:382). But, equally importantly, he also learned a great deal from such comparatively humble sources of up-to-date information as passing visitors,[20] reports transmitted by political informants from within Germany, and various early examples of what would nowadays be called oral history. While in Scandinavian and American exile, Brecht devoted considerable attention to individual eyewitness reports and the clandestine mass-observation material that came his way rather than to the antifascist literary work of fellow exiles, some of it already marred by an outdated picture of life under the swastika. Visits from longstanding acquaintances like Heinz Langerhans, currently gathering testimonies for his study "Deutsche Märtyrer in Konzentrationslagern," and Zenzi Mühsam, widow of the Weimar Republic socialist politician Erich Mühsam who was murdered in the Oranienburg concentration camp in 1934, influenced certain *Furcht und Elend* episodes more than any exile writer's publications probably ever did.

---

[19] Rudolf Olden, *Hitler der Eroberer* (Amsterdam: Malik, 1933); Konrad Heiden, *Adolf Hitler: Das Zeitalter der Verantwortungslosigkeit. Eine Biographie* (Zurich: Europa, 1936) and *Geschichte des Nationalsozialismus: Die Karriere einer Idee* (Berlin: Rowohlt, 1932); Joseph Goebbels, *Vom Kaiserhof zur Reichskanzlei* (Munich: Zentralverlag der NSDAP, 1934); Fritz Sternberg, *Der Faschismus an der Macht* (Amsterdam: Contact, 1935); and Hanns Heinz Ewers: *Horst Wessel: Ein deutsches Schicksal* (Stuttgart, Berlin: Cotta, 1932).

[20] See John Fuegi's claim that "of great importance to the [*Furcht und Elend*] project was the visit of Grete [Steffin's] mother and father from Berlin, whose experiences [were] used as [a] factual basis for writing the play." (*The Life and Lies of Bertolt Brecht* [London: HarperCollins, 1994], 345).

Despite this, there has been a tendency in recent decades to concentrate on Brecht's undoubted indebtedness to literary reflections of life in the Third Reich: such influential exile works as Lion Feuchtwanger's *Die Geschwister Oppenheim* (1933), Heinrich Mann's *Der Haß* (1933), Wolfgang Langhoff's *Die Moorsoldaten* (1935), Friedrich Wolf's *Professor Mamlock* (1935), Willi Bredel's *Die Prüfung* (1935) and *Der Spitzel* (1936), Jan Petersen's *Unsere Straße* (1936), and Ernst Toller's *Pastor Hall* (1938), excerpts from many of which had appeared in the pages of the two leading Moscow-based antifascist journals *Internationale Literatur (Deutsche Blätter)* and *Das Wort*.

In a welcome counterbalance to the academic overemphasis on literary influences, James K. Lyon has explored the role played by the vast array of "general and specific information from newspapers that reached [Brecht] in Danish exile."[21] After outlining the range and significance of the convolute of newspaper articles and cuttings assembled by Brecht and Margarete Steffin mainly during the period 1934–35, Lyon offers a series of examples in support of his implicit hypothesis that many *Furcht und Elend* scenes were substantially dependent on information culled from press reports. He also explores the modifications made to such source material when being shaped into a scene of effective political theater. The status of some other putative sources has, however, remained more open to speculation. Walter Busch, author of the only monograph on *Furcht und Elend* to date, sees the exile SPD's[22] *Deutschland-Berichte*[23] as a vital source of information begging to be dramatized in *Furcht und Elend*,[24] even though the Bertolt-Brecht-Archiv offers no corroborative evidence of Brecht's having accessed them. Herbert Claas, for his part, cites examples of Brecht's recourse to the USSR's rival *Deutschland-Informationen*.[25] On the face of it, it might seem

---

[21] James K. Lyon, "Brecht's Sources for *Furcht und Elend des III. Reiches*: Heinrich Mann, Personal Friends, Newspaper Accounts" in *New Essays on Brecht / Neue Versuche über Brecht*, ed. Maarten van Dijk et al. *The Brecht Yearbook / Das Brecht-Jahrbuch* 26 (Toronto: The International Brecht Society, 2001), 295–305, especially 300–304.

[22] SPD=Sozialdemokratische Partei Deutschlands (German Social Democratic Party).

[23] *Deutschland-Berichte der Sozialdemokratischen Partei Deutschlands (Sopade), 1934–1940*, ed. Klaus Behnken, 7 vols. (Frankfurt am Main: Zweitausendeins, 1980).

[24] Compare Busch's discussion of the scene "Winterhilfe" in *Bertolt Brecht: "Furcht und Elend des Dritten Reiches"* (Frankfurt am Main: Diesterweg, 1982), 41, with the Sopade report for 30 March 1938 (*Deutschland-Berichte* 5, 85).

[25] On the Soviet sources of Brecht's *Deutsche Satiren*, see Herbert Claas, *Die politische Ästhetik Bertolt Brechts vom "Baal" zum "Caesar"* (Frankfurt am Main: Suhrkamp, 1977), 95–96.

unlikely that a politically committed exile writer like Brecht would have simultaneously made use of SPD and KPD[26]/Soviet sources, even during the Popular Front era of grudging SPD–KPD collaboration. Nevertheless, the more flexible young generation of antifascists in exile, among whose number Brecht must be counted, was particularly open to the permissive new Comintern line, even if the old guard remained on the whole reluctant to participate in seemingly heretical Popular Front collaborative politics. Although Brecht may have had good political reasons to cover his tracks in the matter of sources of this kind, the fragmentary evidence available suggests that, while working on *Furcht und Elend*, he did occasionally make use of material from ideologically divergent sources.[27] Unfortunately, such a strategy did not remain without its pitfalls, for the information received from some left-wing antifascist outlets did not always present a reliably balanced picture of life in the Third Reich.

For example, the *Deutschland-Berichte* (compiled between April 1934 and April 1940 by the then-banned Socialist Party of Germany, or Sopade, as it was called in its exile form), which were monthly digests of reports from non-exile Third Reich informants (material smuggled out from Third Reich Germany, to be edited, anonymized, harmonized, and sometimes rewritten), were circulated to subscribers and leading figures within the antifascist movement in exile. In many respects the *Deutschland-Berichte* had similar aims to the *Furcht und Elend* project. Rather than seeing Brecht's play as a catalyst for German homeland resistance to fascism, one critic sees its function as essentially that of enlightening people abroad who knew little about Nazi Germany.[28] In similar terms, the *Deutschland-Berichte* project leader Erich Rinner described the information-gathering exercise's task as "[zu] einer indirekten Beeinflussung der öffentlichen Meinung in der Welt dadurch zu gelangen, daß sie an maßgebende Persönlichkeiten und Institutionen herankommen."[29] To this end, the German material was also made available for distribution in English, Danish, Swedish, and French translations, as of course were many individual *Furcht und Elend* scenes.

---

[26] KPD=Kommunistische Partei Deutschlands (Communist Party of Germany).

[27] Brecht's letter of January 1934 to Kurt Kläber (*BFA* 28:408) makes it clear that he derived information about the Comintern Executive Committee's fascism policy from Radio Moscow, while at the same time monitoring the situation on the ground in Nazi Germany via reports in the exile SPD newspaper *Der Neue Vorwärts*.

[28] Raimund Gerz, *Bertolt Brecht und der Faschismus: In den Parabelstücken "Die Rundköpfe und die Spitzköpfe," "Der aufhaltsame Aufstieg des Arturo Ui," und "Turandot oder der Kongreß der Weißwäscher." Rekonstruktion einer Versuchsreihe* (Bonn: Bouvier, 1983), 78.

[29] Quoted in Peter Longerich, *"Davon haben wir nichts gewusst!" Die Deutschen und die Judenverfolgung, 1933–1945* (Munich: Siedler, 2006), 31.

Targeting a more ambitious audience than Brecht could have ever hoped for, either in Europe or America, the *Deutschland-Berichte* were in theory expected to provide reliable eyewitness reports on the current political climate and major socio-political developments in Third Reich Germany. At the point of circulation, what the Sopade reports usually offered was a digest of prepared written responses to detailed questionnaires forwarded by Sopade border agents ("Grenzsekretäre") in the regions adjacent to Nazi Germany. By the final stage of transmission, the received material had frequently been systematically streamlined by the editors for the sake of political coherence.[30] Like *Furcht und Elend*, the Sopade end product was intended to be used as a basis for informative counter-propaganda ("aufklärerische Gegenpropaganda"[31]). However, coming largely from Social Democrat victims of the NS regime or from homeland informants in various respects dissatisfied with life in the Third Reich, the reports had a tendency to be more personal, impressionistic, and less ideologically perspectivized than Brecht's evocation of Third Reich Germany's fear and misery. Still, they shared with *Furcht und Elend* a need to present a (misleadingly) optimistic picture of the resistance potential of the contemporary situation in Germany.[32] In the assessment of the Sopade leadership, "jede Emigration, je länger sie dauert, [ist] der Gefahr ausgesetzt [. . .], einer Illusionspolitik zu verfallen und demgemäß nicht mehr Ernst genommen zu werden."[33] Misplaced political optimism, especially questions concerning what a character in the "Kreidekreuz" scene (*BFA* 4:349) calls "die Gesinnung" (public opinion, *FM* 12) — i.e., national sentiment, dissent, and possible antifascist resistance — was, of course, not confined to the *Deutschland-Berichte* or to Soviet assessments of the country's mood. We have already encountered some evidence of such rose-tinted "Illusionspolitik" in the case of the high hopes Brecht and his fellow exiles were reported to have placed in the immense role ("gewaltiger Anteil") the Germans in the Third Reich would ideally play in Hitler Germany's defeat ("Bericht über die Stellung der Deutschen im Exil," *BFA* 23:33). We will return to

---

[30] On the editing, reformulation, and alignment of Sopade source material, see Longerich, *"Davon haben wir nichts gewusst!,"* 28–38.
[31] Rinner, quoted in Longerich, op. cit., 31.
[32] According to Friedrich Heine, co-editor of the *Deutschland-Berichte*: "Rinners meiste Arbeit war es, die in den Berichten wiederkehrenden Erwartungen und Hoffnungen und Illusionen zu dämpfen. [. . .] er hat die Berichte [. . .] gemildert, und, wenn sie wollen, verfälscht." (Wolfgang Borgert and Michael Krieft, "Die Arbeit an den *Deutschland-Berichten*: Protokoll eines Gesprächs mit Friedrich Heine," in *Die "Grünen Berichte" der Sopade. Gedenkschrift für Erich Rinner*, ed. Werner Plum [Bonn: Friedrich-Ebert-Stiftung, 1984], 49–119, here 69.)
[33] Letter from Rinner to Wilhelm Sollmann of 24 March 1936, quoted in Longerich, op. cit, 30.

this phenomenon during our discussion of German resistance in Chapter Four. Even in the present context, however, it is perhaps worth noting that in April 1936, after two years' experience organizing and co-editing the *Deutschland-Berichte,* Rinner wrote to Wilhelm Sollmann, former editor-in-chief of *Deutsche Freiheit,* in order to pass on his concern that "die Verfolgung der großen entscheidenden Zusammenhänge" had become "eine Aufgabe, die nach meiner persönlichen Erfahrung selbst von qualifizierten Menschen eher draußen als drinnen erfüllt werden kann."[34] Whether or not Brecht and his own team of informants were sufficiently "qualified" in Rinner's sense of the term, the story of Sopade's *Deutschland-Berichte* has serious implications for any assessment of Brecht's *Furcht und Elend* project as an exercise in counter-informative propaganda. That is to say, individual firsthand reports have in both cases to be treated with circumspection; authenticated evidence concerning conditions and the mood in the Third Reich is likely to be tendentious, even when the goal was objectivity. Most important of all, the bigger picture will at times be easier to grasp from a vantage point beyond Nazi Germany's borders than from inside the Third Reich. In the words of Longerich's evaluation of the *Deutschland-Berichte:*

Es handelte sich im Wesentlichen also um ein publizistisches Produkt, man versuchte, eine sich authentisch gebende, das heißt direkt aus Deutschland kommende Alternative zu den NS-Nachrichtendiensten und zur Berichterstattung der internationalen Presse aus Deutschland aufzubauen. [. . .] Die Deutschland-Berichte sind [. . .] Teil des verzweifelten Kampfes der deutschen Emigration gegen die relativ starke Stellung des NS-Propagandaapparates [. . .]. Sie sind ein Stück aufklärerischer Gegenpropaganda, und es wäre vor diesem Hintergrund naiv, davon auszugehen, dass es den Herausgebern der Deutschland-Berichte nur darum gegangen wäre, einfach ein getreues Bild der Situation in Deutschland zu entwerfen. (Longerich, *"Davon haben wir nichts gewusst!,"* 31)

[Thus it was essentially a matter of a journalistic product, there was an attempt to create an alternative to the NS news service and to the international press reports from Germany, an alternative that presented itself as authentic, in other words one coming directly out of Germany. [. . .] The *Deutschland-Berichte* are [. . .] part of the desperate campaign waged by German émigrés against the relatively robust stance of the NS propaganda apparatus [. . .]. They are a piece of informative counter-propaganda and it would be naïve, given this context, to assume that the sole concern of the editors of the *Deutschland-Berichte* was to present a true picture of the situation in Germany.]

---

[34] Rinner, quoted in Longerich, op. cit., 30.

The *Deutschland-Berichte* phrase "eine sich authentisch gebende, das heißt direkt aus Deutschland kommende Alternative," to the extent to which it also applies to *Furcht und Elend*, raises questions about the relationship between a work presenting itself as a "documentary drama" and the validity of its implicit claims to both authenticity and objectivity.

Models, "Konkretisierung," and the Documentary Mode

To understand the claim made on the title page of *The Private Life* that the work that follows is a "documentary play," it is necessary to see the material in its historical and artistic-generic context. This requires a distinction between the various (in some cases, putative) *sources* for the information dramatized in *Furcht und Elend* and the probable *models* for creating the kind of informative counter-propaganda such a play was intended to present. While working on his play, Brecht clearly had access to many sources, but he also had a restricted number of models for his chosen approach to his documentary work in progress.

Not long before embarking on the *Furcht und Elend* project, Brecht sketched out an "Entwurf für ein Braunbuch" (*BFA* 22:30; Outline for a Brown Book). His use here of the indefinite article suggests that he was thinking of a new work of counter-propaganda comparable to the Popular Front's first *Braunbuch über Reichstagsbrand und Hitler-Terror*.[35] Evidently impressed by the approach taken in that milestone work of political documentation, Brecht declared: "Jetzt muß man natürlich mit um so größerer Wucht die gerichtsnotorische Brüchigkeit der Grundlage der Kommunistenverfolgung darlegen" (*BFA* 28:399; Now of course we must put more energy than ever into exposing the notoriously shaky juridical foundation of the anticommunist campaign: *BBL* 154). ("Brüchigkeit," or "fragility," was a term he would go on to use for the state of the Third Reich's military machine [*BFA* 29:110]). The *Braunbuch*'s strategy of firm rebuttal based on extensive corroborative counter-evidence and its

---

[35] Anon. [Otto Katz, Willi Münzenberg, et al.], *Braunbuch über Reichstagsbrand und Hitler-Terror* (Basle: Universum, 1933). Brecht contributed to the second *Braunbuch* organized by communist exiles in Paris: Anon. [Otto Katz, Willi Münzenberg, Bertolt Brecht, et al.], *Braunbuch II: Dimitroff contra Goering. Enthüllungen über die wahren Brandstifter* (Paris: Carrefour, 1934). Brecht's *Nachlass* contains a plan relating to *Braunbuch II* (*BFA* 22:885–87). While his input remains a matter of conjecture, some of the planned sections (especially "Die Zeugen," "Chancen der Wahrheit, an das Licht zu kommen," and "Der Vernichtungskampf gegen die deutsche Arbeiterbewegung soll moralisch-politisch begründet werden") read like preparations for *Furcht und Elend*.

policy, wherever possible, of allowing documents to speak for themselves would in many respects serve as justification for the fact-based approach Brecht adopted in the case of the *Furcht und Elend* project. The methodological decisions he took after reading the *Braunbuch* corroborate such a conclusion:

> Also jetzt am besten *nur* Dokumente, ausschließlich Montage. Das muß selbst reden! Nur jetzt nichts Gefühlsmäßiges mehr! Die stufenweise Anordnung, allmähliche Entblätterung dieses Anklagebaumes wird jetzt noch wirksamer sein. (*BFA* 28:399)

> [What's needed most is documents, simple montage. Let the facts speak for themselves. No more appeals to sentiments. The tree of indictment will be gradually but all the more effectively stripped bare. (*BBL* 154)]

There was, however, one notable difference between Brecht's Comintern model and his own epic project. The chosen model (i.e., the first *Braunbuch*) puts the emphasis primarily on a single historical incident, although the conduct of the Reichstag Fire trial was at the same time claimed to be indicative of the wave of "Hitler-Terror" raging across the whole of Third Reich Germany after the introduction of the Enabling Act on 23 March 1933.[36] Brecht, in contrast, was determined to present corroborative evidence across the board to support, and not just *claim* representative status for, his chosen illustrations of the "fear and misery" prevalent in the Third Reich as a whole. In this respect, the nation-wide spectrum covered by the *Deutschland-Berichte* would seem to have offered Brecht a more pragmatic model, as too did the sheer sweep of Karl Kraus's *Die letzten Tage der Menschheit* — in its author's words: "ein Drama, dessen Umfang nach irdischem Zeitmaß etwa zehn Abende umfassen würde" (a play whose dimensions, measured in terrestrial terms, would take up approximately ten evenings).[37]

Closer to home, there was a further inspirational model, again a theatrical one, that demonstrably also influenced Brecht's dramaturgical intentions in the case of *Furcht und Elend*: Erwin Piscator's conception of

---

[36] In the wake of the decree of 27 February 1933 that invoked the Reichstag Fire as grounds for securing a whole raft of emergency powers, the Enabling Act (*Ermächtigungsgesetz*) of 24 March 1933 gave the German cabinet the right to rule by decree without reference to either the Reichstag or the president. Together with the Reichstag Fire Decree, it furnished the legal pretext for the creation of the NS dictatorship. From then on, the Third Reich's accomplices had virtual carte blanche to enforce Nazi rule as they liked. Members of the KPD and SPD became the main targets of their lawless attentions.

[37] Kraus, *Die letzten Tage der Menschheit*, 1.

"documentary theater," as set out in *Das politische Theater*.[38] It was clear that any substantial recourse to documentary material would more convincingly broaden the scope from particular instances to the general picture. With Piscator already lined up as a potential director for *The Private Life of the Master Race*, Brecht's sole antifascist work to be published explicitly as "A Documentary Play," and this in an America that had recently experienced a whole wave of left-wing documentary theater,[39] things began to augur well for Brecht's attempt to redesign *Furcht und Elend* for new audiences and new times. But just what did Brecht (and Eric Bentley) mean to signal by calling *The Private Life* "A Documentary Play"?

In the 1960s and 1970s, the spate of German documentary plays and accompanying secondary literature showed very clearly that the epithet "documentary" is not without its ambiguities. It can signify a number of things: a work in which *all* material had been appropriated and quoted verbatim from contemporary historical sources (the most rigorous example being Heinar Kipphardt's *In der Sache J. Robert Oppenheimer*); or a composite work in which fictive elements interface with strategically placed documentary passages (as in Rolf Hochhuth's *Der Stellvertreter*); or one where plot and characters are *entirely fictional*, even though the work draws on substantial authenticated source material to create the requisite illustrative scenario (e.g., Peter Weiss's *Viet Nam Diskurs*); or a work that merely contains a system of *markers of fidelity to source*, while by and large operating with little more than what might be called "the rhetoric of the documentary." In Brechtian contexts, "Konkretisierung" (*BHB* 1:253) is a related term first used of the technique of adding historical detail to an abstract parabolic work like *Der Jasager* to give it the didactic historicity of a political parable-play such as *Die Maßnahme*. In *The Private Life* and the *Aurora* version of *Furcht und Elend*, the material is concretized, thanks to the anchoring of events in a specific location during an identifiable period, with references to the political issues and social circumstances of the time. Selected scenes from *Furcht und Elend* received even more specific framing when they appeared under the umbrella title *The Private Life of the Master Race: A Documentary Play*, although "Konkretisierung" and "documentary" are by no means synonymous concepts. Although the material has been concretized, there are few literal "documents" in either *Furcht und Elend* or *The Private Life*. There is arguably less proper documentation in these depictions of the Third Reich than in *Arturo Ui*. True, the Nazi lead-

---

[38] See Chapter Eight ("Das dokumentarische Drama") of Erwin Piscator, *Das politische Theater* (Reinbek bei Hamburg: Rowohlt, 1963), 70–77.

[39] Brecht and Bentley were both familiar with the presentation of American documentary drama and film in Mordecai Gorelik, *New Theatres for Old* (New York: Samuel French, 1940).

ers' ideological concepts and their political promises are alluded to in certain scenes (e.g. "Volksgemeinschaft," "Rechtsfindung," and "Der Bauer füttert die Sau"),[40] but they are seldom quoted word-for-word. In the final scene, the audience hears the Nazi commentator describing the Führer's triumphant arrival in Vienna broadcast over the radio, but this serves as background noise deliberately used to divide the audience's attention (what Brecht called a "Geräuschkulisse") rather than some form of authenticating acoustic documentation. The only corroborating "document" in the entire play (the song "Moorsoldaten") was not added until the *Private Life* stage (where the scene is entitled "Prisoners Mix Cement"). It is attached to a specified concentration camp setting, "Oranienburg," and dated "1934" (*The Private Life*, 26). While Brecht was indebted to a number of published sources for the details of this scene, it was perhaps the visit of an ex–concentration camp prisoner, Heinz Langerhans, that particularly reinforced the sense of authenticity in this case. Specific details are otherwise generally inserted into the *Furcht und Elend* material to give it the *semblance* of being to some extent a documentary play, yet without receiving what one might call the Piscator Treatment. (What we have termed "the rhetoric of the documentary" is not, of course, an effect to be lightly dismissed in the context of a work of antifascist counter-propaganda.) But since the published *Private Life* adaptation itself contained only seventeen scenes, the process of "Konkretisierung" needed to be retroactively extended to further scenes included in *Aurora* and most subsequent published versions of *Furcht und Elend*. We will return to these quasi-authenticating markers in Chapter Six, but it is worth recalling even at this stage that the names of characters in individual scenes often have a fictive ring (being virtually *noms parlants*, in some cases) rather than adding to any aura of verisimilitude. Thus, the issues usually raised when the documentary mode is signaled in political plays, concerning, for example, the relationship between the documents used and any consequent claims to "objectivity," or relating to tensions between the documentary approach's projected neutrality and any underlying political tendentiousness, seem peripheral in the case of *The Private Life* and the reconstituted postwar *Furcht und Elend*. But two other factors that do come into play are both uniquely specific to Brecht's conception of *Furcht und Elend*.

Like the editors of the Sopade *Deutschland-Berichte* and those exile authors who were obliged to conceal their identities because of relatives or clandestine sources still in Nazi Germany, Brecht also had to protect his informants. For this reason, documentary fidelity frequently had to be reconciled with the need to conceal informants' identities. (Novelists writ-

---

[40] For a chart indicating the standard English titles for the *Furcht und Elend* scenes as they appear in *FM*, see Appendix A.

ing from within the Third Reich about life under a Nazi dictatorship often solved this dilemma by resorting to the use of a nom de plume.) But things tended to be different in the case of drama: for a start, a high-profile anti-fascist dramatist like Brecht was usually less exclusively dependent on a sole eyewitness account than on a whole spectrum of on-the-spot reports. And the truthfulness of his depictions was to some considerable extent guaranteed by publishing under his own name. He once expressed the hope that Hitler would not be able to sleep peacefully at night as long as he was writing. The hope might have been rhetorical (there is no evidence that Hitler had ever heard of Brecht), but such a *Gestus* of authority that the name brings with it was important to the antifascist counter-propaganda in individual *Furcht und Elend* scenes.

In many cases, however, the façade of documentary truthfulness that the framing of the play often created has to be measured against our recognition of the fact that in the world of counter-propaganda activities, any documentary evidence would need to be subjected to a radical selective process (as was even the case with Kipphardt's *In der Sache J. Robert Oppenheimer*). Compared with Piscator's all-embracing, "documentary" method in *Trotz alledem!* and in his production of Toller's *Hoppla, wir leben!*[41] Brecht's approach might appear to make only tentative gestures towards the various complicated conventions of documentary drama. But here another criterion comes into play:

> Wir brauchen nicht wahre, sondern charakteristische Geschichten.[42] Keine großen Geschichten, sondern Geschichten über Größe. Keine erbaulichen Geschichten, sondern Geschichten über Aufbau.[43]
>
> [We don't need true stories, but characteristic ones. Not great stories, but stories about greatness. Not instructive stories, but stories about construction.]

As the word "Aufbau" suggests, these remarks were made in the GDR, although, as has been suggested,[44] they have implications for an interpreta-

---

[41] Singling out the premiere of *Trotz alledem!* as "die Aufführung, in der zum erstenmal das politische Dokument textlich und szenisch die alleinige Grundlage bildet" (*Das politische Theater*, 70) and "der Film [war] Dokument" (72), Piscator declared: "Die ganze Aufführung war eine einzige Montage von authentischen Reden, Aufsätzen, Zeitungsausschnitten, Aufrufen, Flugblättern, Fotografien und Filmen des Krieges und der Revolution." (*Das politische Theater*, 73).

[42] Brecht appears to be echoing Friedrich Engels's letter of April 1888 to Margaret Harkness concerning her 1887 novel *A City Girl: A Realistic Story*. According to this letter (*MEW* 37:42–44), typicality is not so much a matter of truth of detail as the truthful reproduction of typical characters under typical circumstances.

[43] Manfred Wekwerth, *Arbeit mit Brecht* (Berlin: Henschel, 1973), 18.

[44] Busch, *Bertolt Brecht*, 10.

tion of *Furcht und Elend*. While rejecting "true" stories (the very bedrock of documentary literature), Brecht still stresses the need for "characteristic" illustrations, interpreted in *Furcht und Elend* essentially in class, political, region-specific, and historical terms. But this only raises further questions about the relationship between veracity and ideological stance — the nature of antifascist counter-propaganda (especially in a work so dependent on indirect sources and one having to reckon with a constricting Popular Front aesthetic). Before we can gauge the implications of this for an understanding of *Furcht und Elend*, we first need to consider Brecht's perception of the fascism his play attempts to analyze, attack, and undermine.

2: Brecht and Fascism

SUMMONED TO APPEAR before the Congress House of Representatives Un-American Activities Committee (HUAC) on 30 October 1947, Brecht was at one stage of the hearing interrogated about his 1930 "Lehrstück" *Die Maßnahme* (The Measures Taken). Substantial attention had been paid to the work in the FBI's file on Brecht. "Would you consider the play to be pro-Communist or anti-Communist" was the unsubtle opening question he was asked, "or would it take a neutral position regarding Communists?" "In this play," Brecht replied, "I tried to express the feelings and ideas of the German workers who then fought against Hitler." Some surprise was expressed by the chief HUAC investigator, Robert Stripling, upon hearing that German workers were already fighting fascism at that time. "Yes, yes, oh yes," Brecht disingenuously explained, "that fight started in 1923."[1] Presumably, deflecting attention from his play's revolutionary Marxism-Leninism to the possibility that it was built around an antifascist theme might have seemed a shrewd counter-move on Brecht's part. Associating *Die Maßnahme* exclusively with the "feelings and ideas" of a German working class fighting against National Socialism can hardly have suited HUAC's agenda. Although political activist ideas are much in evidence in some scenes of the play, *Die Maßnahme* in fact treats class warfare without even obliquely referring to National Socialism.[2] But then, as Gerd Koch has pointed out (*BHB* 4:129), Brecht was notoriously slow to grasp the importance of Hitler's movement. More to the point, any conclusions that might be drawn about the play's alleged antifascist credentials would depend on just what definition of "fascism" Brecht and

---

[1] "From the Testimony of Berthold [*sic*] Brecht: Hearings of the House Committee on Un-American Activities, October 30, 1947," in *Brecht: A Collection of Critical Essays*, ed. Peter Demetz (Englewood Cliffs, NJ: Prentice-Hall, 1962), 30–42, here 35. In an autobiographical note written in 1943 (*BFA* 27:355), Brecht claims to have been on the register of people to be arrested during the Munich Putsch of 1923.

[2] On *Die Maßnahme*'s political didacticism, see John and Ann White, "Mi-en-leh's Progeny: Some of Brecht's Early Theatrical Parables and their Political Contexts," in *The Text and its Context: Studies in Modern German Literature and Society*, ed. Nigel Harris and Joanne Sayner (Oxford: Lang, 2008), 327–37. It is also conceivable that the attention Eric Bentley paid to the play in "Bertolt Brecht and His Work" (*The Private Life*, 126–27) increased the FBI's interest in the work.

his interlocutors had in mind when the talk was about "fighting Hitler."[3] Was it "fascism" seen as a specifically German regression to barbarism (a view prevalent among intellectual exiles from Nazi Germany at the time of *Furcht und Elend*)? Or "fascism" equated with state-sanctioned eliminationist antisemitism, systematic genocide, and countless other "crimes against humanity"? Or perhaps, given the centuries-old history of European colonialism, a form of ruthless geopolitical totalitarianism associated with the excesses in occupied Eastern Europe resulting from the regime's *Lebensraum* agenda? Strictly speaking, it was none of these in Brecht's case, either at the time of writing *Die Maßnahme* or that of the Washington hearing. The generic conception of fascism to which Brecht initially subscribed was virtually unknown in the West and was certainly not shared by any of the USSR's former Second World War allies.

According to the Bolshevik interpretation of fascism strictly adhered to by the Moscow-based Comintern at the time when Brecht was working on *Furcht und Elend*, National Socialism (or "German fascism," as it was called in the Soviet Union) was not simply ruthless Late Capitalism with the gloves finally off. It represented a further (until then unforeseen) transitional stage in what was taken to be an inevitable historical progression from the imminent demise of Western capitalism to the dictatorship of the proletariat.[4] Accommodating it to the grand historical narrative in this way, those on the extreme Left were still able to interpret their growing struggle against European fascism (in Germany, Italy, and Spain) as one

---

[3] Following established Bolshevik and KPD practice, Brecht tends to use the generic term "Faschismus" when discussing National Socialism. His most important statements on the subject are: "[Faschismus und Kapitalismus]" (Fascism and Capitalism) (*BFA* 22:105–6); "Eine notwendige Feststellung zum Kampf gegen die Barbarei" (A Necessary Observation on the Struggle against Barbarism) (*BFA* 22:141–46); "[Rede zum II. Internationalen Schriftstellerkongreß zur Verteidigung der Kultur]" (Speech at the Second International Writers' Congress for the Defense of Culture) (*BFA* 22:323–25); "Plattform für die linken Intellektuellen" (Platform for Left-wing Intellectuals) (*BFA* 22:326–29); and the essay "Furcht und Elend des Dritten Reiches" (Fear and Misery of the Third Reich) (*BFA* 22:472–77). Brecht's account of the HUAC hearing can be found in his journal for 30 October 1947 (*BFA* 27:247–50; *BBJ* 372).

[4] As Brecht put it, those who regarded themselves as the architects of communism saw it as the inevitable *next* social configuration and the proletariat as the people who had to bring it about. But the time was not yet ripe: "Sie sahen den Faschismus an, und siehe, [der Kommunismus] war noch nicht die nächste Formation: sie mußte also noch kommen. Aus den Propheten für morgen wurden sie einfach die von übermorgen" ("[Einfluß der Gegenrevolution]," [*BFA* 22:48–49; They looked at fascism, and lo and behold [communism] was not yet the next social configuration: thus it was still to come. The prophets of tomorrow simply became those of the day after tomorrow]).

further stage in their preparation for communist world revolution, with the working class the only power ideologically equipped to emerge victorious from such a battle. Given the determination by members of HUAC to trap Brecht into showing his true political colors, they would have been better advised to concentrate on his conception of fascism than to focus on *Die Maßnahme*, an early work that had met with serious disapproval on the KPD Left. There was certainly ample evidence about his political views to serve as ammunition, much of it already in the public domain. As Jan Knopf has observed (*BHB* 4:264), Brecht's standpoint on the question of the relationship between capitalism and fascism was unequivocal, albeit repeatedly expressed with various modifications. While Brecht could never be dismissed as a mere stooge of the Comintern,[5] from the mid-1930s onwards his interpretation of a number of key features of National Socialism nevertheless comes across as a position carefully arrived at *in dialogue with* the new guidelines emanating from the Seventh World Congress of the Third International. The outcome of Brecht's negotiation with a series of dogmatic, often shifting Comintern positions was generally a complex, overly schematic conception of European fascism. While some of its components consisted of an amalgam of Comintern thinking and uncontroversial Marxist-Leninist orthodoxy, Brecht in other respects ploughed his own furrow, especially when it came to the challenging question of whether the Comintern's new-found generic conception of fascism was applicable to Third Reich Germany's current predicament. As we will repeatedly see in the case of the *Furcht und Elend* complex, Brecht's picture of National Socialism, especially during his Scandinavian exile, skillfully combined received wisdom with personal insights.

The various sections of the present chapter that follow are intended to offer a brief account of Brecht's main ideological assumptions concerning National Socialism. While a substantial body of scholarly work on Brecht's

---

[5] During the Cold War, the question of Brecht's indebtedness to Comintern thinking and his role in Popular Front politics soon became a matter of intense ideological wrangling, above all between East and West German *Germanisten*, with both factions often basing their arguments on unsupported claims rather than fresh evidence. For positions taken, see Raimund Gerz, *Bertolt Brecht und der Faschismus*, 59–86; Hans Mayer, *Bertolt Brecht und die Tradition* (Pfullingen: Neske, 1961), 63–82; Werner Mittenzwei, *Brechts Verhältnis zur Tradition* (Berlin: Akademie, 1972), 42–51; Alois Münch, *Bertolt Brechts Faschismustheorie und ihre theatralische Konkretisierung in den "Rundköpfen und Spitzköpfen"* (Frankfurt am Main, Bern: Lang, 1982), 54–70; and *"Das Wort,"* in Hans-Albert Walter, *Deutsche Exilliteratur, 1933–1950*, vol. 4, *Exilpresse* (Stuttgart: Metzler, 1978), 469–89. For a retrospective survey, see Frank D. Wagner, *Bertolt Brecht: Kritik des Faschismus* (Opladen: Westdeutscher Verlag, 1989), 39–40.

theory and critique of fascism has appeared over recent years,[6] with the exception of Wagner's *Bertolt Brecht: Kritik des Faschismus*, these studies make surprisingly little reference to the *Furcht und Elend* complex. The main reason for this omission is no doubt the general tendency to focus on Brecht's antifascist parable plays, as well as his poetry and prolific theoretical writings on the subject. The works in question will be referred to in what follows only when their findings are of relevance to *Furcht und Elend*. However, it is necessary to remind ourselves at this stage that most macrostudies of "Brecht and fascism" inevitably extend beyond the prewar phase depicted in the original *Furcht und Elend* scenes (i.e., 1933–38) and in most cases even beyond the period following Nazi Germany's attack on the Soviet Union thematized in the framing sections of the American stage adaptation *The Private Life of the Master Race* (i.e., 1941–42).

Fascism, Capitalism, and the Role of the German Petty Bourgeoisie

Brecht's essay "Fünf Schwierigkeiten beim Schreiben der Wahrheit" (Five Difficulties in Writing the Truth), written between 1934 and 1935 at a time when he and his assistant Margarete Steffin were already assembling material for the *Furcht und Elend* project, identifies one of the main challenges confronting National Socialism's opponents as the need to be clear about precisely what political phenomenon they were taking on. Brecht dismisses "die weitverbreitete Auffassung [. . .], daß in einigen Ländern schlimme Zustände herrschen, die von der Barbarei herrühren" (the widespread view that in some countries terrible conditions prevail, which originate in barbarism):

> Nach dieser Auffassung ist der Faschismus eine neue, dritte Macht neben (und über) Kapitalismus und Sozialismus; nicht nur die sozialistische Bewegung, sondern auch der Kapitalismus hätte nach ihr ohne den Faschismus weiter bestehen können usw. Das ist natürlich

---

[6] Particularly informative accounts are to be found in: Franz Norbert Mennemeier, "Bertolt Brechts Faschismustheorie und einige Folgen für die literarische Praxis," in *Literaturwissenschaft und Geschichtsphilosophie: Festschrift für Wilhelm Emrich*, ed. Helmut Arntzen et al. (Berlin, New York: de Gruyter, 1975), 561–74; Wolfgang Emmerich, "'Massenfaschismus' und die Rolle des Ästhetischen: Faschismustheorie bei Ernst Bloch, Walter Benjamin, Bertolt Brecht," in *Antifaschistische Literatur: Programme, Autoren, Werke*, ed. Lutz Winkler (Kronberg/Ts.: Scriptor, 1977) 1:223–90; Rolf Tauscher, *Brechts Faschismuskritik in Prosaarbeiten und Gedichten der ersten Exiljahre* (Berlin: Brecht-Zentrum der DDR, 1981); Münch, *Bertolt Brechts Faschismustheorie*; Gerz, *Bertolt Brecht und der Faschismus*; Wagner, *Bertolt Brecht: Kritik des Faschismus*; and Knopf (*BHB* 4:262–72).

eine faschistische Behauptung, eine Kapitulation vor dem Faschismus. Der Faschismus ist eine historische Phase, in die der Kapitalismus eingetreten ist, insofern etwas Neues und zugleich Altes. Der Kapitalismus existiert in den faschistischen Ländern nur noch als Faschismus und *der Faschismus kann nur bekämpft werden als Kapitalismus, als nacktester, frechster, erdrückendster und betrügerischster Kapitalismus.* Wie will nun jemand die Wahrheit über den Faschismus sagen, gegen den er ist, wenn er nichts gegen den Kapitalismus sagen will, der ihn hervorbringt? [. . .] Die gegen den Faschismus sind, ohne gegen den Kapitalismus zu sein, [. . .] gleichen Leuten, die ihren Anteil vom Kalb essen wollen, aber das Kalb soll nicht geschlachtet werden. (*BFA* 22:77–78)

[According to this view, Fascism is a new, third power next to (and above) capitalism and socialism; not only the socialist movement, it is argued, but capitalism also could have continued to prosper, had it not been for Fascism. This is, of course, a Fascist claim, a capitulation to Fascism. Fascism is a historic phase which capitalism has entered into, and in this sense it is both new and at the same time old. In Fascist countries capitalism only survives as Fascism, and *Fascism can only be resisted as capitalism, as the most naked, brazen, oppressive, and deceitful form of capitalism.*

How does someone propose to speak the truth about Fascism, to which he is opposed, if he does not propose to speak out against capitalism, which produces it? [. . .] Those who are against Fascism without being against capitalism [. . .] are like people who want to eat their share of the calf without the calf being slaughtered. (*BAP* 145)]

Both the timing and the phraseology of the above extract betray the unmistakable influence of Georgi Dimitrov's proposals for a radical redefinition of fascism as "the open terrorist dictatorship of the most reactionary, most chauvinistic and most imperialist elements of finance capital."[7] Offsetting the Fifth and Sixth Congresses' parallel demonization of "German fascism" (National Socialism) and "social fascism" (social democracy), previously reviled by Josef Stalin as "twin brothers," Dimitrov sought to open up the way for a new broad-based antifascist campaign — both in Europe and beyond — directed against fascism proper. Unfortunately, many

---

[7] "The Class Character of Fascism," in Georgi Dimitrov, *For a United and Popular Front* (Sofia: Sofia Press, 1935), 115. First laid for approval before the thirteenth plenary session of the Comintern's Executive Committee (ECCI) in December 1933, Dimitrov's report was presented to the Seventh World Congress of the Communist International (Moscow 1935). A later, annotated copy of Dimitrov's proposals, published in his book *Die Volksfront zum Kampf gegen Faschismus und Krieg* (Strasbourg: Editions Prométhée, 1937), is preserved in Brecht's library (*BBB* 267).

staunch diehards in the upper echelons of the KPD and in SPD circles were less than enthusiastic about joining forces with their old enemies in the planned international "Popular Front against war and fascism" — just as they had been at the beginning of the 1930s when an "Einheitsfront" (United Front) of the German Left had been proposed. Under the present circumstances, a desire not to rock the boat by exacerbating potential divisions within various precariously constituted "Volksfront" (Popular Front) alliances could account for Brecht's respectful bows in the Comintern's direction.[8] Admittedly, Dimitrov's definition of fascism might at the time have seemed the next logical step to those who shared his ideological position. After all, the first official Comintern understandings of fascism as a counter-revolutionary tool of monopoly capitalism date back to the early 1920s,[9] and Clara Zetkin had characterized fascism at the Sixth World Congress of the Comintern as capitalism's "qualitatively highest form."[10] Fortunately, thanks to Dimitrov, the focus was now shifting from seemingly endless terminological wrangles to the important practical question of just how European fascism should be combated. The Seventh Congress transformed the Comintern's function from would-be Soviet engine of world revolution to that of organizer of *antifascist resistance at a national level*. In the view of Gerz, Dimitrov's definition was, as far as Brecht was concerned, a necessary, but by no means adequate component of any available fascism theory.[11] From Brecht's German perspective, however, simplistically equating National Socialism with monopoly capitalism, as the Comintern did, risked ignoring the specific contribution that the *Kleinbürgertum* (the German petty bourgeoisie) had made to the strengthening of the NSDAP's stranglehold over Germany. The way forward was clear to Brecht: "Der Nationalsozialismus muß betrachtet werden als der Sozialismus der Kleinbürger" (*BFA* 27:258; National Socialism must be regarded as the socialism of the petty bourgeoisie: *BBJ* 258). This assumption brought with it a number of corollaries. For example:

> Die nationalsozialistische Bewegung wird vom Kleinbürgertum geführt, einer Schicht, die ökonomisch und ideologisch vollständig unselbständig und nicht imstande ist, die großen Aufgaben dieses

---

[8] "Dichter sollen die Wahrheit schreiben" (*BFA* 22:71–74), a preliminary draft of "Fünf Schwierigkeiten," identifies only three difficulties. Despite repeated allusions to the conditions of property ownership, there are at this stage no references to the Comintern position on "German fascism."

[9] For details, see Aristotle A. Kallis, "Fascism — a 'generic' concept?" in *The Fascism Reader*, ed. Aristotle A. Kallis (London: Routledge, 2003), 43–70, here 45.

[10] Quoted from Martin Kitchen: "The Third International and Fascism," in *Fascism*, ed. Martin Kitchen (London-Basingstoke: Macmillan, 1976), 4.

[11] Gerz, *Bertolt Brecht und der Faschismus*, 64.

Jahrhunderts der Technik im fortschrittlichen Sinne zu lösen. (*BFA* 22:27)

[The National Socialist movement is led by the petty bourgeoisie, a social stratum that, both economically and ideologically, is completely lacking in self-sufficiency and incapable of solving in a progressive sense the great challenges of this technological century.]

Brecht's quasi-revisionist position, according to which many of the most important characterizing features specific to German fascism were "die Folgen der Revolution der Kleinbürger" (*BFA* 22:15; the consequences of the petty bourgeois revolt: *BAP* 128), partly accounts for his disappointment at the way in which people like his friend and fellow antifascist writer Lion Feuchtwanger balked at accepting that there was such a thing as "das Phänomen 'herrschendes Kleinbürgertum'" (*BFA* 27:58; the phenomenon of the "ruling petty bourgeoisie": *BBJ* 202–3). That Feuchtwanger was not alone in this, not even within the socialist exile camp, was one of Brecht's problems.

Although deviating dangerously from the Comintern line on certain points of principle, Brecht nevertheless positions himself carefully in relation to Dimitrov's rigid equation of European fascism with finance capitalism. In "Eine notwendige Feststellung zum Kampf gegen die Barbarei" (A Necessary Observation on the Struggle Against Barbarism) of 1935, for example, he declares that the NS regime's "Roheit kommt nicht von der Roheit, sondern von den Geschäften, die ohne sie nicht mehr gemacht werden können" (*BFA* 22:144; brutality does not come from brutality, but from the business deals which can no longer be made without it: *BAP* 160). Echoing Clara Zetkin in his "Plattform für die linken Intellektuellen" (Platform for left-wing Intellectuals, 1937), Brecht pays German fascism the backhanded compliment of calling it "die beste kapitalistische Staatsform dieser Epoche" (*BFA* 22:328; the best form of capitalist state in this epoch: *BAP* 175). His journal for 19 February 1939 emphasizes the Hitler regime's place within a modern political continuum by suggesting that National Socialism might be best understood as a form of "konsequenter Spätkapitalismus" (*BFA* 26:329; consistent late capitalism: *BBJ* 22), although too little is made of the nature of its consistency. Other entries from the late 1930s continue to offer analyses by and large consonant with current Comintern orthodoxy. Yet any émigré German intellectual on the communist Left could hardly ignore the unfortunate fact that Dimitrov's broad-brush explanation of European fascism signally failed to take account of the specific German situation, which was a result of the devastating impact of its armed forces' unexpected defeat in November 1918, the punitive conditions imposed on the country by the Versailles Treaty of 1919, and the destructive economic crises of the Weimar Republic with their particularly harsh impact on the petty bourgeoisie. As far as

Brecht was concerned, to lose sight of all this would be to downplay the role of the very class that had been largely instrumental in bringing about National Socialism's rise to power, and that had done so as much out of self-interest as for purely ideological reasons.[12]

A further jigsaw piece in Brecht's picture of the German petty bourgeoisie's lamentable role during the Weimar period and the early years of the Third Reich was the result of a tendency on the German KPD Left to associate the petty bourgeoisie with social democracy. This becomes a key feature of Brecht's 1939 essay "Warum droht die Abwanderung kleinbürgerlicher und sogar proletarischer Schichten zum Faschismus?" (*BFA* 22:587–88; Why are the Petty Bourgeoisie and Even the Proletariat Threatening to Turn to Fascism?). Although primarily targeting neutral Sweden's Social Democratic Party, the essay's principal charges — reformism, short-termism, a combination of revolutionary rhetoric with slow delivery, and a predilection for abstract utopianism — are also largely relevant to the alleged shortcomings of the German SPD during the Weimar Republic years and beyond. There were arguably even times when Brecht's campaign against the petty bourgeoisie came perilously close to the Stalinist blurring of any substantive differentiation between so-called "social fascism" and fascism proper. What is important for an understanding of *Furcht und Elend*, though, is not any simplistic refusal on the Left's part to differentiate between the two, but the greater charge leveled against the NSDAP of betraying genuine (read: Soviet) socialism: for example, in Brecht's accusation that, in Third Reich Germany, "die Sozialdemokratie [gibt] die Nation preis. [. . .] Die Sozialdemokratie [rückt] immerfort von den Kommunisten [ab], wenn sie die sozialistischen Ideale propagieren" (*BFA* 22:587; Social Democracy sacrifices the nation. [. . .] Social Democ-

---

[12] Neither Brecht's nor the Comintern's interpretation finds support nowadays. Dimitrov's equation of fascism with capitalism and Brecht's emphasis on the petty bourgeoisie have been superseded by recent research, especially Nicos Poulantzas, *Fascism and Dictatorship: The Third International and the Problem of Communism*, trans. Judith White (London: NLB, 1974), showing that the NS regime was relatively detached from any particular social class. For surveys of recent debates, see Pierre Ayçoberry, *The Social History of the Third Reich, 1933–1945* (New York: The New Press, 1999), 209–44; Detlef Mühlberger, "Germany," in *The Social Basis of European Fascist Movements*, ed. Detlef Mühlberger. (London, New York, Sidney: Croom Helm, 1987), 40–139; and Kallis, *The Fascism Reader*, 1–41. Richard J. Evans argues that the NSDAP strenuously wooed the petty bourgeoisie in the early years of coming to power, but a failure to follow through on promises led to widespread dissatisfaction on the part of those affected. See "Building the People's Community" in *The Third Reich in Power, 1933–1939* (London: Allen Lane, 2005), 404–503. Brecht's claims seem to be based more on National Socialism's program than on subsequent performance. Brecht was no lone voice at the time, however.

racy always backs away from the communists, when they propagate socialist ideals: *BAP* 191–92).

While many of Brecht's other, at the time largely unpublished, utterances concerning social democracy's failure to promote genuine socialism come across as often little more than particularizing footnotes to the
Bolshevik equation of fascism with monopoly capitalism, one nevertheless
encounters palpable differences in emphasis between any public stance and
his various cautious remarks of a more private nature. Although Brecht
was generally anxious not to contradict official Comintern policy,[13] those
of his political writings destined for the bottom drawer display a marked
tendency to cast the German petty bourgeoisie in the role of willing agents
of Late Capitalism. There were, of course, other good historical reasons
for such a negative picture. During Friedrich Ebert's presidency, the SPD
of the Weimar years was associated in communist memory with Gustav
Noske's use of right-wing paramilitary (Freikorps) forces to suppress Red
revolutionary uprisings in various parts of Germany, with the assassinations
of Karl Liebknecht and Rosa Luxemburg and the Party's failure to seize
the available opportunities for radically changing German society. All this
was understandably not forgotten during the Popular Front years and, as
we will see, this left its mark on a number of *Furcht und Elend* scenes.

Returning to the subject of the petty bourgeoisie's questionable
behavior in the Third Reich itself, Brecht's journal for 28 February 1942
observed that:

> die ausgloseste aller Klassen, das Kleinbürgertum, etabliert sich
> diktatorisch in der ausweglosesten Situation des Kapitalismus. Die
> Diktatur ist nur insofern scheinbar, als sie sich zwischen den weiter-
> bestehenden Klassen durchsetzt, so das "natürliche" (ökonomische)
> Gewicht des Großbürgertums (Junkertums) zur verschärften Geltung
> bringt und nicht "im Sinn" des Kleinbürgertums regiert; es ist Hand-

---

[13] Knopf (*BHB* 4:263) assigns Brecht's unpublished private comments to the category "kürzere Gelegenheits-Notate, die der Selbstverständigung dienten." Elsewhere he dismisses as a "hartnäckige Legende" the suggestion that Brecht chose
to refrain from entering the fray in print so as to avoid jeopardizing Popular Front
unity; see *Gelegentlich Poesie: Ein Essay über die Lyrik Bertolt Brechts* (Frankfurt am
Main: Suhrkamp, 1996), 142. For others, Brecht's reticence was more a matter of
tactical diplomacy (see Gerz [*BHB* 4:234] for a survey). Gerz elsewhere suggests
(*BHB* 4:236) that Brecht may simply have had too many other projects on his hands
to find time to engage in protracted polemics. Brecht was not the only influential
left-wing figure to disagree with the 1935 Comintern interpretation, although he
was probably unaware of this at the time. In his seminars in the Moscow Party
School, Palmiro Togliatti warned against the mechanical application of the Seventh
Congress's guidelines and questioned the appropriateness of Dimitrov's analysis for
an understanding of the Spanish situation in the mid-1930s.

langertum, Faustlangertum, aber die Faust hat eine gewisse Selbständigkeit; die Industrie bekommt ihren Imperialismus, aber sie muß ihn nehmen, wie sie ihn bekommt, den Hitlerschen. Das Pathologische ist etwas durchaus Klassenmäßiges. (*BFA* 27:63)

[the most hopeless of all classes, the petty bourgeoisie, sets up its own dictatorship when the situation of capitalism is at its most hopeless. The dictatorship is apparent rather than real to the extent that it is established alongside other classes which continue to exist, and thus brings out the "natural" (economic) weight of the upper bourgeoisie (*Junkers*) particularly sharply and does not rule "in the interests of" the petty bourgeoisie; it lends a hand, or a fist, but that fist has a certain independence; industry gets its imperialism, but has to take it as it comes, the Hitler version. The pathology is wholly class-conditioned. (*BAP* 204)]

As has been pointed out,[14] Brecht was able to establish impeccable credentials for the above interpretive scenario by echoing the classic diagnosis of the petty bourgeoisie's predicament offered in Marx's and Engels's *Manifest der Kommunistischen Partei*:

Von allen Klassen, welche heutzutage der Bourgeoisie gegenüberstehen, ist nur das Proletariat eine wirklich revolutionäre Klasse. Die übrigen Klassen verkommen und gehen unter mit der großen Industrie, das Proletariat ist ihr eigenstes Produkt. Die Mittelstände, der kleine Industrielle, kleine Kaufmann, der Handwerker, der Bauer, sie alle bekämpfen die Bourgeoisie, um ihre Existenz als Mittelstände vor dem Untergang zu sichern. Sie sind also nicht revolutionär, sondern konservativ. Noch mehr, sie sind reaktionär, sie suchen das Rad der Geschichte zurückzudrehen. (*MEW* 4:461)

[Of all the classes that stand face to face with the bourgeoisie today, the proletariat alone is a really revolutionary class. The other classes decay and finally disappear in the face of modern industry; the proletariat is its special and essential product. The lower middle class, the small manufacturer, the shopkeeper, the artisan, the peasant, all these fight against the bourgeoisie, to save from extinction their existence as fractions of the middle class. They are therefore not revolutionary, but conservative. Nay more, they are reactionary, for they try to roll back the wheel of history. (Marx-Engels, *Manifesto of the Communist Party* [Moscow: Foreign Languages Publishing House, 1959], 58–59)]

In "Ist das Ideal der Freiheit veraltet?" (Is the ideal of freedom outmoded?), Brecht reminds his readers: "Vor 100 Jahren hat *Engels* vorausgesagt, was das Kleinbürgertum von einer Revolution erhofft" (*BFA* 22:526; A hundred years ago Engels predicted what the petty bourgeoisie expected from

---

[14] Münch, *Bertolt Brechts Faschismustheorie*, 26.

a revolution), citing Engels's list of their aspirations in order to associate the petty bourgeoisie with social democratic reformist thinking rather than truly thorough revolution.[15]

By grafting his dissenting diagnosis of the petty bourgeoisie's failure on to the *Communist Manifesto*'s assessment of the party's predicament, Brecht is able to avoid giving any impression of overtly deviating from the current Comintern line that in his eyes calls for modification.[16] Marx's and Engels's image of a politically powerless petty bourgeoisie at the same time paved the way for Brecht's assessment of Hitler as the epitome of the petty bourgeoisie's unrealistic ideals, as well as implying that the German proletariat was theoretically the sole class neither content to remain a passive victim of Germany's post-Versailles political situation nor willing to become fascism's accomplice. Brecht sums up the petty bourgeoisie's predicament as that of being "ökonomisch nicht eine selbständige Klasse. Es bleibt immer Objekt der Politik, jetzt ist es Objekt der großbürgerlichen Politik" (*BFA* 27:58; not an independent class in economic terms. It is always an object of politics, at the moment the object of upper bourgeois politics: *BBJ* 203). Quite logically, therefore, National Socialism's leader, Adolf Hitler, can be revealed for what he really is: "ein 'bloßer Schauspieler', der den großen Mann 'nur spielt', [. . .] der 'Mann ohne Kern', weil er eben das Kleinbürgertum vertritt, das in der Politik immer nur spielt" (*BFA* 27:58; "merely an actor" who is "just playing" the great man, [. . .] the "man with nothing at the centre," precisely because he represents the petty bourgeoisie, which only ever plays at politics: *BBJ* 203). This damning portrayal of the leader of a social class lacking ideological sincerity and simply playing at politics is designed to prepare the ground for Brecht's devastating attack on Hitler, "der Führer der siegreichen Kleinbürger" (*BFA* 22:877; the leader of the victorious petty bourgeoisie). According to this view,

> [Hitler] ist "phony" nämlich "nur" als Vertreter des Machtanspruchs der kleinbürgerlichen Klasse, nicht persönlich. Innerhalb des Kleinbürgertums ist er nicht phony. Sein Schicksal ist ein echtes, wenn man

---

[15] Brecht's paragraph quotes from Marx's and Engels's "Ansprache der Zentralbehörden an den Bund von 1850" (*MEW* 7:247).

[16] An extract from Dimitrov's address to the Seventh World Congress of the Comintern has been cited as proof that Brecht's "herrschendes Kleinbürgertum" paradigm deviated dangerously from Comintern thinking (Gerz, *Bertolt Brecht und der Faschismus*, 69–70). In the relevant passage, Dimitrov dismisses all talk of "die Macht des Kleinbürgertums oder des Lumpenproletariats über das Finanzkapital" and reaffirms the Comintern definition of "German fascism" as "die Macht des Finanzkapitals selbst." Elsewhere, however, he cautions against the tendency to posit some general model of fascism's development for all countries and all peoples. Brecht's corrective concerning the role of the petty bourgeoisie would seem to respect the spirit of this caveat.

ihn an die Grenzen der kleinbürgerlichen Möglichkeiten prallen läßt, dabei wird er plötzlich eine "Figur" und Hauptrolle. (*BFA* 27:59)

[[Hitler] is "only" *phoney* as representative of the petty bourgeoisie's claim to power, not as a person. Within the petty bourgeoisie he is not phoney. Once you let it collide with the bounds of petty bourgeois possibilities his fate is a real one, and he suddenly becomes a "character" and a leading role. (*BBJ* 203)]

Measured by such uncompromising criteria, Hitler is deemed to be an appropriately pathetic figurehead for a movement positioning itself somewhere between the controlling interests of Germany's *Großkapitalisten* and the aspirations of the *Kleinbürgertum*. Having established this, Brecht is able to suggest that a class that has betrayed its social and political responsibilities in the way the Social Democrats did in the Weimar years has saddled Third Reich Germany with the leadership it deserves, coupled with policies that will lead the nation into a war on so many fronts and in the name of so many incompatible policies that eventual defeat is guaranteed.

Rearmament, War, and the Third Reich's Economy

Noting that the standard approaches to the theme of fascism are differently nuanced in Brecht's work, a leading study argues that the socio-psychological angle tends to remain neglected, while the economic and political dimensions are fundamental to the whole critical project.[17] The most differentiated and comprehensive area of Brecht's analysis is, Frank Wagner suggests, in the field of ideological and cultural criticism. Since *Furcht und Elend*, Brecht's sole non-parabolic antifascist play, is also the only one to bring together the second approach's combination of economic and political analysis, it may be helpful at this stage to give an outline of Brecht's thinking on the NS regime's economic and political objectives during the period (1933–38) covered by his play. This will entail examining his picture of the intertwined issues of job-creation, Third Reich Germany's undercover rearmament, and the regime's large-scale preparation for a war that would ideally make up for the territorial and economic losses suffered as a consequence of the conditions imposed by the Versailles Treaty, as well as in theory solving the nation's alleged internal *Lebensraum* crisis.

At one point in his "Rede über die Frage, warum so große Teile des deutschen Volkes Hitlers Politik unterstützen" (Speech on the Question Why Such Large Parts of the German People Support Hitler's Politics, 1937), Brecht outlines the main reasons why Germany got to its present

---

[17] Frank D. Wagner, *Bertolt Brecht: Kritik des Faschismus*, 13.

predicament, one which made it welcome Hitler and National Socialism with open arms:

> Der unglückliche Vertrag von Versailles beseitigte die deutsche Armee, aber indem er die deutsche Industrie bestehen ließ, ja indem dieselbe durch mancherlei andere Verträge anscheinend profitabler Natur noch gestärkt wurde, blieb die Notwendigkeit einer Armee bestehen, ja wurde noch verstärkt. Es ist offenkundig, daß Deutschland heute mit seinen Gewaltakten den Frieden Europas bedroht. (*BFA* 22:339)

> [The unhappy Treaty of Versailles did away with the German army, but left German industry intact, even strengthened by various other profitable contracts; and, in so doing, the Treaty perpetuated, indeed intensified, the necessity for an army. It is clear that Germany today, by its acts of violence, threatens the peace of Europe. (*BAP* 180)]

Brecht's diagnosis also addresses the problem of the German people's apparent obliviousness to the fact that they were being systematically prepared for a war of monumental proportions. After all, the NS regime's economy was from the outset expressly a war economy, even if incessant propaganda emphasizing job-creation helped deflect public attention from this uncomfortable fact. In Brecht's assessment:

> Spätestens drei Jahre nach der Machtübernahme wurde es für die meisten deutlich, daß die Arbeitsbeschaffung eine Kriegsmaßnahme war; die zahlreichen Versuche von Wirtschaftsplanung dienten offen der Kriegsvorbereitung. (*BFA* 22:339)

> [At the latest, three years after [Hitler's] coming to power it became clear to most people that the work creation programme was a contribution to war; the numerous attempts at a planned economy openly served the preparations for war. (*BAP* 180–81)]

Yet up until the onset of the Spanish Civil War (rightly presented as a major turning-point in *Furcht und Elend*), Hitler and his government had been able to create an impression of having solved the unemployment crisis thanks to a series of ingenious job-creation policies, while in reality all that was on offer was an unsatisfactorily short-term solution: "Freilich sahen jetzt viele, daß durch eine Arbeitsbeschaffung solcher Art die Fütterung von Menschen unheimlich in die Fütterung von Kanonen umschlagen mußte" (*BFA* 22:339; Many now recognized that this sort of work creation would slide eerily over from the feeding of people to the feeding of cannons: *BAP* 181). In the event, Brecht's fears were soon corroborated: in February 1941 he could justifiably declare:

> der Krieg ist zu einer Industrie geworden. Er hängt hauptsächlich davon ab, ob das Öl ausgeht, nicht davon, ob der Fleiß ausgeht. Im

Augenblick sucht Hitler einen Markt für seine "Produkte," einen Kriegsschauplatz. (*BFA* 26:467)

[War has become an industry. It largely depends on whether oil supplies are exhausted, not on whether willingness to work is exhausted. At the moment Hitler is seeking a market for his "products" — a theatre of war. (*BBJ* 134–35)]

"Wie könnte ein Volk des Gedankens verdächtigt werden, es verbessere seine materielle Lage im Krieg?" (How could one suspect a people of thinking that it might improve its material conditions in war?), Brecht asked, before seeking to answer his own question in the following socio-political terms:

> In Wirklichkeit bestimmt aber eben nicht die überwiegende Mehrheit die Geschicke einer Nation im Kapitalismus; ihre Interessen bilden nicht die Gründe für die großen Aktionen: diese Massen sind gezwungen, grundlos, "interesselos" zu handeln. [. . .] Der Kampf der Klassen, Folge der Nichtübereinstimmung der materiellen Interessen der verschiedenen Klassen, verdeckt den wahren, immer höchst realen, materiellen Kriegsgrund (der einer der herrschenden Schicht ist). (*BFA* 21:588–89)

> [In reality, however, it is not the overwhelming majority that determines the destinies of a nation in capitalism; their interests do not form a basis for large-scale campaigns: these masses are compelled to act without reason and "without interests." [. . .] The struggle of classes, consequent on the discrepancies between the material interests of the various classes, conceals the true, always utterly real, material reason for war (which belongs to the ruling stratum). (*BAP* 113)]

In "Rede über die Frage, warum so große Teile des deutschen Volkes Hitlers Politik unterstützen," Brecht once more emphasizes the underlying class dimension of the regime's preparations for the imperialist-expansionist war now looming on the horizon, both in terms of identifying just whose vested interests war represented, as well as which class should in theory have grasped what was happening. His response was simple:

> Nur wenn die Interessen bestimmter besitzender Schichten vor die Interessen der überwiegenden Mehrheit des Volkes gestellt werden sollen, ist eine imperialistische Kriegspolitik nötig. An der deutschen Arbeitsbeschaffung haben die Geschäftsleute [viz. the German petty bourgeoisie] nachweisbar mehr verdient als die Arbeiter. Der Krieg ist selber ein Geschäft, auch derjenige, der verloren wird. (*BFA* 22:340)

> [Only if the interests of particular property-owning classes are valued above the interests of the overwhelming majority of the people does an imperialist politics of war become necessary. The businessmen profited demonstrably more from the German programme of work

creation than did the workers. War itself is a business, even a war which is lost. (*BAP* 181)]

As the following stanza from his satirical poem "Notwendigkeit der Propaganda" (The Necessity of Propaganda) demonstrates, Brecht rightly acknowledges the role played by Joseph Goebbels's Reichsministerium für Volksaufklärung und Propaganda (Reich Ministry for Public Enlightenment and Propaganda) in shaping public opinion on the question:

Nur durch vortreffliche Propaganda gelang es
Millionen davon zu überzeugen
Daß der Aufbau der Wehrmacht ein Werk des Friedens bedeutet
Jeder neue Tank eine Friedenstaube ist
Und jedes neue Regiment ein neuer Beweis
Der Friedensliebe. (*BFA* 12:66)

[Only thanks to excellent propaganda was it possible
To convince millions of people
That building up the army is an act of peace
Every new tank is a dove of peace
And every new regiment new proof
Of the love of peace.]

In Nazi Germany's specific case, war was this time not simply a matter of invading and occupying one's neighbors under the pretext of national self-defense, it was also above all an attempt to exploit their assets. Moreover, as Brecht elsewhere points out, the NS regime's internal war policy in fact looked simultaneously in two directions.[18] Preparations were, on the one hand, being made for an internal "*Vernichtungskampf gegen die deutsche Arbeiterbewegung*" (*BFA* 22:887; struggle to exterminate the German workers' movement) — "der innere Krieg, der mit den furchtbarsten Mitteln geführt wird" (*BFA* 22:71; the war on the Home Front that is being waged using the most horrendous means) — while, on the other, an outward-looking campaign was being directed against Germany's European foes and their allies — allies whom the NS regime chose to present as World Jewry and its political puppets.

Given the fact that the NSDAP's much-trumpeted program of job-creation ("Arbeitsbeschaffung") was inextricably bound up with the regime's intensive re-militarization policy, Brecht needed to explain, at least to his

---

[18] So also did Germany's ostensible peace plans: "Hitlers außenpolitischer Friede ist ein Friede für den Fall, daß die Forderungen erfüllt werden. [. . .] Er hat einen äußeren und einen inneren Kriegsschauplatz, und der Friede ist der Gewaltfriede, der durch Zerbrechung des Widerstands geschaffen werden soll" ("[Haltung der Sozialisten]" [*BFA* 22:299]).

own satisfaction, why so many Germans were prepared to turn a blind eye to the price they would eventually have to pay. Again at the time of Nazi Germany's involvement in the Spanish Civil War, with conflict once more a focal point for much of his thinking, Brecht writes in "Über die Frage des Krieges" (ca. 1937):

> Viele sagten [. . .], daß der Arbeiter keinen Krieg braucht. [. . .] Sie bezweifelten nicht, daß die Grundbesitzer oder die Fabrikanten oder die Bankiers mitunter einen Krieg brauchten; aber sie wußten, daß der Arbeiter ihn niemals braucht [. . .].
>
> Als *die Herrschaft der Kleinbürger* einsetzte, *die nicht gleich und überall als die der Grundbesitzer und Fabrikanten zu erkennen war*, fingen plötzlich auch viele Arbeiter an zu glauben, daß ganze Völker Kriege brauchen, oder sich ihnen wenigstens nicht entziehen können, und daß der Arbeiter zu seinem Volk gehört, ob er will oder nicht, und daß er also auch Kriege brauchen kann oder sich ihnen wenigstens nicht entziehen kann.
>
> Viele Arbeiter ließen sich mit einemmal davon überzeugen, daß die Erfüllung ihrer Arbeiterforderungen in gewisser Weise von der Möglichkeit abhing, daß das Volk, dem sie angehörten, einen Krieg führen konnte oder wenigstens sich ihm nicht entziehen mußte. *Diese Arbeiter wollten nicht den Krieg, aber sie waren bereit, ihn in Kauf zu nehmen, wenn anders ihre so nötigen Forderungen nicht erfüllt werden konnten. Glaubten diese Arbeiter etwas Falsches?*
>
> In einer gewissen Hinsicht glaubten sie nichts Falsches. *Völker, die innerlich so aufgebaut sind wie die unsern, nämlich kapitalistisch, brauchen tatsächlich Kriege, um existieren zu können.* (*BFA* 22:344, our emphases)

[Many people said [. . .] that the worker doesn't need a war. [. . .] They didn't doubt that the landowning class or factory owners or bankers needed a war from time to time; but they knew that the worker never needs one [. . .].

When *the rule of the petty bourgeoisie* commenced, *which was not immediately and everywhere recognizable as that of the landed class and the factory owners,* many workers also suddenly began to believe that entire peoples need wars, or at least cannot avoid them, and that the worker belongs to his people, whether or not he wants to, and thus that he can also need wars or at least cannot avoid them.

All of a sudden many workers allowed themselves to be persuaded that the fulfillment of their demands as members of the working class was in some way dependent on the possibility that the people to whom they belonged were capable of mounting a war or at least could not avoid doing so. *These workers did not want war, but they were prepared to accept one, if their necessary demands could not be met in any other way. Did these workers believe something wrong?*

In a certain respect, they did not. *Peoples that are internally structured like ours are, namely in a capitalist way, do actually need wars in order to be able to exist.*]

Two years later, with Europe-wide conflict over the Czech Sudetenland having been narrowly avoided, Brecht returned to the puzzling question of Germany's passive acceptance of NS foreign policy:

[Die Arbeiterschaft] hat viel geschluckt für die Beseitigung der Arbeitslosigkeit. *Kein* Krieg bedeutet Arbeitslosigkeit, wird das Regime sagen (mit Recht). [. . .] Dann bauen sie eine riesige ratio-nalisierte Industrie auf in einem politisch entmachteten Land und treiben Friedenspolitik! Und Hitler ist nun konsequent: die Grenzen, welche von den Waren nicht überschritten werden können, werden von den Tanks überschritten. Welches auch Waren sind (sowie die sie bedienenden Arbeitskräfte). (Journal entry for 19 February 1939 [*BFA* 26:329–30])

[[Working men] have swallowed a great deal for the abolition of unemployment. *Absence* of war means unemployment, the regime will say (and it is right). [. . .] Then they build a gigantic, rationalised industry in a land deprived of political power, and pursue a policy of peace. At least Hitler is consistent. The borders that goods cannot cross will be crossed by tanks. Which in turn are goods (along with the working men who operate them). (*BBJ* 22)]

The ultimate commodification of the fighting man and the effective way attention was deflected from this by Nazi propaganda images of heroism and self-sacrifice become more the subject of *Mutter Courage und ihre Kinder* (Mother Courage and Her Children) than *Furcht und Elend*, although it is present by implication in some of the *Private Life*'s post-1936 scenes.

In his repeated attempts to explain why so many Germans, especially among the petty bourgeoisie and urban proletariat, were seduced by Nazi pro-war propaganda and behaved as enthusiastically as they did, Brecht was prone to cite as prominent factors: (i) the role played by fear and intimidation in containing all forms of popular dissent, be they political or otherwise; (ii) such measures as the *Kraft durch Freude* (Strength through Joy) and *Schönheit der Arbeit* (Beauty of Work) programs, and (iii) the NS regime's ability to engineer from the outset mass patriotic support through a series of bonding "theatrical" events.

The "Theatricalization" of Politics in the Third Reich

"Die Theatralisierung der Politik durch den Faschismus habe ich schon ein wenig bearbeitet," Brecht modestly observes in his journal for 6 December 1940 (*BFA* 26:443; I have already done some work on the application of theatrical techniques to politics in Fascism: *BBJ*

115). Influenced by Walter Benjamin's concept of the aestheticization of politics,[19] Brecht's writings from the early 1930s onwards keep returning to the function of the Nazis' elaborate program of "Massenveranstaltungen," staged rituals and commemorative events. In Brecht's fictive dialogue "Über die Theatralik des Faschismus" (On the Theatricality of Fascism), a character named Karl comments on "die kleinen Dramatisierungen [. . .], die für den Nationalsozialismus so charakteristisch sind" (the little dramatisations which are so characteristic of National Socialism: *BAP* 195):

> Es ist ja kein Zweifel möglich, daß die Faschisten sich ganz besonders theatralisch benehmen. Sie haben besonderen Sinn dafür. Sie sprechen selber von *Regie*, und sie haben einen ganzen Haufen von Effekten direkt aus dem Theater geholt, die Scheinwerfer und die Begleitmusik, die Chöre und die Überraschungen. (*BFA* 22:563)

> [There is no doubt that the Fascists behave in an exceptionally theatrical manner. They have a particular feel for it. They speak themselves of *Regie* [direction, stage management], and they've adopted a whole range of effects directly from the theatre, the lights and the music, the choruses and the surprise twists. (*BAP* 195)]

Unlike his creator, however, Karl has little to say about the propaganda function of this important political epiphenomenon.

Interviewed by H. C. Loewe in 1935, Brecht declared:

> Das *wirkliche* Theater ist in Deutschland heute auf die Straße verlegt. Dort gibt es Feuerwerke und Militärparaden. Sie sind äußerst modern inszeniert. Die Regie klappt wie am Schnürchen. Bei diesem "Theater" gibt es mehr Besucher als bei dem *Sommernachtstraum* eines Reinhardt. Max Reinhardt, einstmals Deutschlands bedeutend-

---

[19] *"Der Faschismus läuft folgerecht auf eine Ästhetisierung des politischen Lebens hinaus."* (*Das Kunstwerk im Zeitalter seiner technischen Reproduzierbarkeit*, in Walter Benjamin, *Gesammelte Schriften*, ed. Rolf Tiedemann and Hermann Schweppenhäuser [Frankfurt am Main: Suhrkamp, 1973],1, ii, 506 (The logical outcome of fascism is an aestheticizing of political life, *The Work of Art in the Age of its Technological Reproducibility, and Other Writings on Media* [Cambridge, MA: The Belknap Press of Harvard UP, 2008], 41). On the implications of this approach to National Socialism, see Rainer Stollmann, "Faschistische Politik als Gesamtkunstwerk: Tendenzen der Ästhetisierung des politischen Lebens im Nationalsozialismus," in *Die deutsche Literatur im Dritten Reich: Themen — Traditionen — Wirkungen*, ed. Horst Denkler and Karl Prümm (Stuttgart: Reclam, 1976), 83–101, and Ansgar Hillach, "'Ästhetisierung des politischen Lebens': Benjamins faschismustheoretischer Ansatz — Eine Rekonstruktion," in *"Links hätte noch alles sich zu enträtseln. . .": Walter Benjamin im Kontext*, ed. Burkhardt Lindner (Frankfurt am Main: Syndikat, 1978), 127–67.

ster Theatermann, kann heute nicht mehr gegen Goebbels aufkom-
men.[20]

[Nowadays in Germany *real* theatre has been transferred to the streets.
There you find firework displays and military parades. They are staged
in an utterly modern fashion. The staging goes without a hitch. With
this kind of "theater" there are bigger audiences than for *A Midsum-
mer Night's Dream* staged by the likes of Reinhardt. Max Reinhardt,
once the greatest man of German theatre, is nowadays no longer able
to compete with Goebbels.]

Seen by Brecht as prima facie evidence that the NSDAP lacked a serious
political program, the movement's "Massenveranstaltungen" became a fre-
quent target of his satirical writings. Although not part of Comintern analysis (the Bolshevik pot was hardly in a position to call the NS kettle black!),
"Theatralisierung," "Dramatisierung," and "Ästhetisierung" became
recurrent leading concepts in Brecht's thinking about National Socialism's
rhetorical self-presentation. These three to-some-extent-interchangeable
terms are elastic and at times even deliberately ambiguous. Frank Wagner observes of Brecht's interpretative paradigm that the connotations of
aestheticization vacillate between suggesting a diversionary strategy for
discouraging political responses in any form and offering the semblance
of politics as a substitute for a real concrete political program that delivered what the people wanted.[21] Brecht's expository remarks on the subject
tend to operate with an astute mixture of diversion and compensation theory. A whole spectrum of inventive forms of political "Theatralisierung"
is, according to his analysis, deployed in Third Reich Germany in order
to deflect public attention from National Socialism's hollow nature (its
mere semblance of politics) — or in some areas its outright bankruptcy. In
method, this resembles Brecht's argument (addressed below, in our section
on Brecht and antisemitism in the present chapter) that the NS regime's
continual foregrounding of the race issue ("Rassenfrage") was a conscious
attempt to channel attention away from the more important question of
class ("Klassenfrage"). But at the same time, "Theatralisierung" arguably
served another important purpose by pandering to petty bourgeois escap-

---

[20] *Der Arbeiter* (New York), 23 November 1935. Brecht elaborates satirically on
the firework analogy in the third paragraph of his "Briefe um Deutschland" (*BFA*
22:50). While the firework image may have been primarily intended to ridicule the
Nazis' predilection for torchlight processions, it also prefigures Goebbels's "Licht-
dom" son-et-lumière effect used during the 1936 Nuremberg Rally as well as the
closing ceremony for the Berlin Olympic Games of the same year. For illustrations,
see Peter Reichel, *Der schöne Schein des Dritten Reiches: Faszination und Gewalt des
Faschismus* (Munich: Hanser, 1991), 256–57 and 76–77, respectively.
[21] Wagner, *Bertolt Brecht: Kritik des Faschismus,* 178 and 183.

ism.[22] At the stage immediately after the NS regime's coming to power, however, Brecht's "Unpolitische Briefe" (Unpolitical Letters), drafted in response to the Nuremberg Rally's "Reichsparteitag des Sieges" of 30 August 1933, convincingly takes the argument about function in a further, equally significant direction.

Having ridiculed the NS regime's program of contrived pageants, parades, and other spurious festivities (detailed in Stollmann, 84–87), Brecht draws the plausible conclusion: "Vor allem sollte die Einigkeit des Volkes hergestellt werden" (*BFA* 22:12; above all the unity of the people was to be manufactured: *BAP* 126). Despite having frequently charged the NSDAP with overdependence on diversionary tactics, Brecht still allows for the serious possibility that the strategy is also a valuable instrument for fostering a sense of folk — or racial — community (*Volksgemeinschaft* possesses both connotations):

> Diese Einigkeit hatte einige Jahrzehnte oder genauer einige Jahrhunderte lang zu wünschen übriggelassen, da es nicht allen Teilen des Volkes gleich gut ging: einige verdienten zuviel, einige wenig und die übrigen fast gar nichts. Darüber war es zur Uneinigkeit gekommen. Das sollte nun aufhören. (ibid.)

> [This unity had left something to be desired for a few decades, more precisely a few centuries, since things had not been going equally well for all parts of the nation: some earned too much, others a little and the rest hardly anything. That had caused disunity. It was to be stopped. (*BAP* 126–27)]

This bonding function, common to the regime's Wehrmacht parades, quasi-military civilian mass demonstrations, pseudo–folk festivals, youth ceremonies, and even public events (including the 1936 Olympic Games and the stage-managed 1938 *Kristallnacht* pogrom),[23] together with the cultivation of a synthetic sense of belonging to the new *Volksgemeinschaft*, was, of course, by no means incompatible with a diversionary agenda. Bread and circuses were equally necessary if the masses were to be prevented from realizing that "their" *Volksgemeinschaft* was to some considerable extent a pleasurable means to barbaric, aggressive ends. What Brecht identified as the other component of the overall strategy — the establishment of a vast program of building (especially of social housing), job creation, and related social initiatives — was lampooned in his poem on the regime's improvements: "Die Verbesserungen des Regimes" (*BFA* 12:67–68). We will be returning to the question of alleged social "Verbesserungen" in the

---

[22] Stollmann, "Faschistische Politik als Gesamtkunstwerk," 95.
[23] Brecht includes a representative list of such politicized festivities, great and small, in "Briefe um Deutschland" (*BFA* 22:50).

present chapter's section titled "The National Socialist *Volksgemeinschaft* and 'Scheinsozialismus'": in other words, the façade of socialism. In view of the Third Reich's post-1933 program of German remilitarization, a parallel ideological mobilization of the masses and the fact that many items in the regime's calendar of "theatrical" events tended to be of a paramilitary nature, the relationship of much fascist "Theatralik" to prowar propaganda can be seen to possess a far darker side than simply serving the bonding function of offering the people a communal outlet for their long suppressed patriotic feelings and their sense of indignation at having been unfairly defeated in 1918. As Walter Benjamin observed, "*Alle Bemühungen um die Ästhetisierung der Politik gipfeln in einem Punkt. Dieser eine Punkt ist der Krieg*"[24] (*All efforts to aestheticize politics culminate in one point. That one point is war*). National Socialism's obsession with national identity formation was in fact advancing step-by-step towards the point, documented in the framing parts of *The Private Life of the Master Race*, when the most dramatic "theatrical" effects came with the triumphs (and failures) of Germany's armed forces in various theaters of war. "Theatralisierung" thus became more than just a way of forging national cohesion or manipulating escapist dreams for political purposes; it effectively prepared for the time when the sad remnants of a once-proud *Volksgemeinschaft* would eventually be reduced to a fatalist state of mind where they welcomed "den totalen Krieg" and willingly took part in a final, Wagnerian "Götterdämmerung." The events subsumed under Brecht's conception of the "Theatralisierung" of politics amounted to large-scale conditioning for war in all its phases of victory, setbacks, and eventual defeat.

Brecht's writings on "Theatralisierung" pay little attention to the image of Adolf Hitler in his function as would-be charismatic leader of the nation. Given the emphasis on class and class-conflict in his comments on the Third Reich, personality cult may simply have been of little interest to Brecht as a key to the rise of fascism. As we have already observed in the case of Brecht's theoretical critique of National Socialism, and as can be seen in his play *Schweyk* and in the *Kriegsfibel*, when Hitler does enter the picture, it is often in the dubious role of appropriate identification-figure for the hapless petty bourgeoisie. Or in *Arturo Ui*, as a second-rate public orator whose crude rhetoric glosses over the ugly truth about life in the Third Reich by appealing to his audience's patriotism, xenophobia, and a festering sense of injustice. While the cult of the leader-figure does play an important part in a number of general studies of Brecht's views on the NS dictatorship,[25] it

---

[24] Walter Benjamin, *Gesammelte Schriften*, 1, ii, 506. Translation from Benjamin, *The Work of Art in the Age of its Technological Reproducibility*, 41.
[25] For assessments, see Gerz, *Bertolt Brecht und der Faschismus*, 74–75; Mennemeier, "Bertolt Brechts Faschismustheorie," 569–71; Münch, *Bertolt Brechts*

is arguably of limited significance for an understanding of the *Furcht und Elend* scenes, with the obvious exception of the first and last.

National Socialism as a Regime of "Furcht" and "Ängste"

In January 1938 the Moscow German exile journal *Das Wort* published Brecht's poem "Die Ängste des Regimes" (The Anxieties of the Regime). The work begins by presenting the subsequent verses as part of an eyewitness report: "Ein fremder Reisender, aus dem Dritten Reich zurückgekehrt / Und befragt, wer dort in Wahrheit herrsche, antwortete: / Die Furcht" ("Deutsche Satiren," *BFA* 12:68; A foreigner, returning from a trip to the Third Reich / When asked who really ruled there, answered: / Fear: *BBP* 296). The following stanza offers a panoramic account of the fears and anxieties of those living in Nazi Germany:

Angstvoll
Hält der Gelehrte mitten im Disput ein und betrachtet
Erblaßt die dünnen Wände seiner Studierstube. Der Lehrer
Liegt schlaflos, nachgrübelnd über
Ein dunkles Wort, das der Inspektor hingeworfen hat.
Die Greisin im Spezereiladen
Legt die zitternden Finger an den Mund, zurückzuhalten
Das zornige Wort über das schlechte Mehl. Angstvoll
Blickt der Arzt auf die Würgmale seines Patienten, voller Angst
Sehen die Eltern auf ihre Kinder wie auf Verräter.
Selbst die Sterbenden
Dämpfen noch die versagende Stimme, wenn sie
Sich von ihren Verwandten verabschieden. (*BFA* 12:68)

[Anxiously
The scholar breaks off his discussion to inspect
The thin partitions of his study, his face ashen. The teacher
Lies sleepless, worrying over
An ambiguous phrase the inspector had let fall.
The old woman in the grocer's shop
Puts her trembling finger to her lips to hold back
Her angry exclamation about the bad flour. Anxiously
The doctor inspects the strangulation marks on his patient's throat.

Faschismustheorie, 26–31; and Wagner, *Bertolt Brecht: Kritik des Faschismus*, 151–58 and 215–20. On Brecht's response as a professional man of the theater to Hitler's "Theatralik," see John J. White: *Bertolt Brecht's Dramatic Theory* (Rochester: Camden House, 2004), 284–91.

Full of anxiety, parents look at their children as at traitors.
Even the dying
Hush their failing voices as they
Take leave of their relatives. (*BBP* 297)]

The poem moves on, less predictably, from images of the fear of the
oppressed to various examples of things that allegedly give rise to anxiety in the Nazis themselves: an ingenious twist to the phrase "Ängste des
Regimes" in the poem's title:

Aber auch die Braunhemden selber
Fürchten den Mann, dessen Arm nicht hochfliegt
Und erschrecken vor dem, der ihnen
Einen guten Morgen wünscht.
Die hohen Stimmen der Kommandierenden
Sind von Angst erfüllt wie das Quieken
Der Ferkel, die das Schlachtmesser erwarten, und die feisten Ärsche
Schwitzen Angst in den Bürosesseln.
Von Angst getrieben
Brechen sie in die Wohnungen ein und suchen in den Klosetts nach
Und Angst ist es
Die sie ganze Bibliotheken verbrennen läßt. So
Beherrscht die Furcht nicht nur die Beherrschten, sondern auch
Die Herrschenden. (*BFA* 12:68)

[But likewise the brownshirts themselves
Fear the man whose arm doesn't fly up
And are terrified of the man who
Wishes them a good morning.
The shrill voices of those who give orders
Are full of fear like the squeaking of
Piglets awaiting the butcher's knife, as their fat arses
Sweat with anxiety in their office chairs.
Driven by anxiety
They break into homes and search the lavatories
And it is anxiety
That makes them burn whole libraries. Thus
Fear rules not only those who are ruled, but
The rulers too. (*BBP* 297)]

Third Reich Germany is shown to be both the victim and the cause of
a contagious fear in ways that run counter to the regime's all-too-familiar
propaganda claims. The German people, ostensibly all members of a new
Volksgemeinschaft, are shown to be collectively intimidated to the point of
suspecting potential accusers on all sides. In their turn, the regime's agents
fear anything they cannot control — in particular, unpredictable behavior

that might conceivably betoken resistance. While the conclusion — "So / Beherrscht die Furcht nicht nur die Beherrschten, sondern auch / Die Herrschenden" — is obviously not intended to belittle the sufferings of "die Beherrschten," well-chosen images of the NS oppressors' fear make them seem far more irrational and more cowardly than their countless victims. The oppressor-oppressed relationship has been rebalanced.

The poem's various illustrations of the Nazis' overreaction to perceived threats and signs of dissent again invite the application of a compensatory interpretive model, according to which propagandistic images of power, violence, and supremacy can be read as evidence that the country's rulers are less confident of their hold over the people than most propagandistic images and claims would suggest. If such an interpretive model were applied to the full title of Brecht's *Furcht und Elend des Dritten Reiches* (which has seldom happened in the secondary literature to date), then the lessons of Brecht's "Die Ängste des Regimes" would imply that a totalitarian regime that strives inordinately hard to instill abject fear in its subjects does so primarily because at bottom it fears them as putative adversaries and resistance fighters — or, in the case of the KPD, ideological competitors. While fear may be one of the Nazi Party's main weapons, it is at the same time potentially its Achilles heel. The regime's fragility is memorably invoked in both "Die Ängste des Regimes" and *Furcht und Elend* in order to sow the seeds of resistance.

In a letter to Thomas Mann of 1 December 1943, Brecht returns to his thesis of "die Furcht der Herrschenden" with the suggestion that the Nazis might be less in control of Germany than they would like people to think they are. Instead of once again using a sequence of satirical variations on the idea of "die Ängste des Regimes," Brecht now sets out concrete evidence of how the Hitler regime's room for maneuver has been substantially curtailed by the need to keep the lid firmly on potential further resistance on the Home Front:

> Die deutsche Kriegsführung zeigt entsetzlich klar, daß der physische Terror des Regimes zu ungeheuerlichen geistigen und moralischen Verkrüppelungen der ihm ausgesetzten Menschen geführt hat. Jedoch opferten auch über 300 000 Menschen in Deutschland ihr Leben in den meistens unsichtbaren Kämpfen mit dem Regime allein bis zum Jahre 42 und nicht weniger als 200 000 aktive Hitlergegner saßen zu Beginn des Krieges in Hitlers Konzentrationslagern. Noch heute binden die Hitlergegner in Deutschland mehr als 50 Divisionen Hitlerscher Elitetruppen, die sogenannte SS. Das ist kein kleiner Beitrag zur Niederringung Hitlers. (*BFA* 29:318)

> [Germany's conduct of the war shows with terrible clarity that the physical terror to which the regime has subjected the people has left them with hideous moral and intellectual deformities. And yet by 1942 more than three hundred thousand people in Germany had

sacrificed their lives in largely invisible struggles against the regime, while at the beginning of the war no less than two hundred thousand active anti-Nazis were being held in Hitler's concentration camps. Even today the anti-Nazi forces in Germany are tying down more than fifty divisions of Hitler's elite troops, the so-called SS. This is no small contribution to the defeat of Hitler. (*BBL* 374–75)]

At times Brecht may have been surprised and disturbed by the jubilant reception National Socialism enjoyed in both Third Reich Germany and in post-annexation Austria, but his general grasp of the nature of everyday life under the repressive NS regime tends to confirm the role played by fear and intimidation in ensuring subservience. What is more, as we will show in Chapter Three, he presents the regime's exploitation of the fear factor, not in a spirit of resignation, but in order to allow for the possibility — or as the regime would see it: the threat — of meaningful political resistance and local opposition. He juggles in similar fashion with negative and positive elements in the next model to feature in his picture of the Third Reich's power-structure: that of the base-superstructure relationship.

Brecht's Application of the Base-Superstructure Model to the Third Reich

Brecht's journal for 15 May 1942 (at the time of a series of Wehrmacht victories on the Crimean front) begins, perhaps surprisingly, by addressing the debate about whether there was such a thing as a "good" as well as a "bad" Germany:

Die Unterscheidung zwischen Hitlerdeutschland und Deutschland ("Hitler ist nicht Deutschland!") ist naturgemäß, je länger der totale Krieg tobt, desto schwerer einleuchtend vorzutragen. Die Lesebuchfabel, daß das deutsche Volk oder zumindest die deutsche Arbeiterschaft gegen diesen Krieg ist, kann immer weniger den ungeheuren Furor der deutschen Riesenarmeen, die gewaltigen Leistungen der Industrie und die Stabilität der inneren Ordnung in Deutschland erklären. Der Widerstand der Hitlerarmee gegen die Sowjetoffensive in diesem Winter deutet nicht gerade auf brüchige "Moral" hin. [. . .] Wenige Beispiele in der Geschichte beweisen so schlagend die Wahrheit des Satzes, daß das gesellschaftliche Sein das Bewußtsein bestimmt, wie der Einfall des deutschen Volksheeres in die Sowjetunion. (*BFA* 27:95)

[The longer total war goes on, the more difficult, of course, it becomes to demonstrate plausibly the difference between Germany and Hitler's Germany ("Hitler is not Germany!"). Schoolbooks still take the line that the German people, or at least the German working class, is against this war, but this view is increasingly at odds with the terrible fury of the huge German armies, the mighty achievements of industry and Germany's internal stability. The resistance Hitler's army put up during last winter's Soviet offensive does not exactly indicate the collapse of "morale." [. . .] Few examples from history demonstrate as strikingly as the invasion of the Soviet Union by the army of the German people the truth of the proposition that social being determines consciousness. (*BBJ* 231)]

In the eyes of the outside world, the starting-point here seems to imply, Germany is gradually becoming synonymous with Nazi Germany, hence Brecht's pejorative reference to the Wehrmacht forces fanatically fighting on the Eastern front as "Hitler's army." As the ironic use of the word "Widerstand" (resistance) suggests, instead of any resistance within Third Reich Germany, the only discernible resistance at the time was "der Widerstand der Hitlerarmee gegen die Sowjetoffensive" — a state of affairs that Brecht seeks to explain by appealing to Marx's base-superstructure model. However, the picture his diary evokes is patently at odds with the textbook Marxist model of what ought to be happening under such conditions. In the resultant journal entry, we witness Brecht's struggles to explain the events of 1941–42. In fact, just as his class-oriented interpretation of certain features of National Socialism was influenced by Marx's and Engels's thinking on the political role of the petty bourgeoisie, his application of the base-superstructure model is primarily indebted to Karl Marx's *Zur Kritik der Politischen Ökonomie* (*A Contribution to the Critique of Political Economy*). In a diary entry for 18 April 1942, with Third Reich Germany in mind, Brecht refers to "die große Komik, daß sie [middle class German intellectuals] zu führen meinen und geführt werden," citing such self-delusion as exemplifying "die Donquichotterie des Bewußtseins, das vermeint, das gesellschaftliche Sein zu bestimmen" (*BFA* 27:84; The comedy of those who think they are leading but are in fact being led, the don-quixotry of a consciousness which labors under the delusion that it is determining social existence: *BBJ* 222).

As the above journal entry reveals, the locus classicus for Brecht's conclusion is Marx's foreword to *Zur Kritik der Politischen Ökonomie*.

Die Gesamtheit dieser Produktionsverhältnisse bildet die ökonomische Struktur der Gesellschaft, die reale Basis, worauf sich ein juristischer und politischer Überbau erhebt, und welcher bestimmte gesellschaftliche Bewußtseinsformen entsprechen. [. . .] Es ist nicht das Bewußtsein der Menschen, das ihr Sein, sondern umgekehrt ihr gesellschaftliches Sein, das ihr Bewußtsein bestimmt. (*MEW* 13, 8–9)

[The totality of these relations of production constitutes the economic structure of society, the real foundation, on which arises a legal and political superstructure and to which correspond definite forms of social consciousness. [. . .] It is not the consciousness of men that determines their existence, but their social existence that determines their consciousness. (Preface to *A Contribution to the Critique of Political Economy* [London: Lawrence & Wishart, 1971], 20–21)]

According to Marxist-Leninist orthodoxy, the German proletariat should have risen up to oppose their country's war in the East on ideological grounds. The Wehrmacht's huge armies ("Riesenarmeen"), ironically referred to as a people's army ("Volksheer") in the final sentence of Brecht's entry, made a successful massive surprise attack on the Soviet Union in 1941, with no hint of opposition from the German proletariat at large. Vast numbers of Wehrmacht soldiers (the majority of whom, we are meant to understand, were part of a working class sacrificed in the interests of a capitalist cause) were as a consequence now engaged in a life-or-death struggle with their Soviet proletarian "comrades" on the Eastern front.

Brecht tries to explain why working-class German soldiers did not mutiny and specifically refuse to engage in a savage war against a socialist country. His first line of reasoning, almost by way of an excuse, is to suggest that civilian German workers had been disenfranchised and deprived of their traditional leadership. What is more, they had been rendered powerless by "bestimmte gesellschaftliche Maßnahmen" (certain social measures):

Die Arbeiterschaft war daran gewöhnt worden, ihre Interessen durch die demokratischen Institutionen der Parlamente und Parteien der Parlamente, sowie durch die Gewerkschaften wahrzunehmen. Die Auflösung dieser Institutionen usw. machte die Arbeiterschaft organisations- und hilflos. Die Arbeiterschaft, die sich zu schwach sah, ihre internationale Politik zu führen, fügte sich der nationalen Politik ihrer Bourgeoisie. (*BFA* 27:95–96)

[The working class had become accustomed to having its interests represented by democratic institutions, namely parliament and the parliamentary parties, plus the trade unions. The dissolution of these institutions deprived the working class of organised representation and left it helpless. Finding itself too weak to implement its own internationalist policies, it succumbed to the nationalist policies of the bourgeoisie. (*BBJ* 231–32)]

What Brecht offers here is an example of the inhibiting effect of the "base" (Marx's "reale Basis, worauf sich ein juristischer und politischer Überbau erhebt") on the German working class. However, his illustration fails to do justice to the fact that the legal and political superstructure now in place is corrupt and often reinforced by intimidation and propaganda. The workers have as a consequence been deprived of their "institutions" (trades unions, political parties, as well as their vital links with international socialism), a severe blow presented as having thus forcibly deprived them of their channels of self-expression and self-understanding. As a result, the NS regime had it in its power "das Klassenbewußtsein der Arbeiterschaft zu betäuben" (*BFA* 27:95; to [. . .] neutralise the workers' class-consciousness: *BBJ* 231). Up to this point, Brecht could be charged with invoking the base-superstructure model in a mechanistically determinist way. His claim that the proletariat has been rendered "zu schwach [. . .], ihre internationale Politik zu führen" (too weak to implement its own internationalist policies) implies that their obligations to international socialism, assumedly represented by the Comintern and Popular Front antifascist struggle, have been effectively neutralized by the NS regime's draconian measures. However, a further layer of Brecht's explanation concentrates on what prevents the workers from sabotaging what is happening in the East:

> Die Beseitigung der Arbeitslosigkeit, gewisse pseudosozialistische Institutionen, vielleicht auch die Erfassung der Jugend in "volksgemeinschaftlichen" Verbänden, dazu der politische und ökonomische Terror ergaben ein Feld des sozialen Seins, das erst durch einen zerstörenden Krieg erschüttert werden muß, damit es die klassischen Formationen zurückbekommt. (*BFA* 27:96)

> [By eliminating unemployment, introducing a few pseudo-socialist institutions and attracting young people into "one-nation" organisations, while at the same time instituting a reign of political and economic terror, the bourgeoisie created a field of social existence that will have to be demolished by a war of destruction before the classical structure of society can be reinstated. (*BBJ* 232)]

In other words, as a quid pro quo for allowing themselves to be, in the Party's jargon, "gleichgeschaltet" (coordinated) and forcibly integrated into the new Deutsche Arbeitsfront (DAF, German Workers' Front), the workers are guaranteed security of employment coupled with the gratifying sense of personally contributing to the new *Volksgemeinschaft*, a feature of National Socialism discussed in the next section. The totalitarian "superstructure" in question, entailing an asymmetrical ethic of sacrifice, sacrificial patriotism, and unquestioning obedience on the part of the workers, has by and large conditioned them to incline towards different values from those promoted in contemporary socialist countries like the USSR. In an attempt to account for the powerful mass appeal of National Socialism that — Clara Zetkin and Karl Radek had complained at the Fourth World Comintern Congress — was missing from the Bolshevik analysis, Brecht charges the working class with being duped by the NS regime's "Scheinsozialismus." These assertions are also the subject of Brecht's 1937 poem "Die Verbesserungen des Regimes" (The Regime's Improvements), which immediately precedes "Die Ängste des Regimes" in the *Svendborger Gedichte* collection. In both contexts, the welfare, social bonding and economical aspects of the "socialism" allegedly endorsed by the National Socialist German Workers' Party (NSDAP) are unmasked as little more than tokenism.

As we saw, Brecht describes the circumstances he has been exploring as "ein Feld des sozialen Seins, das erst durch einen zerstörenden Krieg erschüttert werden muß, damit es die klassischen Formationen zurückbekommt" (*BFA* 27:96), conceivably as a counterbalance to the vulgar determinist potential of Marx's original base-superstructure model. However, although attempting to draw lessons from a comparison between the situation of Nazi Germany at war with the USSR in 1941–42 and Germany in the First World War, Brecht hardly seems optimistic about the outlook for the proletariat:

Ein Vergleich zwischen dem Verhalten der Arbeiterschaft 1914 und dem 1939 [zeigt], daß das Tiefenfeld des sozialen Seins sogar verstärkte Wirkungen ausstrahlt. Die Schließung des freien Arbeitsmarktes [under the NS regime] hat mit ihrer Verlegung des Schwergewichts der Klassenkämpfe vom ökonomistischen zum politischen Bezirk die Arbeiterschaft in Verwirrung gestürzt, da ihre Organisationsformen damit überholt und veraltet waren; zugleich aber hat sie die Arbeiterschaft endgültig auf den politischen Bezirk getrieben, was sich zunächst freilich nur negativ auswirkt. Die Klage unserer kleinbürgerlichen Corialane, dieses Volk werde wohl immer wieder in imperialistische Abenteuer "zurück"fallen, [. . .] ist natürlich begründet, wenn der Plan besteht, die ökonomisch-politische Basis des Imperialismus zu erhalten. Sie sind keineswegs gegen diesen Plan und hegen eigentlich nur die Befürchtung, die deutschen Massen könnten auch von "neuen" Bewußtseinsstufen aus (Pazifismus, Demokratismus) die unvermeidlichen Tendenzen einer ökonomisch-politischen Basis, ähnlich der von 1918–1933, nicht überwinden. Allerdings würde, was sie nicht wissen und nicht wissen wollen, auch eine solche Basis, poliziert und regional zerstückelt, die vermuteten Tendenzen wieder produzieren. (ibid.)

[A comparison between the behaviour of the working class in 1914 and in 1939 shows that the deep field of social being is emitting even stronger impulses now than then. The closure of the free labour market which transferred the central thrust of the class struggle from the economic to the political sphere plunged the working class into confusion, by making its organisations obsolete and outmoded; at the same time it finally forced the working class into the political sphere — with, initially, only negative effect. The complaints of our petty bourgeois Coriolanuses that the working class will always "backslide" into imperialist adventures [. . .] is of course only valid as long as the plan is to retain imperialism as the politico-economic basis. Bourgeois objectors in fact have nothing against this plan, what they fear is that the German masses, having incorporated "new" components (pacifism, democracy) into their consciousness, might be unable to resist the inevitable appeal of a politico-economic basis similar to the one that existed from 1918 to 1933. Of course — and this they neither know nor wish to know — such a basis, policed and split up into regions, would once again produce the very tendencies they are afraid of. (*BBJ* 232)]

Although struggling to find his way forward to a more constructive framework within which the base-superstructure model could be used with reference to Nazi Germany, Brecht ends with the gloomy prognosis of class stalemate. But earlier on, when applying the base-superstructure model to the Hitler Youth (HJ) movement in "Der Faschismus und die Jugend" (Fascism and Youth), he manages to avoid similarly pessimistic conclusions. Although observing "Das Bewußtsein der deutschen Jugend wird vom nationalsozialistischen Staat mit allen Mitteln planmäßig gestaltet, niemand kann ihn darin hindern. Die Geschichte [. . .] bekräftigt seine Dogmen, sogar die Natur [. . .] bestätigt seine Ideen" (*BFA* 22:348; The consciousness of German youth is systematically molded by the NS state using all possible means, no one can prevent this. History [. . .] strengthens its dogmatic tenets, even nature [. . .] confirms its ideas), this time Brecht avoids resignation, preferring instead to remind himself that:

> indem [die Jugend] älter wird, tritt sie in die Sphäre der Produktion, sammelt sich in den Fabriken und Kontoren und nimmt aktiv teil an dem gigantischen Anschauungsunterricht und Praktikum des gesellschaftlichen Lebens der Nation [. . .]. Die Lehre, daß es keine Klassen gibt, läßt sich natürlich der Jugend leichter erzählen als den Erwachsenen [. . .]. (*BFA* 22:349–50)

> [as [young people] grow older, they enter the sphere of production, come together in factories and offices and engage actively with the vast theoretical and practical educational project that is part of the nation's social life [. . .]. The lesson that social classes do not exist is, of course, more easily conveyed to young people than to grown-ups.]

Further recourse to Marx's base-superstructure model in a series of "Thesen zur Theorie des Überbaus" (*BFA* 21:570–72; Theses on the Theory of Superstructure: *BAP* 107–9) offered Brecht constructive access to certain revealing features of NS Germany's virtually built-in obsolescence. His first "thesis," according to which superstructure-formation is *a process* and to some extent a "selbst entwickelter Faktor" (*BFA* 21:570; an autonomously evolving factor: *BAP* 107), and his fifth "thesis," which states that "die Art, auf die Überbau entsteht, ist: Antizipation" (*BFA* 21:571; The way in which superstructure comes about is: anticipation: *BAP* 108) have important implications for the way in which Brecht dramatizes the relationship of social being to base in the Third Reich context. What is more, the suggestion in his fourth "thesis" that, in the age of imperialism, bourgeois culture (an element that makes up the "Überbau") is essentially international is a crucial assertion, one to which Brecht adds the comment "um wieviel mehr erst die proletarische!" (and how much more is this true of proletarian culture!). Of course, Brecht contemplated any historical phenomenon in terms of its antithesis:

die Dialektisierung aller Kategorien des Denkens ist unvermeidlich, und von jedem Gebiet aus, das dialektisiert ist, kommt man, *wenn nur die politische Komponente gezogen wird*, zur Revolution. (*BFA* 21:571–72)

[The dialectical infusion of all categories of thought is unavoidable, and every area that has been dialectically infused leads to revolution, *as long as the political dimension is inferred.* (*BAP* 108)]

But when applied specifically to the fascist countries of Europe, this helps explain Brecht's unshakeable confidence that resistance of the right kind would eventually materialize.

However, it could be argued that Brecht fails to deploy the Marxist base-superstructure model with sufficient rigor in the case of the NS process of *Gleichschaltung* (co-ordination),[26] a carrot-and-stick policy involving a whole series of coercive measures coupled with inducements affecting virtually all strata of society in the Third Reich. In some contexts, Brecht's literary treatment of the bourgeoisie's capitulation to National Socialism's dictatorial new value system touches implicitly on the phenomenon. It would therefore be rewarding to explore the connections between Brecht's idea that "die Art, auf die Überbau entsteht, ist: Antizipation" and *Furcht und Elend*'s depiction of collaboration, fellow-traveling, willing complicity, and the kinds of moral and political compromise that became an important feature of daily life under the Nazis.

The National Socialist *Volksgemeinschaft* and "Scheinsozialismus"

In an interview with Hanns Johst published in the *Frankfurter Volksblatt* of 27 January 1934, Hitler set out his conception of the Third Reich as a *Volksgemeinschaft*:

Meine Bewegung faßt Deutschland als Körperschaft auf, als einen einzigen Organismus. [. . .] Der Nationalsozialismus nimmt aus [dem] Lager der bürgerlichen Tradition: die nationale Entschlossenheit,

---

[26] Defined as "a process that was in train all over Germany in the period from February to July 1933: the process, as the Nazis called it, of [. . .] *Gleichschaltung*, a metaphor drawn from the world of electricity, meaning that all the switches were being put onto the same circuit, as it were, so that they could all be activated by throwing a single master switch at the centre. Almost every aspect of political, social and associational life was affected, at every level from the nation to the village." (Richard J. Evans, *The Coming of the Third Reich* [London: Allen Lane, 2003], 381.)

und aus dem Materialismus der marxistischen Lehre: den lebendigen, schöpferischen Sozialismus.

[My movement conceives of Germany as a corporate body, as a single organism. [. . .] National Socialism takes national resolve from the camp of bourgeois tradition, and living, creative socialism from the materialism of Marxist dogma.]

While the new *Volksgemeinschaft* was clearly meant to be all things to all men, the main emphasis was on Nazi Germany as a classless society united by a shared ideology:

Volksgemeinschaft: das heißt Gemeinschaft aller wirkenden Arbeit, das heißt Einheit aller Lebensinteressen, das heißt Überwindung von privatem Bürgertum und gewerkschaftlich-mechanisch-organisierter Masse, das heißt die unbedingte Gleichung von Einzelschicksal und Nation, von Individuum und Volk. [. . .] Der deutsche Bürger [. . .] muß Staatsbürger werden und der Genosse [. . .] Volksgenosse. Beide müssen mit ihrem guten Willen den soziologischen Begriff des Arbeiters zu dem Ehrentitel der Arbeit adeln. [. . .] Der Bürger soll sich nicht länger als eine Art Rentner weder der Tradition noch des Kapitals fühlen und durch die marxistische Besitzidee vom Arbeiter getrennt, sondern soll mit offenem Sinn streben, als Arbeiter dem Ganzen eingefügt zu werden.[27]

[People's Community: that means a community of all productive labor, that means the oneness of all vital interests, that means over-coming bourgeois privatism and the unionized, mechanically organized masses, that means unconditionally equating the individual fate and the nation, the individual and the people. The bourgeois must become a citizen of the state; the red comrade must become a racial comrade. Both must, with their good intentions, ennoble the socio-logical concept of the worker and raise the status of an honorary title for labor. [. . .] The bourgeois man should stop feeling like some sort of pensioner of tradition or capital and separated from the worker by the Marxist concept of property. Rather, he should strive, with an open mind, to become integrated into the whole as a worker.][28]

Less than two years later, Dr. Robert Ley, leader of the Deutsche Arbeitsfront, proudly announced that Germany was the first country in Europe to have solved the problem of the class struggle.[29] Claiming, in the wake of the imposition of DAF in place of Germany's traditional

---

[27] *Hitler: Reden und Proklamationen, 1932–1945*, ed. Max Domarus, vol. 1, *Triumph, 1932–1934* (Wiesbaden: Löwit, 1973), 349–51.
[28] English translation in Evans, *The Third Reich in Power*, 497–98.
[29] *Völkischer Beobachter*, 29 September 1935.

unions, that the citizens of the Third Reich were now all "Soldaten der Arbeit" (soldiers of work), Ley set the *Kraft durch Freude* (*KdF*) program in motion to reward workers for accepting the fait accompli of losing their social and political support systems, while exploiting it as a way of appearing to narrow the class divide. *Kraft durch Freude* was clearly one of the pseudo-socialist institutions Brecht was invoking when trying to account for the fact that so many members of the German proletariat had been successfully poached by the National Socialists. "Im Faschismus erblickt der Sozialismus sein verzerrtes Spiegelbild," he argued. "Mit keiner seiner Tugenden, aber allen seinen Lastern" (*BFA* 27:158; In fascism socialism is confronted with a distorted mirror-image of itself. With none of its virtues and all of its vices: *BBJ* 285). He seems to be echoing Dimitrov's reference, near the beginning of his 1935 report to the Comintern, to the German type of fascism, the most reactionary variety that had the effrontery to call itself "National Socialism," though it had nothing to do with socialism.[30]

Although the noun *Volksgemeinschaft* supplies the title for Scene 1 of *Furcht und Elend* and the concept becomes the target of a number of subsequent scenes, the subject seldom figured in Brecht's nonliterary antifascist writings, the most important exception being his critical assessment of the program in "Plattform für die linken Intellektuellen," where Section 5 (*BFA* 22:327) refers to "Der nationalsozialistische Versuch der Einigung" (The National Socialist attempt at unification: *BAP* 174), i.e., the incorporation of all classes into the new *Volksgemeinschaft*. Even here, the term is implied, rather than explicitly mentioned. The reason for this evasiveness on Brecht's part is probably that the concept was already suggested in his various attacks on the NS regime's "Scheinsozialismus," a term calculated to suggest that the NSDAP's façade of "socialism" was little more than a hollow variation on SPD reformist policies, in other words a revival of the "false" socialism all too familiar from Weimar Republic times.[31] This was clearly the main subtext to Brecht's retrospective journal entry for 24 December 1947:

> Der Nationalsozialismus muß betrachtet werden als *der Sozialismus der Kleinbürger*, eine verkrüppelte, neurasthenische, pervertierte Volksbewegung, die für das von tiefer unten Geforderte einen der herrschenden Klasse nicht unliebsamen Ersatz lieferte oder zu liefern versprach. *Die scheinsozialistischen Ansätze müssen also mit dem echten Artikel verglichen werden, nicht mit der "Demokratie."* (*BFA* 27:258, our emphases)

---

[30] Dimitrov, "The Class Character of Fascism," 115.

[31] The charge here echoes that made by Dimitrov in "The Fascist Offensive and the Task of the Communist International in the Struggle of the Working Class against Fascism": "The German type of Fascism, the most reactionary variety of Fascism, has the effrontery to call itself National Socialism, though it has nothing to do with socialism" (*For a United and Popular Front*, 114–93, here 115).

[National Socialism must be regarded as *the socialism of the petty bour-geoisie*, a crippled, neurasthenic, perverted popular movement which produced or promised to produce a surrogate for what was being demanded from lower down the social order, one which would not be too unacceptable to the ruling class. *The pseudo-socialist beginnings must therefore be compared with the real thing and not with "democracy."* (*BBJ* 380, our emphases)]

In "Warum droht die Abwanderung kleinbürgerlicher und sogar proletarischer Schichten zum Faschismus?" (Why are the Petty Bourgeoisie and Even the Proletariat Threatening to Turn to Fascism?), Brecht conceded that the masses had been all too often deceived by the regime's "Scheinsozialismus." Indeed, according to one chronicler of the period, the German public was largely taken in and seduced by NS *Volksgemeinschaft* propaganda.[32] In a deliberate counter-ploy, Brecht attacked the regime's willful "Perversion des Sozialismus" in "[Zweck des Studiums]" (The Purpose of Study) declaring that such a veneer of "National-Sozialismus" (the hyphenation is intended to deconstruct the familiar compound noun in order to draw attention to its falsity) "pervertiert auch die [. . .] Tatsache vom Primat des arbeitenden Volkes zu einer frechen Scheinwahrheit" (*BFA* 22:343).[33] (National-Socialism even perverts the very primacy of the working class into an impudent pseudo-truth). His repeated references to true socialist ideals makes it very clear that in Brecht's eyes the yardstick by which the NS *Volksgemeinschaft* and its half-hearted socialism were to be gauged was the standard allegedly already set by the Soviet Union, rather than the criteria favored by Western bourgeois democracies. In suggesting this, of course, Brecht may have unwittingly invited invidious comparisons between the Third Reich's achievements and the Soviet Union's failure to meet many of its stated targets as the Comintern also did when it tried to contrast German antisemitism with the treatment of Jews in the USSR.

The presence of the seemingly innocuous word "Volk" in the propaganda concept of a *Volksgemeinschaft* was intended to suggest that the new all-encompassing egalitarian society was an ethnic as well as politically classless entity. In his interview with Johst, Hitler declared that even the

---

[32] Evans, *The Third Reich in Power*, 500.

[33] In his satirical critique of Goering's notorious slogan "Gemeinnutz geht vor Eigennutz," Brecht makes the point that "in einem sozialistischen Gemeinwesen besteht kein Gegensatz zwischen dem Nutzen des einzelnen und dem Nutzen der Allgemeinheit" ("Über den Satz 'Gemeinnutz geht vor Eigennutz'" (*BFA* 22:58). The fact that Goering used the slogan in 1938, at the very time of the *Anschluss* and massive mobilization in preparation for outright war on Germany's neighboring countries, leads Brecht to question the motives underlying such a "gutmütiger Satz" (Brecht's phrase).

"red" comrade must become a "racial" comrade, although the converse would obviously never be tolerated. The Third Reich myth of having liberated Germany from all class barriers was such a blatant attempt at stealing historical socialism's clothes that the charge of peddling "Scheinsozialismus" was to become a staple component of Brecht's theoretical and literary attacks on National Socialism. In reality, the *Volksgemeinschaft* was more of an "exclusive-inclusive" construct. As Brecht puts it in "Plattform für die linken Intellektuellen," "Der nationalsozialistische Versuch der Einigung [der Klassen] schließt in sich die Vernichtung, Ausschaltung oder Unterwerfung jener Menschengruppen, welche die nationale Geschlossenheit beeinträchtigen, der Juden und der Arbeiter" (*BFA* 22:327; The National Socialist attempt at unification includes the annihilation, exclusion or subordination of those groups of people who are detrimental to national solidarity, the Jews and the workers: *BAP* 174). Elsewhere, in the context of the regime's *Lebensraumpolitik*, Brecht recalls a recent example of the way in which antisemitic scapegoating had been callously instrumentalized to become an indirect form of national bonding: "Das Bürgertum, das die politische Herrschaft nie bekommen hatte, schuf so ein Nationalgefühl ('gegen die Juden' war 'für die Sudetenbrüder')" (*BFA* 27:64; The bourgeoisie, which had never achieved power, thereby created a feeling of nationhood ["against the Jews" meant "for our brothers in the Sudetenland"]).

National Socialism and Antisemitism

"Schon als Sozialist habe ich überhaupt keinen Sinn für das Rassenproblem selber," Brecht confessed in a letter dated April 1934, an admission made in connection with the Danish production of his parable-play *Die Rundköpfe und die Spitzköpfe* (Round Heads and Pointed Heads): "auf der Bühne wird alles, was damit zusammenhängt, komisch wirken. Ernst dagegen wird das Soziale wirken" (*BFA* 28:414; As a socialist, for one thing, I'm not interested in the racial question as such; on the stage, everything connected with it would have a comic effect. The social question, on the other hand, has an effect of seriousness: *BBL* 172–73). He thereby rejected the widespread assumption that the play in question was about antisemitism: "Es hat bestimmt nicht die Wirkung, zu einer Diskussion der Judenfrage anzuregen. Das geschähe doch nur, wenn es die ungerechtfertigten Leiden der Juden darstellte" (*BFA* 28:414; It certainly does not tend to provoke a discussion of the Jewish question. It would do so only if it depicted the unjustified sufferings of the Jews: *BBL* 172). Once Brecht even suggested flippantly that the rival factions in the play could just as well have been cyclists and pedestrians. If it were not for the contextualizing phrase "Schon als Sozialist," Brecht's confession might simply be read as an attempt to avoid giving the impression that the author of *Die Rundköpfe und die Spitzköpfe* might possibly have contravened Danish regulations by engaging in political activity. However, drawing attention to "das Soziale" (i.e., class war) at the expense of the racial question was a characteristic move. Brecht invariably prioritized the class struggle over the race problem, even if he could not ignore the extent to which class and race were historically intertwined in the Third Reich. This may explain his use of the phrase "das Rassenproblem selber" (meaning the Jewish question when viewed in isolation, rather than against the backdrop of class conflict). Very often the Comintern's preferred "class against class" paradigm colored Brecht's express reactions to Nazi antisemitism, although this was well before full-scale racial cleansing became a major feature of life in the Third Reich. In September 1933, he wrote to Helene Weigel about the German-Jewish émigrés he had encountered in France, dismissing their pipe dreams of acquiring property in Palestine. They are becoming "faschisiert," he felt (i.e. quasi-fascist in the sense that German fascism is being equated with capitalism): "die eigentlichen Angelegenheiten Deutschlands interessieren hier niemand" (*BFA* 28:386; No one here cares about what's really going on in Germany: *BBL* 145). The implication is that, by pinning their hopes on U.S.-financed property acquisition in Palestine, many of the German-Jewish émigrés were behaving like capitalists and losing sight of what was happening to the Nazis' working-class victims back in the homeland.

What Germany's "eigentliche Angelegenheiten" actually were, was at the time a question that divided socialists along ethnicity- and class-based lines, although not always openly. According to Edmund Silberner,[34] Nazi antisemitism was not even touched upon as an agenda issue at the Seventh World Congress of the Comintern. What is more, the Jewish question had only rarely come up at previous congresses, usually in the guise of predictable attacks on the "capitalist imperialism" of the Zionist movement (a factor that may have influenced Brecht's censorious reaction to some of his fellow exiles in France). While not necessarily dictated by narrow Comintern policy, Brecht's response to German antisemitism during the Third Reich nevertheless at times bears signs of a marked indebtedness to then-current Marxist-Leninist thinking. Unfortunately, when eliminationist antisemitism became increasingly systematized, especially during the brief duration of the German-Soviet nonaggression pact (1939–41), criticism of Germany was taboo in Comintern circles and, by extension, in the USSR and its satellites. Little was done at the time that *The Private Life* was written to make amends for this glaring omission.

It was, of course, one thing for Brecht "als Sozialist" to prioritize class over race in his analysis of life under National Socialism, but quite

---

[34] Edmund Silberner, *Kommunisten zur Judenfrage: Zur Geschichte von Theorie und Praxis des Kommunismus* (Opladen: Westdeutscher Verlag, 1983), 322.

another for him to charge the NSDAP with appropriating the discourse and agenda of antisemitism for its own covert political ends. In doing so, Brecht imputes to National Socialism a similar diversionary strategy to the one he had himself already used to explain the movement's theatricalization of politics. Whereas communists deemed the class question to be vastly more important than issues of racial identity, Brecht inverts the pattern in the case of the Third Reich's antisemitic propaganda by arguing that the "Rassenfrage" was deliberately put center-stage for the principal purpose of deflecting attention away from what he took to be the overarching "Klassenfrage."[35] Brecht's most famous exhortation on the subject, his rallying call at the First International Conference of Writers for the Defense of Culture (Paris, June 1935), was probably not intended to advocate the ignoring of the excesses of National Socialist antisemitism, but rather to see it in its proper wider framework. His words were: "Kameraden, sprechen wir von den Eigentumsverhältnissen!" (*BFA* 22:146; Comrades, let us talk about the conditions of property ownership!: *BAP* 162).

As a consequence of his socialist ideology, Brecht converts the problem of antisemitism into a politically functional phenomenon. For example, the three key scenes in *Furcht und Elend* where antisemitism does play a significant role ("Rechtsfindung," "Physiker," and "Die jüdische Frau") all concentrate as much, if not more so, on the capitulation of middle-class intellectuals as on the persecution of the Jews.

"Aus den englischen Briefen," dating from summer 1936 and in all probability written in response to the Third Reich's Nuremberg Race Laws of the previous year, speaks with a heavy-handed irony of the relationship of the new racial legislation to the class question:

> Tatsächlich ist es eine schreiende Ungerechtigkeit, daß einige einzig wegen der Form ihrer Nase nicht das Recht haben sollen, sich an der Ausbeutung ihrer Mitmenschen zu beteiligen, zu einer Zeit, wo sie so unerhört in Schwung gebracht ist. Sollen sie etwa auch vom Kriegsgeschäft ausgeschlossen werden, weil ihre Haare schwarz sind? (*BFA* 22:192–93)

---

[35] Josef Stalin's "antisemitism" operates with a similar diversionary model: "Antisemitism is of advantage to the exploiters as a lightning conductor that deflects the blows aimed by the working people at capitalism": *Works*, 13 (London, Lawrence and Wishart, 1955), 30. Earlier, in "Marxism and the National Question," Stalin had declared in similar terms that "the policy of nationalist persecution [. . .] diverts the attention of large strata from social questions, questions of the class struggle, to national questions, questions 'common' to the proletariat and the bourgeoisie. And this creates a favourable soil for lying propaganda about 'harmony of interests,' for glossing over the class interests of the proletariat and for the intellectual enslavement of the workers" (*Works*, 2, 319).

[In truth, it is a screaming injustice that some people, just because of the shape of their noses, should not have the right to take part in the exploitation of their fellow human beings, just at a time when exploitation is so in vogue. Are they to be excluded from war profiteering as well, just because their hair is black? (*BAP* 167)]

As the tone here suggests, Brecht thought that the race question was, at most, a political smokescreen.[36]

In "Traum des Herrn Chamberlain" (Mr. Chamberlain's Dream), written in the wake of the Munich Agreement's surrender of the disputed Sudetenland to Nazi Germany, Brecht expresses disappointment at the British government's naïvety: "[Die Engländer] haben nichts begriffen von der Methode des Faschismus, den Klassenkampf in Rassenkämpfe zu verwandeln" (*BFA* 22:472; [The English] haven't understood anything of fascism's method of converting class warfare into racial wars). On one occasion, "civilized" bourgeois society's discomfort at the Nazis' racist excesses hands Brecht a stick with which to chastise the hypocrisy of middle-class morality and polite society's general ability to hide behind such question-begging, apolitical categories as "barbarism," "'uncalled-for' excesses," and action "irrelevant" to the common patriotic cause:

So ist diesen Leuten etwa die Judenverfolgung gerade deswegen so ärgerlich, weil sie eine "überflüssige" Ausschreitung scheint. Sie ist ihnen etwas Äußerliches, nicht zur Sache Gehörendes. Sie haben den Eindruck, daß Pogrome für die Eroberung von Märkten und Rohstofflagern nicht nötig sind, also unterbleiben können.

Sie erklären sich die Barbarei in Deutschland nicht als die Folge von Klassenkämpfen; so begreifen sie nicht die Parole des Faschismus, daß die Klassenkämpfe in Rassenkämpfe verwandelt werden müssen. (The essay "Furcht und Elend des Dritten Reiches" [*BFA* 22:473–74])

[This is why such people find the persecution of the Jews, for instance, so exasperating, because it seems such an "unnecessary" excess. They regard it as something extraneous, irrelevant to the business in hand.

---

[36] Diverting attention from the class question to that of race had not always been a Marxist-Leninist strategy. In "Zur Judenfrage," for example, Marx stresses class in relation to questions of nationality and basic human rights. He invokes the "Jewish spirit," but without addressing the question of race. Cf. his dogmatic claim that "Die *schimärische* Nationalität des Juden ist die Nationalität des Kaufmanns, überhaupt des Geldmenschen" (*MEW* 1:664; The *chimerical* nationality of the Jew is the nationality of the merchant, of the man of money in general: "On the Jewish Question," *Early Writings* [London: Penguin, 1992], 239). It is clear from Brecht's letter to Margarete Steffin of 18 December 1944 (*BFA* 27:213–14) that he was sufficiently familiar with Marx's essay on the Jewish Question to have used it in a skirmish with Max Horkheimer and Theodor W. Adorno.

In their view pogroms are not essential to the conquest of markets and raw materials, and accordingly can be dispensed with.

They fail to understand that barbarism in Germany is a consequence of class conflicts, and so they cannot grasp the Fascist principle which demands that class conflicts be converted into race conflicts. (*FM* 94)]

Brecht's left-wing theory concerning the alleged subsidiarity of anti-semitism within the overall NS political program is well summed up in the following extract from his poem "Der Jude, ein Unglück für das Volk" (The Jew, a Misfortune for the People):

Wie die Lautsprecher des Regimes verkünden
Sind in unserm Land an allem Unglück die Juden schuld.
Die sich immerfort mehrenden Mißstände
Können, da die Führung sehr weise ist
Wie sie oft betont hat
Nur von den sich immerfort vermindernden Juden kommen.
Nur die Juden sind schuld, daß im Volk Hunger herrscht
Obwohl die großen Grundbesitzer sich auf den Feldern zu Tode
    arbeiten
Und obwohl die Ruhrkapitäne nur die Brosamen essen, die von
                    der Arbeiter Tischen fallen.
Und nur der Jude kann dahinterstecken, wenn
Für das Brot der Weizen fehlt, weil
Das Militär für seine Übungsplätze und Kasernen
So viel Boden beschlagnahmt hat, daß er
An Umfang einer ganzen Provinz gleichkommt. (*BFA* 12:76–77)

[As the regime's loudspeakers proclaim
In our country the Jews are responsible for all our misfortunes.
The ever-multiplying outrages
Can, since the leadership is very wise
As it has frequently stressed
Only be the work of the ever-diminishing Jewish community
Only the Jews are guilty of the fact that the people are starving
Although the great property owners work themselves to death in the
    fields
And although the Ruhr captains of industry only eat the crumbs that fall
                from the workers' tables.
It can only be the Jew's fault, when
the wheat for the bread is missing, because
The army has requisitioned so much land
For its training grounds and barracks that
Its territory is equal to that of a whole province.]

This inventory of disingenuous accusations serves as a companion piece to Brecht's 1934 poem "Die große Schuld der Juden" (The Jews' Great Guilt,

BFA 14:283), with its black-humored inventory of oppressive features of NS Germany that would not have existed "ohne die Juden." In both poems, pretending to blame everything on the Jews diverts attention, in Brecht's book, from where the blame should really be laid: at the door of capitalism.

Despite the NS boycott of Jewish shops and businesses in 1933, the fact that antisemitism is marginalized in *Furcht und Elend* is in some respects explicable in terms of the work's timescale. Even at the time the play was premiered in May 1938, the outside world still seemed unable — or in other cases unwilling — to grasp the centrality of antisemitism to the NS program, despite *Mein Kampf*, the 1933 boycott of Jewish shops, the Nuremberg Race Laws of 1935, and the systematic "Aryanization" of Jewish businesses and property. The *Kristallnacht* pogrom (9–10 November 1938) and the brutal treatment of Polish "Ostjuden" after the invasion of western Poland were still to come, as was "the Final Solution": the bureaucratically organized mechanized mass slaughter of the Holocaust. At most, one might wonder why *The Private Life of the Master Race* was not refashioned to take more recent historical evidence on board. Only later, in the Soviet Zone of Occupation, does Brecht make a partial conciliatory gesture in respect of the most glaring omission in his documentary play's composite picture of the "Furcht und Elend" of the Third Reich. In a moment of honest confrontation with the horrors of the recent past, he declared in his 1948 "Gespräche mit jungen Intellektuellen" (Conversations with Young Intellectuals):

> Die Vorgänge in Auschwitz, im Warschauer Ghetto, in Buchenwald vertrügen zweifellos keine Beschreibung in literarischer Form. Die Literatur war nicht vorbereitet auf und hat keine Mittel entwickelt für solche Vorgänge. (*BFA* 23:101)

> [The events in Auschwitz, in the Warsaw ghetto, in Buchenwald would doubtless not bear any literary description. Literature was not prepared for such events, nor has it developed any means of describing them. (*BAP* 304)]

However, this would hardly have justified criticism of a play with a setting like that of *Furcht und Elend*, for its chronologically sequenced scenes were limited to a pre-Holocaust, pre-Second World War totalitarianism, the detailed evidence of "Alltagsfaschismus" at grassroots level, and political persecution that was of a lesser order of magnitude. Nevertheless, Dachau already existed in 1933, as had Buchenwald, Sachsenhausen, and a number of other concentration camps and political prisons. And their function, although essentially political at that time, already included a substantial antisemitic dimension.

Only some of the aspects of life in Hitler's Third Reich and the characterizing features of the NS regime's political agenda and practice looked at in this chapter would have lent themselves to treatment within the parable-play format that Brecht tended to prefer in his other antifascist works such as *Die Rundköpfe und die Spitzköpfe*, *Die Gewehre der Frau Carrar*,

Leben des Galilei, Mutter Courage und ihre Kinder, Der Aufstieg des Arturo Ui, and *Schweyk*. In most of these, the overarching macro-parable tends to focus on one, or at most a handful, of features of life under National Socialism and demonstrations of the nature of fascist behavior. Treatment in parable-form, however, ran the risk of simplifying and at times even trivializing the material. In contrast, as the following chapters will show, *Furcht und Elend* successfully brings out virtually all of the other themes relevant to fascism itemized in the present chapter, and while doing so pays due respect to the political complexities of its material, as well as the fabric of experience of "Alltagsfaschismus": the challenges, fear, and alien nature of life under the NS regime.

3: Fear and Misery in Brecht's Depiction of Third Reich Germany

THE CHOICE OF TITLE SEEMS TO HAVE BEEN particularly important to Brecht in the case of the *Furcht und Elend* project, more so than with any of his previous plays. "I sometimes wonder," Eric Bentley, himself responsible for calling the American version *The Private Life of the Master Race*, once confessed, "if the French title of Brecht's work is not the best. It is, simply: *Scènes de la Vie Hitlérienne*" (*The Private Life*, 136).[1] Yet despite the work's changing titles and Bentley's retrospective misgivings, *Furcht und Elend des Dritten Reiches*, as the play eventually came to be known, remains the most challenging of all the various possibilities mooted.

During the early stages of the play's genesis, a number of possibilities were considered for Brecht's work in progress: "Die Angst: Seelischer Aufschwung des deutschen Volkes unter der Naziherrschaft" (Fear: Spiritual Revival of the German People under Nazi Rule); "99%: Bilder aus dem Dritten Reich" (99%: Pictures from the Third Reich), or with the alternate subtitle: "Ein Zyklus aus der Gegenwart" (A Present-day Cycle);[2]

---

[1] "Scènes de la Vie Hitlérienne" was the collective title "Pierre Abraham" (i.e., Pierre Abraham Bloch) used for the scenes that his troupe, Les Comédiens d'Anjou, mounted in Paris in 1939. Details of where the French translations were subsequently published are given in *BFA* 29:630 and *FM* xi.

[2] "99%," the title used for the Paris production, has been interpreted in more than one way. An editorial note to the English translation of "Die Wahl," a scene discussed in Chapter Four, points out that 29 March 1936, when it is set, was "the date of the German election in which 99 percent of the voters voted Nazi" (*FM* 122–23). However, perhaps because "Die Wahl" was not among the scenes included in the Paris production, others have assumed that the reference is to the NS regime's claim that 98.8% of Germans registered a "Yes" vote in favor of the annexation of Austria in the retrospective *Anschluss* plebiscite of 10 April 1938. (The subtitle "Ein Zyklus aus der Gegenwart" arguably ties the title more emphatically to the play's concluding scene, "Volksbefragung.") A Sopade report for April/May 1938 comments that the plebiscite revealed that the dictatorship's methods were becoming less successful, since an 80% approval rate in a free vote would have affirmed the voters' trust, but a 99% return merely highlighted the brutality of the regime. The report argued that such propaganda, far from serving the regime's policies, was now devaluing them (*Deutschland-Berichte*, 1938: 394–95). In a counterattack,

"Deutschland — Ein Greuelmärchen" (Germany — An Atrocity Story), a title combining a respectful nod in the direction of Heinrich Heine's *Deutschland: Ein Wintermärchen* (Germany: A Winter's Tale) of 1844 with a dig at Propaganda Minister Joseph Goebbels's disingenuous complaints that National Socialism's enemies were always peddling malicious "atrocity stories" about dreadful goings-on in the Third Reich; *The Devil's Opera* and *The Devil's Sunday*;[3] and the figurative title "Deutsche Heerschau" (German March-Past) with its implication that the whole of Germany was now one huge ragbag of an army just begging for a rigorous troop review that would reveal its true nature: a spineless nation cowering under totalitarian rule.[4] With the exception of the first title highlighting the discrepancy between omnipresent *Angst* and the regime's boast of having brought about a spiritual revival (*seelischer Aufschwung*) throughout the land, and that based on the troop-review metaphor,[5] the discarded options generally imply an unreservedly negative exposé of the quality of life under National Socialism. Some, perhaps intentionally, echo the reference to "Hitler-Terror" in the first *Braunbuch*'s title, while others signal the fact that the scenes that follow offer the very opposite of the propaganda picture projected to the outside world. Brecht's desire to be seen to present the unvarnished truth about Nazi Germany possibly explains why he opted for the stark, hard-hitting title *Furcht und Elend des III. Reiches*,[6] the one used in *Malik*,

---

Brecht employs the same statistic when referring to "the rest of the German people, the ninety-nine percent" whose interests were not served by Hitler's war ("The *Other* Germany: 1943," *BFA* 23:27). On voter intimidation during the *Anschluss* plebiscite, see Evans, *The Third Reich in Power*, 646–53.

[3] According to James K. Lyon (*Bertolt Brecht in America*, 99), the title "The Devil's Sunday" was suggested by Ferdinand Reyher for the entire cycle. However, it seems more appropriate as a title for "Der Spitzel" alone.

[4] John Willett's translation of "Heerschau" as "March-Past" (*FM* 3) brings out the dynamism of the play's comparison between a collection of scenes being paraded past the audience for the purpose of inspection and, as happened at the Nuremberg Rallies, a situation where Führer and representatives of the German People review their army from an elevated vantage-point. The common denominator is the equation of parading past and being inspected, or in the case of *Furcht und Elend*, being judged.

[5] The inventive ways in which the "Deutsche Heerschau" image was eventually put to use in *Furcht und Elend* will be considered in the "Framing Devices" section of Chapter Four.

[6] This title is generally assumed (e.g., *BFA* 4:524 and *BHB* 1:342) to be derived from Honoré de Balzac's novel *Splendeurs et misères des courtisanes* (1845–47), in which case it would echo the parallel between fascism and prostitution drawn in Brecht's satirical essay "Die Horst-Wessel-Legende" (*BFA* 19:381–89). Although there is a copy of the German translation, *Glanz und Elend der Kurtisanen* (Berlin: Borngräber, n.d.), in Brecht's library (*BBB* 1357), no mention is made of the work

Aurora, the wartime Russian and English versions published in the USSR, and *BFA*, although *Furcht und Elend des Dritten Reiches* was to become the definitive form. The final title was certainly by no means as undemanding as *Scènes de la Vie Hitlérienne*. Its genitive construction "Furcht und Elend *des* Dritten Reiches" (Fear and Misery *of* the Third Reich) opens up a rich number of connotations and permits more readings than would have been the case with the formulation "Furcht und Elend *im* Dritten Reich."[7]

As we saw in Chapter Two, a comparable widening of focus in the title of Brecht's poem "Die Ängste des Regimes" (*BFA* 12:68–70) prepared the ground for a two-pronged treatment of the fear, and on occasions abject terror, of the regime's victims, while at the same time illustrating the equally characteristic uncertainty — even paranoia — experienced by many in National Socialism's vast "army" of henchmen and willing accomplices. Like "Die Ängste des Regimes," the title *Furcht und Elend des Dritten Reiches* refers not just to the mental state and economic predicament of the regime's victims, but also to the fear of lacking authority, and hence of being the target of potential resistance and mockery, experienced by those whom Brecht's "Bericht über die Stellung der Deutschen im Exil" (Report on the Situation of Germans in Exile) once collectively dismissed as "Hitler und seine Hintermänner" (*BFA* 23: 32; Hitler and his backers: *BAP*, 292). Although neither noun appears in individual scene titles, numerous forms of "Furcht" and "Elend" are depicted in Brecht's montage of mini-dramas on the subject. Arguably, there would have been an unfortunate mismatch between the play's title and what it illustrated in many of its episodes if the keywords "Furcht" and "Elend" did not open the door to more connotations than the most obvious, victim-oriented one.

The title's seemingly blunt equation of Third Reich Germany with fear and misery has not, however, always met with approval. One Danish commentator found it unnecessarily limiting:

> gegenüber der nationalsozialistischen mischung aus kapitalismus, idealismus und sozialismus kommt sein materialismus zu kurz; [Brechts] formel für den faschismus ist zu einfach, nur zwei wörter: *elend* und *furcht*. Er unterschätzt seine gegner, weil er rassenpolitik und nationale lebensraum-teorien eigensinnig als verschleierung des wahren

---

in his writings. His knowledge of Balzac came mainly from Georg Lukács. No commentator has adequately demonstrated the significance of such an intertextual possibility.

[7] Despite Brecht's careful consideration of what title would be most effective, one of his closest friends, Walter Benjamin, thought the play was called *Furcht und Zittern des Dritten Reiches* because, as he admitted in retrospect, he was confusing it with Søren Kierkegaard's *Fear and Trembling*. (Details in Erdmut Wizisla, *Walter Benjamin and Bertolt Brecht: The Story of a Friendship*, trans. Christine Shuttleworth [London: Libris, 2009], 149–50).

marxistischen grundkonflikts der beiden klassen stempelt. Die "volksgemeinschaft" des dritten reichs war kein so einfaches fänomen wie
Brechts bild von ihr: ein kleiner kreis von großkapitalisten bedient
sich einer bande psychopaten, um das hungernde volk mit großen
worten in den abgrund zu führen.[8]

[When set alongside the National Socialist mixture of capitalism, idealism, and socialism, [the regime's] materialism is neglected; [Brecht's]
formula for fascism is too simplistic, just two words: *misery* and *fear*.
He underestimates his adversaries because he stubbornly characterizes
racial politics and national geopolitical theories as concealing what
Marxists see as the true basic conflict between the classes. The Third
Reich's "Volksgemeinschaft" was not such a simple phenomenon as
Brecht's picture of it suggests: a small group of big capitalists uses a
band of psychopaths to lead the starving people into the abyss with
their big words.]

While it might be theoretically acceptable to point out what a work's title
fails to mention (as if it is little more than a table of contents), it seems
inappropriate to do so in this case, given that Brecht's play manifestly does
anything but tie National Socialism reductively to two procrustean concepts. On the contrary, *Furcht und Elend* broadens these concepts sufficiently to embrace a rich variety of associations — some, as we will see,
explored specifically in terms of their complex interrelationship.

Of course, it was not only in the context of the *Furcht und Elend* project that Brecht widened the two terms' scope to encompass a vast array of
types of fear and misery. He adopts a similar strategy on numerous other
occasions during the 1930s and early 1940s. In his correspondence, journal entries, political essays, and speeches of the time, the nouns "Furcht"
and "Elend" figure with striking frequency alongside various cognates.
The following is a representative two-part inventory of typical occurrences
(excluding literary usages). Our first examples relate to "Furcht":

"Wiederum sprechen ganze Kontinente das Wort Deutschland mit
der Furcht und dem Abscheu aus" ("Rede an die deutschen Arbeiter,
Bauern und Intellektuellen," *BFA* 22:337)
"Diese Furcht [that of having to pay the ultimate price for remaining
true to one's convictions] beginnt, alle andere Furcht zu überschat-
ten" ("Furcht und Elend des Dritten Reiches," *BFA* 22:476)
"Die Existenz der furchtbarsten Unterdrückungsinstrumente und
der furchtbarsten Polizeimacht, die die Welt je gekannt hat" ("Das
andere Deutschland," *BFA* 23: 432)

---

[8] Harald Engberg, *Brecht auf Fünen: Exil in Dänemark, 1933–1939* (Wuppertal:
Peter Hammer, 1974), 109–10. We have retained the idiosyncratic German of this
passage.

"Die deutsche Kriegsführung zeigt entsetzlich klar, daß der physische Terror des Regimes zu ungeheuerlichen geistigen und moralischen Verkrüppelungen der ihm ausgesetzten Menschen geführt hat" (letter to Thomas Mann, 1 December 1943, *BFA* 29:318)
"Tatsächlich ist nämlich gerade das die Hauptfrage: wie können wir zu Intelligenzbestien werden, zu Bestien in dem Sinn, wie die Faschisten sie für ihre Herrschaft fürchten. Eine Bestie ist etwas Starkes, Furchtbares" ("[Gefährlichkeit der Intelligenzbestien]," *BFA* 22:341)
"Nun besteht tatsächlich eine Furcht vor dem Krieg in Deutschland" (journal entry for 19 February 1939, *BFA* 26:329)
"Die deutschen Arbeiterparteien sind sich [. . .] über die auf jeden Fall furchtbaren Folgen eines Krieges [. . .] sehr bewußt" ("[Nicht Deutschlands Interessen]," *BFA* 22:471)
"Der politische und ökonomische Terror" plaguing the Third Reich (journal entry for 15 May 1942, *BFA* 27:96)

["Once again whole continents speak the word Germany with fear and disgust"
"This fear [of having to pay the ultimate price for remaining true to one's convictions] is beginning to overshadow all others" (*FM* 96)
"The existence of the most frightful instruments of oppression and the most frightful police force which the world has ever known" ("The *Other* Germany: 1943," *BFA* 23:24)
"Germany's conduct of the war shows with terrible clarity that the physical terror to which the regime has subjected the people has left them with hideous moral and intellectual deformities" (letter to Thomas Mann, 1 December 1943, *BBL* 374)
"In fact, the main question therefore is this: how can we become intellectual beasts, beasts in the sense that the fascists fear the threats they represent to their rule" ("The danger of intellectual beasts");
"not that a fear of war does not actually exist in Germany" (journal entry for 19 February 1939, *BBJ* 22)
"The German workers' parties are [. . .] very conscious of what is guaranteed to be the terrible repercussions of a war" ("Not Germany's Interests)
"A reign of political and economic terror" plaguing the Third Reich" (journal entry for 15 May 1942, *BBJ* 232)]

Diverse forms of "Elend" also figure frequently in Brecht's comments on life in Third Reich Germany:

"Als das 3. Reich gegründet wurde, sind viele Schriftsteller eingekerkert, gefoltert, getötet oder aus dem Lande verjagt worden. [. . .] Ihnen ist Unrecht getan worden, unschuldig sind sie ins Elend geraten" ("Bin ich mit Recht aus meinem Lande gejagt worden?," *BFA* 26:307)
"Einige [. . .] Leute hatten ihnen [the petty bourgeoisie] klargemacht, daß ihre elende Lage [. . .] von einer allzu materialistischen Einstellung dem Leben gegenüber herrühre" ("Unpolitische Briefe," *BFA* 22:12)

"[Hitler] wird mit dem riesigen Elend in Deutschland nicht fertig werden" ("Interview," *BFA* 22:27)
"Heute steht dieses Regime, nachdem es Elend über Deutschland und die halbe Welt gebracht hat, vor seinem Sturz" ("Das andere Deutschland," *BFA* 23:30)
"[Das] ungeheure unnötige Elend [. . .], das von dem falschen Aufbau der Produktion herrührt" ("Man muß das Unrecht auch mit schwachen Mitteln bekämpfen," *BFA* 22:61)
"Dem Elend gegenüber reagierte ich als normaler Mensch mit Mitleid, aber [. . .] dann fragte ich mich immerhin: ist das nicht unvermeidlich?" ("Traktat über die Mängel unserer Sprache im Kampf gegen den Faschismus," *BFA* 22:68)
"Aus dem unnötigen Elend soll man kein Geheimnis machen, wie beängstigend es immer auch auftreten mag" ("[Verschweigen der Wahrheit]," *BFA* 22:98)
"[Deutsche Volksgenossen], die [. . .] im Elend gehalten werden" ("Über die Wiederherstellung der Wahrheit," *BFA* 22:93)
"Die faktisch elende Lage von neun Zehntel der Bevölkerung" ("[Die Dauer des Regimes]," *BFA* 22:348)
"Das ungeheure Elend, in das der Nationalsozialismus die Bevölkerung stieß" (journal entry for 26 January 1949, *BFA* 27:299)

["When the Third Reich was founded many writers were imprisoned, tortured, executed or chased from the country. [. . .] An injustice has been done to them, through no fault of their own they have ended up in misery" ("Have I been rightfully expelled from my country?")
"Some of their own people had explained to them [the petty bourgeoisie] that their miserable situation [. . .] was the product of an all too materialistic attitude to life" ("Unpolitical Letters," *BAP* 126)
"[Hitler] will not be able to solve the widespread misery in Germany"
"After it has brought misery to Germany and half the world, this regime is facing collapse"
"The monstrous, unnecessary misery [. . .] which stems from the wrong system of production ("In the Fight against Injustice Even Weak Weapons Are of Use," *BAP* 140)
"As a normal person I responded to the misery with sympathy, but [. . .] then I nevertheless asked myself: isn't it inevitable?" ("Treatise on the Weaknesses of our Language in the Fight against Fascism")
"One should not attempt to conceal unnecessary misery, no matter how disturbing the forms it assumes"
"[German national comrades] who [. . .] are kept by them in misery" (*BAP* 136)
"The demonstrably miserable predicament of nine-tenths of the population" ("The Duration of the Regime")
"The terrible misery the Nazis brought on the people" (journal entry for 26 January 1949, *BBJ* 418)]

The noticeable contrast in Brecht's nonliterary writings between the proliferation of references in them to "Elend" and the limited number of references to "Furcht" becomes yet more pronounced if one extends the search's parameters to include near-synonyms or phrases belonging to the same semantic field, for example, in the case of "Elend," such collocations as "die bestehenden sehr schlechten Zustände" (the existing appalling conditions [from "Rede über die Widerstandskraft der Vernunft" (Speech on the Power of Resistance of Reason), *BFA* 22:334]); "die bedrückenden Maßnahmen" (the oppressive measures, *BFA* 22:299); and oppression ("Bedrückung," *BFA* 21:589).

As can be seen from this sample corpus, in discursive political contexts the terms "Furcht" and "Elend" are more likely to have one unequivocal denotation, whereas in a complex literary work of montage like *Furcht und Elend* we encounter a subtle plurality of connotations. Witness, for example, the starkly prophetic twin suggestions in "Bericht über die Stellung der Deutschen im Exil" that "ein Sieg [Hitlerdeutschlands] würde die ganze bewohnte Welt in [. . .] Elend sehen" (a victory [on Hitler Germany's part] would see the entire inhabited world in [. . .] misery: *BAP* 292), while "die unvermeidliche Endniederlage Hitlerdeutschlands wird unser Land in unausdenkbarem Elend sehen" (*BFA* 23:32; the inevitable final defeat of Hitler's Germany will see our country in inconceivable misery: *BAP* 292). These claims and predictions stand in contrast to the more differentiated treatment of "Elend" in "Die Kiste" and "Der Gefühlsersatz," scenes discussed in detail in the last two sections of the present chapter.

There is one further context, a dramaturgical one, in which Brecht refers to "Furcht" in conjunction with "Elend," and that is in his discussion of the way Epic Theater revolutionizes the traditional Aristotelian preoccupation with cathartic effect. "Was konnte an die Stelle von *Furcht* und *Mitleid* gesetzt werden, des klassischen Zwiegespanns zur Herbeiführung der aristotelischen Katharsis?" he asks in "Über experimentelles Theater" (*BFA* 22:553; What could replace *Fear* and *Pity*, the classical pairing used to create Aristotelian catharsis?); "Wenn man auf die Hypnose [i.e., the theater of empathy] verzichtete, an was konnte man appellieren?" (ibid.; If one were to rule out hypnosis, what could one turn to?). Rejecting the terminology with which catharsis is explained in Aristotle's *Poetics*, Brecht proposes a theater predicated on "Wissensbegierde (anstelle der Furcht vor dem Schicksal)" (desire for knowledge [instead of the fear of fate]) and "Hilfsbereitschaft (anstelle des Mitleids)" (readiness to help [instead of pity]) (*BFA* 22:554). The replacement noun "Hilfsbereitschaft" is code for socialism, or in the Third Reich context, possibly even organized left-wing antifascism. Any serious reading of the title *Furcht und Elend des Dritten Reiches* would have to take such a theoretical proposal into account, given that it has implications not only for what the play's title explicitly promises, but also for how Brecht's antifascist play would have been received. If a work ostensibly about the fear and misery of the Third Reich's victims is the product of a playwright who nails his colors to the mast by stating that his ideal form of theater is one predicated on "desire for knowledge" (i.e., political curiosity, and "readiness to help"), it would be wise to approach the question of Aristotelian or Epic genre with this in mind. We will return to some of the implications of this line of thinking during our discussion of the "Physiker" scene in Chapter Four.

Bearing these factors in mind, we propose to concentrate in the sections that follow on: (i) how the themes of "fear" and "misery" are associated with perpetrators as well as victims, albeit without any blurring of the important distinction between the two;[9] (ii) the complex ways in which *Furcht und Elend* interweaves the two strands; and (iii) how the multi-faceted "Elend des Dritten Reiches" needs to be reconfigured as part of the bigger picture of National Socialism's ethical, political, and historical failure.

Nazi Violence and the Victims' Fear

A draft version of "Eine notwendige Feststellung zum Kampf gegen die Barbarei" (A Necessary Observation on the Struggle Against Barbarism), Brecht's address to the First International Writers' Congress for the Defense of Culture (Paris, June 1935), outlines some of the main challenges facing antifascist German writers in exile. What he says about their predicament throws light on the difficulties he himself must have confronted while trying to present an adequate picture of the violence, fear, and emotional torture characteristic of life in the Third Reich.

> Die Schriftsteller, welche die Greuel des Faschismus erfahren, am eigenen oder am fremden Leibe, und darüber entsetzt sind, sind mit dieser Erfahrung und mit diesem Entsetztsein noch nicht ohne weiteres imstande, diese Greuel zu bekämpfen. Es mag mancher glauben, daß die Schilderung dieser Greuel genüge, besonders wenn großes literarisches Talent und echter Zorn die Schilderung eindringlich machen. In der Tat sind solche Schilderungen sehr wichtig. Hier geschehen Greuel. Das darf nicht sein. Hier werden Menschen geschlagen. Das soll nicht geschehen. Was braucht es da langer Erörterungen? Man wird aufspringen und den Peinigern in den Arm fallen. Kameraden, es bedarf der Erörterungen. (*BFA* 22:142)

> [Writers who experience the atrocities of Fascism at first or second hand, and who are outraged by them, are not therefore in a position

---

[9] See, for example, Arne Johan Vetlesen, *Evil and Human Agency: Understanding Collective Evildoing* (Cambridge: Cambridge UP, 2006) for valuable terminological distinctions.

to resist these atrocities simply by virtue of their experience and sense of outrage, without further ado. Some people may believe that it is enough to describe the atrocities, particularly if great literary talent and genuine anger lend the description urgency. And, indeed, such descriptions are very important. Atrocities are taking place. This cannot be allowed. People are being beaten. This should not be happening. What long explanations could be needed? The reader will surely leap up and restrain the torturers. But comrades, explanations are essential. (*BAP* 157)]

As his Congress addresses of 1935 and 1937 make clear, the kind of political analysis — or return to first principles — Brecht sees as a necessary requirement under such circumstances is one able to do justice to the general relationship between fascism and capitalism, the conditions of property ownership, the political purpose that fascism's barbaric violence is designed to serve, and the question of just who are the primary victims of such a program of targeted atrocities. In spite of the already massive international protest against fascism during the 1930s, insight was still at a premium, according to Brecht, who wrote in his "Rede zum II. Internationalen Schriftstellerkongreß zur Verteidigung der Kultur" (Speech at the Second International Writers' Congress for the Defense of Culture) that "die großen Zusammenhänge [blieben] vielen der von Abscheu Erfüllten ganz dunkel" (*BFA* 22:323; the larger picture remained obscure to many of those who were so filled with disgust: *BAP* 169). The larger picture alluded to here includes not just the permissive terms of the Enabling Act of 1933, but such seemingly disparate elements as the violent invasion of the German Trades Union offices and the seizure of their records in May 1933, the aerial destruction of Guernica, National Socialism's gross mismanagement of the country's economy, the systematic torture of SPD and KPD activists in Gestapo cellars, the German Condor Legion's involvement in the Spanish Civil War, and fascist Italy's barbaric conduct in the Abyssinian War. The overriding fear of the regime's victims is not specifically highlighted in either of these speeches, although the horror ("Entsetztsein," *BFA* 22:142) of many exiles upon hearing of such atrocities is not irrelevant. However, much of the language Brecht uses points to features of Nazi barbarity calculated to induce fear in both the regime's current victims and other potential targets to come, especially the Jews — for example, his references to "die Greuel des Faschismus" (ibid.; fascist atrocities), to the existence of torture chambers ("Folterkeller," *BFA* 22:144), to the victims' silence "wenn die Leiden unerträglich werden" (*BFA* 22:142; when the suffering becomes unbearable), and to "der Schrei derer, die auf öffentlichen Plätzen getötet werden" (*BFA* 22:324; the screams of those who are now murdered in public squares: *BAP* 170), as well as a relatively early acknowledgment of "die Abschlachtungen ganzer Bevölkerungen" (*BFA* 22:324; the slaughter of whole populations: *BAP* 169). In the *Furcht und Elend* scenes, in

contrast, excesses of this order of magnitude are seldom the focus of attention; also, the general tone with which both fear and misery are evoked in
individual scenes is invariably less extreme. One possible explanation for this
lies in the fact that Brecht's Congress addresses were specifically designed
to warn those attending about the dangers of indulging in mere outrage,
to caution against any knee-jerk equation of NS atrocities with regression
to barbarism, and to counteract any inability to move beyond emotional
response to political analysis and collective direct action.

Two other (unrelated) factors have to be borne in mind when one
compares Brecht's references to the Third Reich in his addresses to the
First and Second International Writers' Congresses for the Defense of Culture with the approach taken in *Furcht und Elend*. First, there was the
fact that his limited picture of extremes of violence, intimidation, and fear
in the early years after the Nazi seizure of power was very dependent, as
was suggested in Chapter One, on the information sporadically reaching him about the regime's brutal campaign of terror against its SPD and
KPD enemies. Second, there was always the tactical need, as Brecht saw
it, to minimize the enthusiastic support that Hitler and the NSDAP were
receiving from the people. Back in 1923, Clara Zetkin had already warned
the Comintern against underestimating fascism's heartland appeal to the
masses. Such support could only be explained away by suggesting that
wide-ranging, cross-class support for the Nazi regime was motivated more
by fear and intimidation rather than ideological conviction. In answer to
"die Fragen, warum die Deutschen noch kämpfen" (he was at the time
working on *The Private Life*), Brecht argues that "die Bevölkerung hat die
SS auf dem Genick, außerdem hat sie keine politische Willensrichtung"
(*BFA* 27:200; Why the Germans continue to fight? Well, the population
has the SS on its back, and besides it is without a political will in any direction: *BBJ* 324). For this reason, a number of *Furcht und Elend* scenes treat
the social welfare, job procurement, and community-forging dimensions
of NS internal politics[10] by associating them with elements of fear or by
presenting them as less altruistic than was suggested by the regime's propaganda machine. The ironic titles of certain scenes ("Volksgemeinschaft,"
"Dienst am Volke," "Arbeitsdienst," "Winterhilfe," "Arbeitsbeschaffung,"
"Volksbefragung") alert us to the fact that danger threatens, even when
the NSDAP is doing its utmost to create the impression that the new Germany is the post–Weimar Republic equivalent of a welfare state. National
Socialism's façade of altruism is in many of these scenes revealed to be
manipulative, to come with a price attached, or to be essentially little more
than a strategy for winning over the politically gullible. State interference in

---

[10] This aspect of National Socialism is well documented in Claudia Koonz, *The
Nazi Conscience* (Cambridge, MA: The Belknap Press of Harvard UP, 2002).

people's private life, for example, in the scenes "Winterhilfe" and "Arbeits-beschaffung," quickly leads to gross intrusion and political pressure. Even such nationwide macro-organizations as the network of employment exchanges (referred to in "Das Kreidekreuz"), the ameliorating "Schön-heit der Arbeit" program (in "Die Stunde des Arbeiters"), the SA- and HJ-controlled *Winterhilfswerk* program (in "Winterhilfe") and the policy of *Kinderlandverschickung* (sending children to the countryside to perform agricultural duties, a program referred to in "Die schwarzen Schuhe") become not so much strategies for facilitating social bonding and identity formation as sites of fear and intimidation. As *Furcht und Elend* repeatedly demonstrates, programs targeting economic misery for political purposes are often responsible for creating other forms of "Elend."

Unlike many exile depictions of violence in the Third Reich — works such as Willi Bredel's *Die Prüfung*, Lion Feuchtwanger's *Die Geschwister Oppenheim*, and Wolfgang Langhoff's *Die Moorsoldaten*, that build cumu-latively towards explicit scenes of extreme violence and at times dwell on the victims' fear — Brecht's *Furcht und Elend* already includes such material in one form or another from the very first episode onwards. Scene 1 ends, for example, with a random shooting. Scene 2 begins with a graphic account of a denounced man's brutal arrest at the hands of the Gestapo. In Scene 3, the worker makes a number of risqué critical remarks that could, accord-ing to the SA man, lead to a police arrest, or, since he has also attracted the attentions of the SA, land him in protective custody ("Schutzhaft") in either a prison or a concentration camp. Scene 4 is the first of a number of concentration camp scenes, two of which involve severe punishment beatings and another one the consignment of a group of prisoners to the dreaded punishment bunker ("Strafbunker"). The hapless judge in Scene 5 is confronted with a politically difficult case, the repercussions of which leave him fearful for his future career: one false move and he might be dis-patched to the remote reaches of Pomerania or even a concentration camp. (His predicament is aggravated by the intimidating presence of large num-bers of SA men in the courtroom on the day in question, suggesting that he could become the target of outright violence.) The surgeon in Scene 6 also senses that his career could be on the line; he himself risks being sent to a camp if he correctly diagnoses how a patient from Oranienburg KZ received his multiple injuries. Two physicists speaking clandestinely in Scene 7 are in a state of abject fear of being overheard and denounced for seeking advice from the "Jewish physicist" Albert Einstein. In other scenes, a married couple even fear denunciation at the hands of their son and immediately assume that this will result in imprisonment. A doctor in Scene 8 fears his career aspirations may be compromised because his wife is Jewish. A working-class couple in Scene 15 have to contend with the possibility that a recently freed KPD political prisoner visiting them for the first time since his release could have been tortured by his captors to the point where he might now be in their service as a fifth columnist or mole. In Scene 18, an old woman whose son-in-law has been grumbling about the quality of life under National Socialism and whose daughter keeps a written record of the increases in the cost of living is overcome with fear as her daughter is led away by two SA troopers for interrogation. In the play's final scene, we are explicitly reminded that the act of undercover resistance is being engaged in by the communist cell on the very day that one of their number is about to be executed. In virtually all scenes, the characters in *Furcht und Elend*, fearful of being spied on, denounced, or of inviting unwelcome political attention, are continually looking over their shoulders — either literally or metaphorically.

Unlike the harrowing catalogue of violence in Brecht's addresses to the 1935 and 1937 International Writers' Congresses for the Defense of Culture, many of the above episodes focus on people's fear of intimidation rather than on the regime's actual implementation of extreme forms of violence. Denunciation and its repercussions — from a visit to local Gestapo headquarters through to being sent to a concentration camp — remain more often a possibility than a fact. Much of the torture is thus psychological. Real violence is kept largely in the wings: only in two *Furcht und Elend* scenes do outright atrocities occur on stage, and in both cases it soon becomes a matter of violence interrupted rather than taken to the absolute limit. Elsewhere, threatening gestures accompanied by fears of what might happen tend to dominate the picture.

Foregrounding the *Gestus*: The Semiotics of Fear, Compliance and Dissidence

In a number of Brecht's frequently cited comments on the staging of *Furcht und Elend*, particular attention is drawn to the significance of *Gestus* in the vast majority of scenes. In the case of the dramaturgical writings, *Gestus* has proved to be a rather contentious concept, largely because of its overlapping aesthetic and political connotations.[11] In "Kurze Beschreibung einer neuen Technik der Schauspielkunst, die einen Verfremdungseffekt hervorbringt" (Short Description of a New Technique of Acting which Produces an Alienation Effect) of 1940, for example, Brecht tries to explain the concept within the framework of Epic Theater:

---

[11] Helpful, largely theoretical introductions to the concept can be found in Robert Cohen, "Brechts *Furcht und Elend des III. Reiches* und der Status des Gestus," *The Brecht Yearbook* 24 (1999), 192–207, and Helmut Heinze, *Brechts Ästhetik des Gestischen: Versuch einer Rekonstruktion* (Heidelberg: Carl Winter, 1992). See also White, *Bertolt Brecht's Dramatic Theory*, 228–29.

Es ist der Zweck des V-Effekts, den allen Vorgängen unterliegen-
den gesellschaftlichen Gestus zu verfremden. Unter sozialem Gestus ist der mimische und gestische Ausdruck der gesellschaftlichen
Beziehungen zu verstehen, in denen die Menschen einer bestimmten
Epoche zueinander stehen. (*BFA* 22:646)

[The object of the A-effect is to alienate the social gest[12] underlying
every incident. By social gest is meant the mimetic and gestural expression of the social relationships prevailing between people of a given
period. (*BT* 139)]

This explanation is kept deliberately nonspecific and hence subject to modification, depending on the period and society under scrutiny. Thus, in the
case of a work about the fear and misery of life in the Third Reich, such
otherwise neutral phrases as "der gestische Ausdruck der gesellschaftlichen Beziehungen" and "der allen Vorgängen unterliegende gesellschaftliche Gestus" take on political, and generally by that token more sinister,
contemporary overtones. Social intercourse might now, for example, be
that between an informer and the person spied on, a HJ member and his
conservative parents, or concentration camp prisoners and their overseers.
Even under such circumstances, it would be unwise to lose sight of the
aesthetic link Brecht makes between "das Gestische" and Epic Theater's
"V-Effekt." For any account of the extensive use of *Gestus* in *Furcht und
Elend* is de facto an acknowledgment of it as an important characteristic of
Epic Theater.

Most of Brecht's comments on the staging of *Furcht und Elend* in
fact tend to use *Gestus* with reference to the relatively conventional connotations of "gesture," dominant body language, or gestural manner of
expressing oneself. In the words of "[Über die Aufführung von *Furcht
und Elend des III. Reiches*]" (On Staging *Fear and Misery of the Third
Reich*):

Das Stück zeigt typisches Verhalten der Menschen verschiedener Klassen unter der faschistischen Diktatur, [. . .] die Gestik der Vorsicht,
der Abwehr, des Schreckens usw., aber auch der Auflehnung muß
besonders herausgearbeitet werden. (*BFA* 24:226–27)

[The play demonstrates typical behavior of people from various classes
under fascist dictatorship, [. . .] gestures of caution, fending off, terror, etc., but also that of revolt must be particularly brought out.]

---

[12] In his subsequent translations of the term *Gestus* in *BT* and *The Messingkauf Dialogues*, Willett opts for the neologism "gest." However, when not quoting him, we
have decided to follow his original solution of retaining the German noun *Gestus*
(*The Theatre of Bertolt Brecht: A Study from Eight Aspects*, London: Eyre Methuen,
1959, 172–73 et passim).

While examples of "die Gestik der Auflehnung" will be considered in Chapter Four, what needs emphasizing at this stage is the fact that Brecht does not confine his "Gestarium," as he once called the play (*BFA* 26:477), to the gestures of fear and caution generally associated with life in a totalitarian state. Significantly, he refuses to attribute such "Gesten" exclusively to victims, Nazi perpetrators or particular ethnic groups, although the proletariat and the petty bourgeoisie do loom large in many of the more political *Furcht und Elend* episodes. While the social *Gestus* still remains a relatively neutral concept in 1940 in the theoretical context of "Kurze Beschreibung einer neuen Technik," the approach had already been noticeably politicized in a journal entry of 15 August 1938, on that occasion in an elaboration of Brecht's definition of *Furcht und Elend* as "eigentlich nur ein Gestentafel" (actually only a *Gestus* table). Once more the emphasis is on gestures implying fear, intimidation, and the need for extreme caution: "die Gesten des Verstummens, Sich-Umblickens, Erschreckens usw. Die Gestik unter der Diktatur" (*BFA* 26:318; the *Gestus* of remaining silent, of looking over one's shoulder, of sudden fear etc. The gestures found in a dictatorship). But thanks to this final sentence the idea now becomes regime-specific rather than merely a component feature of a new technique of acting. There is, in fact, hardly a scene in the *Furcht und Elend* complex that does not bear traces of the social semiotics of fear, intimidation, and circumspection on the part of the people whom we are invited to observe, as they try to survive in the shadow of National Socialism.

What is rather surprising, given that this is the case, is the sparse role allocated to stage directions in bringing out the *Gestus* in any particular incident. One can only speculate about why this is the case. Brecht as author knew the subtexts the actors had to bring out, and since *Furcht und Elend* was a work in the production of which he would remain the principal source of advice, there was perhaps less need for lengthy stage directions. When working with Dudow, Busch, and Weigel, Brecht could take a scene's core political *Gestus* for granted. In any case, "[Über die Aufführung von *Furcht und Elend des III. Reiches*]" (dated ca. 1938 in *BFA*) could well be an aide-mémoire of points Brecht needed to stress in his letters to Dudow in respect to the Paris production. If so, too many recommendations about staging detail would have been superfluous between two such experienced, like-minded men of the theater. Alternatively, Brecht's notes about the role of *Gestus* in "99%" could be a way of putting on record what was striking about the performance, a feature to be preserved in future productions. The milestone journal entry for 15 August 1938, beginning with the overconfident statement "*Furcht und Elend* ist jetzt in Druck gegangen" (*Fear and Misery of the Third Reich* has now gone to press: *BBJ* 13) is misleading; Brecht could not yet know about the shenanigans in Prague. It represents another attempt to set the record straight, this time by proving how wrong Lukács was in seeing in the scene "Der Spitzel" a masterpiece of Socialist Realism.[13] This would explain the emphasis on *Furcht und Elend* as a "Gestentafel" or gestural work of montage, a particularly important point to stress in the context of Brecht's association of *Gestus* with "Verfremdung."

For all the emphasis given to *Gestus* in the staging of *Furcht und Elend*, Brecht does not make it sufficiently clear that the term refers to more than simply gesture, body language, facial expression, or other familiar social signals. Language itself is also a *Gestus* within Brecht's theatrical sign-system, as are such signifiers as uniforms or the absence thereof, who sits and who stands during an encounter, an actor's stage-position, and the codes of socio-political interaction: the compulsory "Heil Hitler" greeting, the use of "Volksgenosse" (national comrade) as a form of address, and whether or not civilians in the Third Reich choose to stress their allegiance to paramilitary organizations in public or even in the confines of their own home. If this system of social signals is a feature of much Brechtian Epic Theater in general, it is particularly important in *Furcht und Elend*, inasmuch as it is now a recognized part of the highly politicized codified "Gestik unter der Diktatur." In *Furcht und Elend*'s many tense predicaments, it is also worth noting how frequently the signals given are, unlike those in the sender-receiver conception of semiosis, unconsciously spontaneous rather than deliberate.[14]

As many of the *Furcht und Elend* scenes suggest, "die Gesten des Verstummens" played a well-understood role in the daily life of Third Reich Germany. Those representing the regime gave the right signals, while others were anxious not to be denounced (either falsely or with justification) for saying the wrong thing or failing to abide by the socio-political codes of the day. Or, since they were often not sure what was officially the "right thing" to say or to signal, they found it prudent to hold their tongues. We will come across examples of such revealing silences in the scenes explored in subsequent chapters. But it is worth being prepared in advance for the fact that the *Furcht und Elend* scenes depict many different kinds of silence, most of them accompanied by some sort of physical *Gestus*. There is the silence of *denial*, as the surgeon in "Die Berufskrankheit" prevaricates

---

[13] The role played by "Der Spitzel" and *Furcht und Elend* as a whole in the Moscow "Realism Debate" of 1938 will be discussed below in the second section of Chapter Six.

[14] On iconic and indexical aspects of Brecht's semiotic *Gestus*, see John J. White, "Brecht and Semiotics: Semiotics and Brecht," in *Bertolt Brecht: Centenary Essays*, ed. Steve Giles and Rodney Livingstone (Amsterdam-Atlanta: Rodopi, 1998), 89–108; Id., "Unpacking Mother Courage's Wagon: A Peircean Approach to De-Familiarization in the Plays of Bertolt Brecht," in *C. S. Peirce & les études littéraires. Recherches sémiotiques*, 24 (2004), 133–52; and Manfred Wekwerth, *Schriften: Arbeit mit Brecht* (Berlin: Henschel, 1973), 298–326.

about investigating the conditions under which a concentration camp victim received his injuries or the married couple in "Der Verrat" realize just what violence the husband's denunciation has already caused their neighbor; the silence of *withdrawal* into a protective form of apathy in "Rechtsfindung," when police and legal experts refuse to respond to the judge's desperate questions; the silence of *shock*, as a mother chokes on an apple after realizing she has inadvertently drawn attention to her daughter's dissatisfaction with life under the National Socialists (in "Winterhilfe"); or the boy's inability to recite the words of a brutal war poem he had been forced to learn (in "Das Mahnwort"). But there is also the wordless *Gestus* of political *solidarity*, as when the concentration camp prisoners choose collective punishment rather than point the finger of accusation at one among their number (in "Moorsoldaten"), or the tight-lipped political silence of the released prisoner anxious not to have his former friends worry about whether he might now be a Gestapo agent provocateur (in "Der Entlassene"). There are also other leitmotif-like variations on "die Gesten des Verstummens." For example, those meaningful pauses and empty phrases that might be called "virtual silences":[15] the surgeon's "ach so" (*BFA* 4:380; Oh, I see: *FM* 43), a tactic allowing him time to avoid compromising himself by saying anything more, or the police inspector's "ich habe eine Familie" (*BFA* 4:364; I've got a family: *FM* 28), code for "don't press me, I've got to cover my own back." Or the way the husband in "Die jüdische Frau" plays deaf to everything his wife says to him; the wife's noncommittal shrug of the shoulders at the end of "Der Spitzel" (*BFA* 4:400); or, more blatantly, the husband's crude attempts to silence his wife in "Arbeitsbeschaffung." In many *Furcht und Elend* scenes, "Gesten des Verstummens" have, as their logical counterparts, the "sozialer Gestus" of trying to silence someone else. As Brecht's reference to "Die Gesten des [. . .] Sich-Umblickens, Erschreckens" suggests, wordless fear, anxious glances, and gestures of restraint and self-censorship are part of the general atmosphere of intimidation.

On occasions, the victims' fear is emphasized by the chain-recurrence of one particular leitmotif across a series of scenes. One striking example of this technique is the South German and Austrian word "Obacht," derived from "Hab Acht" (pay attention). This occurs in a variety of contexts, and is sometimes repeated more than once in the early scenes. In "Moorsoldaten," it is used three times to alert fellow concentration camp prisoners that a patrolling guard is approaching. In "Zwei Bäcker," the warning signal is given

---

[15] In some layouts, the length of silent pauses is indicated typographically — for example, in the large spaces between speeches in the layout of "Der Spitzel" in Bertolt Brecht, *Furcht und Elend des Dritten Reiches* (Reinbek bei Hamburg: Rowohlt, 1963), 83–96.

three times as the prisoners exercising in a circle come within earshot of the prison guard. In "Arbeitsdienst," it is said by the student to a young proletarian worker as their Gruppenführer approaches, and in "Das Mahnwort" by *Der erste Junge* to warn the rest of his HJ comrades: "Obacht, der Dicke!" (Watch out, here comes Fatty). Elsewhere, similar verbal gestures are used: "Aufgepaßt!" (Look out) (in "Dienst am Volke") and "Augenblick!" (Just a minute) (in "Physiker"). The sense of fear generated by constant surveillance can sometimes be expressed through other warning reminders whenever outsiders approach: "Sobald jemand kommt, sagt's" (as soon as you see someone coming, give us a shout) says the farmer's wife to one of the children (in "Der Bauer füttert die Sau"): or "Passen Sie mal auf Ihre Zunge auf" (Watch your tongue) and "Halt den Mund von Spanien" (Shut up about Spain) (in "Arbeitsbeschaffung"). Although most of these utterances occur when the threat comes from prison guards — and especially in concentration camps where verbal communication was often forbidden — such warnings also cumulatively suggest that daily life has been so threatened by the possibility of being overheard by spies or informers that the whole of Third Reich Germany has virtually become a concentration camp.

The Fear of the Nazi Perpetrators and Those Who Become Their Accomplices

As we saw in Chapter Two, Brecht's poem "Die Ängste des Regimes" represents a refusal to fall into the trap of seeing NS barbarity exclusively in terms of the victims, although their fear and suffering rightly remains the overriding issue in this satirical work, as it also does in *Furcht und Elend*. In both works, the fear felt by the Nazi perpetrators and their accomplices is inventoried in different ways, again often with reference to "das Gestische." In Brecht's poem on the subject, we hear of the SA's fear of the man who fails to raise his arm in the Hitler salute, and even their general suspicion of anyone who greets them with an innocuous "Guten Morgen." We learn how an epidemic of paranoid suspicion makes the SA break into people's homes and search the lavatories for evidence of dissidence and resistance, and how their accomplices are driven to burn whole libraries of books because of their fear of the real truth about the Nazi regime being revealed. "So beherrscht die Furcht nicht nur die Beherrschten," the relevant stanza (stanza 3) concludes, "sondern auch / Die Herrschenden" (*BFA* 12:69). The appropriate interpretive model here would appear to be a Nietzschean-cum-Freudian compensatory one.[16] The Nazis are depicted

---

[16] Although Brecht was suspicious of psychoanalytical interpretations, this is not the only time he toys with such a paradigm. His journal for 20 September 1944

as always being ready to intimidate and brutalize their fellow Germans, especially their political enemies, because they are at root afraid of them. During the first half of *Furcht und Elend*, such fear as we see displayed by uniformed National Socialists is usually fear of the class enemy: the KPD and SPD, and to a lesser extent (for them) such suspect organizations as the Jehovah's Witnesses because of their pacifist doctrine, Germany's secretive Freemasons, or militant church groups. Fear, according to such a reading, leads to overreaction and violence, and what has been called the "master race syndrome" (*Herrenmenschentum*[17]) displayed by certain characters in *Furcht und Elend* is in effect a compensatory mechanism. The two SS men who make their drunken entrance in the first scene of the play ("Volksgemeinschaft" [*BFA* 4:342]) immediately urinate on stage, a gesture designed to show that they feel they can do so whenever and wherever they want to, as if, animal-like, marking out their territory as the alpha males of the Aryan species. Once they realize they are on alien territory, however, the men's body language begins to change radically and we soon see them backing away in undisguised fear from a district where their class enemies are assumed to be lurking behind every window and closed door, and where they know themselves to be dangerously outnumbered. Their retreat thus takes on a military quality: "Jehn wa mit Rückendeckung" (ibid.; We'd best cover our rear: *FM* 5). Of one we are told: "*Er entsichert seinen Dienstrevolver*" (*BFA* 4:343; *He pushes forward the safety catch on his revolver: FM* 6). Given that the two SS men are in a potentially dangerous situation, theirs is an understandable panic, arguably different from the "Ängste des Regimes" posited in the earlier poem.

Yet such fear is rare in the *Furcht und Elend* scenes in which Nazi perpetrators appear. A more common phenomenon in the scenes dominated by the middle class is the palpable fear of those administrators and state officials (*Beamten*) who have either been coordinated (*gleichgeschaltet*) as a consequence of the NS takeover or who wish to please their new masters but are unable to adjust to the changed circumstances. This is particularly true of the professional classes, as we will see in the case of the judge in "Rechtsfindung" and the schoolteacher and his wife in "Der Spitzel."

(*BFA* 27:205) sets out reactions to Bruno Bettelheim's discussion of "das Verhalten von Konzentrationslagerhäftlingen," in particular "der rapide (galoppierende) Persönlichkeitsschwund," interpreted by Bettelheim as a compensatory reaction to demeaning treatment at the hands of SS guards ("Behavior in Extreme Situations," *Politics*, 1 August 1944). In Brecht's eyes, Bettelheim's findings confirmed Hermann Borchardt's concentration camp experiences, documented in *Die Verschwörung der Zimmerleute*, published in the United States as *The Conspiracy of Carpenters: Historical Accounting of a Ruling Class* (New York: Simon and Schuster, 1943).

[17] Busch, *Bertolt Brecht*, 23.

Their fear of the consequences of their actions is at the same time compounded by their country's collective sense of national disgrace due to
its defeat in the First World War and "the shame of Versailles," as it was
called in reactionary circles. Whether certain forms of fear can be dismissed
as quasi-paranoid or are seen as justifiable will depend on the eye of the
beholder — that is to say, his or her political standpoint. The fear of a
member of the professional middle classes that he might lose his job may
meet with little sympathy on the left-wing, just as the fear of a couple of
drunken SS men running riot in a proletarian district would cut no ice
with the Popular Front. For this reason, in both *Furcht und Elend* and *The
Private Life*, Brecht is inclined to treat the perpetrators' fear as unjustified
overreaction, while taking that of the victims seriously.

These two principal kinds of fear that attracted Brecht's attention are
treated asymmetrically in "Die Ängste des Regimes," as well they deserve
to be, given the fact that in 1930s Germany the fear of the victims far
outweighed that of any Nazi perpetrator. It was only with *The Private
Life of the Master Race*, the Second World War American stage-adaptation
conceived at a time when hostilities were reaching a crescendo of mutual
annihilation on the Eastern Front, that the fear of the perpetrators was
presented as being substantially different from the paranoia and nervous
overreaction of Nazi functionaries on the Home Front. *The Private Life*
is no longer dominated by fear experienced by the proletariat, the petty
bourgeoisie, SA, and Gestapo. Fear is now less often presented within the
framework of class warfare: those soldiers on its armored troop carrier are
from virtually all classes. The war has to a considerable extent broken down
class barriers; all are now united in a sense of impending doom. In *Furcht
und Elend*, the second prologue verse of "Die deutsche Heerschau" had
described those about to be reviewed as "Ein bleicher, kunterbunter /
Haufe" (*BFA* 4:341; a pale, motley crew). Here, it is the adjective "bleich"
alone that carries the burden of suggesting fear, and we are not expressly
told what they are afraid of — presumably not just the war that is being systematically prepared, but also of being called upon to die for *Führer, Volk,
und Vaterland*. In contrast, the description of the *Panzer* soldiers in the
American version leaves nothing to the imagination. It is said of them that
"their faces [are] white as chalk [. . .] they could be puppets" (*The Private
Life*, 1). Presumably, it is extreme fear that makes them resemble inanimate
objects. *Furcht und Elend des Dritten Reiches* contains only one scene ("In
den Kasernen wird die Beschießung von Almeria bekannt") where soldiers
are presented as both petrified and pale with fear. In that scene two young
boys describe the soldiers they have just visited as "ganz käseweiß [. . .]
jetzt haben sie Schiß" (*BFA* 4:432; white as a sheet [. . .] and scared shitless: *FM* 85–86). Of course, the focus in *Furcht und Elend* is of necessity
on forms of fear in a country on the way to war, but still not yet officially at
war. Fear of the war to come is less central a preoccupation than the inter-

nal class war between the National Socialists and their political enemies within Third Reich Germany. Although we encounter a number of SA and SS, few soldiers are on stage in any production of the play. The perpetrators' fear is in fact largely confined to the world of civilians.

Interweaving the "Furcht" and "Elend" Strands: Two Case Studies

Taking our cue from Brecht's "Nicht–Sondern" contrastive model,[18] we conclude the present discussion of the depiction of fear and misery in individual *Furcht und Elend* scenes with an examination of two largely underestimated ones where fear and misery are treated in ways that bring out the interaction between them, and of some respects in which these two essentialist concepts are effectively politicized through the specifics of the scene plots in question.

The subject of our first case study, "Die Kiste" (*BFA* 4:408–9), is a textbook illustration of the fact that the work's "Furcht" and "Elend" strands tend to be intricately interwoven and in this respect contribute towards creating the wider picture that Brecht missed in many of exile literature's responses to the Third Reich. Our second detailed study will be of "Der Gefühlsersatz" (*BFA* 4:443–52), a scene involving a highly plausible, multilayered episode that Brecht had by 1938 already prepared for inclusion, but subsequently jettisoned, allegedly because its subject-matter was not consonant with the project's planned political indictment of the Third Reich specifically.[19] Comparing this scene with the uncontested strengths of "Die Kiste" gives some indication as to what kinds of illustrative material Brecht deemed appropriate to his counter-propaganda campaign against the NS regime. That is to say, in contrast to the communist political correctness that we will observe in "Die Kiste," our analysis

---

[18] Brecht introduces this model in "Kurze Beschreibung einer neuen Technik der Schauspielkunst, die einen Verfremdungseffekt hervorbringt" (*BFA* 22:643). The model's implications and advantages for Epic Theater are discussed in White, *Bertolt Brecht's Dramatic Theory*, 110–12 and 222–23. A neater reformulation of the model can be found in a recent presentation of it as "the 'not A but B' mode of argument" (Martin Swales, "Brecht and the Onslaught on Tragedy," in *The Text and its Context: Studies in Modern German Literature and Society*, ed. Nigel Harris and Joanne Sayner (Oxford: Peter Lang, 2008), 277).

[19] "'Der Gefühlsersatz' gab Brecht nie in Druck, weil er in ihr Verrohung und Unmenschlichkeit geißelte, wie sie nicht nur der Faschismus vorbrachte, sondern auch jede andere kapitalistische Gesellschaft" (Werner Mittenzwei, "Die Szenenfolge *Furcht und Elend des Dritten Reiches*," in *Bertolt Brecht: Von der "Maßnahme" zu "Leben des Galilei"* [Berlin-Weimar: Aufbau, 1973], 193–218, here, 194).

of "Der Gefühlsersatz" will show that the Gnauer family are motivated by greed, rather than politics, and use National Socialism as a mere pretext for their behavior. The scene, good family drama though it may be, offers no exemplary resistance to the Third Reich and thus merely serves to illustrate what the Comintern would see as the cynical capitalist and petty-bourgeois greed characteristic of Third Reich Germany.

According to *The Private Life*, *Aurora*, and *GW* (no location or date is given in the *Malik* proof version used in *BFA*), "Die Kiste" is set in a working-class district in the industrial Ruhr city of Essen in 1934. The scene begins with all the trappings of a rousing left-wing Naturalist melodrama. A widowed mother of two children, the older of whom already suffers from bronchitis, is grieving at the loss of her husband, the family breadwinner and a resolute critic of the NS system. The front door stands open; both family and friends appear to be awaiting delivery of the dead man's corpse, which arrives in a sealed zinc box carried in by some SA men. They deposit the box unceremoniously on the floor, warning the widow before they leave not to make a fuss about the mysterious circumstances surrounding the man's death. For expository reasons, although their inclusion is explained at plot level by their wish to give the bereft family emotional support, two neighbors, a working-class man and his wife, are also present.

The initial impression this short scene makes is one of "Elend": both financial poverty (the penniless woman is now left with two children to bring up) and mental "Elend," in the sense that the woman is at her wits' end, being still unable to understand why her husband died. The man, we are led to assume, was sent to a concentration camp because he had complained about the current starvation wages at his place of work. Even though this is probably the case, no one knows for certain exactly how his end came about: "Sie können ihm doch nichts getan haben" (*BFA* 4:408; They couldn't possibly have harmed him, could they?: *FM* 68) is the wife's knee-jerk response. She is evidently not convinced by the official explanation that the "natural" cause of death was pneumonia. The fact that his body has now turned up in a sealed metal container triggers further suspicion, even if it means that those present in theory still have access to the concealed evidence. Although no one is supposed to open the box, the neighbor is tempted to do so. As he puts it, rising to the bait: "Die haben ja Furcht, daß man das sieht. Sonst brächten sie ihn nicht in Zink" (*BFA* 4:408; They're frightened of people seeing that. That's why they used zinc: *FM* 69).

The NS regime's fear of the truth, and its assumption that anyone highlighting the lies in its propaganda claims is *de facto* engaging in an act of resistance, are leitmotifs running through much of Brecht's political writings during the first half of the 1930s. His essay "[Verschweigen der Wahrheit]" (Hiding the truth, *BFA* 22:98) was already claiming of the National Socialists in 1934, the year in which "Die Kiste" is set: "In Wirklichkeit sind es die Tatsachen, die sie fürchten" (In reality, it is facts they are afraid of). In the antifascist struggle, even the events of such a straightforward scene as this one, pointing to the ugly truth behind the lies, virtually become an act of defiance. However, despite the initial reaction voiced by the worker, it would be wrong to assume that the zinc container is simply part of a strategy to conceal the truth and thus serves as evidence of the perpetrators' fear. If this were its sole or principal purpose, one might wonder why the SA had even bothered to return the body, insulated from prying eyes or not. Corpses were rarely released from concentration camps (or even buried) in the 1930s. For similar reasons, political prisoners set free from so-called "protective custody" were forbidden to disclose anything about their experiences. The intention was not just to conceal the nature of the excesses committed in such places against the regime's enemies, but to tighten the system's stranglehold on the truth. "What happened in the camps was meant to be shrouded in mystery," according to one historian of the period.[20] Fear of the truth coming out was admittedly still a significant factor for a totalitarian regime anxious lest its international image be further tarnished by atrocity stories. One sees this, for example, from the way the full extent of the horrific deeds committed during "Kristallnacht" was quickly concealed from the German people or the fact that political prisoners released from police custody were often not allowed back into the community, but simply re-arrested and transferred to a concentration camp for indefinite further detention. While Brecht's political essays often emphasize the National Socialists' fear of the truth, "Die Kiste" shows that secrecy could also be exploited as an effective form of intimidation. The zinc box itself is obviously an image of concealed facts, but it also represents a physical intrusion into an intimate scene of family grief, as well as a devious form of political entrapment. Realizing this, most of the working-class characters in "Die Kiste" find themselves in a double bind: being reluctant to give in to such intimidation and yet at the same time wary of offering the SA further reason to victimize them. Although divided at the outset about whether or not to open the box, they gradually realize the price that they would pay if found to have done so. The visiting neighbor warns her husband: "Sie holen dich nur auch" (They might come for you too). For a while he still tries to convince the others to stand their ground and do so, but the dead man's widow cautions against such risk-taking: "Ich hab noch einen Bruder, den sie holen können, Hans. Und dich können sie auch holen. Die Kiste kann zubleiben. Wir müssen ihn nicht sehen. Wir werden ihn nicht vergessen" (There's still my brother, they might come for him, Hans. And they might come for you too. The box can stay shut. We don't need to see him. He won't be forgotten, *FM* 69). This decision is arguably not a surrender to force majeure, but a prudent recognition

---

[20] Evans, *The Third Reich in Power*, 95.

of the tangled predicament they find themselves in. "Widerstand war aus-sichtslos," Brecht recalled of the period in the late 1930s when left-wing confidence was at a nadir, "(und groß für das)" (journal entry for 5 January 1948, *BFA* 27:262; Resistance was hopeless (and for that reason great): *BBJ* 383). Despite the temptation to go against orders, the widow and her neighbors in "Die Kiste" decide against satisfying their curiosity by engag-ing in stubborn gestures of disobedience or in grand heroics. Their unfore-seen dilemma could, when viewed from a distance, be interpreted as part of the "Elend" of their circumstances. By 1934 the working-class's resistance capacity is on record as being at its lowest ebb. As this scene demonstrates, the time for concerted action was, as a consequence, not yet ripe. How-ever, the moral and political dilemmas facing the participants in this scene cannot be reduced to a simple fear factor, whether it is a matter of the fear of the victims or that of the perpetrators. Nor can it be contained within the framework of material deprivation (i.e., one connotation of "Elend") or class-on-class intimidation (inevitably creating a climate of "Furcht"). Brecht almost seems to be testing his audience (or readers) by questioning what their response would have been.

The complexities of even such a brief scene as "Die Kiste" appear to challenge Engberg's charge that to focus exclusively on "Furcht" and "Elend" is to create a selective picture of the Third Reich, one unable to do justice to the true nature of the working-class's suffering under the NS regime. Part of the scene's verse epigraph (*Vorspruch*) introduces the dead man with what essentially reads like an epitaph for him: "Er kämpfte für ein besseres Leben / In der großen Klassenschlacht" (*BFA* 4:408; He fought for a better life in the great class struggle), an encoded way of say-ing he was a communist. However, the only information we have about the man's actual contribution to the antifascist struggle suggests a dan-gerous, counterproductive stubbornness of attitude on his part. "Er hat sich nicht ergeben" (he never gave in) may be a backhanded compliment, under the present circumstances. Not cowed, he spoke out against the sub-subsistence wages he and his comrades were being paid and he paid with his life for having done so. The broader problem is that in doing so he may have underestimated the potential consequences. In all likelihood, his family will have to suffer substantial financial burdens in the years to come, his relatives will live under the perpetual threat of collective *Sippenhaft*,[21] fear of losing their jobs, of inadvertently drawing further attention to their political allegiances, and of imprisonment or dispatch to a correc-tive detention camp (*Erziehungslager*). All these putative reprisals could have an impact on any or all of them. The awareness of this predicament

---

[21] *Sippenhaft* is the NS term for the collective punishment imposed on other mem-bers of a family or group for the "crimes" of just one of their number.

gradually colors both their grief and the way those present react to the zinc container. Rather than offering a satisfactory conclusion, the widow's closing words come across as a strategy to make audiences want something better than mere unproductive disobedience. Yet her belief that the dead man will not be forgotten at least gives all present the strength to carry on with the struggle. The scene's setting, its catalyst, central debates, and even the conclusions it reaches are all political, inasmuch as they are predicated on our awareness of the material conditions of working-class life under National Socialism, the role played by fear and intimidation in the "große Klassenschlacht," and the pressing need for reasoned pragmatism when responding to provocation. Material deprivation (the most obvious connotation of the word "Elend" in the play's title) looms large in "Die Kiste," while being for the most part inseparable from various manifestations of fear and a sense of the need for extreme caution.

"Der Gefühlsersatz" (*BFA* 4:443–52), the only scene in the *Furcht und Elend* project not to be authorized for publication by Brecht, is more of a drawing-room intrigue than a "realistic parable" (Brecht's term[22]). It offers a typical picture of the financial and ethical problems facing the petty bourgeoisie during the Third Reich. The action begins with a pervasive sense of gloom, much talk about monetary difficulties, fear of self-incrimination in unguarded moments, indecision in some ways reminiscent of the early part of "Die Kiste." The main difference between the two scenes derives from our having now entered a petty bourgeois milieu, as a consequence of which the principal characters' motivation becomes decidedly less political and driven mainly by greed and hypocrisy. In such a claustrophobic familial setting, the harsh reality of life in the Third Reich still stands in sharp contrast to the regime's propaganda claims about the state of the economy in particular and of post-Weimar society in general. The discrepancy between ideological misrepresentation and reality is prefigured in the prologue's Delphic utterance: "Ein Mäntelchen wurde der Gemeinheit immer umgehängt. Aber jetzt ist es aus Wollstra" (*BFA* 4:443)[23]

---

[22] Brecht's "Gibt es realistische Parabeln? Waren Cervantes, Rabelais, Aristophanes, Lafontaine, Swift Realisten?" (*BFA* 22:539) was written in 1939, in the wake of the "Realismusdebatte." Some of the *Furcht und Elend* "ten-minute" scenes, including "Zwei Bäcker" (*BFA* 22:420), merit consideration as "realistische Parabeln" illustrating certain features of life in Nazi Germany.

[23] "Wollstra" was the trade name for a Third Reich wool-substitute amalgam of wool and synthetic fibers. Ersatz wool was made necessary by the stringent requirements of the first four-year plan's autarkist (or economic self-sufficiency) strategy. Problems with other ersatz materials also figure in "Die schwarzen Schuhe" (*BFA* 4:401–2), "Das neue Kleid" (*BFA* 4:417), with its references to "neue / Schönnamige Kleider [. . .] aus Holz und Papieren. / Die Wolle reservieren / Sie für das Militär," and "Zwei Bäcker" (*BFA* 4:420). According to R. J. Overy (*War and*

(Meanness was always shrouded in a little cloak. But nowadays the cloak is made of synthetic material, *FM* 122).[24] In other words, the mantle of dissimulation that has been draped over the regime's political abuses is now made of ersatz material, and, being threadbare, it is beginning to reveal the shabby reality and moral quagmire that it was originally meant to conceal. (The ersatz motif, a satirical metaphor for the new social revolution that the NSDAP falsely claims to have ushered in, applies both to the state and to the deceptive façade of altruism and selflessness that individual members of the present family try to erect around themselves.) Clearly, the figurative language of the introductory epigraph to "Der Gefühlsersatz," essentially a Brechtian defamiliarization device, would be beyond the reach of most of the characters we encounter in either scene. Whereas the working-class characters in "Die Kiste" speak in simple, no-nonsense sentences, "Der Gefühlsersatz" involves a protracted debate about whether or not family members really care for one another, about material factors and ethical values, and warnings about the foreseeable disruption to the family's plans for a comfortable future. A bold defamiliarizing metaphor is required to introduce "Der Gefühlsersatz" so as to establish our critical distance from the feigned well-meaning intentions and general hypocrisy of a number of the petty-bourgeois characters involved in the altercation.

There are three dimensions to the stage space for "Der Gefühlsersatz": (i) the living-room, occupied by paterfamilias Herr Gnauer (in SA uniform), together with his wife, their daughter Lotte (no BdM[25] uniform), and son Hans (in everyday clothing); (ii) the adjacent sick-room (off-stage) where Herr Gnauer's sister Frieda lies suffering from the terminal stages of stomach cancer; and (iii) beyond their walls, the outside Third Reich world that intrudes upon the home realm in the form of a transparently "loaded" radio propaganda broadcast.

The talk that SA man Gnauer feels they should all listen to on the day in question is given by an officially sanctioned expert. That is to say, *Medizinalrat* Seifner is scheduled to speak on "The Scientist's view of the Four-Year Plan with particular regard to the availability of edible fats" (*FM* 103). The title, with its references to the NS regime's economic strategy as well as to current deficiencies in the supply of fats, suggests that the material

---

Economy in the Third Reich, Oxford: Clarendon, 1994, 31), synthetic production of fuel-, rubber-, fiber-, and oil-substitutes was less a response to current diminishing stocks of raw material than a subtle form of preparation for the Third Reich's planned war economy.

[24] An editorial note to the English translation of "Der Gefühlsersatz" points out that the scene "has no introductory verse, though [the prose epigraph] may be meant as the theme for one" (*FM* 122).

[25] BdM=Bund deutscher Mädel (League of German Girls).

is likely to be highly contentious.[26] Fats, like so many foodstuffs, were in notoriously short supply during the mid-period of NSDAP rule because of the government's harsh economic program, which entailed a whole series of draconian austerity policies. Although this was not yet clear to everyone, Nazi Germany's accelerated drive for economic self-sufficiency (autarky)[27] and the associated four-year plans were key aspects of forward planning on a grand scale for a major European war. In most circles, this would eventually be popularly associated with the infamous *Butter-oder-Kanonen* question alluded to in a number of *Furcht und Elend* scenes. Hermann Goering, plenipotentiary for the implementation of the second four-year plan, was later to make explicit the relationship between extreme food shortages at the national level and the underlying strategy for military victory, suggesting that the German people had to choose between the two, while leaving them in no doubt as to which option a good patriotic German should support. However, the speaker's task in "Der Gefühlsersatz" is not to make a nationalistic plea for material sacrifices *on strategic-economic grounds* (the NSDAP was having to tread more carefully at this precarious stage in the Third Reich's history); instead, it was to put the case for the benefits of less fat, butter, or butter-substitutes, *strictly on health grounds*. His argument, introduced by the claim that it was "eine betrübliche, aber nur allzu bekannte Tatsache, daß der Mensch nicht immer weiß, was zu seinem Besten dient und was nicht" (a regrettable if all too familiar fact that mankind is not always aware what is in its own best interest and what not), leads to the paternalistic assertion that the state knows better what is good for its citizens than they do:

> Mancher unter unseren Volksgenossen sieht bei den großen Maßnahmen, welche die Regierung im Interesse des Volksganzen trifft, vor allem immer darauf, ob sie von ihm größere oder kleinere Opfer verlangen. [. . .] Aber gerade diese sogenannten Opfer sind oft, näher betrachtet, überhaupt keine Opfer, sondern viel eher Wohltaten. So mag mancher, wenn wir an die Ernährung im Rahmen des Vierjahresplanes denken, ein kleinmütiges Ach und Weh anstimmen,

---

[26] On the disastrous impact of the two NS four-year plans on Germany's civilian population, see the discussion of "Der Bauer füttert die Sau" and "Der alte Kämpfer" in Chapter Four.

[27] According to Evans (*The Third Reich in Power*, 345), autarky had been "a basic concept of Nazi economics from the 1920s on." As *Mein Kampf* makes clear, this was mainly because Hitler was mindful of the damage done to the country by naval blockades during the First World War and the colonial and other territorial losses inflicted on the country by the Versailles Treaty. During the 1930s, NS policy repeatedly stressed autarky's military importance for the Third Reich's geo-political aspirations. On the impact of the autarky program, see Overy, *War and Economy in the Third Reich*, 177–204.

daß mal hier ein wenig Milch, mal dort ein wenig Fett fehlt. Und er wird sehr erstaunt sein, zu hören, daß die Wissenschaft ihm sagt, daß dieser Mangel an Fett zum Beispiel eine wahre Wohltat für seinen Körper bedeuten kann. (*BFA* 4:443–44)

[Certain of our national comrades have been known to judge the comprehensive measures which the government takes in the interests of the whole people, according to the degree of sacrifice demanded of the individual judging. [. . .] Looked at closely, however, this presumed sacrifice often turns out to be no sacrifice but an act of kindness. Thus suppose we take nutrition in the context of the Four-Year Plan: a certain amount of petty grumbling might be heard to the effect that there are slight shortages of milk here and of fat there. Those concerned will be surprised to learn from science that such a shortage of fat for instance may constitute a positive act of kindness to their body. (*FM* 103)]

Ironically, it is at the very moment when the broadcaster is on the verge of revealing what the panel of experts has to say on the question of the human body's positive reaction to "fettarme Nahrung" that the Gnauers' doctor returns from examining his patient in the next room. He thus misses the pseudo-scientific NS radio propaganda on behalf of diminished fat intake, only to have left by the time the radio is switched on again. Thus the one man in this scene with sufficient medical competence to be in a position to question the lies being peddled is not present to challenge them (not that the family would have probably believed him, in any case). The fact that all the theater audience needs to hear in this scene is the first and last parts of a much longer broadcast suggests that everything in between is utterly predictable. Nevertheless, *Medizinalrat* Seifner does manage to sign off by striking some disturbing new notes. One example of the Third Reich's politicization of medicine is the speaker's attempted "scientific" justification of economic stringency by invoking Germany's current geo-political predicament:

Allzu fettreiche Ernährung erzeugt eher Krankheit. Fettarme Ernährung garantiert längere Lebensdauer und größere Spannkraft. Nicht umsonst ist der Arbeiter fähiger zu körperlichen Anstrengungen als der sogenannte Intellektuelle. Seine angebliche schlechtere Ernährung ist eben in Wirklichkeit die bessere. Selbst wenn unser Volk also nicht durch seine ökonomische Lage und den Mangel an Kolonien gezwungen wäre, Fett zu sparen und seine Mittel anderweitig zu verwenden, wäre es unserer ehrlichen Überzeugung nach zu seinem Besten, wenn es fettärmer lebte. (*BFA* 4:452)

[Too fatty a diet is more likely to cause disease. A low-fat diet guarantees greater energy and longer life. It is not for nothing that the worker is better fitted for physical effort than the so-called intellectual. His supposedly inferior diet is in reality the better of the two. Thus even if our economic situation and lack of colonies did not force our people to save on fat and apply its resources in other ways we are honestly convinced that it would be in its own best interest to do with less fat. (*FM* 110)]

The broadcast's belated mention of Germany's lack of colonies points back to the Versailles Treaty clause that deprived Weimar Germany of its former colonial possessions, thereby suggesting that the country's old entente enemies are entirely responsible for the present hardship and accountable for the sacrifices Germans are being called upon to make. The subsequent reference to the Third Reich's contemporary economic predicament (the result of the four-year plans) ignores the fact that the present crisis stems not from a lack of colonies, but from a policy that is part of an essentially military agenda. Alluding to the Versailles Treaty is intended to imply that the government has firm geo-political measures in hand to overturn the effects of defeat, while conveniently not frightening the population by revealing that the ultimate consequence will be yet another expansionist war. What began as a specialist radio essay ends up sounding more like a piece of encoded pro-war propaganda. Somewhere along the way, the *Medizinalrat*'s argument that less fat is good for everyone has been swamped by political arguments to the effect that the shortages in question are other people's fault, if also something in the long run surprisingly positive. In a Third Reich pinning its reputation on having brought about a spiritual revival (*seelischer Aufschwung*) in 1933, the proclaimed virtues of autarky have even been reduced to the level of defending a low-fat diet by the latter half of the 1930s! (No date is given for the scene "Der Gefühlsersatz.")

The two excerpts from the radio broadcast that enclose the main body of the scene "Der Gefühlsersatz" establish a clear political context (something not even mentioned by Werner Mittenzwei). They thus provide a neat twist to Herr Gnauer's claim that "die deutsche Ernährungslage" (Germany's food situation) must be treated as a matter of great import to the German people. The equivalents of a prologue and an epilogue supplied by the two extracts are ingeniously linked to the family discussion by the motif of ersatz products (which includes simulated feelings). The challenge for this scene is to move progressively from the ideological frame to a less political family drama without losing either plausibility or the frame's critical thrust. As was to be expected, "Furcht" and "Elend" play only a minor role in the radio talk. Grumblers are alluded to, but only to be dismissed as not worth taking seriously. The pseudo-theoretical medical line adopted by the radio broadcaster is, significantly, received more seriously by the family than was their doctor's advice, advice that they have their own private reasons for not wanting to take too seriously. And it is in their reasons for this behavior that the real clues to the presence of "Elend" can be found.

On the surface, there would appear to be a calculating greed to the behavior of the petty bourgeois Gnauer family, rather than visible evidence

of genuine material deprivation (the obvious form of "Elend"). We learn
that Herr Gnauer's sick sister Frieda is being looked after in their home by
a hired nurse only because they had assumed that it would cost substantially more to put her in a nursing home: a "calculation" in both senses of
the word. Now, however, the doctor's recommendation that she will need
a (costly) operation to prolong her life for a short while — and even that
outcome is not guaranteed — wreaks havoc with their plans. Husband
and wife devote much mid-scene time to rehearsing a series of duplicitous
pseudo-arguments meant to justify not submitting the patient to the risks
of an operation, while at the same time insinuating that it would be kinder
to keep her at home than put her in a clinic (thereby again making serious
inroads into their finances) and taking refuge in the argument that she
should be allowed to die in peace. In another context, much of the family's
predicament in this scene might have served as a pretext to criticize the NS
health service for failing to deliver the kind of support that its claim to be
part of a welfare state might lead one to expect. But a late remark made by
Herr Gnauer disallows such an interpretation:

> Wenn schon durchaus vom Finanziellen geredet sein muß, so gebe
> ich immerhin zu bedenken, daß wir mit dem Sündengeld, das eine
> solche Operation verschlingt, für Lotte gerade jetzt den Laden in der
> Möschstraße für ein Spottgeld aufkaufen können, wo Kott und Söhne
> jetzt bankrott sind als rein jüdisches Geschäft. Das wird nie mehr so
> billig sein. (*BFA* 4:450–51)

> [And if money really has to come into it, then let me point out that the
> monstrous sum such an operation would cost would be just enough
> for us to buy that shop in the Möschstrasse for a knockdown price,
> what with Kott and Sons having gone bankrupt as a Jewish-owned
> business. That's a bargain that won't occur twice. (*FM* 109)]

The possibility that daughter Lotte could be privy to the plan might explain
her callous lack of interest in her aunt's survival, given the danger that she
might no longer be the beneficiary of an "Aryanization" sale of Jewish
property. Such a subtext to the concerted behavior of the entire Gnauer
family, with the noble exception of Hans, the scene's *raisonneur*, puts the
whole dispute in a fresh light. While the regime is busy promoting the idea
that "Gemeinnutz geht vor Eigennutz" (the public interest comes first),
in this particular family profit comes before any vestige of family decency.
The Gnauers are more interested in the material advantages accruing from
National Socialism than in the state's line on a fat-free diet or in the ethics
of its antisemitic policy. With hindsight, some of the earlier exchanges about
what to do with Tante Frieda become increasingly sinister. Tante Frieda has
a right to be more afraid of her own kith and kin than of dying of cancer.

"Der Gefühlsersatz" is an untypical *Furcht und Elend* scene, although
not just for the reason Mittenzwei offers. Surprisingly little fear is expressed

in it, except when it comes to losing money. In fact, the only real fear
expressed in this episode is that of an opportunistic married couple worrying about the financial claims made on them by their dying relative's condition. We see that to the bookbinder, a petty bourgeois supporter of the
regime whose SA uniform typecasts him as such, politics is more a matter of
opportunism than ideological conviction. Herr Gnauer may take pleasure
in the nation's spiritual revival, but he is just as happy to use politics and
nationalism as a stick with which to attack the son who disagrees with him.
One can understand why Brecht might have had misgivings about retaining the scene. The principal justification for doing so would be as evidence
of what effect fascism can have on some members of such an already grasp-
ing family. What has been called "the atomization of everyday life" in the
Third Reich[28] is here convincingly illustrated, and, not for the only time in
Furcht und Elend, at family level. Herr Gnauer and his daughter try to side-
step pressing family responsibilities by escaping to their respective SA and
BdM meetings. The father, when rightly charged with insincerity by Hans,
seeks to exonerate himself by accusing his son of a lack of patriotism. There
may be little overt fear in "Der Gefühlsersatz," but, as even that response
suggests, there is a superabundance of hypocrisy. Indeed, it is difficult to
discern whether the Gnauers ever become genuinely afraid of where their
callousness is leading the entire family. In contrast, one can detect a sense
of genuine spiritual isolation, far outweighing material disadvantage, in the
words of their son who is being threatened with receiving no more pocket
money from his father. His outspoken reaction is not motivated by greed,
but by prudent pragmatism, followed by a rare ethical judgment:

> Dann kann ich nicht mehr zur Schule radeln. Die Schläuche kön-
> nen nicht mehr geflickt werden. Neue aus Gummi kriege ich sowieso
> nicht mehr. Nur Gummiersatz. Die Schule ist auch nur mehr Schuler-
> satz. Und Familie ist Familieersatz. (*BFA* 4:446)

> [Then I won't be able to cycle to school. My inner tubes are past
> mending now. And I can't get new ones of real rubber. Just ersatz
> rubber. Same way school nowadays is ersatz school. And this family's
> an ersatz family. (*FM* 105)]

To sum up, despite the many allusions to economic difficulties, the real
"Elend" in this scene is not material. It lies in what the regime has done
to family, school, and personal relationships as a whole, an "Elend" that is
particularly in evidence in the Gnauers' hypocritical mistrust of all serious
medical help for one of their members. Such "Elend" at family level is in
many ways akin to the combination of material and spiritual "Elend" char-

---

[28] Detlev J. K. Peukert, *Inside Nazi Germany: Conformity, Opposition and Racism
in Everyday Life* (New Haven, CT: Yale UP, 1987), 236.

acteristic of the continual suffering of the German people under the yoke of National Socialist rule. And this was a danger not only confined to the present. We already noted another kind of "Elend" in Chapter One: one invoked in "Bericht über die Stellung der Deutschen im Exil," where Brecht predicts that "Ein Sieg [Hitler Deutschlands] würde die ganze bewohnte Welt in solchem Elend sehen" (*BFA* 23:32). In other words, "Elend" on a comparable scale is not just a feature of present daily life in Third Reich Germany as depicted in the *Furcht und Elend* scenes, it also threatens the future of the entire world. And, as Brecht was evidently well aware, it can even be projected back into the past, as a kind of historical legacy.

The Ultimate "Elend": "Die deutsche Misere"

One possibility, hitherto neglected in the secondary literature on *Furcht und Elend*, is that the phrase "[das] Elend des Dritten Reiches" in the play's title could refer to something far more disturbing than the individual examples of economic deprivation and material misery registered in many of the play's individual scenes. The ultimate connotation of the "Elend" that the play illustrates, we would like to suggest, is a historical phenomenon more akin to what Friedrich Engels once famously called "die deutsche Misere,"[29] a phrase that was quickly to become shorthand for a view of German history as a "special way" (*Sonderweg*), disappointingly lacking in political protest and full-scale revolutions. Brecht's "Notizen zu Heinrich Manns *Mut*" (*BFA* 22:528–37)[30] recalls the "deutsche Misere" thesis specifically in connection with the German Third Reich. Struck in 1939 by the contemporary relevance of Mann's *Der Untertan*, which he regarded as German literature's first great satirical political novel, Brecht evokes Engels's dismissive verdict, adding: "das [deutsche] Bürgertum hat immer noch nicht seine politische Revolution vollzogen" (*BFA* 22: 531–32; the [German] bourgeoisie has still not carried out its political revolution). While not explicitly employing the phrase "deutsche Misere," Brecht nevertheless unmistakably echoes Engels's charge in some of his best-known antifascist works, including the Danish *Ur*-version of *Leben des Galilei* (1938–39) and *Arturo Ui* (1941). At the beginning of Scene 15 of *Arturo Ui*, in a sequence clearly alluding to "die deutsche Misere," one of the Karfiol (Cauliflower) Trust's victims, a greengrocer, comes on stage

---

[29] Letter of 14 July 1893 to Franz Mehring (*MEW* 39:99). The subject of "die deutsche Misere" in other writings by Brecht is treated in Klaus-Detlef Müller, *Die Funktion der Geschichte im Werk Bertolt Brechts: Studien zum Verhältnis von Marxismus und Ästhetik* (Tübingen: Niemeyer, 1967), 89–95.

[30] Heinrich Mann, *Mut* (Paris: Editions du 10. Mai, 1939). Mann's foreword to *Mut* was pre-published in *Das Wort* 4 (February 1939), 105–6.

and sounds the alarm with the words "Mord! Schlächterei! Erpressung! Willkür! Raub!" (Murder! Butchery! Extortion! Despotism! Highway Robbery!), to which a second greengrocer immediately makes the sardonic retort "Und Schlimmres! Duldung! Unterwerfung! Feigheit!" (*BFA* 7:106; And worse! Passivity! Submissiveness! Cowardice!). This pithy, tragi-comical exchange serves as a timely reminder that the economic misery of the NSDAP regime's victims is only one part, albeit for a dialectical materialist an important part, of the overall picture. As the second greengrocer's response is meant to suggest, concepts like "Elend" and "Misere" also apply to the supine behavior of the many people who were in their various ways passively complicit in the "crimes against humanity" and the other outrageous events of 1933–45.

There are clearly as many instances of "Mord! Schlächterei! Erpressung! Willkür! Raub!" in *Furcht und Elend* as there are in Brecht's chronicle of the gangster leader Arturo Ui's systematic rise to power. "Elend," in the more commonly used sense, is experienced in both middle-class and petty-bourgeois circles as well as — and most severely — by the proletariat. As for the German middle class, Brecht was convinced, as we saw in Chapter Two, that they lacked the political conviction and moral fiber to react constructively to their nation's predicament. If there was to be resistance from them, this would only be achieved with the aid of the working class.

> [Die Mittelklassen] haben keinen Plan, wissen keinen Ausweg aus der Wirrnis, sie können weder ein allgemein wirksames, neues, produktives Wirtschafts- und Gesellschaftssystem vorweisen noch ein solches garantieren. Sie sind allein nicht imstande, solche tiefgreifenden Änderungen des Fundaments durchzuführen, als nötig sind, die Freiheit aller Menschen [. . .] zu erzwingen. Zu helfen vermag ihnen nur die Arbeiterklasse. ("Notizen zu Heinrich Manns *Mut*," *BFA* 22:537)

> [[The middle classes] have no plan, cannot think of a way out of their chaotic predicament, they neither possess a generally effective, new, productive economic and social system, nor can they guarantee such a one. On their own, they are not in a position to implement the kinds of far-reaching changes to society's foundations as are necessary to forcibly bring about the freedom of all people [. . .]. Only the working class can help them.]

The emphasis here on the middle class, coupled with the idea that capitalism's victims will gradually form an effective (Popular Front) opposition, is probably attributable to the fact that Brecht's thoughts were to some considerable extent formulated in reaction to Heinrich Mann's *Der Untertan*. The individual scenes of *Furcht und Elend* display little hope of propaganda support for such cross-class political alliances as the Comintern's Popular Front was intended to encourage. As we will see in the next chapter, the most that Brecht could hope to document was local resistance, individual acts of defiance, and occasional political gestures of collective dissent. (He was in retrospect to show no sympathy for the motives of the men behind the 20 July 1944 Bomb Plot; see *BFA* 23:103.) Even at the end of *Furcht und Elend*, the closest the German proletariat come to expressing their hostility to the regime oppressing them is, tellingly, to do so via a plebiscite vote of "No." The continuing ignominy of "die deutsche Misere" is still a major political flaw, one that the pre-war version of the play was specifically designed to persuade those remaining in Germany to overcome. But the play's broad antifascist mission mainly focuses on a typology of levels of resistance, not preparations for some large-scale revolution. As is well known, Brecht was deeply disappointed that the German proletariat, instead of liberating itself by rising up en masse against the National Socialist dictatorship, had, along with Germany as a whole, to be rescued from itself by the Allied Powers, even if one of those powers was the Stalinist USSR.[31] His draft essay "[Wirkung der Doppelniederlage]" (The Effect of the Double Defeat) sums up the ignominy of such a predicament: "zuerst vernichtend geschlagen von Hitler, dann, zusammen mit Hitler, von den Alliierten" (*BFA* 23:104; first thoroughly beaten by Hitler, then, together with Hitler, by the Allies). During his exile antifascist period from 1933 until the end of hostilities in Europe, Brecht continued to pin his hopes on the Popular Front, the KPD, SPD, and other local clandestine resistance movements. *Furcht und Elend* and *The Private Life* reflect these hopes in their different ways.

---

[31] Brecht's journal for 26 December 1947, written in response to Lukács's "Der Briefwechsel zwischen Schiller und Goethe," observes: "Noch einmal keine eigene [Revolution] habend, werden nun wir die russische zu 'verarbeiten' haben, denke ich schaudernd" (*BFA* 27:259). See also in his entry for 9 December 1948: "Allenthalben macht sich [in Ostberlin] die neue deutsche Misere bemerkbar [. . .]. Die Deutschen rebellieren gegen den Befehl, gegen den Nazismus zu rebellieren; nur wenige stehen auf dem Standpunkt, daß ein befohlener Sozialismus besser ist als gar keiner" (*BFA* 27:285), and "die Arbeiter bedenken nicht eben, daß der Zerstörungskrieg gegen die Sowjetunion zwar ohne ihre Billigung, aber nicht ohne ihre Mithilfe gemacht wurde" (ibid.).

4: "Der Widerstand, und zwar der wachsende Widerstand": Brecht's Dramatized Typology of Forms of Opposition

DEFENDING HIS PLAY against certain misgivings, Brecht wrote in mid-April 1938 to Slatan Dudow, who was at the time preparing to direct the first staging of scenes from *Furcht und Elend* in Paris. Brecht's letter contained a response to Dudow's express concern that the work's picture of Nazi Germany was too bleak:

> Ich verstehe Ihre Besorgnis, daß der Abend zu depressiv werden könnte. Ein erhebender Abend kann es ja nun auf keinen Fall werden. Immerhin wird hier, denke ich, die ganze Brüchigkeit des Dritten Reiches in all seinen Einzelteilen sichtbar werden und daß nur Gewalt es zusammenhält. Das ist das Volk, das dieses Regime in einen der größten und schwierigsten Kriege aller Zeiten hineintreiben will. (*BFA* 29:84)

> [I understand your fear that the play may be too depressing. It certainly won't cheer people up. Still, I think it shows how fragile the Third Reich is in all its parts and aspects, that it is held together by violence alone. It shows the people whom this regime wants to drive into one of the biggest and hardest wars of all time. (*BBL* 281)]

Brecht went on to draw attention to what he felt was a crucial feature of the play's cumulative picture of life in the Third Reich:

> Der Widerstand, und zwar der wachsende Widerstand, wird deutlich gezeigt und das in allen Schichten und in allen Graden. (*BFA* 29:84)

> [Resistance, yes, the increasing resistance of every section of the population is shown clearly. (*BBL* 281–82)]

Although not explicit about the specific form taken by that pattern of increasing resistance, Brecht elsewhere expressed a general confidence that within Nazi Germany there would inevitably be a mixture of "Terror und Widerstand in allen Schichten" (*BFA* 29:83; Terror and resistance everywhere: *BBL* 280), and that antifascist elements would gradually infiltrate "selbst [. . .] Schichten, die ihm [the Third Reich] anfänglich entgegenjubelten" (*BFA* 29:86; even [. . .] sections of the population that originally welcomed it [the Third Reich] with cheers: *BBL* 282). Brecht's reference to "Widerstand in allen Schichten und in allen Graden" suggests that the *Furcht und Elend* scenes were meant collectively to offer a spectrum of forms of opposition, ranging from small, seemingly trivial tokens of non-compliance and disapproval to individual acts of effective sabotage and organized, large-scale campaigns of political resistance. Brecht's emphasis on the work's important oppositional component has implications for any reading of *Furcht und Elend* as an epic "Gestentafel" (*BFA* 26:318) involving not just the body language of fear and caution, but also calculated gestures of outright dissidence and acts of political resistance.[1] "Bekanntlich war ja auch das *Braunbuch* nicht einfach deprimierend" (*BFA* 29:86; It's generally known that even the *Brown Book* was rather more than depressing: *BBL* 282), Brecht reminded Dudow in his play's defense.

Expanding on his assertion that the resistance theme was as important a factor as the "Furcht und Elend" mentioned in the work's title, Brecht cited a number of scenes, only four of which were included in "99%: Bilder aus dem Dritten Reich" (99%: Scenes from the Third Reich), as the Paris production was called.[2] Given that the Paris repertoire included "Der Spitzel," "Die jüdische Frau," and "Rechtsfindung," all powerfully dramatic illustrations of middle-class capitulation in the face of *Gleichschaltung,* Dudow's concern might conceivably have related solely to the handful of scenes he had chosen for inclusion in his production, and not the full range available by this time.[3] Brecht's reaction, on the other hand, must apply to the full corpus, since he could not yet know which scenes Dudow would pick. Brecht's letter points to elements of alleged resistance in twelve scenes — i.e., almost half the play:

---

[1] There has been a tendency to interpret Brecht's "Gestentafel" metaphor exclusively in terms of the anxious behavior of German citizens faced with threats (see James K. Lyon, *BHB* 1:346 and *BFA* 4:227). The exception, Robert Cohen, "Brechts *Furcht und Elend des III. Reiches* und der Status des Gestus," *The Brecht Yearbook,* 24 (1999), 196–98, sees such "Gesten" as common to both "Täter und Opfer," as was the case in the poem "Die Ängste des Regimes." Brecht's "[Über die Aufführung von *Furcht und Elend des III. Reiches*]" concludes with the recommendation "auch [die Gestik] der Auflehnung muß besonders herausgearbeitet werden" (*BFA* 24: 227).

[2] Dudow's "99%" consisted of the framing song ("Die deutsche Heerschau") plus eight scenes staged in the following sequence: "Das Kreidekreuz," "Winterhilfe," "Der Spitzel," "Die jüdische Frau," "Zwei Bäcker," "Rechtsfindung," "Der Bauer füttert die Sau," and "Arbeitsbeschaffung."

[3] Brecht initially sent Dudow nineteen scenes to choose from for the Paris production, adding "das Ganze können Sie ja unmöglich spielen" (*BFA* 29:85). Shortly afterwards he informed Dudow that "weitere sechs kleine Stücke" had been written in the meantime (*BFA* 29:90).

Der Bauer *füttert* eben die Sau (scheu über die Schulter blickend); der Physiker *benützt* eben Einstein (laut über die jüdische Physik schimpfend); der Arbeiter [in "Was hilft gegen Gas?"] wirft die Gasmaske in die Ecke; die Soldaten [in "In den Kasernen wird die Beschießung von Almeria bekannt"] geben dem Jungen, der *nicht* "Heil Hitler" sagt, zwei Schlag Essen; der Patient (in "Die Berufskrankheit") *erinnert* den Chirurgen an die Forderungen der Wissenschaft; der Geprügelte *singt* die "Internationale"; der Richter findet *nicht* den Rechtsspruch; die von der Winterhilfe beschenkte Frau erbricht den Apfel; der alte Kämpfer *erhängt sich* demonstrativ; der Bäcker verfälscht auch einmal *nicht* das Brot; die Schwester des in Spanien Gefallenen läßt sich *nicht* den Mund zuhalten; und die Partei (am Schluß) *gibt den Kampf nicht auf.* (*BFA* 29:84–85)

[The farmer *feeds* his sow (while looking fearfully over his shoulder); the physicist *uses* Einstein (while loudly reviling Jewish physics); the worker throws his gas mask into the corner; the soldiers give the boy who does *not* say Heil Hitler two helpings of food; the patient (in "Occupational Disease") *reminds* the surgeon of the requirements of science; the man who has been beaten *sings* "The International"; the judge can *not* arrive at a verdict; the woman who has received a Winter Aid package vomits up the apple; the old soldier *hangs* himself demonstratively; the baker for once does *not* adulterate his bread; the sister of the man who has been killed in Spain does *not* let herself be silenced; and the Party (at the end) does *not give up the fight.* (*BBL* 282)]

On the basis of these — in some cases simplistic — readings, Brecht felt justified in claiming that *Furcht und Elend* demonstrated not only "wie wirkungslos ihr Terror [viz. that of the Nazis] bleiben muß," but also "wie er unfehlbar den Widerstand erzeugen muß" (*BFA* 29:85–86; how ineffectual [the Nazis'] terror is bound to be [. . .] how inevitably it must create resistance: *BBL* 282). The latter claim suggests that Brecht saw resistance as the inevitable dialectical counterpart to oppression and exploitation.[4] As we noted in Chapter One, Brecht's 1938 essay "Furcht und Elend des Dritten Reiches" ends with the question "Wird erst das Elend die Furcht besiegen?" (*BFA* 22:477; Will it be the misery that eventually defeats the fear?: *FM* 96). Brecht would now appear to be experimenting with the *Furcht und Elend* material to try to answer his own question.

Despite his confidence that extreme oppression would lead (dialectically) to acts of resistance and ideological rebellion, Brecht was never-

---

[4] "[Haltung der Sozialisten]" (1937) contains a passage on the relationship between exploitation and radicalization, the early stepping stones towards resistance: "Nicht das Proletariat proletarisiert den Bauern, Handwerker, Angestellten, Intellektuellen, kleinen Geschäftsmann, oder will ihn proletarisieren, sondern der Kapitalismus proletarisiert ihn, muß ihn proletarisieren" (*BFA* 22:299–300).

theless quick to dissociate himself from what he held to be a naïve belief currently in circulation: "das Argument [. . .], Hitler habe durch die Eroberung Österreichs sich ein Wachsen seiner Gegner zugezogen" (the argument [. . .] that by his conquest of Austria Hitler increased the number of his enemies). He dismissed this as unconvincing: "Danach würde er, wenn er die ganze Welt erobert hätte, sich aufhängen können" (*BFA* 29:85; It should follow that if he conquered the whole world he'd have to hang himself: *BBL* 282). Although *Furcht und Elend* ends with Austria's annexation in March 1938, the rationale for concluding the montage of scenes with Hitler's triumphant arrival in Vienna in the scene "Volksbefragung" has nothing to do with any misguided wishful thinking about Hitler's annexation of Austria precipitating an automatic "Wachsen seiner Gegner." Because of the period it covers, *Furcht und Elend* is inevitably less concerned with international opposition to NS foreign policy than with popular dissatisfaction and political resistance *within Germany.* This focus may seem like a continuation of the theme of underground preparation for revolution treated in *Die Maßnahme* (1930) and *Die Mutter* (1933). However, the subject, now even more topical, becomes substantially more complex and problematic in Brecht's *Furcht und Elend.* This is mainly because many of the acts of noncompliance and resistance depicted in the play's individual scenes merely involve dissatisfied individuals who are neither politically motivated to any meaningful degree nor noticeably driven by personal ethical principles. In contrast to what *Die Maßnahme* calls "illegal work," i.e., underground resistance activity intended to prepare for an imminent revolution, few *Furcht und Elend* scenes depict any equivalent acts of organized group-resistance.

"Was da murrt, ist kein Gegner": The Vexed Question of Taxonomy

Fritz Lang once claimed that Brecht was the only European in Hollywood who had an adequate understanding of the German resistance movement.[5] Yet many of the examples cited in Brecht's would-be reassuring letter to Dudow seem contentious when judged by the sophisticated criteria established in recent decades for differentiating between various forms of oppositional behavior. Brecht claims, for instance, that some German soldiers engage in resistance in the scene "In den Kasernen wird die Beschießung von Almeria bekannt" (*BFA* 4:432–33) merely because they reward a boy

---

[5] "Fritz Lang über seine Zusammenarbeit mit Brecht" (*Le Monde*, 9 December 1961), quoted in Wolfgang Gersch, *Film bei Brecht: Bertolt Brechts praktische und theoretische Auseinandersetzung mit dem Film* (Munich: Hanser, 1975), 216.

with a double helping of food for refusing to give the statutory "Heil Hitler" salute. Ironically, the ineffectiveness of such token refusals had already
been demonstrated early on in the play: in the scene "Das Kreidekreuz"
where a worker refuses to respond in kind to an SA man's provocative "Heil
Hitler" greeting. (*BFA* 4:347) When the worker is out of earshot, the SA
man asks the chauffeur who happened to witness the worker's reaction:
"Haben Sie verstanden, was der dahermurmelte? [. . .] *Kann* 'Heil Hitler'
geheißen haben. Muß nicht. Die Brüder hab ich schon gern. *Er lacht schal-
lend*" (ibid.; Could you understand what he was mumbling? [. . .] Might
have been "Heil Hitler." Might not. Me and that lot's old pals. *He gives
a resounding laugh: FM* 10).[6] Unlike the nervous Nazis in Brecht's poem
"Die Ängste des Regimes," the SA man deliberately flaunts the fact that he
is not bothered by the worker's response. In his essay "Furcht und Elend
des Dritten Reiches," Brecht commented on similarly ambiguous gestures
of noncompliance displayed by the bourgeoisie: "Obwohl ab und zu ein
Murren laut wird, was da murrt, ist kein Gegner" (*BFA* 22:476; Even
though now and then the odd grumble is heard. Such grumbles are not
an opposition: *FM* 96). Apparent gestures of dissidence could be deceptive
whichever class they came from.

The trouble with the examples of resistance listed in his letter to
Dudow is not just that Brecht lacked the criteria of later taxonomies for
discriminating between "Widerstand" and "Resistenz" (in Martin Broszat),
"representational resistance" and individual protest (Hüttenberger) or such
lesser phenomena as single-issue dissatisfaction, temperamental nonconformity and ostentatious disobedience (what Löwenthal calls "gesellschaftliche
Verweigerung").[7] Rather, it is the fact that, like the army of informants

---

[6] Two other scenes muddy the waters. In "Der Bauer füttert die Sau," the farmer
cheekily says "Heil Hitler" to his sow when preparing to feed it against regulations.
"Winterhilfe" involves a disagreement between two SA men, who correctly recall
that the daughter of the family failed to say "Heil Hitler" when they arrived with
Winterhilfswerk gifts, and her mother who claims that she did greet them in the
prescribed way. The mother then desperately uses the greeting four times to the SA
men, as if to compensate for her daughter's omission.

[7] On the distinction between "Resistenz" and "Widerstand," see *Bayern in der
NS-Zeit*, ed. Martin Broszat et al., vol. 4, *Herrschaft und Gesellschaft im Konflikt*
(Munich: Oldenbourg, 1981), Teil C, 691–711; a more fluid distinction between
"opposition" and "resistance" is explored in Peukert, *Inside Nazi Germany*, 79–80;
"representational resistance" is distinguished from individual protest in Peter Hüttenberger, "Vorüberlegungen zum 'Widerstandsbegriff,'" in *Theorien in der Praxis
des Historikers*, ed. Jürgen Kocka (Göttingen: Vandenhoeck & Ruprecht, 1977),
118; "gesellschaftliche Verweigerung" is defined in Richard Löwenthal, "Widerstand im totalen Staat," in *Widerstand und Verweigerung in Deutschland, 1933 bis
1945*, ed. Richard Löwenthal and Patrick von der Mühlen (Berlin: Dietz, 1982),
12. For a survey of recent debates about forms of resistance and the advantages of a

contributing to the Sopade *Deutschland-Berichte*, he was obliged because of his exile predicament, as well as on ideological grounds, to assume the presence of resistance "in allen Schichten und in allen Graden" and to exaggerate the subversive potential of a whole spectrum of behavior on a sliding scale from spontaneous nonconformist gestures made in private, on the one hand, to public expressions of dissidence, protest, and organized group resistance, on the other.[8] When judged by modern criteria, the case for assuming dissidence or signs of rebellion, even in such scenes as "Der Spitzel," "Physiker," "Zwei Bäcker," and "Was hilft gegen Gas?" is relatively flimsy. The obvious exception is the speech citing the decisive Russian example of outright revolution spoken by the woman's brother in the penultimate *Furcht und Elend* scene "Was hilft gegen Gas?" (*BFA* 4:439). However, even here we do not learn whether or not his words fell on deaf ears. While there may be signs of an unequivocally dissident mindset elsewhere in some of these scenes (for example, in "Der Bauer füttert die Sau" and "Winterhilfe") they are not necessarily confined to the details cited in the letter to Dudow. But Brecht needed to convince audiences — and probably himself, too — that large-scale organized resistance would eventually grow from such small seeds, even if this had not happened yet.[9]

One of the most positive features of Brecht's presentation of resistance is that it treats it as a dynamic, rather than static, phenomenon. Emerging from a focus on resistance as part of the experience of "Alltagsfaschismus," the picture presented in *Furcht und Elend* comes very close to that explored by the Munich Institut für Zeitgeschichte's Bavaria Project. Here is how Broszat sums up the Project's conception of resistance within the Third Reich:

---

more differentiated approach, see Matthew Philpotts, *The Margins of Dictatorship: Assent and Dissent in the Work of Günter Eich and Bertolt Brecht* (Bern-Oxford: Lang, 2003), 133–66.

[8] See the diagram representing the spectrum of possible types of opposition in Peukert, *Inside Nazi Germany*, 83.

[9] "Man muß das Unrecht auch mit schwachen Mitteln bekämpfen," written ca. 1934, throws light on Brecht's changing attitude to the question of piecemeal resistance versus revolution: "Als sich [. . .] Deutschland faschisierte, [. . .] ging ich nicht so weit wie viele, die bei den großen, auf die völlige Umänderung des gesellschaftlichen Aufbaus gerichteten Unternehmungen einen völligen Zusammenbruch für lange beobachten wollten, aber auch ich sah die zähe und wichtige kleine Arbeit jener oft geringschätzig betrachteten Unternehmungen [. . .], welche viele Menschen tatsächlich retteten, das Unrecht ständig und unermüdlich mit ihrer schwachen Stimme bloßstellten. [. . .] Wir sahen also, daß das Unrecht nicht nur in der endgültigsten, seine Ursachen mit einbeziehenden Weise, sondern auch in der allgemeinsten Weise, d. h. mit allen Mitteln, d. h. auch den schwächsten, bekämpft werden muß." Brecht concludes: "auch auf die schwächsten Mittel kann nicht verzichten, wer das unnötige Elend bekämpfen will" (*BFA* 22:61–62).

The long-standing, exclusive definition of resistance focusing only upon exceptional cases of fundamental and active opposition has produced *an idealized and undifferentiated picture of German resistance.* [. . .] scholars have largely ignored *the primacy of change within resistance* and the interdependence between it and the Nazi regime, and the relationship between the two has been falsely presented as both static and clearly antagonistic. *A revised definition that includes the less heroic cases of partial, passive, ambivalent and broken opposition* — one that accounts for the fragility of resistance and the inconsistency of human bravery — may in the end inspire a greater intellectual and moral sensitivity toward the subject than a definition that includes only the exceptional greatness of heroic martyrdom.[10]

One can imagine the author of the *Furcht und Elend* scenes agreeing with much of this argument, even if his mistrust of the heroic conception of resistance and idealistic motives was motivated by very different political assumptions. Certainly, Brecht's wish to depict "wachsender Widerstand" via a sequence of increasingly effective scenes prefigures some of the thinking in the above passage.

At the time when he was working on Fritz Lang's antifascist film *Hangmen Also Die* (1942), Brecht wrote "Im Zeichen der Schildkröte" (The Sign of the Tortoise), a poem constructed around the images of the "Raubadler des Reichs" (the Reich's predatory eagle), the "Wappentier der Oberen" (heraldic emblem of the upper classes), and the tortoise, "die Kleine," "die Langsame," "das Wappentier der Unteren" (the little, slow one, the heraldic emblem of the lower classes). The tortoise is presented as a symbol[11] of clandestine pacifist resistance:

Und wo die Kleine sich zeigte
[. . .]
Krochen die Tanks aus den Hallen bresthaft
Hoben die Bomber sich kränklich
Vermehrten die U-Boote sich lustlos zögernd:
Kam die Zeugung der Unfruchtbaren und Tödlichen ins Stocken.
(*BFA* 15:77)

---

[10] Martin Broszat, "A Social and Historical Typology of the German Opposition to Hitler," in *Contending with Hitler: Varieties of German Resistance in the Third Reich*, ed. David Clay Large (Cambridge: Cambridge UP, 1991), 25–33, here 26.

[11] John Wexley, also collaborating on the *Hangmen* project, claimed that the Czech government in London exile sent him copies of resistance propaganda leaflets bearing the tortoise emblem, which were circulating in *Reichsprotektorat* factories. Brecht's journal for 18 October 1942 refers to it as "die Schildkröte des slowdowns" (*BFA* 27:129). Brecht's note to the poem when first published attributes the emblem to "skandinavische Widerstandskämpfer" (Bertolt Brecht, *Hundert Gedichte, 1918–1950* [Berlin: Aufbau, 1958], 157).

[And wherever the little one showed itself
[. . .]
The tanks crept out feebly from the factory sheds
The bombers rose in a sickly state
The submarines multiplied hesitantly and unenthusiastically:
The production of unfruitful and deadly things came to a standstill.]

In stark contrast to this image of effective industrial sabotage, *1940*, part of the *Steffinsche Sammlung* (also 1942), presents a gloomy picture within Third Reich Germany of opportunities there for the taking, but not seized:

Die Konstrukteure hocken
Gekrümmt in den Zeichensälen:
Eine falsche Ziffer und die Städte des Feindes
Bleiben unzerstört. (*BFA* 12:97)

[The designers sit
Hunched in the drawing offices:
One wrong figure, and the enemy's cities
Will remain undestroyed. (*BBP* 347)]

There is, however, more than one way of interpreting these conflicting treatments of the resistance theme. "Im Zeichen der Schildkröte" could be intended to suggest that collective organized resistance at factory level was already having an impact in both Third Reich Germany and Nazi-occupied Europe. Alternatively, it could be read as an example of foreign resistance to fascism, an example held up as a model for the German underground. In contrast, "Die Konstrukteure hocken" seems to offer a more honest reflection of the sad fact that there was at the time precious little evidence of resistance on the hoped-for scale within Third Reich Germany. Since the two poems were written at about the same time, Brecht might even have intended them as a form of "Fixieren des *Nicht–Sondern*" (fixing the "not . . . but," *BT* 137).[12] While both poems thematize the possibility of resistance and offer extreme (positive or negative) illustrations, each differs markedly from the spectrum of resistance Brecht had hoped to find in virtually every section of the population and that was, according to him, mirrored in the sequence of *Furcht und Elend* scenes. In the scenes he identified to Dudow, images of opposition to the NS regime tend to be neither as optimistic as the one in "Im Zeichen der Schildkröte" nor as bleak as that in *1940*. Instead, many of the early *Furcht und Elend* scenes

---

[12] This concept is explained in "Kurze Beschreibung einer neuen Technik der Schauspielkunst, die einen Verfremdungseffekt hervorbringt" (*BFA* 22:641–59). On the dialectical structure and didactic advantages of the "Nicht–Sondern" model, see White, *Bertolt Brecht's Dramatic Theory*, 109–12.

are situated in a gray area of complicated ambiguities. Here, even token noncompliance and local opposition (one cannot yet speak of "resistance") are in many cases more a matter of perception than fact.

In "Volksgemeinschaft," for example, usually the first published scene in the *Furcht und Elend* sequence, two drunken SS men become increasingly nervous upon finding themselves in an unidentified working-class district of Berlin on, of all dates, 30 January 1933, the day Hitler became German Reichskanzler. No swastika flags have been hung out to celebrate Hitler's triumphant accession to power, no lights are left on — indeed, there is no sign of life anywhere. The SS men immediately realize that they must have unwittingly strayed onto hostile territory: "Vabrecherviertel. [. . .] Een anständijer Volksjenosse wohnt nicht in so 'ne Baracke" (*BFA* 4:342; Lot of crooks round here. [. . .] Decent comrades don't live in such slums: *FM* 5).[13] However, these two men's strong proletarian Berlin dialect suggests that they have probably severed their links with the working class not long ago. Their hostility to the proletarian district they find themselves in may even be colored by a sense of bad conscience. When someone in one of the buildings eventually opens a window to find out who is there, the two men panic, shooting wildly in all directions until they hear the scream of someone hit, upon which they decide to beat a hasty retreat. Bearing in mind Brecht's poem "Die Ängste des Regimes," it is worth remembering that the two SS men are not actually under attack. On the contrary, on what was officially the first day of Hitler's new Third Reich, a cowering, urban, working-class community has, to its shame, seen fit to lie low and not register any form of protest apart from failing to put flags out in celebration. As we will see, the play's concluding scene, "Volksbefragung," offers a counter-illustration suggesting just how much might be achieved in a proletarian milieu comparable to the one in which "Volksgemeinschaft" is set.

Even in the following scene, "Der Verrat," there is at most merely a suspicion of oppositional behavior, but certainly nothing that could be called genuine resistance.[14] The victim of a political denunciation is alleged to have listened to foreign radio broadcasts ("Rußlandsendungen" in the *Malik*-version, changed to "Auslandsendungen" in all subsequent ones). Yet this charge might be nothing more than malicious insinuation on his neighbor's part.[15] After all, false allegations and political denunciations

---

[13] The Berlin dialect of the original German of this scene is not, and probably could not be, reflected in English translation.

[14] Peukert, *Inside Nazi Germany*, 83, distinguishes "non-conformism" ("individual acts of infringement of the norms") from "resistance" ("calling into question the system as a whole"), something the accused man in this scene is clearly not attempting.

[15] Although Goebbels's "Außerordentliche Rundfunkmaßnahmen" made listening to "enemy" radio stations illegal only at the start of the Second World War, people

based on trumped-up charges were a common feature of daily life in the early years of Hitler's Third Reich, when fear of false — or justified — denunciation created an atmosphere of widespread angst: "Die Ängste des Regimes," in other words.[16]

Schweykian Resistance?

It is with "Das Kreidekreuz," usually published in third place in the *Furcht und Elend* sequence, that a sense of more devious opposition first enters the picture. Much of the worker's[17] cunning is so subtle that his adversary, the SA man, soon no longer feels as in control of the situation as he was when first encountering him. While the confrontation between the two men largely takes place on a one-to-one level, each prefers to treat his opposite number in generic terms. For example, this is how the SA man talks to a member of the working class: "Ihr seid richtige Scheißkerle! [. . .] Keiner traut sich einen Ton von sich zu geben" (*BFA* 4:351; You're a right bunch of turds. [. . .] Not a bloody soul got the guts to open his mouth: *FM* 14). Similarly, the following remark made by the worker to the SA man typifies his generalizing picture of his class enemy: "Ihr könnt doch mehr als einen Trick" (*BFA* 4:349; You people surely know more than one trick: *FM* 11). They are merely sparring with one another. But the important resistance that provides the significant backdrop to this encounter is the clandestine "organizational resistance" of left-wing political cells to ruling National Socialism. What we

---

could attract unwelcome attention for tuning into foreign stations even during the early years of the Third Reich, even when their motives might not have been oppositional (Peukert, *Inside Nazi Germany*, 54). In "Das Kreidekreuz," which *Aurora* dates as happening in 1933, attention is already being paid to the question of whether the worker has a four-valve set, i.e., one capable of picking up foreign stations, or a single-valve "Volksempfänger" restricting reception to Nazi propaganda broadcasts.

[16] According to the standard binary distinction between "affective" or "system-loyal" denunciation and "instrumental" denunciation motivated by self-interest (Robert Gellately, *Backing Hitler: Consent and Coercion in Nazi Germany* [Oxford: Oxford UP, 2001], 192–93), the denouncer here seems to accuse his neighbor purely for reasons of self-interest. In "Der Nachbar," Brecht's companion poem on the same subject (*BFA* 14:238–39), the denouncer tries to justify his action by appealing to civic virtue: "Wir wollen in unserem Haus / Keinen Hetzer haben. [. . .] Die ihn abgeholt haben, sagen / Daß wir uns richtig verhalten haben." Cases of instrumental denunciation outnumbered system-loyal ones by about five to one in the Third Reich (Gellately, *Backing Hitler*, 192–93).

[17] In the "Kreidekreuz" scene, this character is consistently referred to simply as *Der Arbeiter*, never as *Der Kommunist*. This may be intended to reflect the Comintern's desire to construct a Popular Front uniting KPD and SPD on the left.

are witnessing, in other words, is by no means just a private vendetta between two men anxious not to lose face in the presence of the womenfolk.

The confident SA man is quick to taunt the worker by boasting that, later that evening, he will be taking part in an organized raid on a working-class district. He subsequently slips up, inadvertently revealing that Reinickendorf is to be the target, a crass blunder that makes it possible for the worker to rush off and alert his comrades of the attack to come. The worker also gains the upper hand in a number of other ways that evening. Because of his taunts, the SA man gradually loses his dignity in front of the others present. As the scene's title emphasizes, the worker even finds out how the local SA ensures that members of the working class are prevented from obtaining jobs down at the local labor exchange (*Stempelstelle*).[18] What is more, he skillfully communicates a mood of growing dissatisfaction among the German people, as well as insinuating that the Popular Front's agents on the ground are systematically searching out the NS regime's weak spots.

Early on, the SA man plays a practical joke on the worker by surreptitiously draining the man's beer glass without his even noticing it: "Kleiner Trick aus dem Sturmlokal!" (*BFA* 4:348; Little trick they teach you in our squad: *FM* 11). Behind the mask of the ensuing teasing and baiting, the SA man is playing virtually the same game of agent provocateur that he and his comrades play among the queues of the out-of-work down at the labor exchange. However, the worker takes his revenge, hitting on an ingenious way to drink his adversary's beer, with even more effrontery than was the case with the other's ruse. However, this time the trick is part of an agreed wager between the two men. The infuriated SA man then tries to draw the worker onto more dangerous political ground by forcing him to grumble about conditions in the Third Reich. Too shrewd and experienced to fall into such a trap, the worker merely assumes the role of moaner after assurances that he is simply being asked to play a part in a charade and his words will therefore not be subsequently held against him. Entering into the spirit of his assigned part as the devil's advocate, the worker obediently trots out a whole series of predictable complaints concerning the coercive nature of the recruitment method for the hypocritically named *Freiwilliger Arbeitsdienst* (voluntary labor service), about people having to make allegedly voluntary donations to the *Winterhilfswerk* (Winter Relief) fund, the general shortage of food and numerous other bare necessities, the rising cost of living, the far-from-classless *Volksgemeinschaft*, Hermann Goering's notoriously lav-

---

[18] The *BFA*-commentary to "Das Kreidekreuz" defines *Stempelstellen* as: "Melde- und Vermittlungsbüros für Arbeitslose," explaining: "die Wahrnehmung der Meldepflicht und die Auszahlung von Unterstützungsgeldern wurde durch das Abstempeln des Arbeitslosennachweises, der 'Stempelkarte', registriert" (*BFA* 4:535).

ish lifestyle, the number of political denunciations that occur on a regular basis, and the lack of freedom of speech — in short, about almost everything that puts in question National Socialism's pretensions to being a genuinely popular regime oriented toward the people's welfare. Apparently playing the part of archetypal grumbler with such evident relish, the worker at the same time dissociates himself from the complaints he relays to his handful of listeners by feigning to be an ardent supporter of National Socialism. The wit and mental agility with which he scores his points and the comic bravado of his impromptu "performance" leave the worker the uncontested winner after the first two rounds of political sparring. The SA man is clearly disappointed. Everything so far has been too tame for his liking. Seeking to bait his adversary further, he now adopts the role of "Meckerer" (grumbler), this time complaining about the opposition's *cowardice*: "Das Schlimmste ist, daß sich keiner mehr zum Widerstand aufraffen tut" (*BFA* 4:353; The trouble is: nobody bothers to dig his toes in: *FM* 15). Audiences are clearly invited to test subsequent *Furcht und Elend* scenes in the light of this claim.

After trading practical jokes and engaging in much point-scoring political banter within a seemingly innocuous role-playing scenario, the scene's two adversaries tacitly agree to escalate matters by moving on to political jokes. The SA man opens the next round with a currently circulating joke about Goebbels and the two lice, an anecdote reminiscent of numerous familiar *Flüsterwitze* (whispered jokes) then prevalent in the Third Reich about the size of the propaganda minister's mouth.[19] Challenged to outbid this risqué ad hominem joke, the worker responds with the anecdote about Doktor Ley, head of the Deutsche Arbeitsfront, and the cat, an apocryphal joke predicated on the premise that "volunteering" for *Reichsarbeitsdienst* (RAD) is still preferable to ending up in a concentration camp. The worker cleverly covers himself by attributing his anecdote to Ley, a man notorious for his social gaffes. Compared with the SA man's joke about Goebbels, the worker's contribution is in many respects far more subversive. It questions the whole logic behind one of the regime's principal job-creation schemes, while using scatological imagery to criticize the hypocrisy of presenting RAD as *noncompulsory* service. It even serves to remind its listeners that it was Ley's Deutsche Arbeitsfront that had dissolved the German trade unions. Indeed, the worker's joke possibly even manages to suggest that in Third Reich Germany, politics is little more than an elaborate, yet cruel, practical joke played on its people by the NS regime.

"Das Kreidekreuz," which was one of the strongest scenes in "99%," is a clear example of Brecht's conception of humor's potential role in undermining the regime's confidence. This assumption emerges from his retrospective

---

[19] Illustrations can be found in Karl Michael Hillenbrand, *Underground Humour in Nazi Germany, 1933–1945* (London: Routledge, 1995), 32–33.

account of Dudow's production, as recorded in Section B132 of *Der Messingkauf*. There the Dramaturge is asked by the Philosopher to comment on the acting style of the Paris premiere of *Furcht und Elend*. He recalls that "das Außerordentliche war, daß die Spieler diese furchtbaren Vorfälle keineswegs so vorführten, daß die Zuschauer versucht waren, ein 'Halt!' auszurufen." Having referred earlier on to the pervasive climate of fear ("die Furcht der Unterdrückten und die Furcht der Unterdrücker") evoked in the production, the Dramaturge turns to the question of audience reaction:

Die Zuschauer schienen das Entsetzen der Personen auf der Bühne überhaupt nicht zu teilen, und so kam es, daß im Zuschauerraum immerfort gelacht wurde, ohne daß dadurch der tiefe Ernst der Veranstaltung litt. Denn das Lachen schien die Dummheit zu betreffen, die sich hier zur Gewalt gezwungen sah, und die Hilflosigkeit zu meinen, die da als Roheit auftrat. Prügelnde wurden betrachtet wie Stolpernde, Verbrecher wie solche, die Irrtümer begingen oder sich eben täuschen ließen. Das Lachen der Zuschauer hatte sehr viele Schattierungen. Es war ein glückliches Lachen, wenn die Verfolgten ihre Verfolger überlisteten, ein befreites, wenn ein gutes, wahres Wort geäußert wurde. So mag ein Erfinder lachen, wenn er nach langer Bemühung die Lösung gefunden hat: so einfach war es und er sah es so lange nicht! [. . .] Vor allem spielten sie so, daß das Interesse des Zuschauers immer auf den weiteren Verlauf gerichtet blieb, auf das Weitergehen, sozusagen auf den Mechanismus der Vorfälle. Auf das Spiel von Ursache und Folge. (*BFA* 22:800)

[What was so unusual was that the players never performed these ghastly episodes in such a way that the spectators were tempted to call out "Stop." The spectators didn't seem in any way to share the horror of those on the stage, and as a result there was repeatedly laughter among the audience without doing any damage to the profoundly serious character of the performance. For this laughter seemed to apply to the stupidity that found itself having to make use of force, and to the helplessness that took the shape of brutality. Bullies were seen as men tripping over, criminals as men who have made a mistake or allowed themselves to be taken in. The spectators' laughter was finely graduated. It was a happy laughter when the quarry outwitted his pursuer, a contented laughter when somebody uttered a good, true word. That's how an inventor might laugh on finding the solution after a long effort: it was as obvious as that, and he took so long to see it! [. . .] The main thing was that they acted in such a way that the audience's interest was always focused on the ensuing development, the further continuation: as it were, on the mechanics of the episodes. On the interplay of cause and effect. (*BMD* 72–73)]

In other words, the acting style was essentially that demanded of Epic Theater, as advocated in "Über eine neue Technik der Schauspielkunst."

One form of distancing humor, the *Flüsterwitz*, figures only rarely as a form of resistance in *Furcht und Elend*. The "Kreidekreuz" scene ends not with a further exchange of political jokes between the two adversaries, but with an account of a sick practical joke played on left-wing job-seekers down at the local labor exchange, a trick that the maidservant (*Das Dienstmädchen*), having quarreled with her SA fiancé, now fears may even be used to mark her out as persona non grata, as far as the regime is concerned. Two stamps, one official, the other part of a secret trick, dominate the final section of "Das Kreidekreuz": the rubber stamp that job-seekers need to have on their employment card (*Stempelkarte*) in order to gain work or unemployment benefits, and the chalk cross slapped on the back of dissidents,[20] ensuring that they will be singled out for victimization. The latter always cancels out any chance of the former — or it would do, if the worker had not managed to uncover the devious way the SA subvert the welfare system inherited from the Weimar Republic.

The worker in "Das Kreidekreuz" is clearly not acting in an individual capacity. Like the SA man protected by his brown uniform, the worker behaves with the confidence of someone who knows he is part of a large and potentially strong movement. (Until it was outlawed by the Nazis, the KPD was the largest communist organization in the world outside the USSR, and the SPD also remained a force to be reckoned with.) Significantly, the worker may have done more to serve the proletarian cause by alerting his comrades in Reinickendorf and learning about the chalk-cross trick than by scoring points off his opponent. Verbal point scoring amounts to little more than securing Pyrrhic victories, satisfying for worker and audience alike, but in the wider scheme of things merely raising the question of just what constitutes effective political resistance. "Das Kreidekreuz" does, nevertheless, illustrate the advantages of cunning, a virtue frequently recommended in Brecht's writings, as well as showing one way in which oppression can create and strengthen resistance. At the same time, it demonstrates the potential of satire and humor to cut the NS regime's self-important minions down to size.

Subverting National Socialist Propaganda

In the early scenes of *Furcht und Elend*, radio is primarily associated with listening to prohibited foreign broadcasting stations. In contrast, the live

---

[20] As Klaus Völker notes, what under normal circumstances might have been read as a "brotherly" slap on the back from a fellow working-class job seeker here becomes a gesture of denunciation (*Brecht-Kommentar zum dramatischen Werk* [Munich: Winkler, 1983], 175).

transmission from a factory in "Die Stunde des Arbeiters"[21] concentrates on the Propaganda Ministry's extensive use of radio for political purposes, and in doing so presents a hilarious example of political propaganda satirically foiled without any drastic repercussions for those engaged in such a dissident act. Positioned towards the middle of *Furcht und Elend* and coming after a string of scenes depicting middle-class collusion, "Die Stunde des Arbeiters" marks a watershed, inasmuch as it can be read as the play's first convincing depiction of politically motivated group-resistance.

The entire action takes place in the foreman's office in a factory. As a consequence, when the reporter opens his live broadcast with the scene-setting words —

> Wir stehen mitten im Getriebe der Schwungräder und Treibriemen, umgeben von emsig und unverdrossen arbeitenden Volksgenossen. (*BFA* 4:405)

> [Here we are with flywheels and driving belts in full swing all around us, surrounded by our comrades working as busily as ants. (*FM* 65)]

— theater audiences, unlike those listening to the broadcast, will appreciate that he is already misrepresenting the situation. The interviews that follow are conducted in an enclosed location, not just to exclude background noise, but in order to make the fragile situation easier to control. For the same reason, just three ostensibly representative workers have been selected to take part in the scripted interview. And a burly SA man stands menacingly over them to make sure no interviewee puts a foot wrong.

Spoof broadcasts and news announcements were for a brief time stock ingredients of satirical cabaret and *Flüsterwitze* in the early years of the Third Reich.[22] Brecht's scene is palpably indebted to both genres. The very details of the factory setting promise a lively send-up. The (on his part) unintentionally comic associations of the reporter's introduction — "Wir sind heute

---

[21] "Workers' playtime" (*FM* 65), John Willett's title for "Die Stunde des Arbeiters," may give a false impression. Apart from suggesting that the workers at the German factory visited are genuinely having fun at the interviewer's expense, Willett's solution involves an allusion, unmistakable to British audiences, to a wartime program ("Workers' Playtime") broadcast daily, as part of the war effort, on the BBC Home Service from a factory canteen "Somewhere in Britain." The morale-raising lunchtime mixture of variety, music, and comedy, supported by the Ministry of Labour and National Service, was so popular that it ran for twenty-three years. Eric Bentley's title for *Furcht und Elend*'s equivalent, "The Working Man on the Air" (*The Private Life*, 30), comes closer to the tone and propaganda associations of the German original.

[22] For examples, see *Lachen verboten: Flüsterwitze aus den Jahren 1938–1945*, ed. Minni Schwarz (Vienna: Im Weltweiten, 1947), 3:10–11, and Richard Hermes, *Witz contra Nazi* (Hamburg: Morawe & Scheffelt, 1946), 167.

vormittag in der Spinnerei Fuchs AG" (*BFA* 4:405; This morning we are
visiting the Fuchs spinning mills: *FM* 66) — already allow for the possibility
that all may not be what it seems. The association of the fox with cunning,
together with the noun *Spinnerei* (two secondary meanings of *spinnen* are:
to be crazy or *to talk rubbish*), makes a promising prelude to the duplicity
to come. As the individual one-to-one interviews increasingly depart from
plan, the likelihood presents itself that the workers might in fact be taking
revenge on a system that has already exploited them economically and, to
cap it all, now wants to manipulate them for propaganda purposes.

The series of exchanges between interviewer and workers initially
sounds like some grotesque encounter between an obsessive control freak
and a trio of bumbling stooges. Yet the workers may not necessarily be the
gullible fools the interviewer takes them for. They could simply be feigning incompetence in order to make a mockery of the entire propaganda
exercise. As, for example, in the following disjointed exchange with the
broadcast's first interviewee:

> DER ANSAGER [. . .]. Nun, Herr Sedelmaier, wie kommt es, daß
> wir hier lauter so freudige und unverdrossene Gesichter sehen?
> DER ALTE ARBEITER *nach einigem Nachdenken:* Die machen ja
> immer Witze.
> DER ANSAGER So. Ja und so geht unter munteren Scherzworten
> die Arbeit leicht von der Hand, wie? Der Nationalsozialismus kennt
> keinen lebensfeindlichen Pessimismus, meinen Sie. Früher war das
> anders, wie?
> DER ALTE ARBEITER Ja, ja.
> DER ANSAGER In der Systemzeit gab's für die Arbeiter nichts zu
> lachen, meinen Sie. Da hieß es: wofür arbeiten wir!
> DER ALTE ARBEITER Ja, da gibt's schon einige, die das sagen.
> DER ANSAGER Wie meinen? Ach so, Sie deuten auf die Meckerer
> hin, die es immer mal zwischendurch gibt, wenn sie auch immer
> weniger werden, weil sie einsehen, daß alles nicht hilft, sondern alles
> aufwärts geht im Dritten Reich, seit wieder eine starke Hand da ist.
> (*BFA* 4:405–6)

> [THE ANNOUNCER: [. . .] Tell me, Mr. Sedelmaier, how is it that
> we see nothing but these happy, joyous faces on every side?
> THE OLD WORKER *after a moment's thought*: There's a lot of jokes
> told.
> THE ANNOUNCER: Really? Right, so a cheerful jest or two makes
> work seem child's play, what? The deadly menace of pessimism is
> unknown under National Socialism, you mean. Different in the old
> days, wasn't it?
> THE OLD WORKER: Aye.
> THE ANNOUNCER: That rotten old Weimar republic didn't give
> the workers much to laugh about you mean. What are we working
> for, they used to ask.

THE OLD WORKER: Aye, that's what some of them say.
THE ANNOUNCER: I didn't quite get that. Oh, I see, you're referring to the inevitable grouses, but they're dying out now they see that
kind of thing's a waste of time because everything's booming in the
Third Reich now there's a strong hand on the helm once again. (*FM*
66)]

Despite repeated prompting and much telegraphing of the answers that
the NS Reichsministerium für Volksaufklärung und Propaganda wants
to hear, the workers, who are evidently meant to be contrasting Hitler's
Third Reich with the bad old days of the Weimar Republic, repeatedly
wrong-foot the reporter. The fact that they habitually get their verb tenses
wrong already makes them appear to be only quasi-inadvertently sabotaging the broadcast. When one of them points out that on paper they may
appear to earn more in the new Germany, but there were fewer deduc-
tions in the Weimar Republic, the reporter quickly dismisses the point as a
"famoser Witz!" (*BFA* 4:407; a capital joke!: *FM* 67). Indeed, "Die Stunde
des Arbeiters" could be read as a collection of subversive "capital jokes"
and comic double-entendres, with the hapless radio reporter virtually func-
tioning as straight man to the workers' cleverly packaged complaints about
their actual working conditions.

When the second interviewee, Fräulein Schmidt, is asked: "An
welchem unserer stählernen Maschinengiganten arbeiten denn Sie?"
(Which of these steel mammoths enjoys your services?), she responds by
giving the rehearsed "right answer" at the wrong time and in the wrong
context:

DIE ARBEITERIN *auswendig:* Und da ist ja auch die Arbeit bei der
Ausschmückung des Arbeitsraums, die uns viel Freude bereitet. Das
Führerbild ist auf Grund einer freiwilligen Spende zustande gekom-
men und sind wir sehr stolz darauf. Wie auch auf die Geranienstöcke,
die eine Farbe in das Grau des Arbeitsraumes hineinzaubern, eine
Anregung von Fräulein Kinze. (*BFA* 4:406)

[THE WOMAN WORKER *reciting:* And then we also work at deco-
rating our place of work which gives us great pleasure. Our portrait of
the Führer was purchased thanks to voluntary contributions and we
are very proud of him. Also of the geranium plants which provide a
magical touch of colour in the greyness of our working environment,
by suggestion of Miss Kinze. (*FM* 66)]

As we later learn, after receiving a fresh coat of paint for the occasion, the
factory was presented with a picture of Adolf Hitler (standard issue in all
German public buildings at the time) and a generous supply of gerani-
ums, yet the washroom still has only half a dozen taps for 552 workers.
The obvious target of satire here is the NS *Schönheit der Arbeit* (Beauty

of Work) propaganda initiative,[23] now seen in the context of the regime's failure to deliver real improvements on the work front.

As the scene's ironic title implies, "Die Stunde des Arbeiters" is a double-edged episode: first, because the propaganda radio feature being transmitted is specifically devoted to the workers' lives and factory conditions, but second, in the sense that "their hour" has come. They now have a golden opportunity to use the propaganda unit's stage-managed visit to exact revenge. However, caution is required in interpreting this scenario. As was the case with Brecht's *Schweyk* (1943), it is sometimes difficult to decide whether we are witnessing dumb insolence, cunning sabotage, or mere dozy incompetence.[24] This often depends on just who is speaking. For tactical reasons, Brecht eschews the stirring picture of heroic collective resistance evoked in "Im Zeichen der Schildkröte." He does this either in order that audiences can ponder the leading question of just what constitutes genuine resistance under such circumstances or because this scene is set in Nazi Germany and not in some occupied country where in many cases resistance was less like a satirical send-up, being more politically motivated and effectively better organized. Whatever is behind the interviewees' responses, there can be no doubt about the interviewer's blatant hypocrisy. He starts his program by declaring: "Aber wir wollen unsere Volksgenossen selber sprechen lassen" (*BFA* 4:405; But let us get our comrades to speak for themselves, *FM* 66), yet soon finds himself having to waste valuable airtime prompting the chosen few or, failing that, putting scripted sound bites into their mouths. Despite his various diversionary ploys, the scene ends in outright violence on the announcer's part: "*Er schiebt den Arbeiter brutal vom Mikrophon*" (*BFA* 4:407; *He roughly pushes the worker away from the microphone*: *FM* 68). Again, this is something that radio listeners would not be able to see, whereas a theater audience will quickly realize that things have gone drastically wrong onstage.

---

[23] For details, see Peter Reichel, *Der schöne Schein des Dritten Reiches: Faszination und Gewalt des Faschismus* (Munich: Hanser, 1991), 235–43.

[24] Brecht in his journal entry for 27 May 1943 notes: "Auf keinen Fall darf Schweyk ein listiger hinterfotziger Saboteur werden. Er ist lediglich der Opportunist der winzigen Opportunitäten, die ihm geblieben sind" (*BFA* 27:151), a verdict that could to some extent also apply to the worker in "Das Kreidekreuz" and some of the factory interviewees in "Die Stunde des Arbeiters." The claims that *Furcht und Elend* lacks scenes of "schweykscher Widerstand" (James K. Lyon, *BHB* 1:349 and Völker, *Brecht-Kommentar zum dramatischen Werk*, 178) arguably merit revisiting, at least in the case of "Die Stunde des Arbeiters." However, in that of "Das Kreidekreuz," a more fitting analogy would be with the subversive irony of Jonathan Swift's *A Modest Proposal* (1729), singled out as an example of political cunning in Brecht's "Fünf Schwierigkeiten beim Schreiben der Wahrheit" (*BFA* 22:85).

One important difference between the political *Flüsterwitze* that thrived under National Socialism and this scene, with its more veiled comments on the regime, resulted from the nature of radio broadcasting at this stage of its technical development. Since material for the German national radio station, the Deutschlandsender, was seldom recorded and edited before transmission, the jokes and tricks in this fictive scenario would have been sent out "live." No resistance typology has yet been designed to take account of a public humiliation of this order of magnitude. But if such an unlikely event had occurred and had ever been broadcast "on air," the propaganda impact would have been comparable to that of a major political coup for the Popular Front.

The NS regime's concealment of truth is at the center of many other scenes in *Furcht und Elend*, including those dealing with the concentration camps and the regime's escalating preparations for war. There, too, Brecht's play combats the distortions of propaganda with dramatized counter-truths.

Outright Disobedience

"Die Internationale" (*BFA* 4:410; *FM* 110–11), a brief, thirty-two-line scene included in the *Malik* proof version of *Furcht und Elend* but dropped by the time of *The Private Life*, is one of the rare places in the play where the German word for resistance is used, the other being, as we have seen, in "Das Kreidekreuz." Yet what the concentration camp guard in "Die Internationale" is at one stage quick to challenge as "Widerstand" is hardly resistance in any accepted modern sense of the word. Real resistance only occurs towards the end of the scene in question — and when it does, it renders the guard speechless.

"Die Internationale" begins with a flogging taking place in a yard in a concentration camp before the assembled prisoners and SS guards. The first words of the SS man administering the punishment are: "Mir tut der Arm weh. Wirst du Sau deine Internationale noch einmal singen?" (My arm's hurting. Are you or aren't you going to sing us another verse of that Internationale of yours, you pig?). He is angry at having to waste both time and effort inflicting corporal punishment on someone who appears to be a KPD political prisoner. His solution is to force one of the other prisoners to take over the task: "Du da, Genosse, nimm die Peitsche und schlag zu, aber kräftig, sonst kriegst du selber" (Hey, you, comrade, take this whip and beat him, but good and hard or it'll be your turn next). Although setting a concentration camp prisoner against another like-minded prisoner was a standard SS strategy, especially in the case of political prisoners, the SS man still feels the need to concoct a specious reason for ordering a prisoner, clearly also a communist, to take over: "Wie wäre es, wenn ihr [i.e., the assembled inmates] auch einmal eurem Zorn darüber Luft machtet, daß so eine Sau hier die Internationale singt?" (What about you sods showing how angry you feel when you hear a pig like this singing the Internationale?). The response of the man ordered to act is initially one of discernible reluctance. The SS man immediately regains control of the situation: "DER SS-MANN: Widerstand, wie? *Er schlägt ihn. Der zweite Häftling nimmt die Peitsche und peitscht den ersten Häftling*" (THE SS MAN: Stubborn, eh? *He hits him. The second prisoner takes the whip and flogs the first*). If the SS man interprets mere hesitation as a calculated act of resistance, he now receives an object lesson in true resistance's ability to undermine his authority.

What happens in the second half of the scene "Die Internationale" needs to be understood in its dramatic context. This is not the only episode in *Furcht und Elend* involving a punishment beating. "Dienst am Volke" (*BFA* 4:361–62) also begins with an SS man showing signs of fatigue while inflicting another prolonged punishment beating (*Auspeitschung*). This time, however, there are no witnesses, although an SS Gruppenführer does regularly pass by to check that the punishment is being properly administered. When the coast is again clear, the guard carrying out this act of public service ("Dienst am Volke," as the scene title ironically calls it) takes a break, making the prisoner replicate the noise of a beating in order to cover for him. Either because the prisoner plays along with this ruse or conceivably because the guard has political sympathies for his victim, he agrees to the prisoner's request not to be hit on the stomach. However, when the returning SS Gruppenführer's suspicions are aroused, the guard is forced to resume the beating. The scene ends chillingly with the curt, monosyllabic order: "Schlag ihn auf den Bauch" (*BFA* 4:362; Flog his stomach: *FM* 26). Both guard and prisoner are shown to be trapped in the system, seemingly with no hope of being able to alleviate their predicaments.

Unlike "Dienst am Volke," "Die Internationale" moves rapidly on from being another degrading example of someone forced to punish a fellow prisoner. This time, the person charged with administering the punishment rebels by joining his victim in singing "The Internationale." The ensuing action reads like a textbook illustration of Brecht's claim that violence and terror are axiomatically counterproductive, inasmuch as they create resistance:

> *Der zweite Häftling schlägt noch stärker. Der erste Häftling beginnt heiser die Internationale zu singen. Der zweite Häftling hört zu schlagen auf und stimmt in das Lied ein. — Die SS-Leute fallen über die Häftlinge her.* (*BFA* 4:410)

> [*The second prisoner beats harder still. The first prisoner starts singing the Internationale in a hoarse voice. The second stops beating and joins in the song. The SS men fall on the prisoners.* (*FM* 111)]

While it would be naïve to expect defiance of this kind to have had any long-term ameliorative results within what has been called Nazi Germany's "concentration camp universe,"[25] such an overt act of noncompliance could nevertheless help boost inmate morale. From personal experience, Hermann Langbein has stressed that the connotations of "resistance" under extreme conditions differ substantially from those obtaining in the world beyond the electric wire and the watchtowers. In many cases, he recalls, it was a way of combating rampant demoralization and thus of fostering prisoner solidarity.[26] Subsequent *Furcht und Elend* scenes give further examples of heroic forms of resistance that are equally inspiring in this respect. Coming later in the play than "Dienst am Volke," "Die Internationale" could possibly have been intended as the second part of a contrastively constructive scenic model. The timing of the two scenes — *Aurora* gives the setting for "Dienst am Volke" as "Konzentrationslager Oranienburg 1934," while "Die Internationale" is situated next to a clutch of scenes dated 1936 and beyond — suggests that, even in the camps, resistance could be growing ("zwar wachsend"), even if it was usually met with brutal counter-measures.

Historical corroboration of Langbein's remarks about the morale-boosting function of individual acts of resistance can be found in the legendary circumstances of Erich Mühsam's heroic death, which had become well publicized in exile circles as symbolic of the values of the "Other Germany." In all likelihood, this was one of Brecht's principal sources for at least two of the concentration camp scenes in *Furcht und Elend*.[27] Ordered in July 1934, while a prisoner in Sachsenhausen, to sing "Das Horst-Wessel-Lied" as a form of degradation, Mühsam refused point-blank to do so. When his captors threatened to shoot him on the spot, his response was to sing "The Internationale." Mühsam paid for this brave act of defiance with his life. The exiled Expressionist playwright Ernst Toller was so impressed by this courageous act that he cited it in his speech at the 1935 Paris International Writers' Congress for the Defense of Culture[28] and in "Unser Kampf um Deutschland," as well as paying homage to Mühsam in his play *Pastor Hall*. Here is how the event is presented in "Unser Kampf um Deutschland":

Ich will das Gedächtnis an einen deutschen Dichter wachrufen, an Erich Mühsam. In der Nacht vom 27. zum 28. Februar 1933 nach dem Reichstagsbrande verhafteten ihn die Urheber des Reichstags-

---

[25] David Rousset, *L'Univers concentrationnaire* (Paris: Editions du Pavois, 1946).

[26] Hermann Langbein, *". . . nicht wie die Schafe zur Schlachtbank": Widerstand in den nationalsozialistischen Konzentrationslagern, 1938–1945* (Frankfurt am Main: Fischer, 1980), 335–44.

[27] "Dienst am Volke" takes place in the same year as Mühsam's murder. The prisoners in "Die Internationale" respond with the same forbidden socialist song as Mühsam used to express ideological noncompliance, according to Toller's account.

[28] Ernst Toller, "Rede auf dem Pariser Kongreß der Schriftsteller," *Das Wort* 3 (October 1938), 122–26.

brandes. Drei Jahre wurde er im Konzentrationslager seelisch und körperlich gequält. Im dritten Jahre stellten ihn seine Wärter an die Wand des Gefängnishofes und drohten ihm, ihn zu erschießen, wenn er nicht die Nazihymne singe. Er weigerte sich. Sie legten die Gewehre auf ihn an. Erich Mühsam [. . .] straffte sich, er sah dem Tode ins Auge. Und er sang. Er sang: Die Internationale. Die Nazis schossen über seinen Kopf hinweg. Mühsam brach ohnmächtig zusammen. Am Abend des 9. Juli 1934 wurde ihm befohlen, sich beim Kommandanten des Konzentrationslagers [. . .] zu melden. Er, der sich geweigert hatte, Selbstmord zu verüben, sollte mit einem Strick in der Hand vor dem Kommandanten erscheinen. Am nächsten Morgen wurde seinen Freunden mitgeteilt, Mühsam habe sich erhängt. Aber die Wahrheit kam ans Licht. Mühsam war zu Tode gepeitscht und sein Leichnam aufgehängt worden. Sein Tod ist uns Anlaß zur Klage und zur Trauer. Aber darüber hinaus wird er zum Gleichnis jener Tapferkeit, die uns mit Stolz erfüllt, wenn wir an Deutschland denken.[29]

[I want to evoke the memory of a German poet, of Erich Mühsam. On the night of 27–28 February, after the Reichstag Fire, those who had started the fire arrested him. For three years he was subjected to mental and physical torture in a concentration camp. In the third year, his guards put him up against the wall of the prison courtyard and threatened to shoot him if he did not sing the Nazi hymn ["Das Horst-Wessel-Lied"]. He refused. They pointed their rifles at him. Erich Mühsam [. . .] pulled himself up straight and looked death in the eye. And he sang. He sang: "The Internationale." The Nazis fired over his head. Mühsam collapsed unconscious. On the evening of 9 July 1934, he was ordered to report to the commandant of the concentration camp. The man who had refused to commit suicide was to appear before the commandant carrying a length of rope. His friends were told the next morning that Mühsam had hanged himself. But the truth came to light. Mühsam had been beaten to death and his body had been strung up. His death is for us a cause for lamentation and grief. But beyond that, it will be the symbol of that bravery that fills us with pride when we think of Germany.]

Toller goes on to quote from the last letter of the condemned resistance fighter Edgar André, one of Brecht's models for the condemned communist's letter to his son in the *Furcht und Elend* scene "Volksbefragung." Toller concludes:

Oft fragen mich Ausländer, die am deutschen Volke verzweifeln: "Wo, wo ist denn das andere Deutschland, an das Sie glauben?" Und ich erzähle ihnen von Edgar André, von Erich Mühsam, von den hun-

---

[29] Ernst Toller, "Unser Kampf um Deutschland," *Das Wort* 2 (March 1937), 46–53, here 50.

derten von Männern, jungen und alten, die mit der gleichen Würde starben. [. . .] Hier, sage ich ihnen, ist das andere Deutschland! (ibid.)

[Foreigners who despair of the German people often ask me: "Where, where then is the Other Germany that you believe in?" And I tell them about Edgar André, about Erich Mühsam, about the hundreds of men, both young and old, who went to their deaths with the same dignity. [. . .] Here, I say to them, is the Other Germany!]

In collective tribute to one of these representatives of the "Other Germany," an Edgar André Brigade fought on the Republican side in the Spanish Civil War.

Brecht attended the Paris Congress at which Toller spoke so eloquently of Mühsam's supreme act of defiance. As one of the editors of *Das Wort*, he would also have known the printed version of Toller's Paris speech, as well as "Unser Kampf um Deutschland" where Erich Mühsam and Edgar André are jointly cited as exemplary representatives of "das andere Deutschland."[30] Yet while recognizing Mühsam's iconic importance for the Popular Front and for many German writers in exile, Brecht seems to have had little interest in making "Die Internationale" a personal tribute to Mühsam's martyrdom, one comparable in tone and implications to Toller's *Pastor Hall*. Any debt to Toller's picture of Mühsam as a high-profile resistance role model (Pastor Martin Niemöller also figures in *Pastor Hall*) is characteristically depersonalized and desentimentalized in the equivalent *Furcht und Elend* episode. Yet neither "Die Internationale" nor "Moorsoldaten," the scene that replaced "Die Internationale" in *The Private Life*, can hold a candle to the examples of resistance in some of the concluding *Furcht und Elend* scenes. As the Second World War progressed, there was a tendency among the Western Allies to suppress information about the Other Germany's resistance attempts since these hardly helped the strategy of fighting until the Third Reich's "unconditional surrender." This may well have influenced the choice of scenes in *The Private Life*, in contrast to the original teleology

---

[30] Brecht made various contributions to the "Other Germany" debate while working on *The Private Life*, especially in the context of the crusade mounted by Paul Tillich, Alfred Döblin, et al., to show that there was another Germany and Sir Robert Vansittart's controversial theses on the German character and the question of why there had been no German opposition to the attack on the USSR (details in Brecht's journal entry for 8 August 1943 [*BFA* 27:163]). See also the declaration formulated and signed by a number of influential German writers on 1 August 1943 (*BFA* 27:161–62); "The *Other* Germany: 1943," *Progressive Labour*, 3 (March-April, 1966):46–49, German in *BFA* 23:24–30; and "Das andere Deutschland," *The German American* (January 1944):16, German in *BFA* 23:440. *The Private Life* is prefaced by a dedication to "THE OTHER GERMANY."

in *Furcht und Elend* where the largely chronological sequence of examples of resistance is structured according to a gradational principle.

"Und zwar wachsend": The Pattern of Growing Opposition from Scene to Scene

A comparison with Kattrin's increasingly strident opposition to her mother's selfish behavior in *Mutter Courage und ihre Kinder*, opposition eventually culminating in a selfless act of large-scale pacifist interventionism, suggests one possible interpretation of the cumulative ("zwar wachsend") pattern of resistance in *Furcht und Elend*. That is to say, the progression could relate to an increase in the *effectiveness* of direct action in a given situation. In the first half of *Mutter Courage*, Kattrin's diverse altruistic acts — including displays of sympathy for specific victims of the Thirty Years War and attempts at maintaining a consistently critical stance against war per se — carefully chart her gradual development from a naïve, spontaneous, caring person, prepared to put humane values before filial obedience, to something akin to a modern refusenik ready to resort to radical action when justified. Her mother's dismissive verdict "Die leidet an Mitleid" (*BFA* 6:74; She's got a soft heart) questions the misplaced pragmatism of some of Kattrin's well-intentioned acts, including her repeated rescue of hedgehogs, her impetuous saving (and not for the first time) of a baby from a burning building, and the forceful requisitioning of shirts from her mother's wagon in order to make bandages from the material (i.e., merely engaging in what is, in political terms, little more than the equivalent of a reformist gesture[31]). Of course, Kattrin does manage to learn incrementally from her harsh experiences and she adapts consequently to war's challenges. Her ultimate achievement is the saving of the children of Halle in the play's penultimate scene. Yet even if such altruistic heroism does little to hasten the end of hostilities, the play's "open" ending implicitly invites audiences to learn its unspoken political lesson.

Because each of *Furcht und Elend*'s characters is confined to one individual scene, no amount of epic structuring could accommodate the pattern of growing resistance in the same effective, character-based way as one finds in *Mutter Courage*. Nevertheless, a teleological pattern of sorts does still inform the cumulative impression of "wachsender Widerstand." This may be one reason why Brecht put emphasis on the work's "Kontinuität in der Montage" (*BFA* 29:98). In most versions of the play, that continuity

---

[31] On the political background to Brecht's literary treatment of reformism, see John White and Ann White, "Mi-en-leh's Progeny: Some of Brecht's Theatrical Parables and their Political Contexts," in *The Text and its Context*, 331–34.

is highlighted by the through-numbering of scenes. Although presenting a spectrum of resistance "in allen Graden" and "in allen Schichten," the dominant montage of scenes in *Furcht und Elend* creates a plausible semblance of completeness (*Vollständigkeit*), while at the same time bringing out the dialectical interplay between the "fear and misery" of the Third Reich and the growing forces of resistance. Even if the theme of growing resistance may not be treated with the same rigorous chronological linearity one finds in Kattrin's progress towards ethical stature, *Furcht und Elend*'s individual scenes are by and large arranged in a thematically logical order. *The Private Life* and *Aurora* editions help accentuate this by giving the exact location and year of each scene. For example, the scene "Die Berufskrankheit" (original title "Medizin") — in which, according to Brecht's letter to Dudow, "der Patient *erinnert* den Chirurgen an die Forderungen der Wissenschaft" — is so understated in its treatment of dissent that it is appropriately assigned a relatively early place in the sequence: as Scene 7 in *Aurora*, where the setting is explicitly "Berlin, 1934," in a "Krankensaal der Charité" (a ward in the Charité hospital), and as Scene 6 in *Malik* (the scene is omitted from *The Private Life*). Brecht's suggestion to Dudow that this scene's resistance element lies in the way a patient reminds the surgeon of his professional responsibilities hardly does justice to the specific details. The surgeon in fact continues to do his utmost to ignore his obligations under the Hippocratic Oath,[32] as well as his own stated principles of holistic diagnosis. Other patients, in contrast, soon begin to suspect that the new arrival is a victim of Nazi violence (the man has been admitted with injuries allegedly resulting from a fall downstairs, whereas his physical state makes either systematic torture or brutal punishment seem more likely causes). The hospital matron tries to warn the surgeon that the case should be treated with extreme caution, but he merely attempts to pass the buck by ordering that the man be sent to the X-Ray Department straightaway. At this point, an assistant reminds him of his principle that a key step in diagnosis is first to ascertain the patient's social circumstances (*soziale Verhältnisse*). Clearly, a number of those present — including another patient, the matron and at least one of the surgeon's assistants — suspect the truth about the new arrival's condition. Indeed, as is made clear at the end of the scene, this would not be the first time that injured inmates from the nearby concentration camp have been sent to the Charité for treatment. Yet nothing those harboring suspicions say or do in this scene amounts to resistance proper. At most, one of them tries to draw attention to an act of professional hypocrisy (a prevalent "Berufskrankheit" in the

---

[32] Responding in September 1948 to the Nuremberg doctors' trial of the year before, Brecht offers a Marxist diagnosis of their crimes against humanity as examples of "die Selbstentäußerung der Arbeit bei der Medizin" (*BFA* 27:273).

Third Reich, as the scene's title implies). In doing so, he tacitly refuses to accept the shabby discrepancy between the surgeon's stated principles and the overly cautious, supine way he carries out his duties. The surgeon is accompanied on his rounds by a retinue of assistants and nurses, and when answering the question of what in his prehistory makes someone twice decide to tear off his bandages, the stage direction tells us that all heads turn in the direction of the one patient who clearly senses that something wrong is happening. Most of those present merely observe events and, by not speaking out, engage de facto in what is, to all intents and purposes, little more than another cover-up, which could be read as an act of collective complicity. Only at the very end of the scene does one of the assistants reveal that another patient recovering on the ward has been brought to the hospital from the Oranienburg concentration camp. "Also auch eine Berufskrankheit" (*BFA* 4:381; Another case of occupational disease, I suppose: *FM* 44) — the throwaway remark that concludes the scene — is delivered with a grin. The episode thus ends on a sarcastic note, despite the ethical impasse, but not with a gesture of constructive resistance or even one of outright opposition. To agree with Brecht's assessment of the scene's message, one would have to assume that exposing contradictions was under all circumstances an act of genuine resistance, whereas what we in fact witness merely creates a layer of dramatic irony that puts the onus back on the audience.

Any scene-by-scene teleological pattern of overall development in *Furcht und Elend*'s depiction of resistance would, of course, only be meaningful if the full complement of scenes were staged over successive nights (the only practical way the entire play could ever be mounted). Even then, certain structural anomalies would still remain. For example, "Das Kreidekreuz" comes surprisingly early as a scene of subtle resistance — it is not even mentioned in Brecht's letter to Dudow or in the selection suggested in "[Über die Aufführung von *Furcht und Elend des III. Reiches*]" (*BFA* 24:226), although it was in first place in "99%" and is Scene 2 in *The Private Life*. Perhaps it is positioned early so that the worker's challenge to the SA man can establish a yardstick against which to measure the shabby capitulations we witness in the various middle-class scenes to come. While some episodes look premature in *Furcht und Elend*'s continuum of scenes, others seem inexplicably delayed. The ones in which a farmer furtively feeds his sow or a butcher hangs himself in such a way as to display his corpse in his own shopwindow hardly warrant their late position, particularly when judged on the accepted criteria for evaluating the efficacy of any act of resistance. Given that such dissident behavior as there is in them comes across largely as an act of desperation, the clue to their late positioning might instead lie in Brecht's suggestion that resistance would eventually emerge even in those parts of society that welcomed the Third Reich.

The scenes "Der Bauer füttert die Sau" and "Der alte Kämpfer" come in the last third of the play. In *Aurora*, the former is set in Aichach, a rural town just to the northeast of Augsburg, and the latter in "Calw in Württemberg." In *The Private Life*, the former scene's location is given as Schwetzingen. In each case, agrarian constituencies, originally largely pro-NSDAP in the early 1930s, are at this stage associated with dissidence and resistance. As we have seen, Brecht's defensive letter to Dudow puts the stress on the verb (or *Gestus*) when drawing attention to the resistance element in *Furcht und Elend* ("Der Bauer *füttert* eben die Sau," "Der alte Kämpfer *erhängt sich* demonstrativ"), in the first instance emphasizing the clandestine nature of the act by describing the farmer as "scheu über die Schulter blickend," and in the case of "Der alte Kämpfer" by using the verb to emphasize the fact that true resistance takes the form of action, rather than mere verbal outbursts. In all published versions of "Der alte Kämpfer," details in stage directions are again crucial: the butcher displays the deed that he has committed ("*erhängt sich* demonstrativ"), thus inviting others to read the message and draw the conclusions he has drawn. Even an "alter Kämpfer" like him has had to learn to his own cost that the ultimate price of voting for Hitler was economic ruin. The contrast between an illegal act carried out furtively by the farmer and his family and a disenchanted Nazi veteran's demonstration of anger and frustration with the regime he once supported implies growing resistance by highlighting the differences between defiance and the ultimate act of suicide, as well as between those made in private and those exhibited in public. The farmer feeding his sow behind the authorities' back might be acting from largely selfish motives. But the fact remains that both the old militant ("der alte Kämpfer") and the farmer and his family, once willing accomplices of National Socialism, now prefer to see themselves as victims of the regime.

The family's complaint "Wir haben denen ihren Vierjahrsplan nicht gemacht und sind nicht gefragt worden" (*BFA* 4:421; It weren't us as made their four-year plan, and we weren't asked: *FM* 76) identifies the context of "Der Bauer füttert die Sau" as that of Hermann Goering's agricultural directives, promulgated in March 1937 as a consequence of the second four-year plan announced at Nuremberg the year before. Although German farmers and other agricultural workers had initially received many material advantages and financial concessions from the first Third Reich four-year plan (1933–37), small farmers and peasants began to suffer badly thereafter. The Nazi regime's policy, aimed at achieving economic self-sufficiency at national level for the Third Reich's economy, was now becoming increasingly dictated by military considerations. Raw materials required for rearmament and the importation of much-needed cattle fodder were in competition with one another, and farmers as a result suffered from severe problems of supply, shortages of labor, and restrictions on food pricing. The consequence was a highly regulated supply mechanism and an agricultural policy now politically directed, rather than remaining in the hands of the country's economic experts.[33]

The disastrous agrarian impact on the country of the second four-year plan is also equally important for an understanding of the scene "Der alte Kämpfer." Like the farmer feeding his sow, the "old comrade" is presented as having lost his former enthusiasm for National Socialism. Both scenes contain telling references to Hermann Goering's notorious 1936 *Butter-oder-Kanonen* speech.[34] In "Der Bauer füttert die Sau," the farmer himself complains "Mein Korn soll ich abliefern und das Viehfutter soll ich teuer kaufen. Damit der Schtrizi Kanonen kaufen kann" (*BFA* 4:421; I'm supposed to deliver over my grain and pay through the nose for my cattle feed. So that that spiv can buy guns: *FM* 76), while the young Nazi fanatic in "Der alte Kämpfer" echoes Goering's words with the provocative question: "Meinen Sie, mit Butter hätten wir das Rheinland besetzen können?" (*BFA* 4:423; D'you think we could have reoccupied the Rhineland with butter?: *FM* 77). These two scenes are primarily concerned with the cost to the economy, and hence jobs at home, of Nazi Germany's war preparations, whereas other, immediately adjacent, scenes concentrate on the resultant sufferings experienced both on the Home Front and abroad. The gradual shift of focus in *Furcht und Elend* from the Third Reich's internal policies to its aggressive international agenda arguably comes not as late as the time of Germany's annexation of Austria, but with the Wehrmacht's earlier involvement in the Spanish Civil War. This prior context has important implications for the way in which acts of potential resistance are treated in the second half of *Furcht und Elend*.

Conscientious Objection and Pacifist Resistance

According to Brecht's fellow exile and Popular Front associate Alfred Kantorowicz, the Spanish Civil War (1936–39) was welcomed in left-wing circles as the first large-scale antifascist campaign; its effect on those scattered in exile was, according to Kantorowicz, like being liberated.[35] This view was likewise reflected in the Second International Writers' Congress on the theme of the responses of intellectuals to the Spanish Civil War. Brecht

---

[33] For a fuller picture of the relationship between the NS drive to achieve national autarky and the regime's various four-year plans, see Evans, *The Third Reich in Power*, 358–70.

[34] Although Rudolf Hess made a similar speech on the subject on 11 October 1936, the policy was popularly associated with Goering.

[35] Alfred Kantorowicz, *Deutsches Tagebuch* (Munich: Kindler, 1959), 2:425.

attended the Paris part of the Congress together with Ruth Berlau in July 1937, but felt it was too dangerous to attend the Congress's second phase in Madrid because of the Spanish Civil War. There was widespread left-wing support for this first campaign, with Willi Bredel, Mikhail Koltsov and Ruth Berlau leaving for Spain, and a number of Brecht's former theater associates and many left-wing German exiles fighting in the International Brigades against Franco's Nationalists. However, for reasons that have been much debated, Brecht did not join them. For him, antifascism was of a different, purely literary order: "Über den Krieg habe ich zwei Szenen: 'Arbeitsbeschaffung' und: 'In den Kasernen wird die Beschießung von Almeria bekannt' geschrieben," he reminded Dudow (*BFA* 29:85; I've written two scenes about the war: *Arbeitsbeschaffung* (*Job Creation*) and *In den Kasernen wird die Beschießung von Almeria bekannt* (*The Barracks Learn That Almeria Has Been Bombarded*): BBL 282). The emphasis in both of these *Furcht und Elend* scenes is less on the fact that the German Condor Legion, together with a token force of some 50,000 Italian ground troops, was heavily involved in pro-Nationalist operations than on the cost of such an operation to Germans back in the Third Reich. In this, the two *Furcht und Elend* scenes differ radically from Brecht's Spanish Civil War work of 1937: *Die Gewehre der Frau Carrar.* (*BFA* 4:305–37) Clearly, the two scenes cited above can only make sense when interpreted as part of a larger corpus illustrating the extent to which Germany's economy and everyday life under NS rule was becoming progressively sacrificed to the military agenda; they illustrate the consequences of this for ordinary Germans. The fact that both scenes take place in 1937 is particularly significant, given the ever-changing fortunes of the warring Republican and Nationalist sides during the three years of the Spanish Civil War. By 1937 the Popular Front's involvement on the Republican side was gradually beginning to seem like a lost cause, despite the antifascist campaign's auspicious beginnings.

The first "Spanish" scene's title, "In den Kasernen wird die Beschießung von Almeria bekannt," specifies the time of the episode as the day after the bombardment of the Republican-held port of Almeria by the German Navy.[36] The scene itself centers on a humble episode of German local "history from below" — literally so, given the defamiliarizing perspective of two young working-class boys standing in the corridor of a Wehrmacht barracks in Germany discussing the strange change in mood they have just witnessed among the soldiers they were visiting:

DER ERSTE JUNGE Heute sind sie aufgeregt, nicht?
DER ZWEITE JUNGE Sie sagen, weil's Krieg geben kann. Wegen Spanien.

---

[36] For details of the bombardment, see Antony Beevor, *The Battle for Spain: The Spanish Civil War, 1936–1939* (London: Weidenfeld & Nicolson, 2006), 323–34.

DER ERSTE JUNGE Sie sind ganz käseweiß, einige.
DER ZWEITE JUNGE Weil wir Almeria beschossen haben. Gestern abend.
DER ERSTE JUNGE Wo ist denn das?
DER ZWEITE JUNGE In Spanien doch. Hitler hat runtertelegrafiert, daß ein deutsches Kriegsschiff sofort Almeria beschießen soll. Zur Strafe. Weil sie dort rot sind und daß die Roten Schiß kriegen sollen vor dem Dritten Reich. Jetzt kann's Krieg setzen. (*BFA* 4:432)

[THE FIRST BOY: Aren't half worked up today, are they?
THE SECOND BOY: They say it's cause war could break out. Over Spain.
THE FIRST BOY: White as a sheet, some of them.
THE SECOND BOY: Cause we bombarded Almería. Last night.
THE FIRST BOY: Where's that?
THE SECOND BOY: In Spain, silly. Hitler telegraphed for a German warship to bombard Almería right away. As a punishment. Cause they're reds down there, and reds have got to be scared shitless of the Third Reich. Now it could lead to war. (*FM* 85–86)]

The first boy is puzzled by the fact that German people were only recently expressing themselves enthusiastically for Hitler ("Weil er doch die junge Wehrmacht aufgebaut hat" [*BFA* 4:432; Cause he's built up our new armed forces: *FM* 86]), but now they seemed to be frightened by the repercussions of his aggressive policies.

The boys' attention turns to the generosity of the two soldiers who each day give them food parcels. That is decent of them, the first boy decides. (In other words, these acts of charity are very different from the corrupt pseudo-largesse of the NS *Winterhilfswerk* campaigns.) His companion, playing the role of mentor, explains to him the political significance of the soldiers' gesture of solidarity. He points out that the soldiers "sind doch auch nicht bei Millionärs zu Hause. Die wissen doch!" (*BFA* 4:433; ain't millionaires any more than us, you know. They know how it is: *FM* 86). By this last comment he means that although the soldiers have known what it is like to be poor, they are nevertheless not so naïve as to be taken in by the military's attempts to bribe them with special rations in preparation for being dispatched to Spain. Appreciating the fact that the Third Reich's military adventures will be paid for in lives lost and devastating financial sacrifices made largely by the working class, the soldiers respond defiantly by giving some of their food to the two boys to take home to their families. While the boys benefit from such generosity, one of them has also learnt an important political lesson from the experience. Comparing notes about how much food they had been given, they find that the one who always said "Heil Hitler" was given only one helping, whereas the one who greeted the soldiers with a cheery "Guten Morgen" always received double rations. The boys are working class like the soldiers, whereas the latter's Wehrmacht superiors are their class enemies. Thus, while sending troops off to fight on the side of the Spanish Nationalists, the NS regime unintentionally made its own soldiers realize just how morally and politically indefensible Germany's involvement in the Spanish Civil War was, even though engagement was intended to serve as a dry run for the war to come. With their clumsy attempts at buying popular support through material bribery, the Third Reich's powers-that-be unintentionally remind the soldiers what class they come from and of their allegiance to their roots. Once again, NS *Volksgemeinschaft* policies prove to be both patently duplicitous and in the long run counterproductive.

Contrary to the account of this scene in Brecht's letter to Dudow, we have hardly been given an unequivocal illustration of politically effective resistance. Audiences are left to speculate about whether the soldiers have acted out of class solidarity with the boys, out of apolitical compassion, or in a spirit of pacifist opposition to a regime that is about to send them off to fight — and in many cases to die — on its behalf. These possible motives are, of course, not necessarily mutually exclusive. On balance, however, there would appear to be more potential altruism in evidence here than in the following companion scene: "Arbeitsbeschaffung."

Although echoing the important NS propaganda concept of work creation,[37] the scene "Arbeitsbeschaffung" (*BFA* 4:434–37), set in the *Aurora* version in Spandau in 1937, is positioned towards the end of *Furcht und Elend*, logically so, given that it revisits the subject of the Spanish Civil War's impact on the Home Front already broached in "In den Kasernen wird die Beschießung von Almeria bekannt." What the soldiers in the previous scene had feared is by now becoming reality for the families of Wehrmacht forces serving in Spain, and covertly elsewhere too. By 1937, many Germans at home were beginning to suspect Nazi Germany's involvement in the Spanish Civil War. After a short-lived episode in Popular Front history when Republican forces appeared to be gaining the upper hand with the help of the International Brigades, substantial organized Nationalist support from Germany and Italy eventually ensured Republican defeat. The scene's black humor, playing as it does with the idea of "eine Stelle bekommen" — the male protagonist now has a job ("eine Stelle") in the armaments industry, whereas his brother-in-law has also found "eine Stelle," a burial plot a meter below ground level — neatly brings together the double-edged nature of war: as a means of "Arbeitsbeschaffung," underwritten at the same time by human lives and suffering.

Although "Arbeitsbeschaffung" is mentioned in Brecht's letter to Dudow ("*die Schwester des in Spanien Gefallenen läßt sich nicht den Mund*

---

[37] Two major job-creation schemes were launched by the NS government in 1933, one devoted to miscellaneous "Notstandsarbeiten," the other to the autobahn construction program, itself intended to serve a military function.

zuhalten"), it arguably contains more forms of opposition than the one cited by Brecht, for the grieving sister is not the only person at the center of attention. From the outset, it is the Fenns' neighbor, Frau Dietz, who outspokenly voices her suspicions about what is happening in Spain. It is she who suggests that Frau Fenn's brother did not die accidentally, as alleged, while on Luftwaffe training in Stettin. It is she who suspects that he was probably killed in action during the ongoing Spanish Civil War. The cause of his death (whether preparing for a war or participating in one) makes little difference. Frau Fenn ostentatiously puts on mourning at the news and later indicates that her manner of expressing grief is nonnegotiable: "Wenn sie ihn schon abschlachten, dann muß ich wenigstens heulen dürfen" (*BFA* 4:437: If they can slaughter him I have a right to cry: *FM* 90). She will simply not back down, either in order to protect her husband's job or to save her own skin:

> Dann sollen sie mich doch abholen! Die haben ja auch Frauen-Konzentrationslager.[38] Da sollen sie mich doch reinstecken, weil es mir nicht gleich ist, wenn sie meinen Bruder umbringen! Was hat der in Spanien verloren! (*BFA* 4:437)

> [Let them come and get me, then! They've concentration camps for women too. Let them just put me in one of those because I dare to mind when they kill my brother! What was he in Spain for? (*FM* 90)]

Despite the selective way it is presented in Brecht's letter to Dudow, the "Arbeitsbeschaffung" scene is not primarily about a sister's right to mourn her brother or even her assumption that the National Socialists have sacrificed him in "their" war. Like listening to foreign broadcasts or refraining from giving the Hitler salute, one underlying issue of importance raised in this scene is how a gesture — this time one of mourning — might be interpreted by others, especially the Gestapo, given the circumstances under which the woman's brother did in all probability die. The speech quoted above makes it clear that the mourning woman's ultimate grievance concerns what her brother's death symbolizes. Refusing to stop appearing in public dressed in mourning may seem in some respects comparable to the butcher's hanging his body in his own shopwindow in "Der alte Kämpfer." But in declaring herself prepared to be sent to a concentration camp rather than be silenced, Frau Fenn goes an important step further. Her antiwar protest will remain in the public eye, whereas the butcher's suicide was but a final act of despair, evidence of which would soon be airbrushed out of the picture. His corpse and the attached placard (reading "ICH HABE HITLER GEWÄHLT!" [*BFA* 4:426; I VOTED FOR HITLER: *FM* 80]) will be quickly

---

[38] Given that "Arbeitsbeschaffung" is set in 1937, the reference must be to Nazi Germany's first experimental concentration camp for women: Lichtenburg. The camp's specialized function was eventually taken over in 1939 by Ravensbrück.

removed, whereas Frau Fenn's grief and sense of grievance promise not to be erased so easily.

What Brecht fails to mention in his comments on the scene's resistance value is the fact that "Arbeitsbeschaffung" goes on to present in miniature a gradated series of illustrations of how resistance can grow out of even modest acts of opposition. On one level, a neighbor merely suspects the hidden truth behind the airman's death: "Die decken alles hübsch sauber zu" (*BFA* 4:435; They always sweep things under the mat: *FM* 88). More importantly, especially in the light of the virtues enumerated in Brecht's "Fünf Schwierigkeiten" essay, she then expresses her suspicions concerning the links between Herr Fenn's new job, Germany's covert involvement in the Spanish Civil War, and the significance of Frau Fenn's brother's death: "Was üben die denn da? Den Krieg üben sie!" (*BFA* 4:436; What are they exercising at? A war, that's what!: *FM* 89). It was above all her adamant refusal to remain silent that Brecht saw as the bereaved sister's main act of resistance. In contrast, Herr Fenn engages in an elaborate act of denial: "Ich gehöre zu gar nichts. Ich mache meine Arbeit" (*BFA* 4:434; I've not joined nothing. I get on with my work: *FM* 87). He blatantly refuses to acknowledge the mounting evidence that his brother-in-law cannot have died under the circumstances stated in the letter from the airman's commanding officer. Herr Fenn's denial is a textbook example of the tunnel vision characteristic of those prepared to enjoy the short-term benefits of war-capitalism while closing their eyes to the ultimate cost to themselves and others. Herr Fenn remains stubbornly intransigent until the end, his last words being "Halt den Mund von Spanien! [. . .] Sei doch still! Das hilft doch nicht!" (*BFA* 4:437; Shut up about Spain! [. . .] Shut up, will you? It doesn't help: *FM* 90). Undeterred, his wife eventually takes an explicit stand against her husband's position:

> Weil sie dir sonst deine Stelle wegnehmen, drum sollen wir stillehalten? Weil wir sonst verrecken, wenn wir ihnen nicht ihre Bombenflieger machen? Und dann verrecken wir doch? (*BFA* 4:437)

> [Are we to keep quiet just because they might take your job away? Because we'll die of starvation if we don't make bombers for them? And die just the same if we do? (*FM* 90)]

Busch remarks of the playwright's letter to Dudow that it was not always easy to follow Brecht's interpretation of the alleged element of resistance in certain *Furcht und Elend* scenes. He draws attention to one particularly important factor in Brecht's thinking: the part penetrating questions can play in challenging the regime:

> Das Fragen, genauer das Lautwerdenlassen von Fragen allein schon bedeutet Widerstand. Fragen stellen und Fragen provozieren ist für Brecht eine wichtige politische Kunst. Wo nicht mehr gefragt wird, hat der Terror endgültig über den Widerstand gesiegt. (Busch, *Bertolt Brecht*, 44)

In this respect, the responses of Frau Fenn and her intrusive neighbor Frau Dietz might merit consideration as low-caliber resistance. Yet the fact that such doubts are expressed only behind closed doors makes them seem less deserving of the term. Later, Frau Fenn's suspicions become more outspoken, as does her concern with what Brecht once referred to as "die Vorgänge hinter den Vorgängen" (*BFA* 22:520; the events behind the events). It is not merely the dangerous act of seeking answers, but the nature of the questions asked and, in this case, the context that define genuine spoken resistance. On the whole, Busch's comments on "Arbeitsbeschaffung" concentrate less on the scene's concluding questions than on Frau Fenn's decision to don mourning and appear thus dressed before her husband and Frau Dietz and, if she remains true to her resolution, subsequently in public. Audiences may initially be meant to respond to Frau Fenn's actions with empathy. But rather than wallowing in grief for a dead brother, the scene's main identification-figure quickly moves on to the question of what is to be done and the fact that action has to be taken: "Dann macht doch, was hilft!" (*BFA* 4:437; Do something that does [help]!: *FM* 90).[39] None of the other characters in this scene seems to share her belief in the value of interventionist thinking ("eingreifendes Denken," as explained in *BFA* 21:524 and *BFA* 24:182). Her call to action comes nearest to being answered in the play's next and final scene,[40] although, as that scene also suggests, ostentatious protest risks being counterproductive.

Having listed a dozen examples of alleged resistance in his letter to Dudow, Brecht returns to the crucial question of how *Furcht und Elend* should end. "Wir brauchen nicht zum Kampf aufzurufen, wir zeigen den Kampf! Das *Nein* am Schluß scheint mir nicht zu wenig" (*BFA* 29:85; We don't have to call for struggle, we show the struggle! The *no* at the end does not strike me as too little: *BBL* 282). Nevertheless, he promises Dudow, "Ich werde trotzdem noch versuchen, einen positiven Epilog zu schreiben" (*BFA* 29:85; I'll try all the same to write a positive epilogue, *BBL* 282). "Das *Nein* am Schluß," a reference to the last word in the scene "Der fehlende Mann" (The Missing Man), as it was initially entitled, the final word in the last scene of the entire play (an ending used in *The Private Life*, but not in "99%"), is, as one might expect, as much addressed to the audience as to those targeted by the group's propaganda leaflet. The change of scene title from "Der fehlende Mann" to "Volksbefragung"

---

[39] The leitmotif "was hilft," both here and in "Was hilft gegen Gas?" (*BFA* 4:438–40), which in the *Malik* page-proof version follows immediately on from "Arbeitsbeschaffung," would appear to be an allusion to the question "What is to be done?" (Chto delat´?), used by Nikolai Gavrilovich Chernyshevsky (cf. *BBB* 1648) and V. I. Lenin in classic theoretical works of early interventionist socialism.

[40] "Arbeitsbeschaffung" is followed by "Volksbefragung" in all published versions of *Furcht und Elend* except that in *BFA* 4.

shifts the focus at plot level to the German people about to be canvassed in the plebiscite seeking retrospective approval for the annexation of Austria.[41] This scene was in fact already intact and waiting to be used when Brecht assured Dudow of his intention to write a new conclusion to *Furcht und Elend*. That he still felt the need for one may come as something of a surprise, given the undoubted strengths of "Volksbefragung" as the logical conclusion to the work's extensive differentiated treatment of the resistance theme.[42] Nevertheless, some of the problematic assumptions upon which this scene is predicated require contextual reconsideration.

"Die Wahl": NS Vote-rigging and the Problem of Resistance

Before we attempt a reassessment of the function and value of "Volksbefragung" as *Furcht und Elend*'s culminating "resistance" episode, it is worth looking briefly at "Die Wahl" (*BFA* 4: 415–16), another election scene that in the early stages formed part of the cycle. A much shorter scene than "Volksbefragung," it treats another milestone election in Third Reich Germany's inglorious history of vote-rigging. "Die Wahl" appeared as Scene 16 in *Malik*, but was not used in *The Private Life* and *Aurora* and was omitted thereafter from all subsequent versions, except that in *BFA*. While it is not clear why Brecht initially wanted to have *two* election scenes, the inclusion and subsequent exclusion of "Die Wahl" raises a number of important questions. For example, what was the original relationship intended to be between "Die Wahl" and "Volksbefragung"? Although dates for specific episodes were a rare occurrence in the *Malik* version (*Furcht und Elend des III. Reiches*), each of these election-based scenes is prefixed by the indication of an important electoral and plebiscite date in the history of the Third Reich. What is more, the two scenes appear in historically chronological sequence, thus inviting consideration of Scene 27 ("Volksbefragung") in the light of Scene 16 ("Die Wahl"). Patterns of "gegenseitige Verfremdung" clearly

---

[41] The *Anschluss* ballot of 10 April 1938 asked participants to answer the question: "Do you agree to the reunion of Austria with the German Reich carried out on 13 March and do you vote for the [Reichstag] list of our *Führer*, Adolf Hitler?" According to NSDAP statistics, 99.07% of a total vote of 99.59% of the qualified electorate voted "yes."

[42] Brecht's journal entry for 23 November 1938 outlines the kind of ending Epic Theater requires: "[ich brauchte] am Schluß einen Kunstgriff, um auf jeden Fall dem Zuschauer den nötigen Abstand zu sichern. Selbst der unbedenklich sich Einfühlende muß zumindest [. . .], auf dem Weg der Einfühlung [in die Hauptfigur], den V-Effekt verspüren. Bei streng epischer Darstellung kommt eine Einfühlung erlaubter Art zustande" (*BFA* 26:326).

appear to be at work in this instance, encouraging us to engage in an act of "vergleichendes Blättern." We will return to this comparative aspect shortly, when discussing "Volksbefragung" later in the present chapter.

The *Vorspruch* that introduces "Die Wahl" presents a more uncompromisingly violent picture of the National Socialists' manipulation of the voting procedure than one finds in the play's final scene, although this might simply be because the focus in "Volksbefragung" is on "illegale Arbeit"[43] rather than on the corrupt election plus plebiscite machinery itself. Of the press-ganged voters we are told:

> Man trieb sie mit Kolbenschlägen
> Sie hielten sich die leeren Mägen.
> Ein Stöhnen zum Himmel stieg.
> Und fragten wir mit Erbarmen:
> Wo zieht ihr hin, ihr Armen?
> Dann riefen sie: in den Sieg! (*BFA* 4:415)

> [With well-armed thugs to lead them
> And nothing much to feed them
> Their groans rose to the sky.
> We asked them, all unknowing:
> Poor things, where are you going?
> They said "to victory." (*FM* 111)]

Instead of the violence and political coercion described in the *Vorspruch* to "Die Wahl," the propaganda image that the NS ballot organizers attempt to communicate tends to reinforce the importance of such virtues as patriotism, civic duty, obeying the Führer's wishes, and selfless heroism on the field of battle. There is a blatant attempt to create an impression of the regime's desire to lead the people towards the right electoral decision, one duplicitously represented as synonymous with taking "the path to victory." But the interrogating voice of the *Vorspruch*, combined with the use of the first person plural, helps prevent audiences being taken in by the unfolding façade of democratic elections, allowing them instead to perceive the real agenda underlying the vote-rigging procedure.

The election that is the subject of Scene 16, the *Reichstagswahl* of 29 March 1936 following Hitler's sudden dissolution of the German Reichs-

---

[43] For a detailed account of the main connotations of this concept, see the *Kontrollchor*'s hymn "Lob der illegalen Arbeit" (*Die Maßnahme* [1931], *BFA* 3:105–6) and the four agitators' description of their underground activities as "Propaganda zu machen und zu unterstützen die [. . .] Partei durch die Lehren der Klassiker und der Propagandisten, das Abc des Kommunismus; den Unwissenden Belehrung zu bringen über ihre Lage, den Unterdrückten das Klassenbewußtsein und den Klassenbewußten die Erfahrung der Revolution" (op. cit., 105).

tag, was a complex affair. Not only was the NSDAP the sole party to appear on the list of candidates, the ballot box was simultaneously used (as it would be in the 10 April *Anschluss* plebiscite in relation to the events of 13 March 1938) to force voters to register retrospective approval of two recent events that formed part of the build-up to the Second World War: the Wehrmacht's repossession of the Rhineland, confiscated under the terms of the Versailles Treaty, and the systematic remilitarization of the region.[44] The large banner displayed at the scene's polling station emphasizes the geo-political importance of the decisions that voters were being called upon to take. Doubling as an Epic Theater *Tafel* (as explained in Brecht's "Anmerkungen zur *Dreigroschenoper*," BFA 24:58) and as a political propaganda placard, the proclamation "'DAS DEUTSCHE VOLK BRAUCHT LEBENSRAUM' (ADOLF HITLER)" (THE GERMAN PEOPLE NEED LIVING SPACE [ADOLF HITLER]) draws attention to the connection between voting for Hitler and formally approving National Socialism's long-standing expansionist foreign policy. But a vote for the Nazis was not just a vote for more *Lebensraum* for Germans, as the banner implies, it was at the same time a vote for the military aggression that was the NS regime's only acknowledged means of achieving such a goal.[45] The intimidating presence of SA men at the polling station already gives a military complexion to what, under other circumstances, might have been every civilian citizen's democratic right to give expression to his or her political views. Those manning the polling station, including the official in charge, are all in SA uniform. The uniform becomes a form of intimidation.

The SA are not the only people present in this scene. The stage directions focus attention on two proletarian figures: a blind, forty-year-old ex-soldier who lost his eyesight during the First World War and his mother. Through the foregrounding of these two representatives of the working class in this way, audiences might expect that "Die Wahl" would soon become a site of political protest and active resistance, although a nervous, frail old lady and a blind man hardly come across as plausible representatives of antifascist sentiment. As things turn out, although the scene plays with the resistance option, what happens at the polling station will offer a contrast to the various forms of dissidence and resistance that are still to

---

[44] For details of the 29 March 1936 vote, see Evans, *The Third Reich in Power*, 633–37. According to Evans (633), the reclaiming of the Rhineland demilitarized zone was intended as a badly needed "coup to cheer people up" after the recently signed Franco-Soviet pact. However, reports from Sopade observers suggested that it was only the Nazis who celebrated (*Deutschland-Berichte*, 3:303).

[45] As has since been demonstrated, the idea, popularized by Hans Grimm's novel *Volk ohne Raum*, that the German people needed more living space was an NS myth. For details comparing the demographic facts with the myth's literary dissemination, see Uwe-K. Ketelsen, *Literatur und Drittes Reich* (Schernfeld: SH-Verlag, 1992), 199–215.

come in the *Furcht und Elend* cycle — especially in the scenes depicting the impact of the Spanish Civil War on the Home Front. When the blind man's mother anxiously asks whether another war is in the offing, the seriousness of her concern reminds us of the cost to herself and her family of the last one. The question at the end of the *Vorspruch* ("Wo zieht ihr hin, ihr Armen?") and the answer ("in den Sieg!") already draw our attention to the fact that people are being duped into voting for "victory" and forgetting the deprivations that will inevitably follow. The impoverished and incapacitated blind ex-soldier, now dependent on his mother's help, is an example from the past of the price tag attached to war. As if he had not learnt his lesson, the ex-soldier now turns up dutifully to vote for another war, one being prepared for, ostensibly, to make good the losses of the 1914–18 period. (Few pacifist *Furcht und Elend* scenes look even this far back into history!) Although the English translation refers to the ex-soldier as a "WAR VICTIM," it is significant that he is explicitly introduced as a "Kriegsblinder." He is both literally and figuratively blind: his mother has to lead him to the polling booth, and he is symbolically blind to the fact that the coming war, which is at issue in this election, will be disastrous in terms of the number of lives lost, suffering, and Germany's future. Seemingly without demur, he is led forward to cast his vote for a party whose political program is geared to rearmament. In the *Vorspruch* verse, those forcing voters to the polling booth are described as doing so with their rifle butts. This contrasts sharply with the mother's behavior. Having been officiously ordered to do so ("Hierhin!" is the brusque command), she leads her son forward hesitantly, at one stage halting in mistrust, and clearly frightened of the assembled SA men whose stares are intended to intimidate her. This is a classic example of Brecht's even-handed use of *Gestus* in *Furcht und Elend*: the old woman's *Gestus* of fear and the SA men's cocky *Gestus* of being in control of a situation.

When the blind ex-soldier, flanked by two SA men, initially arrives at the polling booth, everyone present greets him with the Hitler salute, i.e., as war *hero* rather than war *victim*. Ritual takes over from here onwards. Much of "Die Wahl" involves illustrations of the Third Reich's theatricalization of politics: for example, the banner bearing Hitler's words, the official's haranguing those present as if he were a commander addressing his troops, the meaningless charade of handing over the voting slip and accompanying envelope, a gesture meant to suggest that the poll will remain secret. These rituals are devised to give the act of voting something of the aura of allegiance-swearing that was central to many NS ceremonies. The scene's various quasi-theatrical procedures appear to create the requisite atmosphere, until, that is, the blind man's mother asks her question about whether there is going to be another war. At this, an uncomfortable silence descends on everyone present. It is left to the official in charge of voting to rescue the situation by praising the blind man at some length and

exploiting for all the propaganda effect he can derive from the occasion the
ex-solder's determination to vote. These are his rhetorical words:

> Der Mann ist kriegsblind. Aber wo das Kreuz hin soll, das findet er.
> Kann manchem Volksgenossen eine Lehre sein. Der Mann hat sein
> Augenlicht froh und freudig für die Nation gegeben. Aber er zögert
> nicht, jetzt, wo sein Führer ruft, von neuem für Deutschlands Ehre
> zu stimmen. Seine Treue zur Nation hat ihm nicht Geld noch Gut
> eingebracht. Das können Sie auf den ersten Blick an seinem Man-
> tel sehen. Mancher ewig meckernde Volksgenosse sollte mal darüber
> nachdenken, was den Mann an die Urne bringt. (*BFA* 4:415)

> [This man was blinded in the war. But he knows where to put his
> cross. There are plenty of comrades can learn from him. This man
> gladly and joyfully gave his eyesight for the nation. But now on hear-
> ing his Führer's call he has no hesitation about giving his vote once
> again for Germany's honour. His loyalty to our nation has brought
> him neither possessions nor money. You need only look at his coat to
> see that. Many a habitual grumbler among our comrades would do
> well to think what has led such a man to the poll. (*FM* 111)]

What has led him to cast his vote? Those wanting to exploit him as a war
hero would no doubt suggest that it was a sense of duty to *Führer, Volk, und
Vaterland* that had been displayed on the Western Front some twenty years
earlier. Some doubting cynics, encouraged by the *Vorspruch* to this scene,
might decide it was the two armed SA men who "led" him to the polling station. And by the warped logic of their fascist ideology, some would
doubtless see his blindness as inspiring evidence of an admirably patriotic
willingness to sacrifice his eyesight for his people. As we will see in the case of
"Das Mahnwort," willingness to die — or make other sacrifices — for one's
country was presented in the Third Reich as the highest act of allegiance to
the Fatherland. Whatever happens in the polling booth, it is clear that neither the blind man nor his mother has the courage to take a stand against the
idolization of war. And even if they did, it is clear that they could do little at
this stage to turn back the tide of pro-war fanaticism. Neither they nor their
compatriots seem to have learnt the lessons of the First World War.

We will return to the implications of this scene towards the end of the
next section, when considering "Volksbefragung," particularly with an eye
to the possible efficacy or futility of political resistance when undertaken
within the framework of a society living under a totalitarian regime.

Organized Political Action

As the similarity in titles suggests, "Volksbefragung" was consciously
designed to act as the counterpart, and contrast, to Scene 1 of the *Furcht*

und Elend cycle. The montage's opening scene, "Volksgemeinschaft," was deliberately set in a working-class district of Berlin on a red-letter day for German National Socialists: 30 January 1933. The concluding scene is located (in *Malik*) "in einer proletarischen Wohnung in Neukölln" on the day of the annexation of Austria (13 March 1938).[46] Although these scenes bear a date,[47] the focus is less on the two watershed events themselves, marked by a torchlight procession in the former case and a triumphant motorcade in the latter, than on the long-term repercussions of these historical moments for the German working class. As we have already noted, both scenes take their titles from NS concepts, one in order to remind audiences of the hollowness of Hitler's claim to be creating a classless *Volksgemeinschaft* and the other to contrast the charade of a carefully orchestrated plebiscite *after the event* with the way it might be exploited to encourage people to signal their collective rejection of the *Anschluss* with a unanimous "No" vote.[48] In one sense, the play's concluding scene is itself potentially a "Volksbefragung" addressed to the country's real (political) audience — and in that respect, arguably more so than the event it actually chronicles.

One obvious difference between the complete play's two framing scenes is the contrast between the pervasive atmosphere of fear and edginess in the former and the mood of growing confidence, despite the incumbent dangers, in the latter. But there are numerous other, not insignificant, differences. For example, the working-class Berlin district in "Volksgemeinschaft" attracts unnecessary attention by pointedly refusing to put out flags to mark the occasion of Hitler's becoming Reichskanzler, whereas in "Volksbefragung" patriotically displaying the flag is cunningly intended to deflect

---

[46] *Stücke* 6, 143 and *GW*, 3:1183, have *Der junge Arbeiter* saying they are "in der Arbeiterstadt Neukölln," whereas *Aurora*, 105 identifies the setting as Hamburg, yet has *Der junge Arbeiter* saying they are "in der Arbeiterstadt Neukölln," and *BFA* 4:441 gives the setting as "In einer proletarischen Wohnung in Neukölln." "Hamburg 1938" was the title and setting for the replacement scene in the Basle production of 1946.

[47] These were not the only scenes in *Malik* to bear a date. "Die Wahl" is dated "29. März 1936" (cf. *BFA* 4:415). Another scene — entitled "Rechtsfindung 1934" when prepublished in *Das Wort* 3 (June 1938), 6–17 — is undated in *Malik*, yet subsequently headed "Augsburg 1935" in *Aurora*, 33.

[48] What Brecht ignores when implying with this scene that the ballot box could be used as a tool of resistance is the possibility that the voting would be rigged. The various intimidatory mechanisms used on such occasions had already been outlined in detail in Sopade's *Deutschland-Berichte* 1934, 347. A contemporary police report (doc. 461) quoted in *Nazism: A Documentary Reader, 1919–1945*, ed. J. Noakes and G. Pridham, vol. 2, *State, Economy and Society, 1933–1939* (Exeter: Exeter UP, 1997), 595, explains how the anonymity of the plebiscite vote of 10 April 1938 was similarly violated.

attention from any suspicion of dissidence or organized resistance activity. The bulk of the "Volksbefragung" scene is also constructed on a series of further contrasts: (i) between the noisy celebration of Hitler's arrival in the Austrian capital and the resistance cell's largely taciturn mood of isolation; (ii) between the applauding crowds and the voices of the few in hiding, conversing in hushed tones to avoid discovery; (iii) between the excited rhetoric of the propaganda broadcast's commentary and the calm, measured words of a condemned father's testament to his son, a dialectical set of contrasts culminating in the single monosyllabic word —"NEIN" — that the group decide to put on their protest leaflet.[49] Their resolve now stiffened by having listened to the reading of a letter from a condemned man to his son, they are no longer so disheartened by the Austrians' ecstatic welcome for Hitler's entourage. "Wir sind doch nicht so wenige" (*BFA* 4:442; There aren't really that few of us after all: *FM* 92), they decide, now reminding themselves that they are part of a vast Popular Front resistance movement that outnumbered any welcoming party that annexed Austria could lay on.[50] The dead man's letter that is the catalyst for this change is presented as "die Abschrift eines Briefes" (a copy of a letter, *FM* 92). In other words, it would appear, despite the dangers involved, to have been mass-duplicated for propaganda circulation purposes: i.e., to help strengthen the sense of political solidarity among the members of the resistance movement.

This moving letter, read out by the only female character present and deliberately masked by a convincingly plausible distracting sound (*Geräuschkulisse*) coming from the radio, combines a measure of justified pathos with a clear-headed political declaration:

> Mein lieber Sohn! Morgen werde ich schon nicht mehr sein. Die Hinrichtung ist meistens früh sechs. Ich schreibe aber noch, weil ich will, daß Du weißt, daß meine Ansichten sich nicht geändert haben. Ich habe auch kein Gnadengesuch eingereicht, da ich ja nichts verbrochen habe. Ich habe nur meiner Klasse gedient. (*BFA* 4:442)

> [Dear son: Tomorrow I shall have ceased to be. Executions are usually at six a.m. I'm writing now because I want you to know I haven't

---

[49] According to Noakes and Pridham, vol. 2, *State, Economy and Society* (doc. 459), 591–92, those engaged in illegal activities soon became wary of distributing propaganda leaflets because experience showed that distribution chains could easily be followed and sources traced. For this reason, the Paris-based Central Committee of the KPD published new guidelines in 1937, switching the emphasis from the distribution of printed pamphlets to propaganda by word of mouth.

[50] The stress on proletarian resistance as the *many* responding to the *few* is indebted to the final part of Percy Bysshe Shelley's "The Masque of Anarchy," Alfred Wolfenstein's translation of which appeared in *Das Wort* 2 (June 1937), 63–65 as: "Sie sind wenige — Ihr seid viel!"

changed my opinions, nor have I applied for a pardon because I didn't commit any crime. I just served my class. (*FM* 92)]

The letter then moves on from the unnamed father's tragic personal circumstances to the needs of the party, while stressing his son's obligations, as well as those of everyone else listening. The letter is sufficiently nonspecific to serve as a rallying cry to resistance fighters of all hues:

> Jeder auf seinen Platz, das muß die Parole sein! Unsere Aufgabe ist sehr schwer, aber es ist die größte, die es gibt, die Menschheit von ihren Unterdrückern zu befreien. Vorher hat das Leben keinen Wert, nur dafür. Wenn wir uns das nicht immer vor Augen halten, dann versinkt die ganze Menschheit in Barbarei. Du bist noch sehr klein, aber es schadet nichts, wenn Du immer daran denkst, auf welche Seite Du gehörst. Halte Dich zu Deiner Klasse, dann wird Dein Vater nicht umsonst sein schweres Schicksal erlitten haben, denn es ist nicht leicht. (*BFA* 4:442)

> [Every man to his post, should be our motto. Our task is very difficult, but it's the greatest one there is — to free the human race from its oppressors. Till that's done life has no other value. Let that out of our sights and the whole human race will relapse into barbarism. You're still quite young but it won't hurt you to remember always which side you are on. Stick with your own class, then your father won't have suffered his unhappy fate in vain, because it isn't easy. (*FM* 92)]

In another context, such an episode might have given rise to the kind of "culinary" sentimentality that Brecht invariably sought to avoid: for example, when it came to the treatment of Pawel's death in *Die Mutter*. The fact that the letter from the father to his son is a montage of documentary material borrowed from a number of real last letters sent to their families by condemned members of the resistance movement[51] transcends emotional specificity in favor of the wider political picture. Nevertheless, we have to be on our guard when it comes to the letter's rhetorical claim that if the son remains mindful of his political duty, the father's death will not have been in vain. This is surely not what gives meaning to his dying. Brecht has arguably laid a trap for any audience tempted to take the father's words at face value (and we will want to argue in a minute that it is not the last trap laid in this scene). Serving as a necessary counterbalance to the scene's emotive emphasis on heroism, the final three speeches after the father's letter has been read out direct attention outwards and upwards to the greater antifascist cause. At this point, the members of the resistance

---

[51] According to Brecht's letter of 7 June 1938 to Wieland Herzfelde, "der Brief in 'Volksbefragung' ist aus mehreren Briefen kombiniert" (*BFA* 29:98–99) — no doubt a strategy devised to protect the identity of the playwright's informants.

group set about deciding what recommendation to voters should stand in their leaflet: "Am besten nur ein Wort: NEIN!" (*BFA* 4:442; Best thing would be just one word: NO!: *FM* 92).

In this powerful concluding scene, the play's rousing finale employs a series of anti-empathic devices (including the stereometric effect created by the simultaneity of dialogue and continuous background noise, contrasts in volume to subvert the emotionalism of Nazi propaganda, and abrupt shifts between emotional and rational content, as well as between the particular and the general) that are instrumental in making sure that "Volksbefragung" avoids the difficulties with emotions that vitiate the endings to other Brecht plays where an exemplary figure dies a quasi-martyr's death. Brecht created a similarly distancing ending for the film *Hangmen Also Die*. Instead of concluding in standard cinematic fashion with the words "THE END," Fritz Lang's film flashed up the statement "THIS IS NOT THE END." "Volksbefragung" supplies a similarly political open ending to the play's treatment of resistance. Unfortunately, the resolute resistance spirit that "Volksbefragung" was intended to illustrate fell very much short of the realities of the real antifascist struggle by the time the scene was first staged.

Returning to the images of vote-rigging and the exploitation of a vote-cum-plebiscite in "Die Wahl," we can perhaps appreciate the shortcomings of the resistance group's naïve plans for exploiting the NSDAP's forthcoming election and plebiscite to their advantage. While it might not have seemed out of order for Brecht to have declared to Dudow, from an exile perspective in April 1938, that "Das Nein am Schluß [i.e., at the end of "Volksbefragung"] scheint mir nicht zu wenig" (*BFA* 29:85), saying "No" may seem less effective if the idea is revisited with the play's earlier depiction of the conduct of the *Reichstagswahl* of 29 March 1936 in mind.[52] What would it mean, for example, if the blind ex-soldier and his mother voted "No"? Or, indeed, if everyone else waiting to cast their votes did so? Probably very little. Noakes and Pridham document the amount of vote-rigging and ideological manipulation that occurred at local level during plebiscites and elections.[53]

While Brecht can hardly have been aware of all of these dispiriting facts at the time of working on the *Malik Ur*-version of "Volksbefragung," he had, with "Die Wahl," already put down one unambiguous marker suggesting that even *Furcht und Elend*'s concluding scene is not necessarily

---

[52] Cf. Völker on the play's ending: "Die Geschichte hat nicht nur das resignativ realistische 'Nein' gegen die 'Volksbefragung' mit Hohn bedacht. Brecht versuchte auch auf Kosten der historischen Präzision an der deutschen Bevölkerung als einem Ort und einem Reservoir der anderen, neuen Zeit festzuhalten" (*Brecht-Kommentar zum dramatischen Werk*, 179).

[53] Noakes and Pridham, vol. 2, *State, Economy and Society* (docs. 459–61), 593–95.

to be construed as the ultimate solution to Nazi Germany's problems. In *Malik* (and only there), because the prior perspective offered by "Die Wahl" tends to militate against an unquestioningly positive reading of "Volksbefragung," the play concludes with a gesture that possibly even suggests naïve political optimism rather than activist pragmatism. To appreciate this, we need to bear in mind that in *Malik* the penultimate scene ("Was hilft gegen Gas?") contains what Theodor Adorno would have called the play's "Dynamitstelle." This comes in the form of the recollections of a German soldier who had served on the Eastern Front fighting the mutinous Russians during the final phase of the First World War. One might conclude that "Was hilft gegen Gas?" points the way to a more pragmatic conclusion to the resistance problem in the Third Reich than either the path of compliance illustrated in "Die Wahl" or the recommendation in "Volksbefragung" that voters ruin the ballot. Klaus Völker rightly presents the reference to the Russian Revolution as "die Konkretion einer Widerstandsmöglichkeit."[54] However, looking beyond these three individual scenes, one can see that, in all versions of *Furcht und Elend*, resistance and revolution remain distinctly separate entities. More so than they did in such earlier (Weimar) plays as *Trommeln in der Nacht*, *Die Maßnahme*, or *Die Mutter*, where "illegale Arbeit" was invariably presented as preparation for revolution rather than the act of resistance on its own.[55]

As we have suggested, the *Malik* version's combination of two voting scenes risks diluting the idealism of "Volksbefragung." If nothing else, it implies that such an optimistic solution has to be viewed with caution. Yet the immediate proximity of "Was hilft gegen Gas?" to the play's concluding scene offsets such a skeptical reaction. It does so by focusing on revolution, rather than token gestures of resistance and dissent that are likely to achieve little. The counterbalancing role played by "Was hilft gegen Gas?" may explain Brecht's determination that the scene should be included among the sequence used in "99%" and his retention of this episode in the seventeen-scene script for the cycle that he constructed in the spring of 1938 (details in *FM* 117).

---

54 *Brecht-Kommentar*, 3:177.
55 In his prefatory remarks leading up to the *Kontrollchor*'s singing of "Lob der illegalen Arbeit," the *Leiter des Parteihauses in Mukden* defines the four comrades' "illegale Arbeit" as preparing for a "Revolutionierung der Welt" (*Die Maßnahme* [1931 version], *BFA* 3:104).

5: Songs, Poems, and Other Commenting Devices in *Furcht und Elend* and *The Private Life of the Master Race*

SONGS AND POEMS PLAY A DIFFERENT ROLE in the genetic history of the *Furcht und Elend* complex than they do in the case of such canonical works as *Mutter Courage und ihre Kinder*, *Der gute Mensch von Sezuan* and *Der kaukasische Kreidekreis*. Instead of his usual practice of establishing a fixed corpus of sung and spoken epic commenting devices relatively early on, Brecht experiments at virtually every stage of *Furcht und Elend*'s evolution with a changing repertoire of prologue verses (*Vorsprüche*), sung or spoken epic inserts, epilogues, and assorted framing devices. The main reasons for this change of approach are to be found in Brecht's repeated attempts to have his play appropriately staged and received during the prewar and wartime years of exile, as well as the need to adjust the work's components to changing historical circumstances.

The Preparatory Poems

A striking feature of the early phase of *Furcht und Elend*'s genesis is the number of scenes for which a companion poem exists.[1] No other play by Brecht stood in such an unmistakable relationship to a series of preliminary sketches in verse. (The symbiotic relationship between Brecht's *Deutsche Satiren* (*BFA* 12:61–80) and a number of his antifascist essays is in some respects a parallel, yet more complicated phenomenon.) Although the various preparatory poems have received sporadic attention, there has been little consensus about their function. One such poem ("Die Ängste des Regimes") was already considered in Chapter Two. Uncharacteristi-

---

[1] The principal preparatory poems and the relevant companion scenes are: "Der Nachbar" (*BFA* 14:238–39) [scene: "Der Verrat"]; "Das Kreidekreuz" (*BFA* 14:236–37) [scene: "Das Kreidekreuz"]; "Die Untersuchung" (*BFA* 14:242–43) [scene: "Rechtsfindung"]; "Der Arzt" (*BFA* 14:237) [scene: "Die Berufskrankheit"]; "Wer belehrt den Lehrer?" (*BFA* 14:247) [scene: "Der Spitzel"]; "Begräbnis des Hetzers im Zinksarg" (*BFA* 11:227–28) [scene: "Die Kiste"]; and "Der dem Tod Geweihte" (*BFA* 14:237–38) [scene: "Der Entlassene"].

cally, however, it does not stand in a close exploratory relationship to just one scene, as the majority of *Furcht und Elend*'s preparatory poems do. Instead, some of its individual lines read more like brief jottings for various planned *Furcht und Elend* episodes. As for their function, the preparatory poems might conceivably represent an attempt by Brecht to identify and explore the plot (*Fabel*) of a particular scene, a function that has elsewhere been proposed for the *Vorsprüche* that introduce the play's individual episodes.[2] Given the importance Brecht attached to establishing the *Fabel* at both writing and rehearsal stages,[3] this is certainly a plausible task for the satellite verses he composed before going on to write the relevant *Furcht und Elend* scenes. As has been pointed out,[4] Brecht liked to repeat the social content of a scene in a *Rollengedicht* (a monologue poem in the first person). He did this in order to identify what was socially and politically representative of any scene's dramatization of particular aspects of life in the Third Reich. However, it is unlikely that this was the verses' main function, especially since the subjective perspective of the *Rollengedicht* genre would risk having a distorting, over-individualizing effect on the process of plot identification. Busch misleadingly suggests that the satellite poems reprise episodes *already drafted or completed*, when in fact their composition nearly always predates that of the relevant scene. His further suggestion that the monologue-like nature of the *Rollengedicht* gives selected characters in the play greater opportunity to speak on their own behalf highlights a significant difference between the various preparatory first-person poems and the play's kaleidoscope of scenes based on interaction between two, three, or more characters. What Brecht achieves by moving inductively towards the play's carefully chosen snapshots of typical life under National Socialism via a series of thematically related poems is more than any simple transposition of core content (or underlying *Gestus*[5]) into another genre could offer. Systematically crossing genre boundaries in this way brings about subtle shifts of emphasis, as well as foregrounding details in the episode's prehistory that often do not figure in the parallel scene. Such fine-tuning could, of course, have been achieved without recourse to a *Rollengedicht*. Elsewhere, for example, Brecht experiments with anticipatory prose sketches,[6] and most other plays by Brecht seem to require no

---

[2] Busch, *Bertolt Brecht*, 22.

[3] The *Fabel*'s importance in Epic Theater is outlined in *Kleines Organon für das Theater* §12 (*BFA* 23:69–70) and *BFA* 23:229.

[4] Busch, *Bertolt Brecht*, 30.

[5] For the suggestion that some preparatory poems essentially involve shifts in *Gestus*, see Wagner, *Bertolt Brecht: Kritik des Faschismus*, 233.

[6] For example, the Berlin dialect prose piece "Mitn Kind müssen Se" (later transformed into "Der Spitzel"), in *Mies und Meck* (*BFA* 18:331).

poetic anticipation at all. So why did he choose to go down this avenue on a number of occasions in the particular case of *Furcht und Elend*?

One possible answer is hinted at in Brecht's theoretical writings of the time. His journal entry for 11 January 1941 notes that during the creation of a character even an epic actor's identification with his or her role can be extremely useful (*BFA* 26:454–55). *Der Messingkauf* likewise stresses the value of limited identification (*Einfühlung*) at the preparatory stage. Having asked the Philosopher "du willst nicht sagen, daß ich eine Figur nachahmen soll, in die ich mich nicht im Geiste hineinversetzt habe?" (*BFA* 22:822; you don't mean I should imitate a character in whom I have not immersed myself mentally?), *Der Messingkauf*'s representative actor (evidently a Stanislavskian!) finds himself on the receiving end of a lecture on the advantages of controlled emotional identification at rehearsal stage, coupled with the general need for its avoidance during the performance proper. The suggestion, first made in *Der Messingkauf* (loc. cit.), that an epic actor's "Sichhineinversetzen" (immersing himself mentally) must be followed by a "Sichhinausversetzen" (mental distancing) recurs, albeit differently formulated, in §53 of *Kleines Organon für das Theater* (*BFA* 23:85–86). However, when it comes to specific preparatory poems, the two essential points at issue in the present context are: (i) whether Brecht transformed composing them into an inductive scene-writing strategy, and (ii) the corollary: whether any of the *Rollengedichte* in *Furcht und Elend* were written specifically with rehearsals in mind. In the case of the scene "Das Kreidekreuz," it has been noted[7] that Brecht created a tangential *Rollengedicht* especially for the maidservant, i.e., a poem using her as the episode's "focalizer,"[8] but not necessarily solely with the needs of the actress playing this part in mind. If our conjecture about the poems' preparatory function is correct, we can assume that just as role-swapping was a useful form of mental distancing for Epic Theater actors (*Kleines Organon* §59, *BFA* 23:88), being permitted via genre-swapping (i.e., through the lens of a *Rollengedicht*) to perceive things temporarily from the perspective of another character could be of great help to all five actors involved in *Furcht und Elend*'s "Kreidekreuz" scene.

One striking feature of the poem entitled "Das Kreidekreuz" is its focus on a subsidiary character, whereas the parallel scene's main interest, as we saw in the previous chapter, lies in the barrage of exchanges between the worker and the SA man. The lack of any reference to the worker in the "Kreidekreuz" poem is instructive, for, unlike the worker and the SA man, the maidservant is anything but a political animal. Her *Rollengedicht* performance remains largely that of an uncomprehending observer display-

---

[7] Busch, *Bertolt Brecht*, 25.

[8] On focalization, see Gérard Genette, *Narrative Discourse*, trans. Jane E. Lewin (Ithaca, NY: Cornell UP, 1980), 189–94.

ing little awareness of the encounter's undercurrent of Schweykian subversion and no appreciation of the irony with which the worker gradually
undermines the SA man's bravado. Damning evidence of the maidservant's
blinkered perspective can be found in the way she recalls hearing about the
trick with the chalk cross played by local Nazi agents provocateurs down at
the job center: how the SA man, in her words, "zeigte [. . .] mir lachend,
wie sie es machen [. . .] Wir lachten darüber" (*BFA* 14:236–37; with a
laugh he showed me how they do it [. . .] We had a good laugh about it).
This is her only response. Using preparatory *Rollengedichte* in this way primarily involves learning to portray the mindset of a given actor's character
and thematizing some of the main issues in the scene. It also helps actors
to understand, both from the outside and the inside, other individual participants in a given scene. It can thus facilitate the ensemble's coming to
terms with the challenge of depicting false consciousness.

The full corpus of preparatory poems in the *Furcht und Elend* complex
is noticeably diverse in both method and function. "Wer belehrt den Lehrer?" (*BFA* 14:247) is exceptionally generalized and comes nowhere near
to communicating the tangled predicament of the teacher and his wife in
"Der Spitzel." "Der Arzt" (*BFA* 14:237) is confined to establishing its episode's starting-point and thus merely acts as a skeletal outline of one of the
play's more intricate episodes: "Die Berufskrankheit." Two other poems,
"Der dem Tod Geweihte" (*BFA* 14:237–38) and "Die Untersuchung"
(*BFA* 14:242–43), do, admittedly, assume something approaching the
Olympian stance of "Mitwisser des Stückeschreibers"[9] (the playwright's
accomplices). In this respect, they are closer to the *Furcht und Elend* complex's various framing poems and songs. And not all of the preparatory
poems that form part of the *Furcht und Elend* complex are *Rollengedichte*.

Framing Devices

From the outset Brecht seems to have recognized that *Furcht und Elend*'s
montage of semi-autonomous scenes — often misrepresented, as we will
see in Chapter Six, as one-act plays — needed an overarching epic frame. In
1938, a series of verses entitled "Die deutsche Heerschau," in part modeled
on Percy Bysshe Shelley's "The Masque of Anarchy,"[10] supplied an introductory "Ballade" (Brecht's term, *BFA* 29:209) for the handful of scenes

---

[9] The phrase occurs in "Die Gesänge," a *Messingkauf* poem on the role of commenting songs in Epic Theater (*BFA* 12:330).

[10] On Shelley's significance for Brecht's "Weite und Vielfalt der realistischen
Schreibweise" (*BFA* 22:424–33) and on the "Shelleynähe" of various satirical
poems by Brecht including "Die deutsche Heerschau," see Hans Peter Neureuter
(*BHB* 2:347). A variant form of Brecht's "Der Kälbermarsch" (*BFA* 14:228–29)

used in Paris. By the time of Dudow's production, Brecht had introductory *Vorsprüche* ready for use in the entire sequence. Other framing possibilities were mooted and sometimes tried out in the coming years. Extracts from *Deutsche Kriegsfibel 1937* (*BFA* 12:88–92) were used in a Russian-language miscellany of thirteen scenes published in 1941.[11] An anonymous English translation of this version[12] went on to incorporate verses 1, 2, 4, and 6 of Brecht's "Lied einer Deutschen Mutter" (*BFA* 15:80), the only single-character-based *Rollengedicht* ever to be included in a stage-version of the play. This "Song of a German Mother" (*BBP* 378) was also used in *The Private Life of the Master Race*. The year 1942 had already seen Brecht casting around for a replacement musical framework (*BFA* 29:231), having rejected a trivial sequence proposed by Erwin Piscator where a pianist strikes up "The Star-Spangled Banner," only to be interrupted by a pistol-toting SS man demanding that "Das Horst-Wessel-Lied" be played instead.[13] "Die deutsche Heerschau," substantial parts of which had already been translated into English in readiness for the planned American stage adaptation, was for the time being replaced by another purpose-written song, on different occasions referred to by Brecht as "Lied der Besatzung des Panzerkarrens," "Chor der Panzerbesatzung," and "Lied der Panzerjäger." In *The Private Life of the Master Race*, this new framing song set to music by Hanns Eisler, composer of the Comintern anthem, remains untitled and, like "Lied einer Deutschen Mutter," is thus deprived of the usual epic "Gestus des Zeigens" (*BFA* 22:641; *Gestus* of showing). As we will try to show later, the German mother's perspective on past events is in any case too problematic to permit any unequivocal didactic function.

Within a relatively short time span, Brecht's scenic montage had been assigned a number of substantially different frames, each of them based on bold presentational paradigms:

(i)   *Furcht und Elend*'s extended metaphor of a "deutsche Heerschau"
(ii) *The Private Life*'s sung comments of the Chorus of Panzer Soldiers, linking the men's individual pasts with their present activities in wartime Nazi-occupied Europe

---

was set to music by Hanns Eisler in 1943 for use in Scene 7 of *Schweyk* (*BFA* 7:235–36).

[11] *Strakh i otchayanie v III. Imperii* (Moscow: Khudozhestvennaya kniga, 1941).

[12] *Fear and Misery of the Third Reich* (Moscow: Khudozhestvennaya kniga, 1941).

[13] Details in James K. Lyon, *Bertolt Brecht in America*, 135. Towards the end of the Second World War, Berthold Viertel considered an alternative frame introducing the male characters in individual scenes via an interrogation that would serve as an exposition to their scene. Details of the proposal are given in Hans-Christof Wächter, *Theater im Exil: Sozialgeschichte des deutschen Exiltheaters 1933–1945* (Munich: Hanser, 1973), 167–69, and Berthold Viertel, *Schriften zum Theater* (Berlin: Henschel, 1970), 216–21.

(iii) an introductory scene, suggested by Piscator, involving a quasi-informal discussion of dictatorship and democracy in the light of the German surrender in May 1945 (details in *FM* xiv)

(iv) the tales of prior civilian life in the Third Reich as told by the deserting Wehrmacht soldiers in Pudovkin's film version in order to justify their defection to the Soviet camp.[14]

Surprisingly, the best known further framing metaphor with substantial satirical potential — that of the "private life of the master race" — remained lamentably underexploited in the American stage adaptation. Perhaps this was simply because one's private life was no longer private in the Third Reich.[15]

As late as 1945, Brecht remained undecided about just which frame to use. "Natürlich ist es durchaus möglich, daß der gegenwärtige balladeske Rahmen allein nicht ausreicht" (*BFA* 29:355; Of course it's quite possible that the present balladesque framework isn't enough by itself: *BBL* 393), he informed Piscator on 2 June, presumably mindful of the new situation brought about by the recent cessation of hostilities in Europe and the rapidly changing global situation. The Swiss theater director Ernst Ginsberg approached Brecht in the following year (letter of 21 September 1946)[16] concerning a forthcoming Basle production of *Furcht und Elend*, inquiring whether it would be possible to make modifications to the final scene so as to create an appropriate conclusion for 1946, or, if this proved impossible, to come up with a new scene for the purpose. Brecht duly responded with a fresh version of the scene, although he must have been aware that Ginsberg's request had serious implications for any continued use of "Die deutsche Heerschau" (confined as it was to the 1933–44 period) as the play's postwar frame.

Back in 1941 Brecht was able to inform Piscator that:

---

[14] Vsevolod Pudovkin, *Ubitsy vychodyat na dorogu* (The murderers are on their way) of 1941–42. The film's framing strategy is described in Wolfgang Gersch, *Film bei Brecht*, 297. Eisler's account of a film scenario discussed by Brecht, Eisler, and Clifford Odets at Fritz Lang's house on 5 June 1942 suggests that a similar frame was under consideration on that occasion. In it, a series of anti-illusionistic flashbacks would present "die Geschichte jedes einzelnen Soldaten [. . .]. Das heißt: Was war notwendig, um diese Leute in den Panzerwagen gegen die Sowjetunion zu kriegen" (Hanns Eisler, *Fragen Sie mehr über Brecht: Gespräche mit Hans Bunge* [Darmstadt-Neuwied: Luchterhand, 1986], 29).

[15] Robert Ley once boasted that in the Third Reich the only time that German citizens were able to have a private life was when they were asleep (Robert Ley, *Soldaten der Arbeit* [Munich: Zentralverlag der NSDAP, 1938], 71).

[16] Quoted in Erdmut Wizisla, "Unmögliche Schlußszene: Typoskript zu *Furcht und Elend des III. Reiches* entdeckt," *The Brecht Yearbook* 22 (1997), 4. For an English translation of this scene, see *FM* 114–15.

Das Stück wäre enorm aktuell, da es das soziale Milieu zeigt, aus dem Hitlers Soldaten kommen, es ist eine riesige Heerschau, die außerdem noch zeigt, was die Leute hier erwartet, wenn sie hier Diktatur kriegen. (*BFA* 29:209–10)

[The play would be exceedingly timely, as it shows the social background of Hitler's soldiers. It's a colossal military review, which has the additional advantage of showing what is in store for the people over here if they get a dictatorship. (*BBL* 337)]

But he has little to say about the satirical "deutsche Heerschau" image, except to note that the individual scenes with *Vorsprüche* linked to the "Heerschau" metaphor were intended to offer "einen Querschnitt durch alle Schichten" (*BFA* 29:83; a cross section of all German society: *BBL* 280). Some exile German audiences and readers (the dust-jacket of *The Private Life* describes it as "a memorable reading experience") might be expected to know that a highlight of the annual Nuremberg Rallies was "Die große Heerschau der vom Nationalsozialismus eroberten Nation" and that regional Gau Party Rallies, organized on the Nuremberg model, contained similar troop reviews.[17] Hence, just as some individual *Furcht und Elend* scenes took their satirical titles from NS concepts, so too did "Die deutsche Heerschau."

Although Brecht has disappointingly little to say about the extended "Heerschau" metaphor, he is gratifyingly informative about the replacement framing song in *The Private Life*. In place by 1942, it is prefaced by the following stage directions:

A band plays a barbaric march. Out of the darkness appears a big signpost: TO POLAND, and near it a Panzer truck. Its wheels are turning. On it sit twelve to sixteen soldiers, steel helmeted, their faces white as chalk, their guns between their knees. [. . .] The soldiers sing to the tune of the Horst Wessel Song. [There follow the first three stanzas of their song]. (*The Private Life*, 1)[18]

---

[17] For details, see Karlheinz Schmeer, *Die Regie des öffentlichen Lebens im Dritten Reich* (Munich: Pohl, 1956), 108 and 117, and Hans-Ulrich Thamer, "Von der 'Ästhetisierung der Politik': Die Nürnberger Reichsparteitage der NSDAP," in *Faszination und Gewalt: Zur politischen Ästhetik des Nationalsozialismus*, ed. Bernd Ogan and Wolfgang W. Weiß (Nuremberg: Tümmel, 1992), 95–104. The concluding day of the *Reichsparteitage der NSDAP*, the *Tag der Wehrmacht*, was devoted exclusively to a large-scale troop review. Arguably, Brecht's "Deutsche Heerschau" metaphor is a counterfactual to this particular day's events, rather than to the Nuremberg Rally as a whole.

[18] This 1943 version of seventeen reordered and substantially reframed scenes is traditionally referred to as an adaptation for the stage ("Bühnenbearbeitung" was Brecht's term), although in theory the description also applies to "99%" and vari-

The vehicle in question is, strictly speaking, neither a Panzer (Bentley's "Translator's Note" refers to it as "an armored troop-carrying truck"[19]) nor a "Blitzkrieglastwagen," the term used in Brecht's journal entry for 20 May 1942 (*BFA* 27:99; Blitzkrieg vehicle: *BBJ* 234). It is a half-track troop carrier. Brecht informed Berthold Viertel (*BFA* 29:236) that it would appear four times accompanied by a ballad and by Hanns Eisler's variations on the melody of the Horst Wessel song.[20] As a visual leitmotif linking war with capitalism, this would have presented a far more frightening image than its iconic counterpart, Mutter Courage's wagon, ever could.

Paul Dessau, who wrote and performed the "Heerschau" score for Dudow's Paris production, had been replaced in America by Hanns Eisler, whose initial offering was rejected by Brecht as "Filmkitsch" (journal entry for 20 July 1945, *BFA* 27:226) and thereafter discarded.[21] Eisler's score had at one transitional stage been considered for *The Private Life*, but in the event a new song for the "Chorus of the Panzer Soldiers" was used. Brecht not only changed composers from time to time, he was also often unsure which framing device to adopt — or even if one was needed at all. "Die deutsche Heerschau" featured neither in the 1941 Soviet adaptation

---

ous other later productions of *Furcht und Elend* based on a selected set of scenes and framed in different ways.

[19] The vehicle, for which Brecht uses a variety of descriptive terms, is a simulacrum of the SdKfz 7 armored half-track. This troop carrier's main function in the early war years — both during the invasion of France and subsequently on the Eastern Front — was "to move divisions of highly mobile infantry swiftly in behind the [advancing] tanks to press home the advantage" (Richard J. Evans, *The Third Reich at War, 1939–1945*, [London: Allen Lane, 2008], 162). We have found no evidence of any replica of such a military vehicle ever being deployed in productions of *The Private Life*. This was a lost opportunity since such an image would have had the advantage of contrasting the iconic machine itself, by then synonymous with the Wehrmacht's "Blitzkrieg" strategy (see Brecht's journal for 8 June 1940, *BFA* 26:377) and the white faces of the exposed frightened infantrymen ensconced on it.

[20] There is a substantial subtext to the fact that the words of "Die deutsche Heerschau" were at one stage designed to be sung to the tune of the Nazis' "Horst-Wessel-Lied." For the background, see Brecht's 1935 satirical prose piece "Die Horst-Wessel-Legende" (*BFA* 19:381–89) and *BFA* 19:686–89. One draft of the song (details in *BFA* 14:582) is amusingly entitled "Das Horstdussellied."

[21] The original music for "99%" was the work of "Peter Sturm" (i.e., Paul Dessau). It was performed by Dessau on percussion and piano. Although Dessau *sang* the words of the *Vorstrophen* in Paris, they were usually *spoken* in subsequent productions, according to Eike Middell et al., *Exil in den USA* (Berlin-Weimar: Aufbau, 1979), 338. On Brecht's misgivings about the "Horst-Wessel-Lied" parody, see Eisler, *Fragen Sie mehr über Brecht*, 84, and Albrecht Dümling, *Laßt euch nicht verführen: Brecht und die Musik* (Munich: Kindler, 1985), 52.

nor in Pudovkin's film, presumably because its liberal dose of what Brecht called "in die Augen fallende Verfremdungen" (*BFA* 24:521; alienation devices that hit you in the face) risked being censored as "formalist." Yet having initially scheduled "Die deutsche Heerschau" for Volume 3 of the abortive *Malik* edition of his *Gesammelte Werke*, Brecht put it to one side, only resurrecting it in the *Aurora* edition of 1945, after which it became a firm fixture. The song of the Panzer soldiers that had such a high-profile role in *The Private Life* disappeared from use, virtually for good. This degree of chopping and changing raises questions about the relative merits and disadvantages of the framing devices used at various points in *Furcht und Elend*'s stage history. Why in the case of *The Private Life*, for example, was "Die deutsche Heerschau" jettisoned in favor of a weaker "Rahmenlied," ostensibly buttressed by a series of bland commenting verses? Was the change dictated by historical and cultural differences between 1938 Europe and wartime America? And if so, why did Brecht subsequently reinstate the original frame? In the absence of explanatory statements from Brecht or his collaborators, any answers to these questions must remain speculative.

Like the scenes it introduces, "Die deutsche Heerschau"[22] presents the Germany of the years 1933–38 as systematically preparing for war. "Herrgott, es gibt doch nichts mehr, was nicht für den Krieg ist!" (My God, there's nothing left that's not for war) a character complains towards the end of the play, in "Arbeitsbeschaffung" (*BFA* 4:436; *FM* 89). Although the extended metaphor of reviewing the troops as they march past elaborates ingeniously on this idea by finding the "troops" not up to scratch, the scenario can still be read in different ways. Obviously, the majority of male figures we encounter in the individual scenes are civilians soon to be drafted into the armed forces. A pathetic ragbag of recruits-in-waiting, they offer a counterfactual picture to the heroic image of the Nordic warrior that NS propaganda sought to project. A more specific variation on the contrast between façade and reality offered by Busch[23] posits a systematic juxtaposition of the shabby participants in the play's social panorama with heroic images familiar from NS propaganda newsreels, where cohorts of representative groups formed of military detachments and civilians march in formation past their leaders or, by extension, past the play's audience. Although Busch makes no mention of the actual title used for the troop review that formed part of the NSDAP's annual Nuremberg Rally, the play's allusion to this fixture in the program of events actually strengthens his interpretation. By the time of *The Private Life*, with a savage expansionist war being waged on the Eastern Front resulting in an extremely high toll in human lives, the metaphor receives a new twist, as

---

[22] For the German text of the four introductory verses of "Die deutsche Heerschau" and John Willett's English translation, see Appendix B below.
[23] Busch, *Bertolt Brecht*, 16.

the Panzer Chorus reports how "out of the factories and out of the kitchens and out of the breadlines / we fetched the men for our Panzer" (*The Private Life*, 25). Some time between 1938 and 1943, the Nuremberg-inspired original troop-review image has given way to that of loading onto a war wagon the various representative types whom the audience encounters in the American adaptation's selection of scenes. The new frame still retains a figurative dimension, for the omnivorous troop carrier is a cross between the allegorical Moloch image familiar from Fritz Lang's film *Metropolis* and a modern Ship of Fools. But whereas the pre-war *Furcht und Elend* cycle ended on a note of resistance, *The Private Life*'s "Panzerkarren" grinds to a halt, "vereist in der Gegend von Smolensk," as Brecht explained to Max Reinhardt (*BFA* 29:231; covered with ice in the Smolensk region: *BBL* 347–48). After which, as Eric Bentley crisply puts it, "the play ends with the Nazis singing of failure to the tune of their victory hymn."[24]

A variant reading of the "Heerschau" frame would see the civilian "army" the audience is invited to inspect as essentially a synecdoche for an already militarized nation. Brecht once described his play as an attempt to capture

> die seelische Verfassung der Armee des totalitären Staates, *die ja die ganze Bevölkerung umfaßt* (so daß sich das Ausland ein Bild von der Brüchigkeit dieser Kriegsmaschine bilden kann). (*BFA* 29:110, our emphasis)

> [the state of mind prevailing in the army of the totalitarian state, *which is a cross section of the population as a whole* (to give people outside Germany an idea of the fragility of this war machine). (*BBL* 292, our emphasis)]

In the pre-1939 scenario, the work thus reviews a figurative army, consisting of members of the cowering, capitulating society that makes up the real Wehrmacht's hinterland, whereas *The Private Life* — less convincingly — attempts to bring out the causal factors (including *Gleichschaltung*, widespread fear of victimization, misery, and moral capitulation) linking the debacle in Russia to the earlier Third Reich phase of civilian conditioning for total war. One common denominator, whichever interpretation one decides on, is the way the presentational metaphor recurs as a leitmotif running the breadth of the entire play from the introductory metaphor ("Dort kommen sie herunter / Ein bleicher, kunterbunter / Haufe") across each subsequent verse ("Dort kommen SS-Offiziere," "Es kommen die SA-Leute," "Dann kommen die Herren Richter" and so on). What could have been relatively autonomous scenes are in this way integrated into the symbolic troop review or, in *The Private Life* version, into a pattern of events leading from the "private" fear and misery of pre-1939

---

[24] Bentley, "Bertolt Brecht and His Work," in *The Private Life*, 135.

Germany via wholesale conscription to the disastrous failure of the Wehrmacht's massive Russian offensive.

Despite the troop-review/march-past image's undeniable binding function, it has often been assumed that the title "Die deutsche Heerschau" (at one stage under consideration for the entire *Furcht und Elend* cycle) referred simply to the first four verses.[25] Yet when Brecht pre-published a number of individual *Furcht und Elend* scenes in *Das Wort*, and assigned them an appropriate *Vorspruch*, the relevant prologue verse was in many cases followed by the attribution "Aus 'Die deutsche Heerschau,'"[26] thus stressing the continuity between the first four verses and all thirty-four "prologue" verses (some *Vorsprüche* have two). The erroneous assumption that the prologue's title only referred to the four verses introducing the play could have been influenced by the admittedly marked contrast between the first-person plural verses (an example of what Brecht called "reimlose Lyrik mit unregelmäßigen Rhythmen" [rhymeless verse with irregular rhythms]) and the mocking march-beat of the majority of *Vorsprüche* prefacing individual scenes. Yet this is by no means an insuperable interpretive challenge if one views the shift in style in the context of other works by Brecht. In *Die Dreigroschenoper* and *Mutter Courage und ihre Kinder*, for instance, Brecht creates an effect of what he calls reciprocal defamiliarization ("gegenseitige Verfremdung") by intercalating songs in contrasting styles. In "Die deutsche Heerschau," comparable antithetical styles and registers are easily accounted for by reference to changes in subject matter or mood, as we leave the reviewing rostrum to descend, metaphorically speaking, to inspect individual behavior at grassroots level. While the initial prologue verses radiate an assured sense of political omniscience (be it that of the dramatist, the acting ensemble, or even the audience), the *Vorsprüche* satirize what is about to happen, at the same time as briskly establishing the political context.

---

[25] Possibly influenced by Brecht's distinction between introductory "Balladenstrophen" — which he initially hoped W. H. Auden would translate — and the "Zwischensprüche" (already translated by Ferdinand Reyher and Hans Viertel), some commentators reason that only the initial "prologue" verses constitute "Deutsche Heerschau." For example, Busch, *Bertolt Brecht*, 22, distinguishes between the "Prolog 'Die deutsche Heerschau'" and the *Vorsprüche*. James K. Lyon (*BHB* 1:345) makes a similar distinction between the "Prolog *Die deutsche Heerschau*" and what he terms "die lyrischen Mottos" to the individual scenes. Joachim Lucchesi and Ronald K. Shull, *Musik bei Brecht* (Frankfurt am Main: Suhrkamp, 1988), 655, talk of "Vorstrophen" and "Verbindungsstrophen."

[26] See, for example, the *Vorsprüche* to "Arbeitsdienst," "Die Stunde des Arbeiters," and "Die Kiste," prepublished under the collective title "'Deutschland — Ein Greuelmärchen': Aus dem gleichnamigen Szenen-Zyklus," *Das Wort* 3 (July 1938), 35–39.

In relinquishing "Die deutsche Heerschau" in favor of a completely
new frame for *The Private Life*, "a play he considered conventional enough
for American audiences to understand,"[27] Brecht of course did more than
merely replace one extended framing song with another. The new Chorus
of the Panzer Soldiers is only one part of a complex, multi-layered framing strategy involving sung elements at both the beginning and end of
the play, as well as in the gaps between its three constituent parts. Added
to which, "a voice speaking out of the darkness,"[28] referred to throughout simply as "The Voice," comments on individual scenes, while "Lied
einer Deutschen Mutter" (deprived of its title, but in English translation
introduced with the words "A WOMAN'S VOICE SINGS" [*The Private
Life*, 109]) supplies what is to all intents and purposes a second epilogue.
If anyone still needed ammunition with which to attack Georg Lukács's
assumption that with *Furcht und Elend* Brecht had returned for good to
the Socialist Realist fold, these interlocking "kommentarische Elemente in
der Darstellung" (*BFA* 22:713; commenting elements in the depiction),
involving all three genres, cross-cut with the intermittent *Geräuschkulisse*
supplied by the armored troop carrier's loud engine, offer ample evidence
to the contrary. Such an abundance of epic paraphernalia arguably reflects
the conditions under which *The Private Life* was conceived for staging in America. It bears unmistakable signs of having been created "for
Broadway."[29] As this suggests, Brecht felt the need to court an "Aristotelian" audience conditioned by Stanislavskian theater and method acting,
while at the same time working with epic, "anti-Aristotelian" counterbal-
ances (e.g., the display throughout entire scenes of a backdrop of swastika
flags or a placard giving information about location and date "in enormous
black letters" [*The Private Life*, 2 et passim]). On his own terms, Brecht
may have created a relatively "closed" Aristotelian structure for U.S. audiences, but for that very reason he needed to design a more complex distancing frame than *Furcht und Elend* originally possessed: for example,
through the clustering of scenes into parts, the use at the end of each
part of emotive "curtain" silences in lieu of the usual disembodied Voice's
comments, and the supplementing of "Lied einer Deutschen Mutter" (set
by Eisler for solitary voice and piano to contrast with the boisterous singing of the Panzer chorus) with a military marching song and three further
historicizing verses from the Panzer chorus to culminate in a grand finale.
In general, emotional scenes in *The Private Life* for this reason come at the

---

[27] Lyon, *Bertolt Brecht in America*, 132.

[28] Translator's Note, *The Private Life*, n.p.

[29] Lucchesi and Shull, *Musik bei Brecht*, 656. In fact, it made its debut at the
Wheeler Hall of the University of California, Berkeley on 7 June 1945, to be followed by an off-Broadway reprise at the New York "Theatre of all Nations" five
days later (details in Lyon, *Bertolt Brecht in America*, 133–41).

end of each part, while the final strategic location of the archetypal grieving German mother's lament near the end of Part Three induces a powerful dramatic effect via the exploitation of controlled empathy. In contrast to Aristotelian theater's gratuitous emotionalism (as Brecht saw it), the feelings generated by "Lied einer Deutschen Mutter" create what he regarded as acceptable empathy ("eine Einfühlung erlaubter Art," journal entry for 23 November 1938, *BFA* 26:326). There are various other residual problematic features to *The Private Life*'s hybrid combination of Aristotelian and epic elements, ones that Brecht eventually avoided by cutting the Gordian knot and readopting "Die deutsche Heerschau" as the frame for future productions of *Furcht und Elend*. Earlier, we expressed surprise that the highly effective "Heerschau" frame had been summarily rejected in favor of a combination of weaker framing song and the Voice's frequently bland comments. What follows is intended to substantiate this charge.

The Voice, usually speaking in the first-person plural and often seeming to speak collectively for the entire NS regime and its accomplices, serves a variety of functions in *The Private Life*. At times it delivers retrospective comment rather than mere scene-setting information; elsewhere it offers a mixture of both and at other times little more than floating generalizations. Substantial differences in quality and function can be found in the case of the following juxtaposition of *Vorsprüche* used in *Furcht und Elend* with corresponding verse-comments spoken by the Voice. Our first pair introduces "Der Verrat" / "The Betrayal":

> Dort kommen Verräter, sie haben
> Dem Nachbarn die Grube gegraben
> Sie wissen, daß man sie kennt.
> Vielleicht: die Straße vergißt nicht?
> Sie schlafen schlecht: noch ist nicht
> Aller Tage End. (*BFA* 4:344)

> [The next to appear are the traitors
> Who've given away their neighbours.
> They know that people know.
> If only the street would forget them!
> They could sleep if their conscience would let them
> But there's so far still to go. (*FM* 6)]

In *The Private Life*, the above German *Vorspruch* is more loosely translated as:

> Thus neighbor betrayed neighbor.
> Thus the common folk devoured each other
> and enmity grew in the houses and in the precincts.
> And so we went forth with confidence

> and shoved onto our Panzer
> every man who had not been slain:
> a whole nation of betrayers and betrayed
> we shoved onto our iron chariot. (*The Private Life*, 3)

The *Vorspruch* to "Der Verrat" focuses on the act of denunciation and the fact that it might even be more injurious to the accusers' reputations than to their victim. The bald statement "sie haben dem Nachbarn die Grube gegraben" foreshortens the chain of events leading from arrest to interrogation, verdict and, after protective custody, possible death in a concentration camp. What is more, the denouncers are shown to be more fearful of the possibility that they might be treated as people not to be trusted ("Vielleicht: die Straße vergißt nicht?"). The lines "noch ist nicht / Aller Tage End" put into words the fear that their actions will leave them with much unfinished business in the community when the war is over. Even before the scene has begun, the *Vorspruch* has established a picture of the fear of "the oppressors" as well as the predicament of "the oppressed," as distinguished in section B132 of *Der Messingkauf* (*BFA* 22:799). Little of this is to be found in the verse from *The Private Life* with its blandly bleak image of "common folk devour[ing][30] each other and [growing] enmity in the houses and in the precincts." At most, these lines possibly justify the Panzer soldiers' proud claim to have consigned "a whole nation of betrayers and betrayed" to their armored troop carrier. Gone now, though, is any lingering sense of guilt or fear that they might one day be called to account. In its place comes collective boasting about the way the Third Reich's war machine press-ganged its citizens into military service. Any coming to terms with Third Reich Germany's past will have to be the audience's task, for it looks unlikely in the case of the characters we meet on stage.

The *Private Life* verse-comment — in contrast to the positioning of the original *Furcht und Elend Vorsprüche* — *follows* the scene in the above pairing, whereas in the illustrations from "In Search of Justice" / "Rechtsfindung" offered below, it comes first. In *The Private Life*, the verse creates a bridge between the play's picture of legal conditions in Nazi Germany in 1935 and the Nazis' subsequent misdemeanors in occupied France.

> And there are judges also on our Panzer,
> clever at taking hostages, picking out a hundred victims
> accused of being Frenchmen

---

[30] The verb echoes the metaphor of fascism as "cannibalism" that was popular in Soviet antifascist discourse at this time. See, for example, Edmund Silberner, *Kommunisten zur Judenfrage*, 209.

and convicted of loving their country,
for our judges are trained in the German Law
and know at last what is demanded of them. (*The Private Life*, 49–50)

Dann kommen die Herren Richter
Denen sagte das Gelichter:
Recht ist, was dem deutschen Volke nützt.
Sie sagten: wie sollen wir das wissen?
So werden sie wohl Recht sprechen müssen
Bis das ganze deutsche Volk sitzt. (*BFA* 4:363)

[The judges follow limply.
They were told that justice is simply
What serves our People best.
They objected: how are we to know that?
But they'll soon be interpreting it so that
The whole people is under arrest. (*FM* 26)]

The *Vorspruch* to "Rechtsfindung" identifies the legal-political context by quoting from Reichsrechtsführer und Reichskommissar Hans Frank's notorious decree that "Recht ist, was dem deutschen Volke nützt"; it then goes on to prophesy that "die Herren Richter" will create a nightmare situation as a result of which the entire German people will eventually end up behind bars. In contrast, the stanza introducing "In Search of Justice" moves the time frame on from a setting given in *Aurora* as "1934" to a wartime situation where zealous German administrators are already imposing punitive conditions on the citizens of occupied territories. In a neat twist, the defamiliarizing image of bundling even compliant judges onto what is now referred to as a "Panzer" (perhaps the noun is intended to accentuate the link between conditioning for war and a corrupt militarized legal system) has the effect of equating the judiciary's draconian application of Nazi law in Poland with sitting in a tank and firing at unprotected civilians.

Such qualitative differences between the above sample of *Furcht und Elend* verses and those in *The Private Life* are not untypical. The framing elements in *Furcht und Elend* and those supplied by the Panzer Chorus and the Voice in *The Private Life* are differently weighted and serve divergent purposes. The *Furcht und Elend Vorsprüche* establish their episode's pre-war context from a critical standpoint. Satirical wordplays, ridiculing rhymes, and a bag of assorted one-off presentational tricks make a substantial contribution to the caustic humor with which "Die deutsche Heerschau" introduces its material. In contrast, the Voice's portentous pseudo-comments in *The Private Life* frequently fail to situate or preemptively undermine their scenes in an adequate way. Too often they seem content to imply a link between wartime situations and features of earlier private life in the Third Reich. In doing so, they lack an adequately aggressive vantage point. In later scenes, they become shorter and more generalized, as if genuine critical comment was by now superfluous. The Voice continues to concentrate myopically on the loading of individual characters onto the armored troop carrier (though some of them would have needed little persuasion!). As a consequence, the new frame devotes too much attention to the figures' present predicament on the Eastern Front at the expense of the original *Furcht und Elend*'s focus on the daily experiences of people living under threat from the NS regime's surveillance systems and on the wider consequences of social regimentation. We will revisit this feature at the end of the present chapter, where we explore the frame's role in creating *The Private Life*'s double time-structure and the importance of this for an appreciation of the play's uncontainable undercurrent of political optimism vis-à-vis the question of the antifascist struggle.

An endnote to *GW* reproduces "eine spätere Epilogstrophe" (*BBA*, 429/06):

> Wir haben sein Heer gesehen
> Es wird ihm bleiben stehen
> In Sumpf und Niederlag.
> Wir würden lachend drauf zeigen
> Wär's nicht unser Bruder und Eigen
> Was da verkommen mag. (*GW* 3:2*)

> [We'll watch them follow the band till
> The whole lot comes to a standstill —
> A beaten, bogged-down élite.
> We'd laugh till we were crying
> If it weren't for our brothers dying
> To bring about his defeat. (*FM* 122)]

It is clear from the terms in which this stanza was subsequently presented[31] that the undated replacement epilogue could possibly have been used in some GDR productions. As we saw in Chapter Four, Brecht spent a considerable time searching for a satisfactory conclusion to the play.[32] He seems to have abandoned the above replacement epilogue-verse — which was just as well, given its inability to furnish a conclusion pointing in the

---

[31] Werner Hecht et al., eds., *Bertolt Brecht: Sein Leben und Werk* (Berlin: Volk und Wissen, 1971), 113.

[32] Writing to Max Reinhardt in May 1942, Brecht returns to the question of *Furcht und Elend*'s conclusion: "Als Epilog könnten die Schauspieler an die Rampe treten und (inhaltlich) dem Publikum sagen: Ihr aber, wenn ihr diesen Wagen aufhaltet — und haltet ihn auf, um Gottes willen, haltet ihn mit Gewalt auf! — vergeßt nicht, daß Gewalt nicht genügt in einer Welt, die so kalt ist" (*BFA* 29:232).

right political direction and capable of delivery in an appropriate tone. In any case, "Plebiscite"/"Volksbefragung" already contained a stirring call to arms in the shape of a condemned father's letter to his son. It would have been foolhardy for Brecht to abandon this scene, especially given the "Aristotelian" catharsis of closure that it offered American audiences, with its positive valorization of resistance that had, prior to *The Private Life*, been put into question by "Die Wahl" and, more radically, by "Was hilft gegen Gas?" Although Brecht had originally tried to persuade Dudow to include "Was hilft gegen Gas?" in "99%," this did not happen. Of course, one can see why it would have been unwise for an exile writer to include such pro-revolution propaganda in *The Private Life*. Even with the USSR having now become the United States' ally, this would have been an imprudent move. At a time when the Second World War was coming to an end, German resistance was largely an unrealistic hope and ran counter to the Allies' policies for a defeated Third Reich Germany.

Fortunately, the American version's overdetermining, at times even confusing, multiplicity of epic devices was limited to the second brief phase of *Furcht und Elend*'s complicated history. In preparation for his planned return to Europe, Brecht reverted to the "Heerschau" frame, now expanded to give a broader panoramic picture than was offered in the Paris, Soviet, or American productions, and depending on a sharper arsenal of commenting devices. In doing so, he also successfully returned the play to *Aurora*'s concretization of episodes leading up to and including the historical *Anschluss* turning-point without any longer extending the time-frame to the period of the German Army's rout in Russia.[33]

"Das Mahnwort"

"Das Mahnwort," one of *Furcht und Elend*'s underestimated scenes, appears as Scene 23 in *Malik* and Scene 21 in *Aurora*. It is tempting, in view of the tendency for increasing amounts of documentary material to be included in some of the later *Furcht und Elend* scenes, to assume that the episode must be based on an actual poem with this title. However, no

---

[33] *The Private Life* was the first version of the play to include systematically place and date for each individual scene, information in most cases subsequently transferred to *Aurora*. Although individual scenes generally have the same date in both versions, a few are different: Oranienburg becomes Esterwegen and Schwetzingen is changed to Aichach. While it is possible to speculate about why some dates were also changed (e.g., 1934 to 1935 for "In Search of Justice," 1938 to 1936 for "The Old Nazi," and 1938 to 1937 for "Two Bakers"), such subtleties would be lost on non-German audiences and readers.

source has been located to date. Jürgen Kreft confesses to having drawn a blank about Brecht's putative source here:

> Ich weiß nicht, ob dieses Mahnwort authentisch ist oder von Brecht erfunden. Ich habe Zweifel, nicht so sehr, weil es mir bei der HJ nicht begegnet ist, sondern weil es im Reim und Rhythmus eher wie ein von Brecht für diesen Zweck gemachtes Gedicht wirkt. So ist z.B. als Reim auf *Sieg* in einem Nazi-Gedicht *Krieg*, auch noch *flieg* (*flieg, deutsche Fahne, flieg!*), jedenfalls kaum *gib* zu erwarten. Entsprechendes gilt für die fünf Hebungen in der vierten Zeile. Die Nazi-Lyrik war meist säuberlich konventionell gearbeitet. Auch der Vers: "Und dann schieße, steche, schlage" fällt ziemlich aus dem Rahmen der eher neuromantisch getönten Nazi-Kriegslyrik, paßt aber gut zu Brechts Anti-Kriegstexten. Freilich ist die Nazi-Lyrik nicht so einheitlich, daß ein derartiges Mahnwort-Gedicht nicht doch in ihr hätte Platz finden können.[34]

Whether or not such a source poem existed, the scene remains the sole example in *Furcht und Elend* of the NS regime's appropriation of German literature for propaganda purposes, as well as representing a rare occurrence of the phenomenon in Brecht's antifascist plays as a whole.

In *Aurora*, the scene's setting is given as "Chemnitz, 1937. Ein Raum der Hitlerjugend." Two items are on the HJ *Heimabend* program that evening. First comes training in gas mask use, an exercise soon to become obligatory for the German armed forces and even for civilians in key posts, although here implying that the country must prepare itself against enemy attack and thus misleadingly suggesting that the forthcoming war will be a "defensive" one on a beleaguered Germany's part. This is followed by a test to see if the boys can recite the NS pro-war propaganda poem "Das Mahnwort." Whereas gas mask training re-awakens horrific images of the effect of mustard gas during the First World War, the poem "Das Mahnwort" relies on archaic clichés and heroic rhetoric to make modern warfare appear more acceptable, despite still-recent memories of the Western Front.

The first stanza of "Das Mahnwort" encourages the young boys to learn to confront death bravely: "Lern dem Tod ins Auge blicken / Ist das Mahnwort unserer Zeit" (*BFA* 4:431; Thou shalt gaze on death unblinking — / Saith the motto of our age —: *FM* 84). They will be better equipped, it assures them, to fight and die for their country if they go off to battle in the right spirit: "Wird man dich ins Feld einst schicken / Bist du gegen jede Furcht gefeit" (*BFA* 4:431; Sent into the fray unflinching / Heedless of the battle's rage: *FM* 84). Ironically it is only *fear* from which they are promised immunity, not the threat of death itself. This seductive assurance

---

[34] Jürgen Kreft, "Realismusprobleme bei Brecht," http://kgg.german.or.kr/kzg/kzgtxt/68_13.pdf (accessed 26 February 2009).

is followed by the insidious suggestion that death in battle is in any case the true purpose of being a German in the Third Reich (i.e., this is "das Mahnwort unserer Zeit"). The poem offers not one exhortation ("Mahnwort"), but two. Willett translates the poem's title as "The Motto" (*FM* 83), which may capture some of the German noun's connotations, but misses others. Whereas the first stanza is about the need to steel oneself for the task to come, the second turns to the deeds of selfless heroism the boys will be called upon to perform on the field of battle.[35]

> Und dann schieße, steche, schlage!
> Das erfordert unser Sieg.
> Sei ein Deutscher, ohne Klage
> Dafür stirb und dafür gib. (*BFA* 4:431)

> [Victory is ours for gaining.
> Beat, stab, shoot them so they fall.
> Be a German uncomplaining
> Die for this and give your all. (*FM* 84–85)]

The episode, viewed in its entirety, functions as a timely exhortation not to be deceived by the false NS rhetoric of belligerent idealism deployed to brainwash young people in preparation for the ultimate sacrifice. The focus on the practicalities of gas mask training suggests that the scene, unlike the propaganda poem, is essentially about the ugly realities of conflicts to come.[36] As Scenes 22 and 23 in *Aurora* subsequently remind us, German soldiers were already fighting and in some cases laying down their lives in Spain.

Although the "Mahnwort" scene includes a number of boys without gas masks, attention quickly concentrates on the one who is apparently unable to master the two stanzas of the poem. That he is not the only person without a gas mask is politically significant; Chemnitz, an industrial working-class city, would have contained many inhabitants unable to rise to such a luxury as a gas mask, as well as many others with ideological reasons for not wanting to be constantly reminded that the NS regime was on the brink of taking the country to war again. Having to pay for one's

---

[35] For the Third Reich HJ background to this scene, see Gregor Athalwin Ziemer, *Education for Death: The Making of a Nazi* (London, New York: Oxford UP, 1941).

[36] The threat of gas warfare is also alluded to in "Was hilft gegen Gas?" (*BFA* 4:438–40). Here we learn that the gas masks the HJ boys are being trained to use are defective. Instead of fear and fatalism, however, this scene leads to the political conclusion that the correct answer to the gas threat must be concerted action: i.e., emulating the behavior of the mutinying soldiers at the end of the First World War by refusing to fight, as well as going on to depose the rulers who sent them off to war.

gas mask in this context emblematizes the fact that the regime is systematically impoverishing the poor in order to prepare for its capitalist war. It is a somewhat insidious variation on the shabby fact, only gradually revealed in "Das Kreidekreuz," that the SA man had to pay for his own jackboots. They were not standard issue.

As the victimized boy struggles to recite the second verse of "Das Mahnwort," he produces a fragmented — i.e., in Brechtian terminology, "estranged" — version of the jingoistic lines that are the bone of contention:

> Und dann schieße, steche, schlage!
> Das erfordert unser . . .
> [. . .]
> Das erfordert unser . . . Sieg.
> Sei ein Deutscher . . . ohne Klage . . . ohne Klage
> Sei ein Deutscher, ohne Klage
> Dafür stirb . . . dafür stirb und dafür gib. (*BFA* 4:431)

While the boy is able to recite the first stanza faultlessly, his rendition of the second is halting and repetitive. He appears to have difficulty saying certain words. Such bellicose concepts as "unser Sieg" and "dafür sterben" cause him to stall. For the same reason, he keeps returning to the line "Sei ein Deutscher, ohne Klage," as if deferring the last line, possibly because he knows that he has not got what it takes to become a German "ohne Klage."

Although most of the HJ boys think that Pschierer (no first name is given) is simply unable to learn the assigned poem, despite the fact that he had been trying to do so for five weeks, the scene contains sufficient circumstantial evidence to suggest more profound motives for both his failure to acquire a gas mask and his inability to recite "Das Mahnwort" to his Scharführer's satisfaction. As a third boy, who evidently knows Pschierer better, informs the others: "Er kann es doch schon lang" (*BFA* 4:430; He's known it off for ages: *FM* 83), a claim perhaps borne out by the speed and accuracy with which he recites the first stanza and the significant pattern of what he balks at saying in the second one. Another boy's suggestion that it is ultimately fear that underlies Pschierer's hesitation ("Er bleibt doch nur stecken, weil er Furcht hat" [*BFA* 4:430; He only gets stuck cause he's frightened: *FM* 83]) comes no nearer to the truth than the rumor that Pschierer is being picked on because he declined a dubious invitation to go to the cinema in the company of his homosexual Scharführer. Another, more probable, reason for the lad's systematic victimization is suggested by the Scharführer himself: "Du lernst wohl was andres zu Hause, wie?" (*BFA* 4:431; I bet you learn something different at home, don't you?: *FM* 85). With this, Pschierer stands accused of belonging to a family that rejects NS policies, in particular the regime's preparations for war. The Scharführer's final words express surprise about all the fuss being made: "Als ob das schwer wäre!" (Now what's so difficult about that?). Such a dismissive remark is meant to suggest how easy it ought to be for good patriotic Germans to recite a two-stanza poem about dying for their country. But it is the content of the poem that Pschierer has difficulties with, not just having to learn and recite it faultlessly under such intimidating circumstances.

"Die Moorsoldaten"

In contrast to the unsolved status of the poem "Das Mahnwort," one song — first included in *The Private Life* and retained in all subsequent editions of the *Furcht und Elend* cycle — is convincingly authenticated. Because the scene in which it occurs treats the crucial issue of the antifascist Popular Front, "Die Moorsoldaten," written by Johann Esser and Wolfgang Langhoff, original score by fellow prisoner Rudi Goguel,[37] makes an important contribution to the play's resistance theme. The "Moorsoldaten" scene was added in 1942 to replace "Die Internationale."[38] Like "Das Mahnwort" and the socialist revolutionary hymn "The Internationale," the song

---

[37] The scene's source was Wolfgang Langhoff, *Die Moorsoldaten: 13 Monate Konzentrationslager. Unpolitischer Tatsachenbericht* (Zurich: Schweizer Spiegel, 1935), 175–95. (Further citations appear in the text.) According to a letter to Wieland Herzfelde of July/August 1935 (*BFA* 28:518), Brecht read Langhoff's account in conjunction with work on *Furcht und Elend*. Presumably out of respect for his source, Brecht dates it "1934," possibly to suggest that German victims of the NS regime were already anticipating the spirit of the Popular Front before the campaign was officially set in motion. By 1934, the song already served an important resistance function in a number of "wilde KZs" and was no longer confined to the Emsland camp complex. For a detailed analysis of the original song, see Guido Fackler, *"Des Lagers Stimme": Musik im KZ. Alltag und Häftlingskultur in den Konzentrationslagern, 1933 bis 1936* (Bremen: Temmen, 2000), 219–20.

[38] Ilja Fradkin, *Bertolt Brecht: Weg und Methode* (Leipzig: Reclam, 1977), 176, interprets "Moorsoldaten" as a thematically analogous scene to "Die Internationale." While both scenes show concentration camp prisoners moving from cowed obedience to dangerous acts of resistance and each takes its title from the song that serves as a catalyst, Brecht's reason for replacing the one scene with the other probably has more to do with differences than similarities. The two prisoners in "Die Internationale" are not endowed with specific attributes, whereas those in "Moorsoldaten" are situated on a politically differentiated spectrum. "Moorsoldaten" thus contributes to the Popular Front debate in a way that the scene it replaced arguably could not. On this context, see Werner Herden, *Wege zur Volksfront: Schriftsteller im antifaschistischen Bündnis* (Berlin: Akademie, 1978), 38–52, and Raimund Gerz, *Bertolt Brecht und der Faschismus*, 76–86.

"Die Moorsoldaten" is plot-motivated, whereas most material considered so far tends to operate at a metadiegetic level.

There were understandable reasons for replacing a concentration camp scene centering on "The Internationale" with "Prisoners Mix Cement," as "Moorsoldaten" is called in *The Private Life*, and also for positioning the new episode much earlier: as Scene 3 in *The Private Life* and Scene 4 in *Aurora*. Unlike "The Internationale," the rallying song and marching hymn of world socialism, the song "Die Moorsoldaten" soon became specifically associated with the history of KPD underground activities in the early concentration camps (the "wilde KZs," as they were called). Originally performed as part of Langhoff's *Zirkus Konzentrazani* cabaret in Börgermoor Concentration Camp complex (Emsland), it served as "a key song of resistance of most prisoners of the camps between 1933 and 1945."[39] And in the world beyond the camps it went on to enjoy an iconic status comparable to that of the Brecht-Dudow film *Kuhle Wampe*'s "Solidaritätslied."[40] Hanns Eisler's score and Paul Robeson's and Ernst Busch's famous performances and recordings of the song soon ensured its international standing, as did Langhoff's and Bredel's published accounts of the powerful bonding function it had for the NS regime's early political prisoners. In the words of another KPD prisoner: "Vor allem war es das Lied, das die Kameraden fest zusammenschweißte, ihnen moralischen Halt, sowie physische Kraft verlieh und in ihnen Lebenszuversicht wachhielt."[41] However, the song's actual status in 1934, when the play's

---

[39] Joanne McNally, "'Die Moorsoldaten': From Circus-cum-Cabaret to International Anthem," in *Words, Texts, Images*, ed. Katrin Kohl and Ritchie Robertson (Oxford: Peter Lang, 2002), 215. When the song is introduced in Act II of another play written in the same year as *Furcht und Elend*, one prisoner is reluctant to join in the singing because the song is, he claims, "verboten!" (*Pastor Hall*, in Ernst Toller, *Gesammelte Werke*, ed. Wolfgang Frühwald and John M. Spalek, vol. 3, *Politisches Theater und Drama im Exil, 1927–1939* [Munich: Hanser, 1978], 298).

[40] For accounts of the political significance of "Die Moorsoldaten" in the 1930s, see Werner Mittenzwei, "Die Verbreitung der Wahrheit: Langhoffs 'Die Moorsoldaten'" in *Kunst und Literatur im antifaschistischen Exil, 1933–1945*, vol. 2, *Exil in der Schweiz*, ed. Mittenzwei et al. (Leipzig: Reclam, 1978), 162–66, and *Kunst und Literatur im antifaschistischen Exil, 1933–1945*, vol. 1, *Exil in der UdSSR*, Klaus Jarmatz et al. (Leipzig: Reclam, 1979), 238–39.

[41] Reported by one of Heinz Hentschke's informants in Inge Lammel and Günter Hofmeyer, eds, *Lieder aus den faschistischen Konzentrationslagern* (Leipzig: Friedrich Hofmeister, 1962), 6. In the year when Langhoff's *Die Moorsoldaten* was published, the song's origins were also documented in Anon. (Willi Bredel), *Als sozialdemokratischer Arbeiter im Konzentrationslager Papenburg* (Moscow, Leningrad: Vegaar [Verlagsgenossenschaft ausländischer Arbeiter in der UdSSR], 1935), 27–28. Willi Dickhut, who was in Börgermoor Camp together with Langhoff and

new concentration camp scene is set, remained ambiguous. Singing the song back then could just as well have been a tacitly sanctioned group activity as a life-threatening act of outright disobedience. But how could Brecht know this?

His journal entry for 16 February 1943 records a visit from Heinz Langerhans, an old comrade from the Weimar days now working in exile on his study *Deutsche Märtyrer in Konzentrationslagern*. Brecht's visitor misleadingly informed him that "Die Moorsoldaten" was "in allen Lagern verbreitet und erlaubt" (*BFA* 27:149; known and permitted in all the camps: *BBJ* 277). While Langerhans was for that reason inclined to see the song as a Nazi-sanctioned "Sklavenlied" (a song for slaves), Brecht preferred to concentrate on just how it was sung in the camps and what it meant to the prisoners:

> Bei der Negation im letzten Refrain "*nicht* mehr mit dem Spaten ins Moor," auf das Nein warteten immer alle geil und stampften beim Nein auf, daß die Baracke wackelte. (*BFA* 27:149)

> [As for the negative in the last chorus and "*no* more with the spade on the moor," everybody waited eagerly for that "no" and stamped when the "no" came, so that the hut shook. (*BBJ* 277)]

However, other prisoners' recollections of the song's status in Börgermoor — including Langhoff's, which Brecht had read — suggest that any contrast between its being *banned* or *allowed* was an oversimplification:

> Manchmal, wenn wir ins Moor marschierten, etwas abseits vom Lager, forderten auch die SS-Begleiter: "Los, das Moorlied!"
> Dann sangen wir mit Begeisterung. Im Lager selbst sangen die Genossen gedämpft oder summten vor sich hin: "Wir sind die Moorsoldaten und ziehen mit dem Spaten ins Moor." Das Lied wurde zu einem Kampflied und munterte manchen auf, der schon resignierte. (Dickhut, 198)

> Zwei Tage darauf [i.e., after the song's first performance] wurde das Lied verboten. Wahrscheinlich wegen der letzten Strophe, die ja auch wirklich mehrdeutig ausgelegt werden kann. Trotzdem waren es die SS-Leute, die immer wieder und wieder das Lied zu hören verlangten und es gegen die Kommandantur durchdrückten, daß wir auf den weiten Märschen zum Arbeitsplatz das Lied sangen. (Langhoff, 163)

---

after the war edited the GDR reprint of *Die Moorsoldaten*, largely confirms Langhoff's account, but offers an illuminating treatment of the song's disputed status (Willi Dickhut, *So war's damals . . .: Tatsachenbericht eines Solinger Arbeiters, 1926–1948* [Stuttgart: Neuer Weg, 1979] 181–230). (Further citations appear in the text.)

Langhoff recalls numerous occasions on which the illicit song was performed, even though the Lagerkommandant had expressly forbidden it: "'Jetzt singen wir als erstes das Börgermoorlied. Aber leise, daß es die Posten nicht hören.'" (Langhoff, 214) According to this account, the song was also invariably sung before prisoners were to be moved on to another concentration camp or prison: "'Auf Wiedersehen, Kameraden'. Leise wird das Börgermoorlied angestimmt" (Langhoff, 230). The singing of the last verse (viz. the sixth verse in the original Börgermoor version reproduced together with the musical score in Langhoff, 159–62) was especially important to the prisoners, and on occasions even to their guards. McNally emphasizes the "*strategic ambiguity* inherent [. . .] in the final verse, which could be interpreted as being released from the camp as well as from Fascism."[42] But the final stanza could also generate cathartic feelings of aggression, rather than mere pious hopes for a better future. This was very clear on the occasion of the song's first performance at the *Zirkus Konzentrazani*:

> Bei den Worten, "Dann ziehn die Moorsoldaten *nicht* mehr mit dem Spaten ins Moor" stießen die sechzehn Sänger die Spaten in den Sand und marschierten aus der Arena, die Spaten zurücklassend, die nun, in der Moorerde steckend, als Grabkreuze wirkten.[43]

Far from being an expression of strategic ambiguity, as McNally claims, the final refrain, when delivered in the way described above, became a collective gesture of solidarity and opposition. To sing it was a deliberate *Gestus* of resistance.

In 1934, the year when "Prisoners Mix Cement" is set in *The Private Life*, a situation thus existed where the "Moorsoldaten" song could be officially banned at the camp in which it was first performed — and from where it was smuggled out to other camps and prisons — and yet still be requested by individual guards. Usually the final verse was only included "when the inmates could be sure that no hostile ears were listening,"[44] or when singing it was a calculated act of insubordination or a reckless gesture

---

42 McNally, "Die Moorsoldaten," 219.

43 Lammel and Hofmeyer, *Lieder aus den faschistischen Konzentrationslagern*, 17.

44 McNally, 225. According to McNally, "the size of the audience, and number of voices joining in with the song, would depend on where the event was being held: these could range from 20 to 30 (sleeping quarters), 150 in the dayrooms, and 400 to 500 in the washrooms" ("Die Moorsoldaten," 226). Comparable figures are given in Aleksander Kulisiewicz, *Adresse: Sachsenhausen: Literarische Momentaufnahmen aus dem KZ*, ed. Claudia Westermann, trans. Bettina Eberspächer (Gerlingen: Bleicher, 1997), 27. Kulisiewicz, who was a prisoner in Sachsenhausen from 1940 until 1945, makes a distinction between clandestine "illegal" performances confined to relatively small groups, and "die offiziellen Konzerte" attended by four hundred to five hundred inmates. He recalls "die illegalen Veranstaltungen" of

of solidarity on the political prisoners' part. To this must be added, if one is to do justice to the song's complex role in Brecht's "Moorsoldaten" scene, that from 1933 onwards prisoners were frequently forced to sing religious or political songs central to their convictions as a form of degradation.[45] At the time of writing "Moorsoldaten," Brecht was obviously able to exploit a far richer spectrum of possibilities than the recollections of Langhoff, Bredel, Langerhans, or Ernst Toller's play *Pastor Hall* offered him.

Presumably for dramatic reasons, Toller and Brecht employ a shorter version of "Die Moorsoldaten" than the full six verses reproduced in Langhoff.[46] However, the song's reduction to three verses should not be read as prima facie evidence of *Pastor Hall*'s influence on *The Private Life*. The song had already been shortened in this way in Lilo Linke's English rendition in her translation of Langhoff's *Die Moorsoldaten*,[47] published in the same year as the German original. In fact, the most compelling evidence for Brecht's not sharing either Langerhans's or Toller's conflicting assumptions about the song's status is the ingenious way in which each of the verses of "Die Moorsoldaten" serves a different function in the "Prisoners Mix Cement" scene in *The Private Life*.

Near the beginning of the scene (*The Private Life*, 27), a work-party of prisoners is ordered by their guard to sing the first verse (verse 1 in Langhoff's *Die Moorsoldaten* and in all other published versions of the song), a command that at this stage would make it seem like little more than a "Sklavenlied" in Langerhans's pejorative sense. In later occurrences of the song in "Prisoners Mix Cement," the situation changes substantially. When the SS man patrols for a second time in the direction of the work party, it is the Pastor — in the German original referred to as the *Bibelforscher*, translated in *FM* as Jehovah's Witness — who alerts them to the impending danger, and Brühl, the Social Democrat, who sings a further verse to allay the guard's suspicions. "Up and down the guards are marching" is appropriately the first line to be sung on this occasion (*The Private Life*, 28), although, confusingly, in Brecht's source (Langhoff's *Die Moorsoldaten*) this is in fact the fifth of six stanzas, and the second in Brecht's shorter three-stanza *Aurora* version of *Furcht und Elend*. Brühl's quick

---

those years: "zuletzt sangen wir das Moorsoldatenlied, Arbeiterlieder und ganz leise die Internationale" (Kulisiewicz, *Adresse: Sachsenhausen*, 26).

[45] On prisoners being forced to sing songs as a form of public humiliation or while being tortured, see Shirli Gilbert, *Music in the Holocaust: Confronting Life in the Nazi Ghettos and Camps* (Oxford: Clarendon, 2005), 116–17 and 134.

[46] While both playwrights use the same verses (1, 5, and 6), the middle stanza in W. H. Auden's version of the song for Stephen Spender's English translation of *Pastor Hall* (Toller, 1939, 74, 97–98) is not the same.

[47] Wolfgang Langhoff, *Rubber Truncheon: Being an Account of Thirteen Months Spent in a Concentration Camp*, trans. Lilo Linke (London: Constable, 1935).

thinking saves the situation and the guard again moves off. Not long after, however, the political squabbling among those in the work party reaches a dangerous crescendo, as Brühl, the SPD man, starts shouting at, and then threatening, the KPD man with his shovel. The Pastor once again warns his fellow prisoners that they are putting themselves in danger of reprisals; and as a diversion another figure, referred to in *The Private Life* as "the Non-Political Man," begins to sing the last verse (*The Private Life*, 29). In almost all published editions of Brecht's play over the past half-century, Brühl is said to sing the *third* verse and the *Bibelforscher* the *last* one. But in the three-verse adaptation of "Die Moorsoldaten" for the American stage (which no longer implies a longer song), the third and the final verse are *one and the same thing*.[48] The verse that in the *Furcht und Elend* "Moorsoldaten" scene is referred to as the *third* is in fact the *fifth* in the original "Moorsoldatenlied," the third in this latter version being one of the omitted verses. What all versions but the authorized American adaptation in *The Private Life* erroneously refer to as the *third* verse is, in fact, the *fifth* (less contentious) one. To point this out is not pedantry. The well-documented resistance associations of the final, highly provocative verse of "Die Moorsoldaten" endow the concluding part of this important scene with a particularly charged significance. The three verses used in *The Private Life* are: (i) a scene-setting verse, (ii) one concentrating on the omnipresent threat from the guards, and (iii) the utopian last verse projecting the vision of a world where camp life is a past chapter and the prisoners are once more free to live their own lives, a vision that some of their guards might well count as resistance and others might share. In *The Private Life*, this dangerously subversive final verse, sung by the Non-Political Man, reminds his fellow prisoners that their oppression cannot last forever: "One day we shall say rejoicing: / Home, now you are mine again!" (*The Private Life*, 29). In true Popular Front spirit, the verse is thus used to advise them to bury the hatchet and find common cause so that such a future can come about. This is precisely how the scene ends, with all the prisoners refusing to point a finger of accusation after singing what has once more become *their* song. The third and final verse clearly plays a leading instrumental role in transforming them from a collection of bickering sectarian individualists into a potentially disciplined resistance cell. It is not just the explosive nature of this last verse in contrast to the two preceding ones, but the specific context in which it is sung that gives it a distinctly revolutionary connotation.

---

[48] Whether Brecht was influenced by *Pastor Hall* is uncertain. "Friedrich Halls Flucht: Dritter Akt des Dramas *Pastor Hall*" was published in *Das Wort* 4 (January 1939), 42–51 and Stephen Spender's and Hugh Hunt's translation of the play (*Pastor Hall: A Play in Three Acts*, London: John Lane The Bodley Head) appeared the same year. Eric Bentley, as translator of *The Private Life* for New Directions, is likely to have known of the Spender-Hunt translation.

If the complex status of "Die Moorsoldaten" and its various verses is not taken into account, it looks as if the entire group of prisoners had suddenly seen the light and acted in a spirit of newfound political solidarity. This would hardly suit Brecht's purpose, as can be seen from his differentiated treatment of the resistance theme discussed in our last chapter.

"Lied einer Deutschen Mutter"[49]

Ana Kugli has suggested that the original "Lied einer Deutschen Mutter" addressed the theme of the losses suffered by all the mothers and wives of soldiers of the time (*BHB* 2:350). When spoken by an inanimate female voice coming from offstage, it moves from being the song of a specifically *German* mother to one expressing largely archetypal feelings. Untitled when inserted towards the end of the third and final part of *The Private Life* (109), the song was conceivably intended to widen the play's perspective to the destructiveness of *all* wars, thus shifting the subject, uncharacteristically for Brecht, from the Third Reich to an essentialist evocation of misery and suffering. Nevertheless, removing the title does not depersonalize the singer's words with one wave of a magic wand; many details still remind us that the *Rollenlied* is specifically that of a German mother. Her story is in fact very much part of the "private life of the Master Race." She blames herself both as a mother and as a politically naïve person for much that has happened. At the same time, though, she tries to excuse herself by finally appealing to the advantages of hindsight: "Had I known what today I know, / I'd have hanged myself from a tree"; "I knew not that arms saluting Him [Hitler], / Will wither where they grew"; "And knew not that who goes with Him, / Never comes back." This strategy for coping with loss and culpability is both problematic in political terms and unsatisfactory within the context of *The Private Life*'s theme of the German people's responsibility for the Third Reich's crimes against humanity. The mother's apologetic *Gestus* combines lamentation (if I had known then what I know now) with a diluted form of self-accusation, tempered by the idea that hindsight was a luxury not available at the time.[50] In the

---

[49] The original four verses of "Lied einer Deutschen Mutter" (*BFA* 15:80) were written alongside a number of other poems by Brecht about the cost of war to the Home Front and developments on the Eastern Front, including "Ich lese von der Panzerschlacht," "Und was bekam des Soldaten Weib?" (used in *Schweyk*), "An die deutschen Soldaten im Osten," and "Jeden Tag greifen die Roten Armeen an."

[50] Two further stanzas (reproduced in *BFA* 15:360) were not used in *The Private Life*, but were added to create the version recorded by Lotte Lenya for the U.S. Office of War Information. These merely compound the mother's combination of confession and self-exoneration: how could she foresee, she protests, that her son

context of *The Private Life* version of *Furcht und Elend*, this would have been a questionable — rather than question-posing — note for the play to end on.

Bentley's English translation of "Lied einer Deutschen Mutter" is positioned between "The Sermon on the Mount" and "Plebiscite." Thus framed, it acquires a different set of connotations from the ones it had when it appeared in *Hundert Gedichte*. In *The Private Life*, the mother's dependence on a religious framework to give her the strength to confess her sins of omission seems sadly inadequate when set alongside the direct action taken by the proletarian resistance group in the play's concluding "Plebiscite" scene (although, as we have suggested in Chapter 4, even this concluding scene may be more challenging and problematic than most interpreters and audiences have assumed). In the scene preceding the "Song of the German Mother," i.e., "The Sermon on the Mount," we learn that the dying man has recently been trying to discuss war with his fanatical Nazi son, but they "always got to quarreling" (*The Private Life*, 107). Even the Pastor tries to fob the dying man off with evasive religious clichés: "'Blessed are the peacemakers'" (107) or "We are all in God's hands" (108). Thus, the likelihood that the mother in the *Rollenlied* that follows could have exercised any positive influence on her son looks remote, even if she had been more aware of what was happening to him and of the crimes committed by the Wehrmacht in Germany's name. Her combined confession and carefully protective self-accusation seem as unconstructive as the Pastor's responses. The mother's only concrete thought (that if she had known then what she now knows, she would have committed suicide) comes across as desperation. Like Brecht's Galileo, she confines the indictment to her own behavior without any considered reference to the regime that was to a large extent responsible for transforming her son into the monster he became. The fact that she learns too late that people who go off to war, as her son did, "never come back" and that his proudly worn uniform will eventually become his "winding sheet" has, as an unfortunate corollary, the fact that her son himself had no real opportunity to recognize the error of his ways any more than he and she had to join forces to help create a better world. Were it not for other adjacent scenes, this song's contribution to the ending of *The Private Life* would have been as dispiriting as the parts of "99%" about which Dudow had once complained.

---

would eventually become one of National Socialism's *Folterknechte* or that, thanks to the regime that her son fanatically supported, "[Deutschland] würd werden / Zu Asche und blutigem Stein." The repeated use of Old Testament language and imagery here suggests that she is content to see confession and lamentation as appropriate responses to her original failure to comprehend just where her son's ideology was leading.

The Private Life's Multi-layered Finale

After the "Song of the German Mother" has been sung, two further components conclude the third part of *The Private Life of the Master Race*. First, "A band plays a barbaric march" (*The Private Life*, 113);[51] this is then followed by the last three verses of the Panzer-soldiers' song.[52] The men on the armored troop carrier initially sang three verses as a form of prologue to the entire play (comparable in this respect to the function of the first four verses of "Die deutsche Heerschau" in *Furcht und Elend*), three more at the end of Part Two, only one at the start of Part Three (there is little left to boast about after the historical turning point in the German Army's Russian offensive), and now they finally take stock of what has happened on the Eastern Front up to the end of Part Three. The mood has predictably become one of pessimism and defeatism. The visual picture of the German soldiers is as pitiful as, and possibly modeled on, Allied newsreel images of the mass surrender of General von Paulus's Sixth Army after the Siege of Stalingrad. This final parody of a troop review offers a savage caricature of Nazi propaganda's heroic image of the victorious soldier:

> When the lights go up the armored car is seen, stationary, frozen on the Eastern Steppes. The soldiers are wrapped up strangely. They try to keep warm with women's furs and underclothing. But they have also come alive. They beat their arms against their bodies to keep warm. One runs round and stares at the motor (ibid.).

While still singing their words to the tune of "Das Horst-Wessel-Lied," a reminder of earlier, seemingly more propitious circumstances under which they would have done so, the Panzer soldiers now display a new mood of bitterness and honesty:

> Two years of conquest in our iron chariot—
> And then it stopped before the world was won.

---

[51] The march is not identified, but given the fact that the Panzer soldiers subsequently sing of how their "conquest [. . .] stopped before the world was won," the most likely candidate would be "Es zittern die morschen Knochen," with its notorious refrain "Wir werden weitermarschieren / Wenn alles in Scherben fällt; / denn heute gehört uns Deutschland / und morgen die ganze Welt" (Hans Baumann, *Macht keinen Lärm: Gedichte* [Munich: Kösel & Pustet, 1933], 16).

[52] In *The Private Life*, the song of the Panzer soldiers runs to ten four-line stanzas distributed across the three constituent parts of the play. When reproduced at the end of *Aurora*, these are, wherever possible, conflated to form twelve-line stanzas.

At times we fear that we have made too long a journey;
We'll see no more the Rhineland and the sun.

For as we eastward drove and it was winter,
Our chariot stuck on Volga's bloody strand,
In the third year snow fell upon the Führer's laurels;
We were defeated in the poor man's land.

Enslaved ourselves, we tried to enslave the others.
By force subdued, we grew by force too bold.
Death beckons from the left and from the right. O brothers—
The road back home is long, and it is cold![53]

References to "two years of conquest" (i.e., dating from the launch of the German Army's Operation Barbarossa against the Soviet Union in June 1941) and snow falling on the Führer's laurels "in the third year" (i.e., during the winter of the Stalingrad defeat and a series of reversals in the Caucasus) situate these verses in the latter phases of Wehrmacht activity on Soviet territory. More significant than the military situation of the time, however, is the fact that these soldiers are finally beginning to show some insight into the contradictions in their collective behavior and the nature of their worsening predicament. The final stanza gives belated expression to their awareness that Germany's "enslaved" armies are at the same time themselves engaged in the subjugation of vast occupied territories. The second stanza's reference to being "defeated in the poor man's land," alluding to the NS propaganda's picture of the USSR as a failed social experiment, at the same time recalls Brecht's conviction that only true socialism could defeat capitalist fascism (*BFA* 22:329). While this last (of three) epilogues fails to end in a spontaneous uprising, it does suggest that even if internal German resistance was disappointingly rare, defeat might still eventually come from the right quarters. There is a similarity between the soldiers' situation as they sing their final chorus and the one recalled by the brother in "Was hilft gegen Gas?"

Ich war 1917 an der Ostfront. Die im Schützengraben gegenüber haben das gemacht, was hilft. Sie haben ihre Regierung weggejagt. Das war das einzige, was half, und es war das erste Mal in der Weltgeschichte, daß es gemacht wurde. (*BFA* 4:439)

[I was on the Eastern front in 1917. The fellows in the trenches opposite did something that [did help]. They threw out their government. That was the only thing that was any good, and it was the first time in the history of the world that anyone did it. (*FM* 114)]

---

[53] Ibid. For a "Rollengedicht," dated 1942, giving an account of the historical background to the second stanza, see Brecht's "Lied der polnischen Juden in der Sowjetunion" (*BFA* 15:69–70).

At the time in history at which the third part of *The Private Life* ends, the German Army found itself in a predicament comparable to that of the Imperial Russian Army in 1917. Among the Panzer soldiers, the possibility of collective resistance still cannot be ruled out, but in *The Private Life* it is merely one option among others signaled in this complex finale.

One commentator talks of *The Private Life* scenes being characterized by a recurrent alternation between a collective voice (the chorus of the Panzer soldiers) and the words spoke by the lone Voice.[54] Yet as we have seen, the Voice tends to use the first-person plural and to speak on behalf of a collective. The interplay between the Voice (words always spoken by the one same person) and the "Chor" (many soldiers singing in unison) has implications for the treatment of the resistance theme, even at this late stage in the play. The differences in function between the original *Furcht und Elend* "Heerschau" and the various scenes' *Vorsprüche*, on the one hand, and the Voice's verses and the song of the Panzer soldiers, on the other, are significant in a number of important respects, as our conclusion to this chapter will attempt to show.

There is, of course, a substantial disparity in overall time span between *Furcht und Elend* and *The Private Life*. Because of the time of composition, the scenes in the former version are inevitably confined to the period 1933–38, while the latter's virtually contemporary frame includes images from the Eastern Front, as well as fast-forward moves to cover the period from 1941 to the first half of 1943 (at the latest). Unlike *Furcht und Elend*'s "Heerschau" verse frame, the one used in *The Private Life* is as a consequence set substantially later than the play's individual constituent scenes, with the imminent defeat of the Axis forces now having become a seemingly foregone conclusion. One might, of course, see the missing years as in some way connected with the Molotov-Ribbentrop nonaggression pact of 23 August 1939 (after which all critical references to Nazi Germany were taboo in the USSR and in foreign Communist Party circles). *The Private Life* thus conveniently leapfrogs the period covered by the pact, its frame focusing instead on the later period of the war, when Stalinist Russia had become America's ally and the Red Army was finally making up for the USSR's failure to take "German fascism" seriously in the early 1930s. The result in the case of *The Private Life* is a play in which, in a manner reminiscent of *Der kaukasische Kreidekreis*, the outer frame is predicated on the defeat of the reactionary forces that dominate the framed episodes. (Pudovkin's film adaptation approaches its material from a similar angle.) The move from the original "Heerschau" frame to the new one is important in other ways as well. The implications are part structural and part thematic in nature.

---

[54] Busch, *Bertolt Brecht*, 13.

In the 1945 *Aurora* edition, the first to contain virtually the full complement of available *Furcht und Elend* scenes, the addition of dates to each episode created a stronger sense of teleology, as well as generally emphasizing the continuity between the montage's individual scenes As a consequence, two parallel narratives are progressively developed from scene to scene: the image of a fascist country systematically preparing for a large-scale war, while increasing its hold on the people until they become, to borrow Ute Frevert's apt phrase, a "kasernierte Nation,"[55] and that of "Widerstand, und zwar wachsend." This sense of patterns becoming progressively more pronounced from scene to scene results in part from the inevitable lack of historical distance in the *Vorsprüche* from the episodes they introduce. The situation is substantially different in *The Private Life*. Here, a later (almost contemporaneous Second World War) perspective is brought to bear, especially through the song of the Panzer soldiers. Our response to each scene is now dictated by hindsight knowledge that most of the people encountered will end up on the armored troop carrier, taking part in a vast military campaign that will eventually end in failure or victory, depending on one's perspective. If it were not for the "Plebiscite" scene and the Panzer soldiers' moments of insight after the final part of the sequence, *The Private Life* would probably have ended up appearing too defeatist. But this danger is offset by a contrapuntal dimension to the new structure, something barely possible in *Furcht und Elend*. The historical vantage point that informs *The Private Life* as a result of the commentaries in the spoken and sung elements attenuates the sense of increasing gloom that the original scenes created. Grouping the seventeen scenes that make up *The Private Life* into three chronological clusters (covering the periods 1933–34, 1935, and 1936–38) — sometimes even assigning them a new date for their new purpose — divides up the period from Hitler's seizure of power to the annexation of Austria into three consecutive interlinked *phases*. In contrast to the highly focused individual *Vorsprüche*, the stanzas spoken in *The Private Life* by the Voice and, to a larger degree, the words sung by the Panzer soldiers assume a greater autonomy, especially since the soldiers comment more frequently on experiences at the front than they recall their individual backgrounds. The end effects of this restructuring and the deployment of a different perspective are: (i) less concentration on the cause-and-effect pattern that Brecht was intent on bringing out in his original treatment of the Third Reich (see *BFA* 22:698); (ii) a dilution of the frame's satirical power; and (iii) a general tendency to divert attention away from "private life" (a theme so central to the "Alltagsfaschismus" approach) towards the military situation during the final phases of the war

---

[55] Ute Frevert, *Die kasernierte Nation: Militärdienst und Zivilgesellschaft in Deutschland* (Munich: Beck, 2001).

in Europe. Thus, Brecht is not just adapting his work stylistically and historically to the presumed expectations of an American audience; he introduces at the same time a new teleological double-pattern into *The Private Life*, one that for obvious reasons could not have been included in *Furcht und Elend*.

6: Epic Structure, Alienation Effects, and Aristotelian Theater

"**D**ER SPITZEL," ONE OF THE MOST POWERFUL SCENES depicting the German bourgeoisie's intimidation by and gradual accommodation to the dictates of National Socialism, was the first part of *Furcht und Elend* to be prepublished in *Das Wort*.[1] The story of Georg Lukács's uncharacteristically positive reaction to this one scene, Brecht's surprised response, and his subsequent theoretical amplifications has been told a number of times, albeit seldom with reference to *Furcht und Elend,* the antifascist work that was at one stage a vital piece of evidence in what has been called "one of the richest controversies in the history of Marxist aesthetics."[2] This episode was a significant early milestone in *Furcht und Elend*'s mixed reception. Brecht had never before been accused of finally abandoning Epic Theater — and praised virtually in the same breath for doing so.

The controversy's starting point, a reassessment of German Expressionism in *Das Wort* and *Internationale Literatur (Deutsche Blätter)*,[3] predicated on the thesis that the movement was an irrational phenomenon that had paved the way for National Socialism, made the "Expressionismusdebatte" a convenient label for the clashes to come. Brecht himself occasionally referred to its latter stages as a "Formalismusdebatte," but in the context of the Zhdanovist and Lukács camps' concerted campaign of attacks on modernism and Epic Theater, he had good reason to see it as above all a "Realismusdebatte." The term "Debatte" was, it has to be said, something of a misnomer, for the schism was publicly enacted as a one-sided polemic. The reason for this was that Brecht was generally reluctant to retaliate in print against left-wing attacks on his work or to engage in

---

[1] Bertolt Brecht, "Der Spitzel," *Das Wort* 3 (March 1938), 3–10.
[2] Eugene Lunn, *Marxism and Modernism: An Historical Study of Lukács, Brecht, Benjamin, and Adorno* (Berkeley, Los Angeles, CA: California UP, 1982), 75.
[3] For documentation, see Hans-Jürgen Schmitt, ed., *Die Expressionismusdebatte: Materialien zu einer marxistischen Realismuskonzeption* (Frankfurt am Main: Suhrkamp, 1975), and David R. Bathrick, "Moderne Kunst und Klassenkampf: Die Expressionismusdebatte in der Exilzeitschrift *Das Wort*," in *Exil und innere Emigration*, ed. Reinhold Grimm and Jost Hermand (Frankfurt am Main: Suhrkamp, 1973), 89–109.

any form of dispute that risked opening up further theoretical rifts between the Popular Front's various literary factions.

In the present chapter's consideration of *Furcht und Elend*'s epic, defamiliarizing, and strategically inserted "Aristotelian" elements, the initial focus will be on 1938, the year of the completion of the original montage cycle, the Paris premiere, and its reception at the hands of Socialist Realism's leading Moscow advocates. This was a time when the main issue exercising those contributing to the realism controversy in the pages of *Das Wort* and *Internationale Literatur (Deutsche Blätter)* was the question of just what forms of depiction were appropriate to exile writing's antifascist struggle. Unfortunately, Brecht complained in a preface to "Über reimlose Lyrik mit unregelmäßigen Rhythmen," a piece written for *Das Wort*, but never published there, "die Diskussion [wurde] zum großen Teil etwas allgemein geführt und die Bestimmungen [blieben] etwas vage" (*BFA* 22:1014; the discussion [was], to a large extent, conducted in somewhat general terms and the definitions [remained] somewhat vague). The opposition's ideological pronouncements, targeting above all Epic Theater, tended to be riddled with generalized accusations of decadence, formalism, and ideological deviation, rather than engaging in any detailed analysis. Brecht's impassioned plea to his critics in "Praktisches zur Expressionismusdebatte" (*BFA* 22:421), "exkommuniziert nicht die Montage!" (don't excommunicate montage!), gives some idea of the quasi-religious fervor with which he felt his opponents were delivering their ex cathedra pronouncements on matters aesthetic. "Die Rede ist wieder vom Realismus, den sie jetzt glücklich so heruntergebracht haben wie die Nazis den Sozialismus" (The talk is once again of realism which they have blithely debased, just as the Nazis have debased socialism: *BBJ* 6), Brecht wrote in his journal for July 1938 (*BFA* 26:313) in response to Lukács's "Marx und das Problem des ideologischen Verfalls."[4] "Die Realismusdebatte blockiert die Produktion, wenn sie so weitergeht" (*BFA* 26:321; The Realism Debate will gum up production if it goes on like this: *BBJ* 15), he was soon to warn.

For Brecht the playwright, at the time working on *Furcht und Elend* alongside a number of other antifascist projects, one overriding personal concern was how to avoid exclusion from the ranks of the Soviet Comintern–organized cultural Popular Front, while continuing to experiment with Epic Theater's interventionist realism. Most writers engaged in the debate, Brecht observed in disgust, "wollen [selber] nicht produzieren. Sie wollen den Apparatschik spielen [. . .]. Jede ihrer Kritiken enthält eine Drohung"[5]

---

[4] Georg Lukács, "Marx und das Problem des ideologischen Verfalls," *Internationale Literatur (Deutsche Blätter)*, 7 (1938), 103–43.

[5] Quoted in Walter Benjamin, *Versuche über Brecht*, ed. Rolf Tiedemann (Frankfurt am Main: Suhrkamp, 1981), 168.

(they themselves don't want to produce. They want to play the apparatchik [. . .]. Every one of their criticisms contains a threat). More than any of his other antifascist projects, *Furcht und Elend* was Brecht's pragmatic response to what soon risked becoming an aesthetic cul-de-sac. As he defined the problem facing him:

> die Theoretiker, die letzthin die Technik der *Montage* als reines Form-prinzip behandelten, begegnen [in *Furcht und Elend*] der Montage als einer praktischen Angelegenheit, was ihre Spekulationen auf einen realen Boden zurückführen mag. ("Anmerkung zu *Furcht und Elend des Dritten Reiches*," BFA 24:226)

> [the theoreticians who recently dealt with the *montage* technique as a purely formal principle, treat montage [in the case of *Fear and Misery*] as a practical concern, something that may put their speculations back on firm ground.]

Sadly, there is little evidence that this ever happened, either at the time or in later contributions to what has since been dubbed the Moscow "Methodenstreit."[6]

Lukács, *Furcht und Elend des Dritten Reiches*, and the "Realismusdebatte"

Furcht und Elend's reception at the hands of Moscow's *Kulturpolitiker* got off to an unusually good start. In an essay published in *Das Wort* (judged to be "ein Kind der Volksfront"[7]) in the same year as "Der Spitzel," Georg Lukács praised the scene in glowing terms, implying relief that Brecht had abandoned "formalist" Epic Theater and had finally decided to align himself with a realist, if not, strictly speaking, Socialist Realist, aesthetic:

> Brecht hat in der dritten Nummer des *Wort* einen kleinen Einakter [. . .] veröffentlicht, in welchem er den Kampf gegen die Unmensch-lichkeit des Faschismus bereits in einer bei ihm neuen, vieltönigen und abgestuften realistischen Weise führt; er gibt dort ein lebendiges, durch *Menschenschicksale* vermitteltes Bild vom Schrecken des faschis-tischen Terrors in Deutschland.[8]

---

[6] See Werner Mittenzwei, "Der Streit zwischen nichtaristotelischer und aristo-telischer Kunstauffassung: Die Brecht-Lukács-Debatte," in *Dialog und Kontroverse mit Georg Lukács: Der Methodenstreit deutscher sozialistischer Schriftsteller*, ed. Wer-ner Mittenzwei (Leipzig: Reclam, 1975), 153–203.

[7] Fritz Erpenbeck, "Nachwort," in *Das Wort, Registerband* (Berlin: Rütten & Loening, 1968), 5.

[8] Georg Lukács, "Es geht um den Realismus," *Das Wort* 3 (June 1938), 112–38, here 138. In the following year, citing *Die Gewehre der Frau Carrar*, "Der Spit-

[Brecht published in the third number of *Das Wort* a small one-act play in which he conducts the fight against fascism's inhumanity in a, for him, new, many-hued, and differentiated realistic manner; there he presents a vivid picture of the horror of fascist terror in Germany, communicated by means of accounts of individual human suffering.]

Three years later, Lukács repeated this positive reaction in *Wie ist Deutschland zum Zentrum der reaktionären Ideologie geworden?* But soon after, having discovered that "Der Spitzel," far from being an autonomous one-act play, was part of a large-scale montage of scenes (montage was one of his bêtes noires), Lukács removed the passage singing its praises from all subsequent reprints of "Es geht um den Realismus."[10] He also made no mention of "Der Spitzel" in *Die Zerstörung der Vernunft*,[11] of which *Wie ist Deutschland zum Zentrum der reaktionären Ideologie geworden?* was a precursor.

Reacting to the compliment (more the result of ideological wishful thinking than sensitivity to literary detail on Lukács's part), Brecht noted in a journal entry of 15 August 1938:

> Lukács hat den "Spitzel" bereits begrüßt, als sei ich ein in den Schoß der Heilsarmee eingegangener Sünder. Das ist doch endlich aus dem Leben gegriffen! Übersehen ist die Montage von 27 Szenen und daß es eigentlich nur eine Gestentafel ist. (*BFA* 26:318)

> [Lukács has already welcomed the "Spy" as if I were a sinner returned to the bosom of the Salvation Army. Here at last is something taken straight from life! He overlooks the montage of 27 scenes, and the fact that it is actually only a table of gests. (*BBJ* 13)]

Lukács's unexpectedly condescending pat on the back and Brecht's response to it need to be seen in context. As the reference to a "Montage von 27 Szenen" shows, Brecht tends to think of the *Furcht und Elend* cycle as a whole. Individual scenes prepublished in *Das Wort* after the appearance there of Lukács's misrepresentation were framed by such explanatory headings as "'Deutschland — Ein Greuelmärchen': Aus dem gleichnami-

---

zel," and "Rechtsfindung 1934" as evidence, Lukács's Hungarian compatriot and fellow Moscow exile Julius Hay reacted equally positively to Brecht's recent work in "Put´ k realizmu" (The Path to Realism), *Teatr*, 2–3 (1939), 32–39.

[9] Georg Lukács, *Wie ist Deutschland zum Zentrum der reaktionären Ideologie geworden?* [Written in 1941]. (Budapest: Akademiai Kiadnó, 1982), 180–81.

[10] Robert Cohen argues that Lukács realized his mistake some time later and, as a result of his having retracted his earlier published opinion, full and bowdlerized versions of the relevant essays were simultaneously circulating. "Brechts *Furcht und Elend des III. Reiches* und der Status des Gestus," *The Brecht Yearbook* 24 (1999), 193.

[11] Georg Lukács, *Die Zerstörung der Vernunft*, Berlin: Aufbau, 1954.

gen Szenen-Zyklus" and "Zwei Szenen aus dem Zyklus 'Furcht und Elend des Dritten Reichs.'" Given the connection we noted in Chapter Three between *Gestus* and Brechtian alienation, referring to the play's individual scenes as collectively forming a "Gestentafel" was on Brecht's part a further, less explicit rebuttal of Lukács's reductionist image of montage.[12] Over the years, literary montage had been progressively demonized by Lukács and his acolytes as either the product of deliberately haphazard structuring processes, more akin to Surrealism's "automatic writing," the psychological meanderings of Joycean interior monologue, or as a quasi-Naturalist technique that bombarded the reader with a disorienting plethora of random fragments gleaned from the surface of everyday life in a manner reminiscent of John Dos Passos's *Manhattan Transfer* and Alfred Döblin's *Berlin Alexanderplatz*. "Die *Montage*," Brecht remarked of such a prejudice in February 1939, "gilt als Kennzeichen der *décadence*. Weil durch sie die *Einheit* zerrissen wird, das *Organische* abstirbt!" (*BFA* 26:328;[13] *Montage* is viewed as a characteristic feature of decadence. Because unity is torn apart by it, and the organic whole dies: *BBJ* 21). Stressing *Furcht und Elend*'s "Kontinuität in der Montage" (*BFA* 29:98) amounted to taking a private, one-man stand against all those contemporaries who failed — or were unwilling — to appreciate that montage could also be the result of highly conscious structuring procedures and not some dreadful example of what Brecht himself once dismissed as "*anarchische Montage*" (*BFA* 22:440). This may explain his frustrated complaints about "Theoretiker, die letzthin die Technik der *Montage* als reines Formprinzip behandelten" (*BFA* 24:226; theoreticians who recently treated the *montage* technique as a purely formal principle). As far as Brecht was concerned, montage could just as well be a matter of socio-political *content* as of epic *structure*, and this it certainly was in the case of *Furcht und Elend*. At the same time, he found himself at odds with his contemporaries' inability to appreciate the

---

[12] For example, as early as "Reportage oder Gestaltung: Kritische Bemerkungen anläßlich eines Romans von Ottwalt," *Die Linkskurve* 7 (1932), 27–30, and 8 (1932), 26–31, and later in *Der historische Roman* and "Marx und das Problem des ideologischen Verfalls," *Internationale Literatur (Deutsche Blätter)* 7 (1938), 103–43.

[13] Left-wing attacks on montage were common well before the late 1930s. Contributions crucial to the present subject are: Lukács, "Größe und Verfall des Expressionismus," *Internationale Literatur (Deutsche Blätter)* 1 (1934), 153–73; Ernst Bloch, *Erbschaft dieser Zeit* (Zurich: Oprecht & Helbling, 1935); and Hans Günther, "Erbschaft dieser Zeit?" *Internationale Literatur (Deutsche Blätter)* 3 (1936), 87–90. The most virulent skirmishes conducted in *Das Wort* were in response to Günther's polemical review of *Erbschaft dieser Zeit*. Günther took particular exception to Bloch's defense of certain modernist features of Expressionist literature, above all the social-critical role played by montage.

connection between literary montage and the defamiliarization techniques used in Epic Theater to highlight the cause-and-effect patterns that it was genuine realism's task to highlight (*BFA* 22:710–12).

At the time of writing "Es geht um den Realismus," Lukács probably knew little about the broader *Furcht und Elend* concept. Even later, he was likely to have been familiar with at most a handful of prepublished scenes.[14] His *Skizze einer Geschichte der neueren deutschen Literatur* suggests[15] that he still regarded these as either freestanding one-act plays or short sketches in need of further elaboration. He stubbornly maintained this view despite Brecht's repeated attempts to stress in *Das Wort* that the individual *Furcht und Elend* scenes had been conceived as parts of a cycle linked together by the *Vorsprüche* that comprised the macro-commenting device "Die deutsche Heerschau." Not having access to the contents of the cycle in its entirety, at one stage not even knowing that individual scenes formed part of a cycle, was by no means just Lukács's predicament. It was that of many other contemporary commentators. The Soviet editors of *Internatsional'naya literatura* also labored under the impression that Brecht had written a series of independent short plays. "The plays enthralled us so much," Timofei Rokotov wrote to Brecht, "that I turned to the secretary of the Paris League of German Writers with the request that he send us [. . .] the manuscripts."[16] *Sovetskoe iskusstvo* and *Internatsional'naya literatura* each published contributions conveying the impression that *Strakh i otchanaya-nie v III. imperii* (as the play's translation was called in the USSR) was simply a convenient umbrella title for a miscellany of autonomous one-act

---

[14] Apart from "Der Spitzel," Lukács could have known the following scenes prepublished in *Das Wort*: "Rechtsfindung 1934," 3 (June 1938), 6–17; "Arbeitsdienst," "Die Stunde des Arbeiters," and "Die Kiste," published under the collective title "Deutschland — Ein Greuelmärchen," 3 (July 1938), 33–39; and "Die jüdische Frau" and "Arbeitsbeschaffung," published as "Zwei Szenen aus dem Zyklus 'Furcht und Elend des Dritten Reiches,'" 4 (March 1939), 3–10. He may also have encountered individual scenes published in other European exile journals, including: "Das Kreidekreuz," *Die Sammlung*, 1 (1934), 641–42; "Physiker 1935," *Die Neue Weltbühne*, 1 (26 May 1938), 646–47; and "Die Bergpredigt," *Maß und Wert*, 2 (1939), 842–44.

[15] Georg Lukács, *Skizze einer Geschichte der neueren deutschen Literatur* (Berlin: Aufbau, 1953), 141.

[16] Letter of 14 August 1939 on behalf of the editorial board of *Internatsional'naya Literatura*, quoted in David Pike, *Brecht and Lukács* (Chapel Hill, NC, London: North Carolina UP, 1983), 216. Rokotov's reference is to the *Furcht und Elend* scenes published as one-act plays in the French left-wing journal *Commune*. See also [Anon.], "Odnoaktnye p'esy Bertol'da Brechta" [One-Act Plays by Bertolt Brecht], *Internatsional'naya Literatura*, 8 (1938), 259 and Timofei Rokotov, "Malen'kie p'esy B. Brechta" [Short Plays by B. Brecht], *Sovetskoe iskusstvo* (7 August 1941).

plays.[17] If the idea that Brecht had responded to "Alltagsfaschismus" with a series of conventional, "Aristotelian," antifascist mini-dramas might at the time have seemed plausible to some, any detailed analysis of the rhythms and ingenious segmentalization of the individual scenes that made up the *Furcht und Elend* complex — including "Der Spitzel" itself — would have soon revealed that the work's montage was more than just a variation on the innovative macro-structure described in Brecht's early accounts of Epic Theater. It was also a striking feature of the internal structure of most of *Furcht und Elend*'s longer scenes, and, on the whole, the most important ones. In any case, as Brecht's comments elsewhere make clear,[18] the individual *Furcht und Elend* scenes were too diverse, often too brief, and always overtly framed as parts of a discontinuous montage structure characteristic of Epic Theater, to pass muster as one-act plays. The proliferation of signals coupled with substantial internal evidence indicates that the individual scenes were parts of a macro-montage as well as micro-montage structures in their own right.

In Brecht's theoretical writings, the term "Montage" first came to prominence in his famous two-column scheme contrasting "Dramatische" and "Epische Formen des Theaters."[19] Although this remains the locus classicus, Brecht's journal entry for 15 August 1938 reminds us that there is another important context, one central to the *Furcht und Elend* project: "Die Montage, so sehr verfemt, entstand durch die Briefe Dudows, der für die kleine proletarische Spieltruppe in Paris etwas brauchte" (*BFA* 26:319; montage, a process that has been so thoroughly condemned, arose here out of letters from Dudow who needed something for his little proletarian theater-group in Paris: *BBJ* 13–14). Brecht elsewhere spells out what lay behind this claim:

---

[17] Brecht at different stages uses the terms "Szenenfolge," "Szenenzyklus," and "Zyklus" for the scenes comprising the *Furcht und Elend* complex (*BFA* 29:99, *BFA* 22:438, and *BFA* 29:110, respectively). In her letter to Benjamin of 24 October 1937, Margarete Steffin refers to "2 kleine stücke [. . .] aus einer reihe einakter" (*BBA* 2173/67). Benjamin's article on "Brechts Einakter" appeared in *Die Neue Weltbühne*, Heft 26 (30 June 1938), 825–28. Brecht still used the term "Einakter" in the early stages of work on *Furcht und Elend* (e.g. *BFA* 29:86). This suggests either that the project at one point changed from being a miscellany of autonomous pieces to a structured cycle or that Brecht found it more diplomatic to present the collection as a series of one-act plays than as a work of montage.

[18] Brecht's reference (letter to Dudow of late July 1937) to short plays, to be performed alongside *Die Gewehre der Frau Carrar*, together with his comment "Sie sehen, ich komme auch zur kleinen Form, auf diese Weise" (*BFA* 29:36), hardly suggests scenes of a length traditionally associated with one-act plays.

[19] "Anmerkungen zur Oper *Aufstieg und Fall der Stadt Mahagonny*" (*BFA* 22:79).

Damit das Stück sogleich, unter den ungünstigen Umständen des
Exils, aufgeführt werden konnte, ist es so verfaßt, daß es von winzigen
Spieltruppen (den bestehenden Arbeitertruppen) und teilweise (in der
oder jenen [*sic*] Auswahl der Einzelszenen) gespielt werden kann.[20]
Die Arbeitertruppen sind sowohl außerstande als auch unwillig, die
Einfühlung des Zuschauers herbeizuzwingen; die wenigen zur Ver-
fügung stehenden Artisten beherrschen die epische Spielweise, ausge-
bildet in den theatralischen Versuchen des letzten Jahrzehnts vor dem
faschistischen Regime. ("Anmerkung zu *Furcht und Elend des Dritten
Reiches*," BFA 24:226)

[To allow it to be performed immediately, under the unfavourable
circumstances of exile, it is written in such a way that it can be performed by tiny theatre groups (the existing workers' groups) and in
a partial selection (based on a given choice of individual scenes). The
workers' groups are neither capable nor desirous of conjuring up the
spectators' empathetic feeling: the few professionals at their disposal
are versed in the epic method of acting which they learnt from the
theatrical experiments of the decade prior to the fascist regime. (*FM*
97)]

The conditions under which Dudow's production had to be put on by a
combination of a small amateur theater troupe with little professional experience and a handful of "Artisten" trained in the techniques of Epic Theater
was in some respects peculiar to the 1938 Paris context. Rising to the challenge, Brecht devised "eine Reihe kleiner Stücke (zu zehn Minuten)," "ein
Zyklus kleiner und kleinster Stücke" (*BFA* 29:36, 82; a series of short plays
(ten minutes), several short and very short plays that I've grouped together:
BBL 258, 280). Some of these were capable of being "carried" by amateurs;
others, because of length or subtlety, demanded professionals. Given this
unique situation, Brechtian montage became associated not just with early
1930s Epic Theater, but also with Dudow's eclectic borrowing from a variety of contemporary sources, including agitprop, political revue, and satirical cabaret. A case could also be made for seeing the play in toto as either a
montage of gestures or a Bakhtinian "carnival" of stylistic registers. Yet as far
as Moscow was concerned, *Furcht und Elend* cried out for swift recategori-
zation as a prime example of all that was wrong with "formalist" montage.
But what about that other important feature of Brechtian Epic Theater: the

---

[20] In a letter to Piscator of late July 1941, Brecht is adamant that the full complement of scenes had to be staged together (*BFA* 29:209). His change of position
possibly reflects differences between the precarious exile context of 1938, when a
writer was fortunate to have even parts of such a work staged, and the new optimism resulting from the USSR's entry into the war against Nazi Germany after
Germany's breaking of the Nonaggression Pact with the USSR in 1941.

alienation device or "V-Effekt"? Having read August Strindberg on one-act plays,[21] Brecht noted in a journal entry for 12 October 1948:

> Es scheint mir möglich, auch für Zustandsschilderungen (mehr oder minder naturalistischer Art) eine Verfremdungstechnik auszubauen; wenngleich sie vorerst wohl nur für Stücke mit echter Fabel etwas ergibt. (*BFA* 27:274)
>
> [It seems to me possible to construct a technique of alienation for depicting states (of a more or less naturalistic type); even if in the first instance it turns out only to be fruitful for plays with a real plot. (*BBJ* 394)]

If it was nothing else, *Furcht und Elend* was undoubtedly a play constructed from a documentary amalgam of many "real plots," although hardly in Strindberg's sense. The obvious question one is left with is: why has there been such disagreement about whether *Furcht und Elend* was, in Brecht's terms, a work of Aristotelian drama (Socialist Realism, according to his Soviet contemporaries) or just another example of Epic Theater?

Brecht's "Trojan Horse" Tactic

In the case of *Die Rundköpfe und die Spitzköpfe,* Brecht made a helpful list of examples of alienation in the Copenhagen production (*BFA* 24:215–16). While he could have done something similar with *Der Aufstieg des Arturo Ui* and *Die Horatier und die Kuriatier,* he was adamant that another of his recent antifascist plays, *Die Gewehre der Frau Carrar,* was a work of Aristotelian (empathetic) drama (*BFA* 24:225) that could only be *made epic* ("episiert") by the insertion of documentary film material. However, in the increasingly ad hominem context of the Moscow "Realismusdebatte," Lukács's obsession with montage seems to have diverted attention, Brecht's as much as his critics', from the equally crucial issue of whether or not *Furcht und Elend* was paradigmatic Theater of Alienation. At times Brecht seems content to account for potential anti-illusionist devices in the Paris production by highlighting the exigencies of the moment. He notes, for example, that:

> wegen materieller und zensureller Schwierigkeiten konnten zunächst durch die zur Verfügung stehenden kleinen Arbeitertruppen nur einzelne Szenen aufgeführt werden. Mit einfachen, nur andeutenden Dekorationen (etwa vor und unter beleuchteten Hakenkreuzfahnen). (*BFA* 24:226)

---

21 August Strindberg, *Werke,* trans. Emil Schering, part 1, vol. 12, *Kammerspiele.* Munich-Leipzig: Georg Müller, 1911.

[Censorship problems and material difficulties have hitherto prevented the available small workers' theatre groups from performing
more than a few isolated scenes. Using simple indications of scenery
(for instance, playing against dimly lit swastika flags). (*FM* 97)]

Although the reference to the scant means at their disposal has an apologetic ring, Brecht and Dudow were doing more than simply making the
best of adverse circumstances. Indeed, other comments suggest that they
were well aware of the fact. On one occasion, Brecht even drew attention to the cunning way in which certain *Furcht und Elend* scenes actually
deployed covert forms of alienation behind a deceptive façade of realism:

> Das Stück ist ein Szenenzyklus, der das Leben unter der braunen Dik-
> tatur behandelt. Bisher montierte ich 27 Einzelszenen. Auf einige von
> ihnen paßt das "realistische" Schema X entfernt, wenn man ein Auge
> zudrückt. [. . .] Auf das Ganze paßt es überhaupt nicht. ("Über den
> formalistischen Charakter der Realismustheorie," *BFA* 22:438)[22]

[The play consists of a cycle of scenes treating life under the Brown
dictatorship. Up to now I have assembled 27 individual scenes. The
"realistic" X-schema is loosely applicable to some of them, if you close
one eye. [. . .] It is not at all applicable to the entire work. (On the
Formalist Character of the Realism Theory)]

One elsewhere comes across further revealing admissions on Brecht's part
that, despite appearances to the contrary, *Furcht und Elend* is a work of
Epic Theater. In an undated draft piece in his *Nachlass*, Brecht admits
that:

> die Sprechweise des Alltags, das Interieurdetail, der Fortfall chorischer
> Elemente und sogleich in die Augen fallender Verfremdungen lassen
> das Stück schwerer als andere als ein Stück des epischen Theaters
> erkennen ("Anmerkung zu *Furcht und Elend des Dritten Reiches*,"
> *BFA* 24:521).

[the everyday manner of speaking, the interior detail, the omission of
choric elements and alienation devices that hit you in the face immediately make the play harder than others to recognize as a piece of
Epic Theater.]

By conceding that this was an exceptional work, a case where it would be
"harder" for the uninitiated to detect elements of defamiliarization, Brecht
implicitly draws attention to the fact that *Furcht und Elend* was actually work-

---

[22] The reference is presumably to Arno Holz's essay *Die Kunst: Ihr Wesen und ihre
Gesetze*, culminating in the famous German Naturalist formula "Kunst = Natur
– x," where "x" stands for "die jedweiligen Kunstbedingungen" (Berlin: Issleib,
1891), 118.

ing with covert estranging strategies. Such a deliberate paradigm shift looks like a uniquely Brechtian version of the "Trojan horse" tactic frequently used in the Popular Front's war against fascism after it had been recommended by Dimitrov at the Seventh World Congress of the Comintern in 1935.[23] There may, in sharp contrast to Brecht's earlier strikingly anti-illusionist works, be fewer "sogleich in die Augen fallende Verfremdungen" in *Furcht und Elend* (the plural here signifying estranging *devices*) — or so it may seem, "wenn man ein Auge zudrückt." The methods employed at times appear to be at odds with Brecht's customary assumption that effective alienation goes hand in hand with ostentatious anti-illusionism and requires staging specifically designed to conform with the epic principle that, as Brecht wrote in "Vergnügungstheater oder Lehrtheater?" (Theatre for pleasure or theatre for instruction?), "das 'Natürliche' mußte das Moment des *Auffälligen* bekommen" (*BFA* 22:109; What is "natural" must have the force of what is startling: *BT* 71). Skeptical scrutiny is thus called for in this matter, but this certainly does not necessarily mean that defamiliarization must be — or has been — abandoned. As we will see, there are as many defamiliarizing devices in *Furcht und Elend* as in *Die Rundköpfe und die Spitzköpfe* or *Arturo Ui*. They are simply of a different kind.

What follows in this chapter is a selective exploration of some of the ways in which defamiliarizing devices were smuggled into what has, with some justice, been called a work of "dialectical realism" (i.e., definitely not "realism" in Lukács's sense).[24] *Furcht und Elend* resorts to covert alienation devices and cleverly disguises the extent to which individual scenes are in many respects still examples of camouflaged Epic Theater, not just token gestures of compliance with the artistic *Diktats* of the Popular Front or the

---

[23] Brecht appears to have taken this advice to heart in the case of *Furcht und Elend*. His letter of 11 March 1937 to Johannes R. Becher makes it clear that he was not averse to applying Dimitrov's Trojan horse approach to the tactics of dramaturgical camouflage. Complaining about Julius Hay's response to Bernhard Reich, "Zur Methodik der antifaschistischen deutschen Dramatik" (*Das Wort* 2 (January 1937), 63–72) Brecht declares "der Aufsatz ist ein Angriff auf jede Tarnung auf dem Theater, er will Dimitroffs trojanisches Pferd partout nicht auf die Bühne lassen" (*BFA* 29:20). Reich's survey included a discussion of *Die Rundköpfe und die Spitzköpfe* and Friedrich Wolf, *Das Trojanische Pferd: Ein Stück vom Kampf der Jugend in Deutschland* (Moscow: Vegaar, 1934), a work on the subject of clandestine resistance during the Third Reich. This was probably why Brecht took exception to Hay's "Angriff auf jede Tarnung," even when it came to dramatic tactics. Another classic illustration of the Trojan horse tactic was the way in which copies of "Fünf Schwierigkeiten beim Schreiben der Wahrheit" circulated in Germany disguised as a first-aid manual.

[24] The term "dialektischer Realismus" was used by Berthold Viertel, quite possibly at Brecht's instigation, in "Der Dramatiker Bertolt Brecht," *Austro-American Tribune* (1 July 1945), 10.

Zhdanovist Socialist Realist aesthetic. But, more significantly, it provides evidence of Brecht's current interest in exploiting his recognition of the fact that the alienation effect is also a procedure found in everyday life.[25]

It was, of course, understandable in the second half of the 1930s that a number of German and Hungarian Marxist exiles associated with the German-language journals *Das Wort* and *Internationale Literatur (Deutsche Blätter)* should have had a vested interest in believing that Brecht had finally repented of his formalist ways. "Soll er sich hundertmal ärgern über die Lukásschen Theorien," Fritz Erpenbeck wrote to Willi Bredel, a fellow *Das Wort* editor, "wenn er sie in der Praxis (trotz seiner inneren Widerstände) dennoch befolgt."[26] Although Lukács's conciliatory reaction came in an article provocatively entitled "Es geht um den Realismus," Brecht insisted in private that *Furcht und Elend was* a piece of realistic drama (*BFA* 22:438). But this claim was one made strictly on Brecht's own terms. As he explained elsewhere, "*Realistisch* heißt: den gesellschaftlichen Kausalkomplex aufdeckend" (*BFA* 22:409; *Realistic* means: exposing the complex of social causes). He charged those in the Lukács "Clique" intent on heating up the Realism Debate with employing a conception of "realism" that was itself essentially formalist.[27] In an earlier part of his letter to Bredel (quoted in *BFA* 22:1038), Erpenbeck explained why Moscow's purist line was nonnegotiable, arguing that the Popular Front was at stake, that it was a matter of winning over the masses. Much later, during the Cold War years, doubtless for equally pressing cultural-political reasons, GDR Brecht scholars rushed to side with Lukács's original verdict. One of them, Werner Mittenzwei, spoke unreservedly of Brecht having *turned towards* Socialist Realism,[28] while another, Hans Kaufmann, talked of his *abandoning* alienation in the case of *Furcht und Elend.*[29] There was even a parallel tendency in the West, to some extent born out of Schadenfreude, to conclude that Brecht had put aside his notorious alienation effects — at least for the time being. Subsequently influenced by Brecht's comments on the epic features that Lukács had ignored, remarks only published in 1973, two years after Lukács's death, much secondary literature on both sides of the Iron Curtain eventually appeared to accept that *Furcht und Elend*'s macro-

---

[25] The arguments in support of this claim are set out in "Kurze Beschreibung einer neuen Technik der Schauspielkunst, die einen Verfremdungseffekt hervorbringt" (*BFA* 22:655–57).

[26] Letter of 20 July 1938 (quoted in *BFA* 22:1039).

[27] In, for example, "Über den formalistischen Charakter der Realismustheorie" (*BFA* 22:439–43).

[28] Werner Mittenzwei, *Bertolt Brecht: Von der "Maßnahme" zu "Leben des Galilei"* (Berlin-Weimar: Aufbau, 1965), 250.

[29] Hans Kaufmann, *Bertolt Brecht: Geschichtsdrama und Parabelstück* (Berlin-Weimar: Aufbau, 1962), 193.

and micro-montage-structures were essentially what still identified the play as a work of Epic Theater.[30] Unfortunately, there has been little comparable reexamination of the work in respect of Kaufmann's equally dogmatic claim about the suspension of alienation. The general tendency since then has been to restrict discussion of *Furcht und Elend*'s generic status to the procrustean terms dictated by the historical Realism Debate, either by assuming that Lukács's remarks in "Es geht um den Realismus" about a paradigm change were largely correct, or following in Brecht's footsteps by reasoning that it was first and foremost the overarching montage-structure that made *Furcht und Elend* a work of Epic Theater. However, despite these shifting verdicts, it would be unwise to forget that many of the essays in Benjamin's *Versuche über Brecht* (1966) use examples from *Furcht und Elend* — a work that Benjamin had seen in Dudow's production in 1938 — to illustrate what is generally understood by "Epic Theater."

The main exception to the tendency to accept Lukács's verdict, a GDR piece by Günter Hartung on "*Furcht und Elend des Dritten Reiches* als Satire,"[31] comes as part of a wide-ranging discussion that took its cue from Brecht's 1938 essay "Weite und Vielfalt der realistischen Schreibweise" (*BFA* 22:424–33; Breadth and Variety of the Realist Mode of Writing: *BAP* 220–28). This situates the play within the context of a broad spectrum of competing conceptions of realism. Despite being in important respects indebted to Hartung's approach, we only partly agree with his choice of evidence and do not always accept his conclusions. Hartung interprets as political satire some of the features we feel are best subsumed under the rubric of "alienation," while we intend to posit covert alienation devices in scenes not even covered by Hartung.

After a refreshingly unbiased account of *Furcht und Elend*'s shameful treatment in the late 1930s at the hands of Soviet *Kulturpolitiker* on the extreme Left, Hartung traces the play's long satirical pedigree, from Menippean satire, Juvenal, German class-based satire ("Ständesatire"), Brant's *Narrenschiff*, and Grimmelshausen's *Simplicissimus* to Kraus's *Die letzten Tage der Menschheit*.[32] Mindful of Dudow's work in agitprop, revue, and cabaret,

---

[30] For example, Franz Norbert Mennemeier, *Modernes Deutsches Drama: Kritiken und Charakteristiken*, vol. 2, *1933 bis zur Gegenwart* (Munich: Fink, 1974), 60–65, and Jan Knopf, *Brecht-Handbuch: Theater. Eine Ästhetik der Widersprüche* (Stuttgart: Metzler, 1980), 147–48.

[31] Günter Hartung, "*Furcht und Elend des Dritten Reiches* als Satire," in *Erworbene Tradition: Studien zu Werken der sozialistischen deutschen Literatur*, ed. Günter Hartung et al. (Berlin-Weimar: Aufbau, 1977), 57–118. (Further citations appear in the text.)

[32] Kraus's play became of particular importance to Brecht while he was writing his antifascist plays (see *BBB* 712). His journal entry for 15 July 1942 records the wish to produce *Schweyk* again, interspersed with scenes from *Die letzten Tage der*

Hartung also considers the play's satire against a second, this time contemporary, backdrop: that of Brecht's indebtedness to left-wing political cabaret:

> das kommunistische Laientheater hatte [. . .] die Linie der proletarischen Revue weitergeführt und sich vornehmlich kleiner satirischer Formen aus dem Reservoir des Kabaretts bedient, bis in den Jahren 1929/30 die Tendenz zu geschlosseneren Großformen herrschend wurde. [. . .] In der Praxis der Spieltrupps führte das sowohl zum beinahe regulären Stück, *zur halbnaturalistischen oder dokumentarischen Wiedergabe des "konkreten Einzelfalls"* [. . .], zu großangelegten Revuen oder zu nichtnaturalistischen, stark verallgemeinernden Stücken [. . .]. (81, our emphasis)[33]

Whereas Hartung sees *Furcht und Elend* against the backdrop of the "popular" sub-genres within which many of Dudow's amateur actors had been accustomed to work, we propose to examine selected scenes and local devices to show how Brecht transposes scenarios and techniques from (above all) contemporary political cabaret and the satirical *Flüsterwitze* prevalent in the Third Reich,[34] while subversively integrating them into an epic framework. The methodological justification for this can be found in Brecht's essay "Verfremdungseffekte in der chinesischen Schauspielkunst" (Alienation Effects in Chinese Acting). Here Brecht asks which Chinese theatrical devices

---

Menschheit, "so daß man oben die herrschenden Mächte sehen kann und unten den Soldaten, der ihre großen Pläne überlebt" (*BFA* 27:114). Some satirical techniques in *Furcht und Elend* appear to be indebted to specific scenes in Kraus's play. But whereas *Schweyk* took its cue from *Die letzten Tage der Menschheit* by depicting "die herrschenden Mächte," those in power remain largely in the wings in *Furcht und Elend*.

[33] Fritz Erpenbeck was the first to draw attention to the importance of these traditions for an understanding of *Furcht und Elend* in his *Lebendiges Theater: Aufsätze und Kritiken* (Berlin: Henschel, 1949), 279–80. For related material, see *Deutsches Arbeitertheater, 1918–1933: Eine Dokumentation*, ed. Ludwig Hoffmann and Daniel Hoffmann-Ostwald, 2 vols. (Berlin: Henschel, 1972) and Gudrun Klatt, *Arbeiterklasse und Theater: Agitprop-Tradition — Theater im Exil — Sozialistisches Theater* (Berlin: Akademie, 1975).

[34] Our argument draws on the following useful anthologies and studies of the German *Flüsterwitz* in the Third Reich: Hans-Jochen Gamm, *Der Flüsterwitz im Dritten Reich* (Munich: List, 1963); Richard Hermes, *Witz contra Nazi* (Hamburg: Morawe & Scheffelt, 1946); Karl Michael Hillenbrand, *Underground Humour in Nazi Germany, 1933–1945* (London: Routledge, 1995); Gudrun Pausewang, *Erlaubter Humor im Nationalsozialismus (1933–1945)* (Frankfurt am Main: Lang, 2007); Peter Poddel, *Flüsterwitze aus Brauner Zeit* (Munich: Hornung, 1954); *Lachen verboten: Flüsterwitze aus den Jahren 1938–1945*, ed. Minni Schwarz, 4 vols. (Vienna: Im Weltweiten, 1947); and *Vox populi — Die Hitlerei im Volksmund,* ed. Kurt Sellin (Heidelberg: Freiheit-Verlag, 1946).

can be regarded as "ein *transportables Technikum*" (*BFA* 22:206; a transportable piece of technique: *BT* 95); that is to say, a device or strategy capable of adaptation and integration into Epic Theater's repertoire of distancing devices. For as well as borrowing socially satirical effects from various contemporary political sub-genres, *Furcht und Elend* continues to deploy other alienation devices from Epic Theater's familiar arsenal of distancing strategies. These two forms of critical distancing, via open structure and local alienation devices, can already be seen operating in tandem in Scene 1.

"Volksgemeinschaft" Revisited

As was noted in Chapter Four, the scene title "Volksgemeinschaft" refers to the propaganda myth that one of the National Socialists' main achievements was to have turned Germany into an egalitarian society where social barriers — of class, if not race or political persuasion — had been swept aside. The time when the *Furcht und Elend* scene is set, 30 January 1933, was theoretically the date when such a process was set in motion. Not surprisingly, the scene's action, location, and the two protagonists' behavior put a question mark next to NS propaganda claims concerning the Third Reich's status as a unique "Volksgemeinschaft."

Although the scene title quotes the concept in High German, from then on the noun "Volksgemeinschaft" occurs in regional dialect. Like almost everything else the two SS men say, the Nazi slogans they enthusiastically parrot are in broad *Berlinisch*:

> DER ERSTE Nu sind wir oben. Imposant, der Fackelzug! Jestern noch pleite, heut schon in die Reichskanzlei. Jestern Pleitejeier, heute Reichsadler.[35]
> *Sie lassen ihr Wasser.*
> DER ZWEITE Und nu kommt die Volksjemeinschaft. Ick erwarte mir een seelischen Uffschwung des deutschen Volkes in allerjrößten Maßstab.
> [. . .]
> DER ZWEITE Meenste, er schafft die Volksjemeinschaft?
> DER ERSTE Er schafft allet! (*BFA* 4:342–43)

> [THE FIRST: Top dogs, that's us. That torchlight procession, impressive, what? Broke one moment, next day running the government. Rags to riches in a single day.

---

[35] Possibly, the boastfulness of this remark was intended to recall the title and rhetoric of Joseph Goebbels's autobiographical success story: *Vom Kaiserhof zur Reichskanzlei*, published in 1934. If so, then Goebbels's self-satisfied tone is undercut by being translated into Berlin dialect.

They make water.
THE SECOND: And now it'll be a united nation. I'm expecting the
German people to have an unprecedented moral revival.
[. . .]
THE SECOND: Think he'll really make us a united nation?
THE FIRST: He'll make anything. (*FM* 5–6)]

Scene 1 would lose much of its intended impact if the dialect spoken in it
and its relationship to the specific urban location lacked clear socio-political connotations. It would also do so if audiences were unfamiliar with
the propaganda clichés being spouted (for example, the reference to what
the NS movement's leaders referred to as "der seelische Aufschwung des
deutschen Volkes" under the new regime) — or if people failed to spot the
contradiction between how these two men talk and behave and the fact
that they come on stage resplendent in the uniform of SS officers.[36] As we
saw earlier, Brecht's putative source for the scene is the newspaper report
of an incident involving two SA men.[37] Indeed, given the SA's massive
presence in the triumphant torchlight procession of 30 January and their
notorious aggressiveness in the days thereafter, this is what most audiences
would expect the two thugs to be. But the stage directions are unequivocal
("*Zwei SS-Offiziere torkeln die Straße herunter*," *BFA* 4:342; Two SS officers lurching down the street, *FM* 5); indeed, they need to be in the SS in
order to establish the play's marked emphasis on class warfare.

Because the two SS men speak in broad dialect, some commentators
have invoked "regional authenticity" in an attempt to link the feature with
German Naturalist literature, where fidelity to dialect was attempted in a radically experimental way that had no real equivalent in its French, Russian, and
Scandinavian counterparts.[38] Sometimes dialect is associated with the claim

---

[36] At this stage, the ranks of the SS were still largely drawn from the lower strata
of Third Reich society. The SS was not the rigorously selected elite of later years,
according to Richard Grunberger, *A Social History of the Third Reich* (London:
Weidenfeld & Nicolson, 1971), 137.

[37] James K. Lyon's entry on *Furcht und Elend* (*BHB* 1:40–41) cites a cutting from
the *Berliner 12 Uhr Blatt* of 7 February 1933 as a possible source for "Volksgemeinschaft." The incident in question occurred in the week after Hitler came to
power. A pair of men in SA uniform were reported to have opened fire on two
communists, killing one. No district is specified, nor is the reader told whether
the culprits were apprehended. The material, assuming it was Brecht's source, is
modified so that SA men become SS men, the unnamed Berlin street is located in a
working-class district within walking distance of the city center, and the incident is
moved back from the night of 6–7 February 1933 to 30 January.

[38] On one occasion Brecht himself adopts this line of reasoning: In "Über die
Verwendung von Prinzipien" (ca. 1940) he declares that "beinahe jede neue Aufgabe erforderte neue Methoden," while going on to note that there are "Ausfüh-

that *Furcht und Elend* is a work that lays great store by verisimilitude, even in the case of regional language. "Nur natürliche Sprache [wird] verwendet," Hartung claimed in respect of the *Furcht und Elend* cycle as a whole, adding that "sogar Dialektpartien [kommen] vor" (74). More cautiously, Bentley explains that "the dialogue of the scenes in *The Private Life* is naturalistic but the play is not naturalism" (*The Private Life*, 132). What nevertheless comes as something of a surprise, given that the language used in "Volksgemeinschaft" arouses expectations of further varieties of regional discourse to follow, is the virtual absence of broad dialect elsewhere, even in the proletarian scenes set in Saxony, the Ruhr, Upper Silesia, and other Berlin districts.[39] It has been suggested that "there would have been great scope for using dialect, but there is no mention of this in any of the reports, an indication that Brecht was not really reverting to realism."[40] While agreeing, we would argue that dialect is used on important occasions primarily as a form of defamiliarization, and seldom resorted to for the purpose of adding local color.

According to Hartung (84), Brecht had initially intended to put a number of already available scenes into dialect, but he failed to get around to doing so; although a Berlin dialect prose version entitled "Mitn Kind müssen Se" (*BFA* 18:331) does exist in the case of "Der Spitzel," writing a regional version of a scene as a form of five-finger exercise is not the same as transforming High German dialogue into dialect. More revealing for our purposes is the fact that in 1938, as his references to *Furcht und Elend* in "Über die Verwendung von Prinzipien" suggest, Brecht drafted a significant portion of dialogue in dialect for Scene 3 ("Das Kreidekreuz"), but took the plan no further (details in *BFA* 4:524). The reason for this is not hard to imagine. Had there been a consistently plausible use of dialect in all *Furcht und Elend* scenes set in working-class milieus, the result would have been an impression of linguistic fidelity to real settings, something that Lukács might have relished. However, even Hartung's assumption that in

---

rungen, in denen der Nutzen stilisierter Redeweise in der Dramatik gezeigt wird; aber in *Furcht und Elend des Dritten Reiches* finden sich Stücke [i.e., scenes], die im Dialekt verfaßt sind, mit phonetisch getreuer Wiedergabe der Sprechweise von bayrischen Bauern und Berliner Dienstmädchen" (*BFA* 22:677). But by alluding solely to "Der Bauer füttert die Sau" and "Das Kreidekreuz," he ignores Scene 1's use of dialect. The contrasting there of language with content for defamiliarization purposes puts this scene into the "neue Methoden" category.

[39] One possible exception is the working-class register used by the servant Mari in "Rechtsfindung" (*BFA* 4:374). Rather than being in pronounced regional dialect (*Aurora*, *The Private Life*, and *FM* set the scene in Augsburg), her ungrammatical utterances may simply be meant to emphasize the fact that she is an uneducated woman trying to help out someone who is her social superior.

[40] Hugh Rorrison, Introduction to Bertolt Brecht, *Plays: Two*, trans. John Willett (London: Methuen, 1987), xxvii–xxviii.

"Volksgemeinschaft" dialect is used for satirical purposes fails to explain Brecht's unwillingness to repeat such an effect. Only by interpreting the rationing of dialect as a controlled alienation device can one link this feature to the way the play's presentational strategy varies from scene to scene, thereby preventing any reassuring horizon of expectation from developing. Continually changing register, sociolect, and even genre allows Brecht to establish patterns of reciprocal defamiliarization ("gegenseitige Verfremdung") between the constituent parts of the *Furcht und Elend* cycle.

There is, apart from German Naturalism, one other important literary precedent for the use of dialect in the opening "Volksgemeinschaft" scene. At the time when *Furcht und Elend* was being written, there already existed an established cabaret tradition of using dialect to satirize the hollow rhetoric of the Nazi political leadership. This might explain the use in "Volksgemeinschaft" of regional dialect to establish a satirically critical stance at the very beginning of the *Furcht und Elend* cycle, yet without repeating the same approach in other scenes. The following extract from a poem using the tactic is to be found in Hardy Worm's "Die Nationalstrolchisten" (1933):

> An der Spitze von det Janze:
> Goebbels im Heldenjlanze!
> Mimt des Vaterlandes Retter
> Uff der Schmiere blutje Bretter.
> Alle sind hurrabejeistert,
> Wenn er ihr Jehirn verkleistert.
> Beifall tobt durchs volle Haus,
> Läßt er weiße Mäuse raus.
> Stilljestanden! Hand zum Schwur!
> Hakenkreuz uff roter Fahne,
> Stramm bezahlt von Thyssens Jelde,
> Is das Sinnbild der Kultur.[41]

In the above example, defamiliarization results from a direct contrast between the NS propaganda minister's impassioned rhetoric — ironically, High German–speaking Goebbels was also Gauleiter of Berlin — and the working-class perspective supplied by the East Berlin dialect. In the case of Brecht's "Volksgemeinschaft" scene, a far more serious ideological point is made about class roots, political allegiances, and betraying one's origins. "Halte Dich zu Deiner Klasse" (Stick with your own class, *FM* 92) are virtu-

---

[41] Quoted from Volker Kühn, *"Deutschlands Erwachen": Kabarett unterm Hakenkreuz, 1933–1945*, vol. 3 (Weinheim-Berlin, Quadriga, 1989), 23–24. According to Kühn, op. cit., 329, the poem/song, intended to mimic the style of Goebbels's newspaper *Der Angriff*, was performed at the cabaret "Die Pille" before being subsequently printed in the satirical magazine *Die Ente*. The *Berlinisch* of the above poem is untranslatable, not least because it would be inappropriate to imply that a certain English dialect bears any resemblance to the German original.

ally the father's last words of advice to his son in "Volksbefragung" (*BFA* 4:442). Given the literary associations of East Berlin's sociolect (especially thanks to the urban fiction of Max Kretzer, Arno Holz, Johannes Schlaf, and, above all, the Alfred Döblin of *Berlin Alexanderplatz* fame), *Berlinisch* came to be associated with the proletariat in the "Red" districts of the Reich capital, notably Wedding, Reinickendorf, Neukölln, and especially the area around the Alexanderplatz itself. The spectacle of the two SS men speaking in a way that suggests their roots were not so long ago in the proletarian world they are now drunkenly lurching through was probably intended to suggest that they have betrayed the working class from which they come. Such class traitors, boasting of having taken part in punitive raids on various proletarian districts of the city, are evidently being tacitly accused of falling for the NSDAP's claim to be a "German Socialist Party" (i.e., *the* appropriate Socialist Party for post-Weimar Germany). The same charge is also implicit in the scene's contrast between the pseudo-egalitarian political clichés the two SS men parrot and the mindless way they think and behave. What is more, the images of cowardice and fear associated with both SS and proletariat in "Volksgemeinschaft" stand in direct contrast to the play's final scene. Also set in Berlin, "Volksbefragung" shows a working-class district becoming the focus of organized resistance. Although dialect performs an important critically distancing function at the beginning of the play, no comparable process of linguistic defamiliarization is required in the last scene. As we saw in Chapter Four, politically "correct" behavior (in the form of organized group resistance) is now on display and critical distance as a consequence becomes superfluous. Ironically, "Volksgemeinschaft" was not used in "99%" or in *The Private Life*, perhaps because its dialect was a hindrance to understanding.

Brecht's theoretical writings seldom associate dialect with linguistic mimesis of the kind found to varying degrees in such Naturalist plays as Gerhart Hauptmann's *Vor Sonnenaufgang*, *De Waber*, and *Die Weber*. He does, however, occasionally present its deployment as a useful defamiliarization strategy. In November 1935, he was asked in an interview with Victor Jerome, the chief cultural officer of the Communist Party of America,

> how he would treat the language in a play about a slave insurrection in nineteenth-century America led by an educated slave (later correspondence confirms that it was Nat Turner). [. . .] His solution here constituted a striking example of his now famous "estrangement" [. . .]. Brecht would have had the slaves, who normally spoke dialect, employ Standard English. "This is revolutionary," he claimed. Verisimilitude mattered little to him.[42]

---

[42] Reported in James K. Lyon, *Bertolt Brecht in America*, 15–16. The interview (*BBA*, 341/46–51) was recorded in German and translated into English by Elisabeth Hauptmann.

If people who habitually speak dialect are depicted on stage using an estranged version of the language of their "masters," the effect is comparable to having a cabaret version of Joseph Goebbels, the personification of NS rhetoric par excellence, spout verse in *Berlinisch*. The alien register estranges the discourse's political content. It does this in "Volksgemeinschaft" (although seldom in "Das Kreidekreuz" and "Der Bauer füttert die Sau," where other estranging properties are deployed). This may explain why one preparatory exercise recommended in "Kurze Beschreibung einer neuen Technik der Schauspielkunst, die einen Verfremdungseffekt hervorbringt" (Short Description of a New Technique of Acting which Produces an Alienation Effect) to help actors achieve the requisite distance from their characters was to speak their lines in dialect at rehearsal stage: "Prosa kann verfremdet werden durch ihre Übersetzung in den heimischen Dialekt des Schauspielers" (*BFA* 22:645; Prose can be alienated by translation into the actor's native dialect: *BT* 139). Brecht is concerned with rehearsal techniques that could help actors establish critical distance from their stage personas. Yet if actors thereby achieved a skeptical "take" on their lines, this would inevitably be communicated to the audience, thereby discouraging empathy.

"Physiker"

Berlin dialect is not the only sociolect used in *Furcht und Elend* for the specific purpose of critical defamiliarization. The "Physiker" scene treats the predicament of a pair of Third Reich physicists (labeled simply X and Y, as if they were guinea pigs being exhibited for demonstration purposes,[43] or conceivably in order to mimic the anonymity their clandestine behavior requires) in the aftermath of their academic discipline's *Gleichschaltung*.[44] In this respect, the scene uses technical jargon in a more sophisticated way than would be required to underwrite their professional expertise. There is no indication that they speak anything other than High German, but in

---

[43] Eric Bentley seems to have later on taken a leaf out of Brecht's book, for the scene "In Search of Justice" (*The Private Life*, 50–70) refers to two figures simply as Judge A and Judge B.

[44] The fact that the physicists' attention is focused on a complex research problem is not immaterial to this picture of life after the *Gleichschaltung* of non-Aryan physics. As has been pointed out in Alan D. Beyerchen, *Scientists under Hitler: Politics and the Physics Community in the Third Reich* (New Haven, CT; London: Yale UP, 1979), 53–54, Jewish physics had hitherto been associated with independent research, whereas the NS Reichserziehungsministerium prioritized teaching, i.e., dogmatic academic leadership, in the universities.

order to have the right effect their discourse needs to be very remote from common daily usage.

Even before they open their mouths, the *Vorspruch* conjures up the atmosphere of fear and suspicion under which these two Göttingen researchers now work:

> Es kommen die Herren Gelehrten
> Mit falschen Teutonenbärten
> Und furchterfülltem Blick.
> Sie wollen nicht eine richtige
> Sondern eine arisch gesichtige
> Genehmigte deutsche Physik. (*BFA* 4:382)

> [Enter the local Newtons
> Dressed up like bearded Teutons —
> Not one of them hook-nosed.
> Their science will end up barbarian
> For they'll get an impeccably Aryan
> State-certified physics imposed. (*FM* 44)]

In the original German *Vorspruch* (where "Newtons" play no role), the context of "eine arisch gesichtige / Genehmigte deutsche Physik," coupled with the reference to "falschen Teutonenbärten" (an allusion to the hirsute appearance of the leading "Aryanizing" Nazi physicist Philipp Lenard[45]), neatly caricatures the illogicality and unethical nature of the NS regime's racially motivated scientific program by highlighting *facial*, and thus, according to NS thinking, *racial* features. The satirically emphasized façade of Lenard's "Teutonenbart," synecdoche for the whole misguided process of creating an exclusively *national* academic discipline, contrasts as much with the scene's evocation of former international academic cooperation as did the SS officers' uniforms with what should have been their true class interests in "Volksgemeinschaft." In order to ensure that the physicists do not come across as mere victims of totalitarianism, the "Physiker" scene has to go beyond evoking the climate of fear and mistrust in which they are forced to work. It has to present them as problematic figures. They may have suddenly found themselves in direct contact with the acknowledged world expert in their field, a person whose advice it is illegal, and hence highly dangerous to seek, because in the NS regime's

---

[45] Together with Johannes Stark, Philipp Lenard led the NSDAP's campaign against "Jewish physics" in the 1930s. While Lenard's four-volume *Deutsche Physik* was the main theoretical weapon in the systematic Aryanization of the discipline, Stark spearheaded the antisemitic campaign against Einstein. An account of the campaign's impact specifically on Göttingen, where *Aurora* sets this scene, can be found in Beyerchen's "Göttingen — 1933," in *Scientists under Hitler*, 15–39.

eyes he is the embodiment of decadent Jewish physics. But that by no means automatically makes them into resistance fighters. On the contrary, their displays of tunnel vision ostensibly shelter them from any sense of moral responsibility for the new regime under which they suffer.[46] For this reason, Brecht resorts to a further ingenious form of verbal estrangement in order to predispose audiences to view them critically from a certain distance.

The contradictions in the two men's behavior are far from being as unequivocally comic as *Der Messingkauf*'s account of the Paris production might lead one to expect from scenes of the play.[47] Alone in their laboratory, the two physicists turn, with a mixture of excitement and nervous anxiety, to the letter they have just received from Albert Einstein. (A stage direction at one point in this scene describes one of them as paralyzed with shock.) For a long time they remain so tight-lipped about the letter's source that we only learn of the eminent physicist's identity towards the end of the scene. Although we are given a considerable amount of detailed information about the content of Einstein's letter, as far as most people in the auditorium are concerned, the two German physicists could just as well be reading a densely formulated communication in an incomprehensible foreign language:

> Y   *liest:* Es handelt sich um zwei willkürliche kontravariante Vektoren, *fi* und *nü*, und einen kontravarianten Vektor *t*. Mit deren Hilfe werden die Komponenten eines gemischten Tensors zweiter Stufe gebildet, dessen Struktur demgemäß
>
> $$\Sigma^{-lr} = C_{hi}^{-l}$$
>
> ist.
>
> X   *der mitgeschrieben hat, bedeutet ihm plötzlich zu schweigen:* Augenblick!
> *Er steht auf und geht auf Zehenspitzen zur Wand links. Er hört anscheinend nichts Verdächtiges und kehrt zurück. Y liest weiter, mitunter jedoch auf ähnliche Weise unterbrochen. Sie untersuchen dann das Telefon, öffnen schnell die Tür usw.*
>
> Y: Für ruhende, inkohärente, nicht durch Spannungen aufeinander einwirkende Materie ist $T = \mu$, die einzige von O verschiedene

---

[46] According to Section 3, sub-section ii, of Brecht's note "Das Denken als ein Verhalten" (ca. 1930): "Das technische Denken (Berufsdenken, wissenschaftliche Denken) [. . .] führt den Denker aus der Gemeinschaft der Menschen heraus, macht ihn zu ihrem objektiven Feind, isoliert ihn (als Spezialisten, der nur den Arbeits*teil* bewältigen darf), so daß er mit Leichtigkeit zu mißbrauchen oder zu überwältigen ist" (*BFA* 21:421–22).

[47] For Brecht's account of the Paris production, see our discussion of "Das Kreidekreuz" in Chapter Four.

Komponente der tensoriellen Energiedichte. Infolgedessen wird ein statisches Gravitationsfeld erzeugt, dessen Gleichung unter Hinzufügung des konstanten Proportionalitätsfaktors 8 πϰ

$$\Delta f = 4\pi\varkappa\mu$$

liefert. Bei geeigneter Wahl der Raumkoordinaten ist die Abweichung von $c^2 dt^2$ sehr gering. (BFA 4:382–83)

[Y *reads:* The problem concerns two arbitrary countervariant vectors *psi* and *nu* and a countervariant vector *t*. This is used to form the elements of a mixed tensor of the second degree whose structure can be expressed by

$$\Sigma^{-lr} = C_{hi}^{-l}$$

X *who has been writing this down, suddenly gives him a sign to shut up:* Just a minute.
He gets up and tiptoes over to the wall, left. Having evidently heard nothing suspicious he returns. Y goes on reading aloud, with other similar interruptions. These lead them to inspect the telephone, suddenly open the door, etc.

Y: Where matter is passive, incoherent and not acting on itself by means of tensions $T = \mu$ will be the only component of the tensional energy depth that differs from O. Hence a static gravitational field is created whose equation, taking into account the constant proportionality factor 8 πϰ will be

$$\Delta f = 4\pi\varkappa\mu$$

Given a suitable choice of special coordinates the degree of variation from $c^2 dt^2$ will be very slight. (FM 45)]

At this point the physicists are interrupted by the sound of a slamming door, as if someone were rushing off to denounce them to their superiors. Once their fears have been allayed, they return to their clandestine discussion until, that is, X blurts out "Aber was sagt Einstein zu . . ." (But what's Einstein got to say about . . .). After which they clumsily rush to cover their tracks: "Ja, eine echt jüdische Spitzfindigkeit! Was hat das mit Physik zu tun?" (BFA 4:383–84; What a typical piece of misplaced Jewish ingenuity. Nothing to do with physics: FM 45–46). The two physicists' hamfisted attempt at damage control gives us some sense of their existential dilemma: on the one hand, desperate for scientific help; on the other, fearful of being sent to a concentration camp if they are denounced or caught red-handed. In their attempt to proclaim their innocence, they end up speaking the language of their oppressors while at the same time unintentionally offering an appropriate verdict on their own betrayal of their discipline: "Was hat das mit Physik zu tun?" This is a question directed at the audience, as well as any potential informant. Clearly, these two physicists are not taking a heroic stand in principle against the regime's draconian "Aryanization" of physics. Nor are they protesting against the nationwide *Gleichschaltung* of Germany's academic institutions. Judged on Brechtian criteria, these two cowering academics are not far short of being archetypal "Tuis."[48] This is why they become the target of Epic Theater's critical defamiliarization devices.

On first encounter, "Physiker" would appear to be one of the most unapologetically "Aristotelian" of all *Furcht und Elend* scenes. It is hardly surprising, therefore, that it was given pride of place at the beginning of Part Two of *The Private Life*. It offers a powerful evocation of the two physicists' fear of being discovered and of what that might lead to, combined with a sense of the sheer intellectual "Elend" of two German scientists riskily soliciting help from experts now living abroad — in this case, as it turns out, from one of the most illustrious of exiles from the Third Reich. Because the NS "Deutsche Physik" program has made their discipline a virtual caricature of science in the eyes of the outside world, these two physicists are automatically excluded from civilized international scholarly debate. Despite — or even because of — the weight of emotive material, the "Physiker" scene can also be read as camouflaged self-referential commentary on the virtues of "Überdenflußdenken" rather than "Imflußdenken," to recall a metaphor Brecht used in his "Anmerkungen zur *Dreigroschenoper*" (*BFA* 24:59) to sum up the main difference in perspective between Epic and Aristotelian Theater. In order to appreciate the dramaturgical subtext here, we need to remember that Brecht was prone to cast himself in the role of the Einstein of Epic Theater.[49]

The fact that the language and nervous behavior of the two physicists and that of Einstein's letter differ as much as Aristotelian and Epic Theater do appears plausible under the circumstances. "Physiker" is set in Göttingen University at the height of the NS campaign against Jewish Physics, whereas by this time Einstein was already a Fellow of Princeton Univer-

---

[48] While Brecht's petty-bourgeoisie theory possibly accounted for the behavior of the majority of characters in early *Furcht und Elend* scenes, the alacrity with which the professional middle classes in the next cluster accommodate themselves to *Gleichschaltung* needs to be seen in the context of the conception of the intelligentsia's predictable behavior that formed the core of Brecht's "Tui"-project. According to Brecht, "die goldene Zeit der *Tuis* ist die liberale Republik, aber den Gipfel erklimmt der Tuismus im Dritten Reich" (*BFA* 26:448). "Dieses Land [i.e., Third Reich Germany] zerschlägt mir meinen 'Tuiroman,'" Brecht complains in a journal entry for 18 April 1942 (*BFA* 27:84). On the "Tui" concept, see *Brechts Tui-Kritik: Aufsätze, Rezensionen, Geschichten*, ed. Herbert Claas and Wolfgang Fritz Haug (Berlin: Argument, 1976).

[49] For details, see Mordecai Gorelik, "Brecht: 'I am the Einstein of the New Stage Form,'" *Theatre Arts*, 41 (March 1957), 72–73 and 86–87.

sity's Institute for Advanced Study and still very much in touch with the international scientific community (which is why the physicists' request for help was forwarded to him by Mikowsky in Paris). The staccato language of the two physicists is excited, expressing both joy and surprise that their letter should have been answered so promptly. The register then becomes nervously halting, as it dawns on them just what risks they are exposing themselves to; as the tension mounts, their speech often becomes clipped to the point of being monosyllabic, and the ensuing exchanges are frequently accompanied by paranoid gestures. Einstein's written communication, in contrast, is impersonal, clear, measured, and invariably focused on technical detail. It is also cautious: there is nothing in the letter we hear read out that would implicate the two physicists by expressly addressing them or that might suggest some form of conspiratorial networking between Göttingen and Princeton. While the stylistic contrast is contextually motivated, what the juxtaposition emphasizes is the productiveness of a style of communication reminiscent of Epic Theater's "Wissenschaftlichkeit" in contrast to the dangers of emotional behavior under such circumstances. By the end of the scene, as so often happens in Brechtian theater, the physicists have themselves clearly taken on board the object lesson they have just received. In the words of the concluding stage directions: "*Erleichtert nehmen sie ihre Notizen wieder vor und arbeiten schweigend weiter, mit allergrößter Vorsicht*" (*BFA* 4:384; *Relieved, they again bring out their notes and silently resume work, using the utmost caution*: FM 46).

The rigorously presented scientific content of Einstein's letter to X and Y takes up about two-thirds of the scene and would, together with the two protagonists' accompanying gestures and various meaningful silences, require at least fifteen minutes delivery time. According to the notes in the *BFA* edition, "In dieser Szene werden wissenschaftliche Begriffe und Formeln verwendet; sie repräsentieren jedoch keine konkrete physikalische Theorie" (*BFA* 4:537).[50] Nevertheless, an editorial attempt to throw light on some of the technical terminology hardly reaches the point where even the educated nonspecialist could understand the letter's content. In any case, it was not Brecht's intention to make such a specialist scientific dia-

---

[50] A number of postscripts were added to Brecht's letter to Wieland Herzfelde of 22 July 1938, including the following: "In der Szene 'Physiker' scheinen mir die Formeln nicht richtig, aber ich bin leider kein Physiker und kann aus dem mir von einem solchen zugeschickten Manuskript nicht genau lesen, wie man die Zeichen hinmalen soll. [. . .] Kannst Du [. . .] einen Fachmann fragen? Das sollte ja am liebsten stimmen!" (*BFA* 29:105) Brecht appears to be implying here that defamiliarization can be a by-product of technical accuracy, not just the fictive formulae of invented characters. Perhaps it was the fact that the letter to the two physicists is supposed to have come from Einstein that prompted Brecht to make such a request.

logue readily accessible to the audience. They are not meant to grasp much more than the general gist of what X and Y are being told; indeed, they are more likely to concentrate instead on the two men's body language and speech acts than on Einstein's explanation. The use of opaque technical vocabulary may in part be a way of highlighting the scientists' blinkered vision (or *déformation professionnelle*), presented, as it was in *Leben des Galilei*, as a special case of ideological "false consciousness." The demeaning spectacle of two highly intelligent adults reduced to such abject fear is a phenomenon that will soon be commented on by the Jewish wife in the scene following immediately on from "Physiker":

> Was seid ihr für Menschen [. . .]? Ihr erfindet die Quantentheorie und den Trendelenburg und laßt euch von Halbwilden kommandieren, daß ihr die Welt erobern sollt, aber nicht die Frau haben durft, die ihr haben wollt. (*BFA* 4:388)

> [What sort of people are you [. . .]? You work out the quantum theory and the Trendelenburg test, then allow a lot of semi-barbarians to tell you you're to conquer the world but you can't have the woman you want. (*FM* 50)]

Yet it is not being ordered about by savage barbarians that the physicists have most to fear, but being caught red-handed by their academic peers, every one of whom has the ability to become a potential informer, in their eyes.

The stage directions to "Physiker" put the emphasis on the gestures displayed in such a predicament. We are told at one point that Y gives the impression of being conspiratorial (*BFA* 4:382), a formulation that suggests the two physicists might at first even be boyishly excited by the idea of taking part in such cloak-and-dagger activity until, that is, they are overcome by fear. The focus on *Gestus,* discussed in Chapter Three, rather than on complicated dialogue, creates a situation comparable to that of watching silent cinema or a foreign film without the aid of subtitles. In some of Brecht's epic plays, *Gestus* is defamiliarized through techniques of overacting, thereby establishing a discrepancy between the content of the utterance and the speaker's body language. In this instance, however, instead of the physicists' body language contradicting what is said, gesture is foregrounded in inverse proportion to the (for the average audience) minimal semantic content of their specialist dialogue. The scientific passages in Einstein's letter are read out with increasing enthusiasm, but such a mood is regularly interrupted by attacks of naked fear. Contradictory behavior of this kind is crucial to our impression of the two physicists, not as scientists, but as human beings. "What sort of people are you?" will soon be the question the Jewish wife asks her husband and his type, not "What sort of doctors are you and your kind?"

Walter Benjamin claimed that gesture tends to become particularly important in Epic Theater when a character is interrupted in what he or she is doing.[51] Although it was not included in the Paris production that Benjamin saw, Brecht's "Physiker" scene epitomizes this principle in two respects. First, in the obvious sense that whenever the dialogue is halted by some outside noise, the two men suspect that they are possibly being overheard. Second, when they are cocooned in their specialized jargon, genuine communication with the outside world, including those in the theater auditorium, has been effectively disrupted and all that can be registered is the social *Gestus*. Judged by Benjamin's criterion, "Physiker" has the makings of highly effective Epic Theater. Structurally, it is a scene of repeated interruptions and, at the same time, it works with variations on two basic plot situations: a complex three-way scientific exchange between like-minded people and a classic wartime "The-Walls-Have-Ears" scenario. For once, the scene is not split, as it often is in Epic Theater, between two visible parts of the stage, but between what is visibly happening while the physicists are talking and the mere possibility of someone lurking outside this controlled sphere. In this respect, "Physiker" is a further illustration of the Trojan horse tactic by virtue of the way it taps into Epic Theater's ability to exploit "[nicht] sogleich in die Augen fallende Verfremdungen." Just as Standard English did in the American Nat Turner context cited above, professional communication becomes dialogue defamiliarized; the audience is excluded, just as it will be in other ways in "Die jüdische Frau," the scene following in the usually preferred sequence of *Furcht und Elend*. "Die jüdische Frau" too is a scene constructed on the basis of a series of "[nicht] sogleich in die Augen fallender Verfremdungen," this time not interrupted by potential threats from outside, but comprising a fragmented situation that results from the central figure's repeated change of tactics.

"Die jüdische Frau"

Although "Die jüdische Frau" is an instructive illustration of the use of epic fragmentation ("epische Diskontinuität") within an individual scene,[52] it has little to do with the kinds of unstructured montage that were anathema

---

[51] Having seen the Paris production, Benjamin concluded: "Gesten erhalten wir um so mehr, je häufiger wir einen Handelnden unterbrechen." ("Was ist Episches Theater?" In *Versuche über Brecht*, ed. Rolf Tiedemann [Frankfurt am Main: Suhrkamp, 1981], 19; English translation in Benjamin, *Understanding Brecht*, 18). Benjamin's example of an interrupted family row is similar to the maidservant's repeated intrusions upon the Furke family in the early parts of "Der Spitzel."

[52] In the words of a "Nachtrag zur Theorie des *Messingkauf*," "Die Fortführung der Fabel [beim epischen Theater] ist hier diskontinuierlich, das einheitliche Ganze besteht aus selbständigen Teilen" (*BFA* 22:701).

to Lukács and his camarilla. Eric Bentley, for example, talks of the American version's "system of interruptions which break up the play into the atomic elements of which it consists" (*The Private Life*, 133). The scene broadly divides into three consecutive sections: (i) the telephone calls that Judith Keith, the Jewish wife, makes in preparation for going into exile that same day; (ii) her various rehearsals of the difficult exchange she expects to have with her husband Fritz when he finds out that she is leaving him to go to Amsterdam; and (iii) the married couple's actually brief, but shabby parting. While "Die jüdische Frau" is preceded by an introductory *Vorspruch*, the eventual culminating encounter between wife and husband has been cleverly preempted by a series of surrogate prologues in the form of the one-sided telephone calls and an equally one-sided rehearsed dialogue. What is more, the first two sequences are themselves repeatedly fragmented, with each phone call and rehearsal dummy run coming across as almost a mini-drama in its own right.

Rehearsing and role-playing had, as self-referential modes of anti-illusionism, always had a key part to play alongside Epic Theater's various other distancing and estranging strategies. One has only to think of Polly Peachum's demonstration of how she would run Macheath's gang in his absence (*BFA* 2:265–67), Shen Te's demonstration of her preparedness to fight tooth and nail to protect her child (*BFA* 6:248–49), and Azdak's illustration of how he would face the challenge of being a judge in Grusinia (*BFA* 8:159–62). The main structural departure in "Die jüdische Frau" lies in the fact that instead of being witness to a single rehearsal or demonstration, audiences eavesdrop on a whole series of repeatedly modified versions of how the marital breakup might eventually unfold. Even most of the successive telephone calls in the first part of the scene can be read as oblique rehearsals for the Jewish woman's final face-to-face leave-taking from her husband. Moreover, the pattern of the phone calls is one of variations on the truth concerning what is about to happen, or in Epic Theater terms, a form of reciprocal estrangement that is arguably the overall principle of the entire scene.

Unlike the phone calls, the preemptive rehearsals are conducted in a vacuum. Judith Keith repeatedly constructs fresh scripts for the inevitable encounter, testing out how she might handle her husband's potential reactions, and yet not seeming to come to a satisfactory conclusion. As a result, when he does return home, audiences cannot help but measure the callousness of his actual behavior against a scenario that the Jewish wife (or "woman," the ambiguity is deliberate) never imagined, even in her worst moments. Rehearsals of this kind prefigure events still to occur. When it does take place, the encounter between husband and wife has already been in several ways estranged by the numerous competing perspectives supplied by the various phone calls and rehearsal scenarios. If communication over the telephone was never easy for the protagonist, matters become even more fraught later on. Despite Judith Keith's pre-scripted exchanges, the final leave-taking is soon marred by the alacrity of her husband's willingness to see the back of his Jewish wife, coupled with his pathetic denial of the significance of her leaving for a long period of self-imposed exile, taking her winter coat with her.

Judith Keith's rehearsals (an ingenious Brechtian experiment with "inductive theater"[53]) are epitomized by one particular touchstone phrase. When, in the ultimate confrontation, the doctor-husband eventually says, in a part-statement, part-question: "Du weißt, daß ich unverändert bin, weißt du das, Judith?" (*BFA* 4:389; You know I haven't changed, you do, don't you, Judith?: *FM* 51), the audience has already been conditioned to dismiss his claim. One of his wife's early imagined exchanges in fact started with the words "Sage nicht, du bist unverändert, du bist es nicht!" (*BFA* 4:387; Don't tell me you haven't changed; you have!: *FM* 48). Even though each of Judith Keith's rehearsed versions fails to predict what will eventually happen, almost everything that is said or done in the final minutes of this scene has in some way been prepared for — and estranged in one sense or another — by the wife's earlier dummy runs. For this reason, the audience is able to tap into the complex subtext of the short concluding dialogue with a heightened — and extremely partisan — awareness.

Epic Theater's juxtapositions, Brecht observed in his "Anmerkungen zur *Dreigroschenoper*," are theater's equivalent of cross-referring from one page or part of a book to another ("vergleichendes Blättern," *BFA* 24:59). Such acts of bringing together in the audience's mind occur as a result of highly structured local montage pairings *within* individual *Furcht und Elend* scenes and *between* pairs of scenes (for example, in the parallels and differences between "Volksgemeinschaft" and "Volksbefragung," or between the latter and "Die Wahl"). In a real-life situation, it would be unlikely for a series of carefully rehearsed speeches to be spoken out loud and for them to have elements in common, even though they are addressed to different people. Hence Mittenzwei's and Busch's characterization of this part of "Die jüdische Frau" as quasi-interior monologue,[54] a verdict that, given the Zhdanov camp's proscription of interior monologue in Soviet fiction at this time, adds a further layer of evidence in support of Brecht's claim that *Furcht und Elend* marked no simple return to Lukácsian realism.

The actor would be well advised, Brecht noted in his journal entry of 15 August 1938 (*BFA* 26:319), to study the "Street Scene" before playing

---

[53] On "induktives Theater," see Brecht's "Haltung des Probenleiters (bei induktivem Vorgehen)" (*BFA* 22:597–99) and "Über den Bühnenbau der nichtaristotelischen Dramatik," § 3 (*BFA* 22:229–34).

[54] Werner Mittenzwei, *Das Leben des Bertolt Brecht oder Der Umgang mit den Welträtseln* (Frankfurt am Main: Suhrkamp, 1987), 1:592; Busch, *Bertolt Brecht*, 27.

one of the short scenes. The theoretical essay to which he is referring, "Die Straßenszene: *Grundmodell einer Szene des epischen Theaters (1940)*" (*BFA* 22:370–81; The Street Scene: A Basic Model for an Epic Theatre: *BT* 121–29), argues that eyewitness behavior after a street accident can serve as an instructive paradigm of Epic Theater's approach to more complex political problems. Reconstructions are by definition "epic" because they look back, often dispassionately, at past events: "Das Ereignis hat stattgefunden, hier findet die Wiederholung statt" (*BFA* 22:372; The event has taken place; what you are seeing now is a repeat: *BT* 122); "Die Vorführung hat einen Vorfall zum Anlaß, der verschieden beurteilt werden kann" (*BFA* 22:381; The performance's origins lie in an incident that can be judged one way or another: *BT* 128). This, above all else, explains the need for discussion "zur Klärung der Schuldfrage" (*BFA* 22:373; with a view to fixing the responsibility: *BT* 122). It can take the form of an exchange of views between the sole eyewitness and those who only came upon the scene after the event or one between a number of witnesses with different perspectives on just what has happened. Each eyewitness's performance, according to Brecht, is marked by repetition. Epic Theater's staged reconstructions and rehearsals thus invite a differently nuanced relationship to events. The "Straßenszene" model allows for two possibilities: the eyewitness saw what really happened and will be able to help those around him arrive at the truth. Alternatively, "er kann einen Vorgang erfinden und diesen demonstrieren" (*BFA* 22:379; he can fabricate an incident and demonstrate it: *BT* 127).

Judith Keith would appear to belong to the first category of witness identified in "Die Straßenszene," whereas, as we will shortly see, the reconstruction attempted by the schoolteacher and his wife in "Der Spitzel" puts them into the second. Some features of Brecht's model are, of course, absent from both these *Furcht und Elend* scenes. For example, the question of guilt (in the sense of "who was responsible for the accident?") is only tangential to "Die jüdische Frau" and even less applicable to "Der Spitzel." The emphasis Brecht puts on the accident's reconstruction having a socially practical significance (*BFA* 22:373) is also rather peripheral to both, if any such social significance is meant to be recognized by all characters involved in a given scene. Whereas the observer is central to Brecht's model and is more the focus of interest than the culprit, Judith Keith and the schoolteacher and his wife are part victims and part accident-prone. Of even more significance, given the minimal presence of "in die Augen fallender Verfremdungen" in "Die jüdische Frau" and "Der Spitzel," is Brecht's reference to his "Straßenszene" model as "[ein] Beispiel allereinfachsten, sozusagen 'natürlichen' epischen Theaters" (*BFA* 22:371; an example of completely simple, "natural" epic theatre: *BT* 121).

As deployed in "Die jüdische Frau," the deconstruction of a racially mixed marriage and the rehearsal of the parting to come may seem as artificial as those expository staged monologues to which many German

Naturalists took exception. "Es müßten einige Grundbeispiele des Ein-
ander-etwas-Vormachens im täglichen Leben beschrieben werden" (*BFA*
27:126; a few basic examples from daily life of people demonstrating-
something-to-one-another ought to be described: *BBJ* 258), according
to Brecht's journal entry for 10 October 1942, an observation written at the time of work on *The Private Life*. Admittedly, Judith Keith's
rehearsed scenarios may come across as somewhat less contrived than the
"Straßenszene" model suggests, given that they follow on immediately
from the various telephone calls she makes to her few remaining friends
and relations in order to smooth the path towards leaving her husband.
Yet Fradkin sees both the telephone conversations and rehearsal sequences
as "monologisch"[55] — which in a sense they are, although in radically
divergent respects. However, they are more plausible than a theatrical
monologue would be, if spoken in an everyday situation. Judith Keith's
rehearsals each involve an *imagined* dialogue between the wife and her still
absent husband, a dialogue that will never take place in any of the forms in
which it is rehearsed. In contrast, audiences have to assume that her phone
calls, while these may come across as equally one-sided because audiences
are unable to hear what is said at the other end of the line, are closer to
genuine dialogue than her rehearsed leave-takings. The result in both sections is a complicated eavesdropping situation where audiences either have
to reconstruct the missing husband's reactions or the unheard half of a
telephone dialogue.[56]

In Brecht's oeuvre, the one-sided telephone call is a device unique to
Furcht und Elend.[57] (Characters do not use telephones in parable plays.)
The device fulfills Epic Theater's demand that audiences must not remain

---

[55] Ilya Fradkin, *Bertolt Brecht: Weg und Methode*, 174.

[56] The scene's multiple phone calls and rehearsals could be read as variations on
Brecht's "Nicht-Sondern" paradigm. But whereas in the familiar "Nicht-Sondern"
scenario frequently used in Epic Theater, "das Publikum [dichtet] im Geist andere
Verhaltungsweisen und Situationen hinzu" (*BFA* 23:300), in "Die jüdische Frau"
the protagonist does this on their behalf. Because the words spoken by the friends
and professional acquaintances Judith Keith rings cannot be heard and are not
repeated on-stage by her, audiences are invited to engage in a unique form of what
Brecht called "Ko-Fabulieren" ("[Vom Epischen zum Dialektischen Theater 2],"
BFA 23:301).

[57] "In a sense," John Fuegi notes in his account of staged Epic Theater, "one can
see [Brecht's] theatre as a silent theatre in the way that we speak of silent films
[. . .]. One of Brecht's main objectives [. . .] seems to be that the play would be
intelligible to an audience sitting on the other side of sound-proof glass" (*Bertolt
Brecht: Chaos according to Plan* [Cambridge: Cambridge UP, 1987], 25). The relationship to the unheard other party during Judith Keith's various telephone calls
is in some respects analogous to the wordlessness of the unspeaking characters in
silent movies. This can be read as a further illustration of Brecht's tactic of using

passive, but should engage dialectically with what they are shown. In the early part of the scene, the audience, full of "curiosity" (a prerequisite of Epic Theater, as we have seen), focuses mentally as much on the people at the other end of the line as on Judith Keith herself. In a way that experience tells us would be unlikely in real life, the audience for "Die jüdische Frau" is expected to grasp the general gist of what is said by the people she phones, not because the addressees are types, but on account of the predictably defensive hypocrisy displayed by most of the middle-class people she rings. Judith Keith's reaction to what is said by the person to whom she is talking ("Warum sollte ich so was denken?" [*BFA* 4:385; What put that idea into my head?: *FM* 46]) allows the audience to deduce the subtext of their words. She is in this particular instance clearly responding to a denial that prior arrangements for regular games of bridge between the Keiths and a colleague and his wife have collapsed because of the Keiths' mixed marriage. The year 1935, the date that Brecht subsequently appended to this scene, was the year of the Nuremberg Race Laws. Judith Keith's response — "Das weiß ich doch, daß ihr nicht so seid, und wenn, das sind doch unruhige Zeiten und alle Leute passen so auf" (*BFA* 4:386; I know you're not that sort, but what about it, these are unsettled times and everybody's being so careful: *FM* 47) — even offers Frau Schöck a fig leaf behind which to conceal her apparent desire not to come across as a fair-weather friend, while at the same time making it very clear to the audience that this is precisely what she and her surgeon husband have become. Slightly less transparent is Frau Keith's response to her sister-in-law, whom she has asked to look after her husband once she has left for Amsterdam: "Warum möchtest du nicht? — So wird es aber doch nicht aussehen, bestimmt nicht für Fritz" (*BFA* 4:386; Why not? — Nobody'd think that, anyway not Fritz: *FM* 47). Perhaps she is trying to convince Fritz's sister that she will not be incriminating herself by demonstrating solidarity with her own brother, who made a mistake in choosing someone the NS regime would consider a racially unsuitable wife. Or maybe she is simply trying to second-guess the probability of receiving such a response. What results from the telephone exchanges is a series of palimpsests of her *friends'* hypocritical reactions to her embarrassing Jewish status. It is for once they who are the main targets of the usually satirical estranging device. Shifting the focus, Fradkin talks in exceptionally positive terms of Judith Keith's magnanimity:

> Es kostet sie Überwindung, mit diesen Leuten zu sprechen, die unverbindliche Plauderei, mit der sie, ein Mensch von empfindsamem Ehrgefühl, ihren Schmerz und ihre bange Sorge verdeckt, kostet sie eine gewaltige Willensanstrengung, doch sie tut dies für ihren Mann,

---

familiar, quasi-realistic devices for the purpose of estrangement in the case of the *Furcht und Elend* project.

aus Sorge um ihn, damit er nach ihrer Abreise nicht einsam und verlassen zurück bleibt.[58]

Yet despite the audience's inevitable sympathy for the protagonist,[59] they are still left feeling that her generosity of spirit, even towards her husband, is ideologically misplaced. In a move to prevent the scene from slipping from poignancy into self-indulgent sentimentality, Brecht allows Judith Keith to compromise herself by saying in one of her rehearsed speeches: "Was tue ich ihnen? Ich habe mich doch nie in die Politik gemischt. War ich für Thälmann?" (*BFA* 4:388; What am I doing to them? I've never had anything to do with politics. Did I vote Communist?: *FM* 49). From then on, she blames virtually everything on her husband and "them" (i.e., the National Socialists) without ever returning to the uncomfortable matter of her own personal complicity in what is happening in Third Reich Germany.

The device of the one-sided telephone conversation, usually used to create suspense in films and in much modern Aristotelian drama, is more likely to have been influenced in the case of "Die jüdische Frau" by contemporary satirical cabaret.[60] The "Telefongespräch" had by the time of *Furcht und Elend* long been a staple part of stand-up political cabaret. As has been pointed out, the one-sided telephone call has the advantage of allowing audiences to create their own picture of the person at the other end of the line:

> Das Pointierungsgitter des Telefongesprächs hat [. . .] den Vorteil, daß Einwände des verdeckten Gesprächspartners fingiert werden können, Einwände, die dieselbe Form haben, als würden sie auf Publikumseinwände erfolgen. Die sprachliche Form dieses offenen Dialogs läßt also eine Rezeption als Publikumsdialog zu.[61]

---

[58] Fradkin, *Bertolt Brecht: Weg und Methode*, 175.

[59] Brecht observes: "Bei dem Stück *Furcht und Elend* ist die Versuchung für den Schauspieler, eine Spielweise anzuwenden, die für Stücke aristotelischer Dramatik am Platz ist, größer als bei andern Stücken dieser Sammlung" [i.e., Malik, vol. 3] ("Anmerkung zu *Furcht und Elend des Dritten Reiches*" [*BFA* 24:226]; English translation in *FM* 97). His references to the solutions adopted in "99%" make it clear that the temptation needed to be either resisted or offset by the acting style familiar from Epic Theater.

[60] The subject is covered in Benedikt Vogel, *Fiktionskulisse: Poetik und Geschichte des Kabaretts* (Paderborn: Schöningh, 1993), 195. Vogel offers a detailed analysis of the cabaret sketch "Telefongespräch mit Tante," performed by Wilhelm Bendow at the "Wilde Bühne" in 1921. Another possible influence on the present scene is the telephone discussion of the arrangements for the funeral of Archduke Ferdinand in Scene 3 of the "Vorspiel" to Karl Kraus, *Die letzten Tage der Menschheit*, 12–16.

[61] Vogel, *Fiktionskulisse*, 175.

Yet whereas political cabaret's use of such fictive scenarios is comically satirical, Brecht gives the device a much darker function in this scene because Judith Keith has to hide her real plans from her friends, her husband, and from the Gestapo.

The rapid mood shifts during different adjacent parts of "Die jüdische Frau" are another feature of this play's particular montage technique. This has its counterpart in "Der Spitzel," an episode that has much in common with "Die jüdische Frau" when it comes to the deployment of covert defamiliarization devices and the maximizing of epic discontinuity at scene level.

"Der Spitzel"

Although entitled "Der Spitzel" in the singular, the scene in question implies that there may well be a number of potential political informers waiting in the wings to criticize, or even denounce, the teacher and his wife. But there are also times when, for lack of reliable information, audiences are likely to share the couple's suspicion that their own son, Klaus-Heinrich, is the person most likely to denounce them because of the unguarded critical comments one of them makes about life under the NS regime. Before the boy leaves the house, he has heard his father vehemently attack the NS press[62] as well as declaring that *he*, as Klaus-Heinrich's father, is the person to decide what is fit material for his son to read, not the local HJ Gruppenführer. The boy has even been ordered to switch off the radio, another source of orchestrated Nazi propaganda of which the Gruppenführer would doubtless approve. In other words, if Klaus-Heinrich wanted to denounce his parents, he would probably have sufficient cause to do so, having overheard much incriminating evidence. Indeed, he would be praised for doing so. Boys in the HJ, his parents know, are deliberately encouraged to report everything.[63]

---

[62] The son's question concerning what he has read in the newspaper ("Machen alle Geistlichen das, Papa?" [*BFA* 4:393]) is an allusion to the campaign of trumped-up charges of homosexuality and pedophilia that the Goebbels press waged against the Catholic Church from 1935 onwards. Its purpose was to diminish the Church's moral credibility as a center of political opposition. Show trials of hundreds of priests followed in Munich and Koblenz in 1936 and 1937. As is clear from reports in the *Völkischer Beobachter* (31 July 1935), the campaign was well underway by the middle of the year in which "Der Spitzel" is set, in that other great bastion of German Catholicism: Cologne.

[63] According to reliable accounts, members of the various branches of the HJ, down to the lowest rank (i.e., that of "Pimpf"), were particularly zealous in denouncing their teachers, classmates, religious instructors, and on occasions even their parents.

In focusing on a situation where the scene's most likely spy or denouncer may have left the room before some of the teacher's most damning remarks have even been made, "Der Spitzel" effectively replicates the mood of uncertainty all too familiar in totalitarian states where it is often difficult to ascertain whether or not one is in the presence of a putative informer. Lukács expressly praised the scene's "Bild vom Schrecken des faschistischen Terrors in Deutschland," but what "Der Spitzel" actually highlights is the extent to which, in such a surveillance society, the pervasive fear of everyday fascism is a complex product of actual danger, imagined threats, and the omnipresent climate of suspicion. In the Third Reich, it has been claimed, "what counted was not whether there really were informers everywhere, but the fact that people thought there were."[64] As Klaus-Heinrich's father succinctly puts it, "Gegen alle liegt was vor. Alle sind verdächtig. Es genügt doch, daß der *Verdacht* besteht, daß einer verdächtig ist" (*BFA* 4:397; They've something against everyone. Everyone's suspect. Once the suspicion's there, one's suspect: *FM* 59). "Einen Judas hast du mir geboren!" he at one stage complains, blaming his wife:

> Da sitzt er bei Tisch und horcht, während er die Suppe löffelt, die wir ihm hinstellen, und merkt sich alles, was seine Erzeuger sagen, der Spitzel! (*BFA* 4:399)

> [A Judas, that's what you've borne me. Sitting at the table listening, gulping down the soup we've given him and noting down whatever his father says, the little spy. (*FM* 60)]

Anyone present, even in such a behind-closed-doors family situation, is a potential denouncer in the eyes of someone aware of having dangerously overstepped the mark. Nevertheless, a sullen adolescent (as a HJ "Pimpf" Klaus-Heinrich is in the 10–14 age-bracket), witnessing his parents' behavior and perhaps making a mental note of what they say, might be doing so simply because this is what the HJ encourages him to do. Or, if he does inform on them, he could be merely getting back at the grown-ups, in line with his alleged general vindictiveness (*BFA* 4:396). Or he could be attempting to intimidate, and thus find ways to exploit, his parents. After all, his father admits to having confiscated their son's pet frog for the neglected creature's own good. Klaus-Heinrich probably also knows that his parents have in the past attempted to bribe the *Blockwart*[65] with generous presents and had even taken on the man's daughter as a housemaid,

---

(Robert Gellately, *The Gestapo and German Society: Enforcing Racial Policy, 1933–1945* [Oxford: Clarendon, 1990], 156).

[64] Evans, *The Third Reich in Power*, 105.

[65] On the *Blockwart* system's organization and the duties of each individual *Blockwart*, see Evans, *The Third Reich in Power*, 108–9. Only 12% of denunciations,

thinking thereby to ingratiate themselves with her father. In doing so, they have unfortunately admitted another potential spy into their midst. But the maid is neither the real nor the only threat to the family. Husband and wife have also become wary of even close relatives and professional colleagues. "Sag so etwas nur deiner Mutter, und wir können in den schönsten Salat kommen," the husband warns his wife (*BFA* 4:392; If you mentioned anything of the sort to your mother we could land in a proper mess: *FM* 54). They feel the need to keep their distance from another teacher, who has an NS school inspectorate case (another form of legalized intimidation) currently hanging over his head. They also steer clear of the Lemke family, who never miss an opportunity to rub their noses in the fact that they are "nicht luftschutzfreudig genug" (*BFA* 4:392; slack about civil defence, *FM* 53). Such a failure almost begs to be reported to the local Gestapo as an act of dissidence. To crown it all, young Klaus-Heinrich's world consists of a whole army of potential spies: "Jeder Schüler ein Spitzel," in the words of the scene's *Vorspruch* (*BFA* 4:391; Every schoolboy's a spy: *FM* 52).

The first verse of this *Vorspruch* presents an inverted image of the traditional relationship between teacher and pupil, with politically indoctrinated schoolchildren at liberty to give their would-be educators a painful lesson about the power of youth under the new regime:

> Es kommen die Herrn Professoren
> Der Pimpf nimmt sie bei den Ohren
> Und lehrt sie Brust heraus stehn.
> [. . .] Sie müssen
> Von Himmel und Erde nichts wissen.
> Aber wer weiß was auf wen? (*BFA* 4:391)

> [Here come the worthy schoolteachers
> The Youth Movement takes the poor creatures
> And makes them all thrust out their chest.
> [. . .] So now marking
> Is based not on knowledge, but narking
> And on who knows whose weaknesses best. (*FM* 52)]

The second verse offers a similarly topsy-turvy picture of the family relationships:

> Dann kommen die lieben Kinder
> Sie holen die Henker und Schinder
> Und führen sie nach Haus.
> Sie zeigen auf ihre Väter

---

most common among the lower middle class, were politically motivated by 1936, according to Evans, *The Third Reich in Power*, 101–2.

Und nennen sie Verräter
Man führt sie gefesselt hinaus. (*BFA* 4:391)

[They educate traducers
To set hatchet-men and bruisers
On their own parents' tail.
Denounced by their sons as traitors
To Himmler's apparatus
The fathers go handcuffed to gaol. (*FM* 52)]

This two-part *Vorspruch* (a rarity, most *Furcht und Elend* scenes are prefigured by only one verse) offers a defamiliarized picture of customary adult-child relations as a comment on power structures in the Third Reich in general. Two verses are in this instance required to show the way the pupils' conditioning at school now gradually invades the household realm. Rather than being mere victims of the new power structure, however, the teacher and his wife, Herr and Frau Furcke, tend to come across as sad, yet at the same time ridiculous figures. Their angst-ridden mood is established at the outset by a series of comic sequences. The time, for example, when the husband declares that within the four walls of his own home he is at liberty to say whatever he likes, only to be cut short whenever the maid enters the room: a classic display of "die Gestik des Verstummens," as Brecht called it. Being repeatedly silenced in mid-sentence is an example of what Henri Bergson called "comedy of repetition," as is the father's complaint that "man kann eben nicht in einem Land leben, wo es eine Katastrophe ist, wenn es regnet" (*BFA* 4:392; it's quite intolerable, living in a country where it's a disaster when it rains: *FM* 53–54), and variations thereon, coupled with his wife's continual references to how wonderful things were in "the good old days," i.e., during the Weimar Republic. Such repeated comic scenarios initially establish a mood of general amusement at the two grown-ups' nervous behavior. However, once the Furckes discover that Klaus-Heinrich is no longer in the house and they cannot remember what parts of their conversation he may have overheard and then try to imagine where he can have gone, a further distancing mechanism is brought to bear, one that again functions as part of a Trojan horse defamiliarization strategy.

Aware of the danger they could be in, Klaus-Heinrich's parents decide to concoct a less incriminating version of what Herr Furcke might have actually said. The wife sets the attempt to devise a smokescreen in motion:

Können wir nicht ausdenken, was du gemeint haben kannst bei deinen Bemerkungen? Ich meine, er hat dich dann eben mißverstanden. [. . .] Wir müssen uns alles genau zurechtlegen, und zwar sofort. Wir dürfen keine Minute verlieren. (*BFA* 4:397)

[Couldn't we work out what you could have meant by your remarks? Then he could just have misunderstood you. [...] We must straighten everything out right away. There's not a minute to spare. (*FM* 59)]

At this stage, the Furckes' chief problem is that they do not know exactly when Klaus-Heinrich left the living room, a difficulty compounded by the fact that neither of them can recall the precise order in which Herr Furcke's various incriminating remarks were made. Added to which, they suspect that anything they decide to incorporate into their new version of what was said then risks being officially construed as evidence of either a guilty conscience or guilt itself. The scene's *Vorspruch* has already established that the word of a boy in the HJ is more likely to be believed than that of any adult currently under Gestapo suspicion.

The acts of reconstruction and defensive reformulation engaged in by husband and wife in their frantic retrospective attempt to put the record straight are, like Judith Keith's rehearsals in "Die jüdische Frau," reminiscent of Brecht's "Straßenszene" model. Whether or not the end-result is denunciation, "Der Spitzel" also centers, figuratively speaking, on a (political) accident — or rather, an accident still waiting to happen, given the teacher's rash outspokenness and his various blatant errors of judgment. Just as witnesses to a street accident will compare notes on what they have seen, give their version of events, and even apportion blame, so for Klaus-Heinrich's parents the sequence of remarks that could be used as evidence of their treachery has to be carefully reconstructed. Because they do not know how many and which incriminating comments Klaus-Heinrich overheard or what his response has been in the meantime, their repeated attempts at closing the living-room door when their son has already bolted may be focused on what might still turn out to be an accident that never happened or a "Straßenszene" model deprived of a clear narrative. To be sure, "Die Straßenszene" was only intended to offer a *basic model* of Epic Theater's approach. Inevitably, the situation in "Der Spitzel" is far more complicated, mainly due to the imponderables noted above. And the desperate, tragi-comic way in which Klaus-Heinrich's parents try to piece together an exonerating version of events that Sunday afternoon makes for a radically different response on the audience's part to the serious comparison of eyewitness perspectives that the "Straßenszene" essay describes. What is more, the Furckes' "Einander-etwas-Vormachen" at times differs from the essay's paradigmatic post-accident reconstruction because of the way the couple's roles perceptibly change as the reconstruction unfolds. After repeated attempts to correct her husband's claims about just what he did say, the wife begins to assume the role of interrogator: "Du tust ja schon direkt, als sei ich die Polizei!" she complains at one stage (*BFA* 4:396; You're acting absolutely as if I were the police: *FM* 58). This is not an unjustified complaint, for there are moments when it seems more likely that the wife will denounce her husband than

Klaus-Heinrich will inform on his parents. Her phraseology becomes more noticeably influenced by Nazi propaganda as their desperation grows. Like the two scientists at the end of "Physiker," in trying to come across as convinced National Socialists, husband and wife end up presenting something that is little more than a caricature of the NS regime's propaganda clichés.

As also happened in "Die jüdische Frau," a montage structure, a form of epic discontinuity involving the segmenting of individual sequences, divided up in this case either by the maid's intrusions or by the ominous presence — or absence — of Klaus-Heinrich, creates space for the necessary critical distance. This time in a more strikingly anti-illusionist way, the effect of discontinuity is in part achieved through the intermittent insertion of periods of silence, indicated by typographical blanks and a stage blackout technique. But these blackouts and pauses for critical reflection also risk creating dramatic tension. (That is, after all, what meaningful pauses are normally used for in drama.) Thus, "Der Spitzel" centers on a predicament that is on the surface just as likely to produce Aristotelian Theater's "Spannung auf den Ausgang" as Epic Theater's "Spannung auf den Gang" (eyes on the finish; eyes on the course: *BT* 37), to borrow the terms Brecht used in his notes to the opera *Aufstieg und Fall der Stadt Mahagonny* (*BFA* 24:79). Early on, the scene twice plays with audience expectations of what the eventual outcome will be: (i) in the second *Vorspruch* verse, with its picture of children as spies and denouncers, and (ii) in the wife's anxious reference to a recent denunciation in the community, one that was evidently acted on: "Und der Junge, von dem Schmulkes erzählt haben? Sein Vater soll noch immer im Lager sein" (*BFA* 4:395; What about that boy the Schmulkes were telling us about? They say his father's still in a concentration camp: *FM* 56). This is the fate that husband and wife both fear will be the possible consequence of being denounced by their son. In the final few minutes of the scene, their efforts to prepare for such a contingency become ever more frantic — and ever more ridiculous — as they struggle to decide whether or not Herr Furcke should wear his Iron Cross, then dither about where Hitler's picture is best displayed, whether the maid should be slipped a ten-Mark bribe, and resolutely decide to pack a case with some underwear for him to take into custody. After all this panic, Klaus-Heinrich's seemingly innocent reappearance comes as an anticlimax: "Hast du nur Schokolade gekauft?" "Was denn sonst? Klar" (*BFA* 4:400; Did you simply go out to buy chocolate? Whatever else? Obvious, isn't it?: *FM* 61). Thereafter, Brecht plays with his audience by replacing this "Aristotelian" cathartic ending with a situation leaving "den Vorhang zu und alle Fragen offen" (the curtain down and all the questions open), to use the words of *Der gute Mensch von Sezuan* (*BFA* 6:278). The husband's question as to whether his son is telling the truth and his wife's shrug of the shoulders opens the door to more destabilizing possibilities: not only in the sense that fear has been shown to be more a matter of the unknown than of certainties, but because Klaus-Heinrich's mother and father now find themselves faced with a further dilemma. Although they desperately need to believe their son, their immediate response suggests that they no longer feel able to do so. They struggle to find a way to defuse a potentially incriminating scene, while at the same time suspecting that any such move could still be counterproductive. Rather than create a situation where audiences wholeheartedly empathize with Herr and Frau Furcke as they panic in their no-win situation, Brecht structures his scene so as to create epic distance vis-à-vis the adult protagonists, while still allowing room for the obvious implication that they should have sought a real solution to their predicament — i.e., a political one. After all, as we saw in Chapter Three, *Furcht und Elend* was supposed to be less an illustration of theater working cathartically with fear and pity than one of curiosity and willingness to help.

By the time he came to consider how the scene should be handled in *The Private Life*, Brecht, writing to the U.S. version's potential director Max Reinhardt in May 1942, included a few lines from one of the alternative *Vorsprüche* he was still toying with as a possibility:

> Und da ist auch ein Lehrer auf unserm Karren / Ein Hauptmann jetzt, mit einem Hut aus Stahl / Der erteilt seine Lektionen / Den Fischern Norges und den Weinbauern der Champagner / Denn da war ein Tag vor sieben Jahren / Verblichen zwar, doch vergessen niemals / Wo er [der Lehrer] im Schoß seiner Familie gelernt hat / Spione zu hassen. (*BFA* 29:231)

> [And in that truck there rides a teacher / A captain now with helmet of steel / he gives his lessons to / the fishermen of Norway and the wine growers of Champagne / For seven years ago on a certain / faded but never forgotten day / he learned in the bosom of his family / to hate informers. (*BBL* 347)]

Brecht then added the further suggestion, apparently never taken up, that "unter einer großen, aufgehängten schwarzen Schrift, Datum und Adresse des Lehrers angebend, 'Der Spitzel' gezeigt wird" (*BFA* 29:231; under a big black and white sign indicating the date and the teacher's address, *The Informer* is played: *BBL* 347). In the published New Directions text, the Voice's English verse is simply followed by a placard bearing the details "COLOGNE 1935" (*The Private Life*, 71). Yet it is important to recognize that Brecht did briefly consider adapting the epic frame to supply "documentary" detail to serve as a form of ad hominem naming and blaming. While this might have worked in the case of an accusatory, grandly historical play like Rolf Hochhuth's *Der Stellvertreter*, it is difficult to see what the desired effect would have been in the case of *Furcht und Elend*'s cycle of semi-fictive scenes of "Alltagsfaschismus" in the Third Reich. Since the scene was fictive, the protagonists also were, and hence beyond the reach of international law. Conceivably, exile documentary theater of the 1930s could never have the same kind of accusatory impact that West German political theater of the 1960s was frequently able to achieve.

"Alltägliches Theater" and "Alltagsfaschismus"

"[Es] kommt mir vor," a character says of Brechtian Epic Theater in "[V-Effekte, Dreigespräch]," "als hättet ihr einfach aus der Komödie soundso viele Elemente genommen und sie in das ernste Stück gesteckt" (*BFA* 22:398; It seems to me as if you simply borrowed so-and-so many elements from comedy and inserted them into a serious play: "Alienation Effects: A Three-way Discussion"). The discussion was not about *Furcht und Elend*, but it could easily have been. Yet if that had been the case, the term "Komödie" would need to be sufficiently elastic, as Hartung has shown, to include elements of the stand-up revue sketch, political satire's apocryphal anecdotes, and the subversive *Flüsterwitz*. Brecht's interest in these sub-genres and, more generally, his experimental exploration of the advantages of what one might call "illusion-based alienation" had little to do with the concessions to American tastes that one encounters in *The Private Life*. Rather, his radically new approach to Trojan horse defamiliarization strategies is highly significant in the present context for other reasons. First, because Brecht believed that epic actors had much to learn about distancing technique from real-life situations:

> [der Schauspieler] benützt dieses Mittel [Verfremdungen] eben so weit, als jede beliebige Person ohne schauspielerische Fähigkeiten [. . .] es benützen würde, um eine andere Person darzustellen, das heißt ihr Verhalten zu zeigen. (*BFA* 22:642)

> [[the actor] uses these means [alienation devices] just as any normal person with no particular acting talent would use them if he wanted to portray someone else, i.e., show how he behaves. (*BT* 136)]

Second, and more important, because this insight justified for Brecht the smuggling of alienation devices into quasi-realistic scenes, and invariably doing so more with an eye to influencing audience response than to winning the approval of often hostile left-wing *Kulturpolitiker* or bypassing the prejudices of dyed-in-the-wool "Aristotelian" audiences. What was at stake during the Realism Debate and the ensuing antifascist campaign was above all Epic Theater's relationship to life. If "Die Straßenszene," predicated on the assumption "Es besteht kein elementarer Unterschied zwischen dem natürlichen epischen Theater und dem künstlichen *epischen Theater*" (*BFA* 22:380–81; the elements of natural and of artificial epic theatre are the same: *BT* 128), could provide a basic model for an "anti-

Aristotelian" scene, Epic Theater could in its turn furnish constructive models with which to dissect everyday political behavior without sacrificing either the requisite distance or minimizing human suffering, especially when a work's serious subject was the "fear and misery" of life in the Third Reich. This, rather than any similarity between comedy and Epic Theater's camouflaged defamiliarization strategies — or even its use of comic scenes to sugarcoat the pill of Popular Front didacticism — is the main reason for Brecht's retention of both alienation devices and subtle structural "epic" features in this, his most impressive dramatic contribution to the fight against National Socialism. *Furcht und Elend* was no surrender to Aristotelian expectations, nor did it require any outright abandonment of Epic Theater. It was a tactical move appropriate to the demands of the occasion.

Concluding Remarks

THE YEAR 1938 BROUGHT both a high point and an unpredictable set-back in the fortunes of Brecht's *Furcht und Elend* project. The Paris premiere of "99%" (21–22 May) was an undoubted success, especially among the German exile community, and it was an event that would prove particularly important for Walter Benjamin's ongoing crusade on the play-wright's behalf, the collective fruits of which would eventually be pub-lished by Suhrkamp in 1966 under the title *Versuche über Brecht.* One of the peculiarities of *Furcht und Elend*'s reception is the fact that a work that was in many respects so untypical of Brecht's mainstream anti-illusionist Epic Theater should have played such a major role in Benjamin's under-standing of the playwright's achievements. Because he was still primarily associated with *Die Dreigroschenoper* and his austerely didactic plays of the early 1930s, the exiled Brecht desperately needed Slatan Dudow's pro-duction to succeed, not least because this play was both politically and aesthetically far more important than *Die Gewehre der Frau Carrar*, a more parochial depiction of (Spanish) fascism that Dudow had directed in Paris to much acclaim the year before. In the event, *Furcht und Elend* was to set new standards for innovative forms of Epic Theater, within a framework where many of the defamiliarizing effects operated in ways that were cun-ningly camouflaged for covert resistance reasons.

Benjamin's wholeheartedly positive review of "99%," published in *Die Neue Weltbühne* on 30 June 1938, was only matched in enthusiasm by Brecht's own glowing accolade in *Der Messingkauf.* The latter was one of the most detailed accounts he had until then given of a specific per-formance of one of his works, although perhaps for that reason the praise was attributed to his fictive alter ego, the Dramaturge. Both Benjamin's and Brecht's responses make it clear that *Furcht und Elend* had enjoyed a production guaranteed to serve as a model for the Popular Front anti-fascist theater of the time. One only has to set this achievement alongside the comparatively muted reception of Friedrich Wolf's *Professor Mamlock*, Ferdinand Bruckner's *Die Rassen* or Ernst Toller's *Pastor Hall*[1] to appre-ciate the qualitative difference between melodramatic, quasi-Aristotelian treatments of life in the Third Reich and *Furcht und Elend*'s new form of Brechtian theater, conceived as an act of "eingreifendes Denken" based on

---

[1] See details in Gerz, *Bertolt Brecht und der Faschismus*, 256–81.

political analysis. Later that same year, Brecht nevertheless found himself in a desperate predicament: unable to get the work published before the onset of the Second World War and all too aware that his analysis might soon be overtaken by events. To compound matters, professional theaters in Europe were becoming increasingly reluctant to stage works critical of the Third Reich. As a consequence, Brecht's last-ditch plea (through the medium of documentary drama) to those on the Left in Third Reich Germany to rally to the resistance cause went largely unheard. By the time the work reached the United States, he found himself preaching to the converted among Free Europe's wartime allies.

Comparing his timing with that of other, at the time high-profile, antifascist writers (Bredel, Feuchtwanger, Langhoff, Petersen, Heinrich Mann, and Wolf, for example), one might wish to charge Brecht with having spent so long meticulously preparing his various *Furcht und Elend* scenes that many previously available opportunities for the work's dissemination had slipped through his fingers. One of the main reasons behind such a delay can be found in Brecht's letter to Dudow of 19 April 1938, clearly a muchneeded rallying call to the ensemble in the run-up to the Paris premiere. (Brecht had a penchant for penning last-minute encouraging letters suitable for displaying on bulletin boards for the cast and production team to read.) In this instance, he seeks to explain why the exile antifascist situation demanded such high standards in respect of historical and artistic detail, as well as in matters pertaining to the staging of *Furcht und Elend*:

> Wir kritisieren das Hitlersystem, und von der Schärfe der Kritik hängt alles ab. Die hängt aber wieder ab von der Schärfe der Darstellung [. . .]. Lahmheit, die von mangelnder artistischer Kraft herrührt, wirkt in diesem Fall als politische Lahmheit. Welche Autorität haben wir schon im Exil, wenn nicht diejenige, welche die Qualität verleiht? Wir kritisieren das Dritte Reich, wer weiß, wer wir sind? Das Dritte Reich hat zehn Millionen Soldaten! Also muß die Kritik für sich sprechen. Wir bezweifeln die Dauer des Dritten Reiches, da müssen doch zumindest unsere Arbeiten Zeichen von Dauer an sich tragen. (*BFA* 29:88)

> [We're criticising the Nazi system, and everything depends on the incisiveness of our criticism. [. . .] In this case feebleness resulting from insufficient artistic talent will have the effect of political feebleness. What authority can we have in exile other than that conferred by quality? We stand up and criticise the Third Reich. But nobody knows who we are, whereas the Third Reich has ten million soldiers. So the criticism has to speak for itself. We doubt the durability of the Third Reich. Then our work must show the hallmark of durability. (*BBL* 284–85)]

Unfortunately, Brecht and his collaborators were to pay the price for such painstaking perfectionism. *Furcht und Elend* had to be put on the back burner for many months while his major works of antifascist poetry and fiction still reached their intended readerships. Undeterred, he remained convinced of the project's importance. The steadfastness of purpose that we observed in Chapter One, combined with Brecht's trust in the play's potential stage impact when properly directed and performed, confirmed his faith in *Furcht und Elend* and buoyed him up over the coming dark years.

Did the *Furcht und Elend* complex deserve Brecht's confidence and continued support? Judging from much of the secondary literature on the play to date, some must have thought not. However, among the work's admirers, scholars who have repeatedly demonstrated their belief in the play's artistic and political importance — including Benjamin, Bentley, Busch, Fradkin, Hartung, Knopf, Kuhn, Lyon, Mittenzwei, and, of course, Willett — the arguments of one particular advocate, Wolfgang Emmerich,[2] stand out. Emmerich is one of the few critics to judge Brecht's various achievements alongside the antifascist works of literature written by his leading contemporaries. While the Third Reich gave rise to a number of important antifascist works, Emmerich argues that few contributed "zur Aufdeckung des Kausalkomplexes in Sachen Faschismus, zur Analyse der Bewußtseinsverfassung der breiten Massen und damit zur praktischen Bekämpfbarkeit des Nationalsozialismus" (223) in the way that Brecht's writings did. Questioning the cognitive value of work by virtually all left-wing antifascist writers, with the debatable exception of Feuchtwanger, Langhoff, Wolf, and Seghers, Emmerich blames the KPD and SPD for their lamentable failure to do justice to fascism's massive power base among the petty bourgeoisie, the unemployed in the countryside, and the youth. Brecht, in contrast, is credited with insight into the relationship between National Socialism, capitalism, and the working class. He is singled out for praise as the one exile writer to raise — and address — the questions that many of his contemporaries failed even to consider. Ignoring artistic criteria, Emmerich's emphasis is firmly on Brecht's rare political competence in the field of the analysis of fascism, not on his specific strengths and achievements in depicting, caricaturing, and strengthening resistance to National Socialism. A similar, exclusively ideological focus can also be found in the various studies of "Brecht and Fascism" cited in our list of Works Consulted. Yet any assessment of the *Furcht und Elend* complex within its broader aesthetic and historical context, must, we would argue, evaluate it as a work of literature and not simply regard it as a piece of dramatized ideological doctrine. We have tried to redress this imbalance in the present study, not

---

[2] Wolfgang Emmerich, "'Massenfaschismus' und die Rolle des Ästhetischen: Faschismustheorie bei Ernst Bloch, Walter Benjamin, Bertolt Brecht," in *Antifaschistische Literatur: Programme, Autoren, Werke*, ed. Lutz Winkler (Kronberg/Ts.: Scriptor, 1977), 1:223–90.

by comparatively assessing *Furcht und Elend*'s ranking within the hierarchy of Brecht's own Epic Theater or by setting it off against the antifascist work of other German exile dramatists, but by literary analysis of individual scenes and their socio-political significance, by testing the work's value as a piece of contemporary documentary drama, and by assessing the propaganda value of the cycle's overall montage structure. The evidence such an approach offers is arguably of greater value than the mere demonstration of Brecht's political credentials or his unmitigated faith in the work.

Given that the *Furcht und Elend* project meant so much to him during his campaign against fascism, it may be difficult to understand why, in the early postwar and subsequent GDR years, Brecht never radically rethought his cycle of scenes or framed his account of life in the Third Reich to meet contemporary political circumstances, as he had done in the case of *Arturo Ui* and *Leben des Galilei*. Perhaps it was always technically less difficult to update his parable plays of the 1930s than to rework a documentary play. Or perhaps Brecht was loath to rewrite *Furcht und Elend* because any depiction of the Third Reich was uncomfortably dependent on a number of still-contentious issues. For example, there was the embarrassing question of the diminishing role of the Stalinist USSR–orchestrated Popular Front in Germany's limited resistance activities, the country's failure to liberate itself (even during the final months of the war), as well as the GDR policy of regarding fascism as having nothing to do with East German history, but seeing it as an essentially capitalist skeleton in the Federal German Republic's closet. Tellingly, the most frequently quoted line from *Arturo Ui* — "Der Schoß ist fruchtbar noch, aus dem das kroch!" (*BFA* 7:112; The womb from which it crawled is still fertile) — was usually interpreted as being aimed exclusively at West Germany, and not at the GDR's own "unbewältigte Vergangenheit." In general, the complex fluctuations in the political interpretations of *Furcht und Elend*, from the pre-war years, Brecht's Scandinavian and U.S. exile, and subsequent to his return to liberated Europe and eventually the GDR, have still to be analyzed from a nonbiased standpoint.

For a long time two prejudices hung over *Furcht und Elend*, in spite of Brecht's vigorous campaigning on the play's behalf. First, there was the generally shared assumption, one we have been at great pains to refute in the present study, that the work represented a major retreat from Brechtian Epic Theater to Socialist Realism, a volte-face sometimes interpreted as a necessary renunciation of modernism in the interests of the Popular Front antifascist literary campaign. While an undeterred Brecht patiently drew attention in private correspondence (and even in the pages of *Das Wort*) to the work's use of montage, alienating "Gesten," and various anti-illusionist commenting devices, the legend of the Marxist Prodigal Son's return to the family of communism has persisted with surprising tenacity. Such an entrenched view is not to be attributed to Lukács's growing influence on antimodernist revisionism or to the dominance of the Socialist Realist aesthetic in Eastern Bloc Europe. Rather, it is evidence of the staying power of the received wisdom, according to which any mimetic approach to contemporary socio-political problems increased in importance as the European struggle against fascism took center stage. Although *Die Gewehre der Frau Carrar* and *Furcht und Elend* are still frequently seen as noncontentious illustrations of such a paradigm shift, little distinction tends to be made between the two works' respective modi operandi. During the late 1930s, Brecht was, of course, invariably prepared to redefine "realism" to suit his purposes. At the same time, he provocatively appended the heading "*Ein Stück des epischen Theaters*" to a commentary on *Furcht und Elend* (*BFA* 24:521), as well as forewarning readers of the American translation, using Eric Bentley as his spokesman, that "the piece will be widely misunderstood unless it is interpreted as Epic Theater" (*The Private Life*, 132). Sadly, the warning fell largely on deaf ears. *Furcht und Elend* for a long time remained the subject of stubborn misunderstandings in far too many quarters, perhaps because people doggedly sought out the qualities that they wanted to find in the work, or possibly because they were reluctant to abandon the widespread assumption that, like the hero of some German Expressionist play, the Brecht of the essay "Über experimentelles Theater" had chosen to reinvent himself in the interests of the antifascist cause. In the face of such prejudice and to ward off further misunderstandings, Brecht became adept at concealing defamiliarization techniques, although for understandable reasons without resorting to subliminal effects. Moreover, he became skilled at finding ways of communicating plausibly realistic pictures of life under "Alltagsfaschismus," while at the same time leaving himself room for the creation of a necessary critical political standpoint.

The second misgiving was that *Furcht und Elend* was in one respect or another "bad theater": either too prolix or politically far too dogmatic or even badly acted into the bargain. Misgivings about the work's prolific length, the quality of the performances in Los Angeles (University of California, Berkeley, 7 June 1945) and New York (by The Theatre of All Nations, at the Pauline Edwards Theater, New York City College, 12 June 1945), and qualms about the fragmentary montage structure were mirrored in the work's low-key American reception in comparison with that of the canonical plays in the Brecht repertoire. In contrast to the earlier uninformed judgments in the case of *Die Mutter*, *Furcht und Elend*'s reception was vitiated more by an inability to appreciate montage structure and concealed defamiliarization devices than an outright antipathy towards Epic Theater in its new form.

In contrast to such audience incomprehension, the New Directions book publication of *The Private Life of the Master Race* was received extremely positively (details in *BFA* 4:532). And it was not the only augur of a better U.S. reception to come. While a one-act piece entitled *Justice* (presumably "Rechtsfindung") had the dubious honor of being the last

German play produced in New York (April 1939) before the commencement of what became known in the theater world as the "war seasons," in the mid-1940s no work by Brecht was staged in America as often as *The Private Life*. One reason for this was that documentary drama at the time generally enjoyed greater popularity here than politically didactic parable plays. The work's wartime reception in the United States was at best guarded, yet the impression it made on audiences was by no means as negative as accounts dating from 1944 suggest. Individual scenes from *The Private Life* went on to play a not inconsiderable role in U.S. political life, with individual episodes frequently performed for the benefit of union members (as had happened in earlier years for the benefit of Soviet soldiers about to depart to fight on the USSR's Western Front). Extracts from *The Private Life* even formed part of the official cultural program laid on for the international delegates attending the San Francisco Founding Congress of the United Nations on 24 October 1945. Further afield, numerous professional and amateur productions were in subsequent years staged in Great Britain, most Western European countries, and South America. Radio versions of selected scenes were broadcast in Great Britain (1940), Denmark (1947), Sweden (1954), and Poland (1956). In the twenty-first century, new productions have been staged in a number of German cities, as well as in France and Britain. However, the Berliner Ensemble's iconic landmark production of ten scenes from the cycle (1957–63), set in motion by Brecht himself during the last year of his life and staged with Helene Weigel in the cast, will always remain proof of just how compelling genuine Epic Theater could be in the right hands — even if the production only offered fewer than half of the available scenes.

The production problems created by the sheer length of the *Furcht und Elend* montage have continued to challenge directors and theater ensembles from Brecht's early exile years up to the present day. As has frequently been argued, the work's uniquely fragmented epic structure, considered in a number of chapters in the present study, lends itself admirably to a whole series of *ad hoc* productions comprising either individual scenes, sometimes juxtaposed with other antifascist material, or larger configurations usually including the corpus that has come to be recognized as comprising the work's major scenes: viz. "Das Kreidekreuz," "Der Spitzel," "Rechtsfindung," and "Die jüdische Frau." Nevertheless, far too little attention has been paid to the damage done to the *Furcht und Elend* complex by such cherry-picking approaches. As we have attempted to demonstrate in our analyses, much of the play's overall picture of life in Third Reich Germany — from the onset of totalitarian oppression, surveillance, and various other forms of "fear and misery," to individual displays of dissent, subversion, and politically organized resistance — depends on the cumulative structure of the entire cycle. As one might expect in the case of a work of Brechtian political montage, the whole is greater than the sum of its parts

— or would be, if the play was staged in its entirety over more than one evening. The conception of epic structure originally formulated in Brecht's "Anmerkungen zur Oper *Aufstieg und Fall der Stadt Mahagonny*" implies the notion of quasi-autonomous scenes, whereas in some cases, above all in the case of the *Furcht und Elend* project, only a limited semblance of autonomy within the framework of an overall macro-montage structure is to be discerned. The contrast between early Epic Theater's alleged principle of "Jede Szene für sich" (rather than "Eine Szene für die andere") needs reexamining in the case of *Furcht und Elend*'s montage structure. The difference has underestimated implications for the play's reception. Brecht's interest in the resistance theme, for example, depends, as we demonstrated in Chapter Four, on its belonging to a pattern designed to emphasize its nature as "zwar wachsend," rather than consisting of a diffuse array of individual displays of personal dissatisfaction, local grievances and desperate measures. To ignore the extent to which the entire *Furcht und Elend* complex is the quintessential example of what Brecht once heralded as the new "Kontinuität in der Montage" is essentially to do an injustice to the play's generic integrity. And that, as we have tried to show, is essentially to depoliticize the work, a work that is both politically and historically a major new achievement within Brecht's series of experiments with Epic Theater. While Brecht was rightly unhappy at the way epic montage was treated by some of his critics as a technical matter (a "Formprinzip"), the form was in this case politically dictated and crucial to the picture of the Third Reich he sought to present. During the exile period, it may have been to his advantage that selective presentation tempered the politics, while still emphasizing the playwright's antifascist stance.

One of the principal underlying assumptions in the present study is that *Furcht und Elend* is best approached as a documentary work, the result of meticulous research drawing on a vast range of contemporary sources of information. Given the importance of this aspect of Brecht's "Zyklus aus der Gegenwart," we felt strongly while working on the present study that the play required substantially more historical and political exegesis than it had hitherto received, especially considering the twenty-first century's ever-increasing distance from the period in question. Of course, Brecht's use of copious source material, impressive though it is, was no guarantee of socio-political accuracy. For this reason, the present study also approaches the cycle of scenes by testing them against present-day historical knowledge about what life was actually like in the Third Reich. In many cases, Brecht proves to be a fairly reliable commentator on the five years from the Nazis' coming to power in January 1933 to Third Reich Germany's annexation of Austria in 1938 (where *Furcht und Elend* ends) or the war on the Eastern Front (at times vividly evoked in the frame to *The Private Life*). Obviously, no one should expect an exile writer always to have his finger on the pulse of a nation that had changed so fundamentally since his departure. Nevertheless, what still surprises about *Furcht und Elend* is the palpable accuracy of its picture, especially in the case of "Alltagsfaschismus": National Socialism experienced at grassroots level. Not only are the historical facts and collective mood-swings convincingly depicted, the play also captures the various ways in which people living in a threateningly brutal surveillance society think, express themselves, and interrelate.

There is, however, one major respect in which *Furcht und Elend* risks becoming an untrustworthy companion through the labyrinthine complexities of the fear and misery of daily life in the Third Reich. We are, of course, referring to Brecht's self-evident indebtedness to Marxist-Leninist thinking about class warfare, and, more immediately, the contemporary Comintern approach to German "fascism."

As we saw in Chapter One, Brecht had declared that his antifascist activities were always of a purely literary nature. Yet one does not always gain this impression from some of his pre-war utterances: for example, his address to the Second International Writers' Congress for the Defense of Culture, with its declaration "Diesen Kriegen wie jenen anderen Kriegen, von denen wir sprachen, muß der Krieg erklärt werden, und dieser Krieg muß als Krieg geführt werden" (*BFA* 22:325; We must declare war on these wars, as on every other war of which we have spoken, and our war must be prosecuted as a war: *BAP* 171). Such rhetoric, clearly formulated for maximum impact at an intellectual writers' conference, would doubtless have rung hollow to real resistance fighters operating underground at the time. It was not that Brecht was hubristic enough to assume that, in the war on fascism, the pen was mightier than the sword. His purpose was not to suggest that exile German antifascist writing was at the time comparable to the practical resistance work that so many *Furcht und Elend* scenes call out for. Rather, his agenda was a substantially different one. As he makes clear, above all in letters written during the American exile period, the play's task was to give National Socialism's enemies outside Germany a clearer picture of just what kind of regime they were fighting, and, as a consequence, a clearer strategy ("know thine enemy") and greater national resolve to enter the fray, a necessary lesson for those not yet engaged in the struggle against fascism. The principal questions arising from Brecht's use of documentary drama to explore life in the Third Reich was whether his picture was correct and — above all — balanced.

Clearly, there are few scenes in *Furcht und Elend* that depict genuine, dyed-in-the-wool Nazis. Too often, even characters who appear on stage wearing Nazi uniforms or who might be seen as "Hitlers Hintermänner" come across as more motivated by opportunism, peer pressure, and fear than by ideology. We encounter very little unequivocally antisemitic behavior in the play, although the impact of the regime's racial laws is flagged in a number of scenes. The preparations for a new war are repeatedly emphasized, although, like the characters on stage, we learn less about the expansionist purpose of the war to come than many Germans did from Nazi propaganda or even a cursory reading of *Mein Kampf.* While a number of scenes memorably evoke the role played by psychological intimidation, rather than brute force, *Furcht und Elend* makes remarkably little reference to the enthusiasm with which the people greeted the new regime. That only comes in "Volksgemeinschaft" and "Volksbefragung." It is as if Brecht wanted to suggest that popular enthusiasm for the NSDAP and its charismatic leader was more a fiction of NS propaganda than a reality. This is, of course, not unconnected with the stress that Brecht puts on the part played by fear and intimidation in persuading the German people to acquiesce in Hitler's plans for Germany and its European neighbors. While recent historical scholarship has done much to document the nature and effect of intimidatory surveillance in the Third Reich, Brecht's play helps its audience to penetrate further into the minds of both the perpetrators and their class and racial enemies.

In "The *Other* Germany: 1943," Brecht suggested that "the exile's trade is: hoping" (*BFA* 23:25). Our treatment in Chapter Four of resistance within the Third Reich's borders revealed a picture of ever-increasing hope that effective resistance could still be possible, coupled with a reluctance on the German people's part to engage in any large-scale uprising. Not surprisingly, the working class is regularly presented as the driving force behind acts of dissidence and resistance, whereas the petty bourgeoisie and the professional middle classes come across as compliant fellow-travelers. Given that the core *Furcht und Elend* scenes covered only the first five years of NS rule, it is understandable that the thematization of resistance is all too circumscribed, and that other forms of opposition (from the church, the military, anarchic youth groups, and lone idealists) also remain few and far between. Too much emphasis on these sources of resistance would not have suited the playwright's purposes. If Brecht had once hoped that critical distance would give exile audiences able to influence events within Nazi Germany itself the impetus to intensify resistance, by the time the play ends, and even more so during the period covered by *The Private Life*, such hopes had generally been dashed. "Die deutsche Misere" had once again become a reason for political recriminations.

Sometime during 1940, with the war that had been so long in preparation now in its second year, Brecht begins to consider just what value *Furcht und Elend des Dritten Reiches* would have for future audiences ("die Nachgeborenen"), once the slaughter had ended and rebuilding commenced. This is his conclusion:

> *Furcht und Elend des Dritten Reiches* werden nach dem Untergang dieses Reiches keine Anklage mehr sein, wenn auch vielleicht immer noch eine Warnung. ("Über die Verwendung von Prinzipien," *BFA* 22:678)

> [After the fall of this Reich, *Fear and Misery of the Third Reich* will cease to be an accusatory work, but will perhaps remain a warning.]

Appendix A: *Furcht und Elend* Scene Titles and Their English Equivalents

BFA German titles are given in alphabetical order. The corresponding English titles are those used in *FM*. Other titles are sometimes used in *The Private Life*.

Arbeitsbeschaffung	Job creation
Arbeitsdienst	Labour service
Das Kreidekreuz	The chalk cross
Das Mahnwort	The motto
Das neue Kleid	The new dress
Der alte Kämpfer	The old militant
Der Bauer füttert die Sau	The farmer feeds his sow
Der Entlassene	Release
Der Gefühlsersatz	Ersatz feelings
Der Spitzel	The spy
Der Verrat	A case of betrayal
Die Bergpredigt	The Sermon on the Mount
Die Berufskrankheit	Occupational disease
Die Internationale	The Internationale
Die jüdische Frau	The Jewish wife
Die Kiste	The box
Die schwarzen Schuhe	The black shoes
Die Stunde des Arbeiters	Workers' playtime
Die Wahl	The vote
Dienst am Volke	Servants of the people
In den Kasernen wird die Beschießung von Almeria bekannt	News of the bombardment of Almería gets to the barracks
Moorsoldaten	Peat-bog soldiers
Physiker	The physicists
Rechtsfindung	Judicial process
Volksbefragung	Consulting the people
Volksgemeinschaft	One big Family
Was hilft gegen Gas?	Any good against gas?
Winterhilfe	Charity begins at home
Zwei Bäcker	Two bakers

Appendix B: The First Four Verses of "Die deutsche Heerschau" in German and English

DIE DEUTSCHE HEERSCHAU

Als wir im fünften Jahre hörten, jener
Der von sich sagt, Gott habe ihn gesandt
Sei jetzt fertig zu seinem Krieg, geschmiedet
Sei Tank, Geschütz und Schlachtschiff, und es stünden
In seinen Hangars Flugzeuge von solcher Anzahl
Daß sie, erhebend sich auf seinen Wink
Den Himmel verdunkeln würden, da beschlossen wir
Uns umzusehn, was für ein Volk, bestehend aus was für Menschen
In welchem Zustand, mit was für Gedanken
Er unter seine Fahne rufen wird. Wir hielten Heerschau.

Dort kommen sie herunter
Ein bleicher, kunterbunter
Haufe. Und hoch voran
Ein Kreuz auf blutroten Flaggen
Das hat einen großen Haken
Für den armen Mann.

Und die, die nicht marschieren
Kriechen auf allen vieren
In seinen großen Krieg.
Man hört nicht Stöhnen noch Klagen
Man hört nicht Murren noch Fragen
Vor lauter Militärmusik.

Sie kommen mit Weibern und Kindern
Entronnen aus fünf Wintern
Sie sehen nicht fünfe mehr.
Sie schleppen die Kranken und Alten
Und lassen uns Heerschau halten
Über sein ganzes Heer. (*BFA* 4:341)

THE GERMAN MARCH-PAST

When He had ruled five years, and they informed us
That He who claimed to have been sent by God
Was ready for His promised war, the steelworks
Had forged tank, gun and warship, and there waited
Within His hangars aircraft in so great a number
That they, leaving the earth at His command
Would darken all the heavens, then we became determined
To see what sort of nation, formed from what sort of people
In what condition, what sort of thoughts thinking
He would be calling to His colours. We staged a march-past.

See, now they come towards us
A motley sight rewards us
Their banners go before.
To show how straight their course is
They carry crooked crosses
Which double-cross the poor.

Some march along like dummies
Others crawl on their tummies
Towards the war He's planned.
One hears no lamentation
No murmurs of vexation
One only hears the band.

With wives and kids arriving
Five years they've been surviving.
Five more is more than they'll last.
A ramshackle collection
They parade for our inspection
As they come marching past. (*FM* 3)

Bibliography

Primary Literature

(i) Bertolt Brecht

Strakh i otchayanie v III. Imperii. Translated by Semyon Kirsanov. Moscow: Khudozhestvennaya kniga, 1941.

Fear and Misery of the Third Reich. Translated by anon. Moscow: Khudozhestvennaya kniga, 1942.

The Private Life of the Master Race: A Documentary Play. Translated by Eric Russell Bentley [assisted by Elisabeth Hauptmann]. New York: New Directions, 1944.

Furcht und Elend des III. Reiches: 24 Szenen. New York: Aurora, 1945.

Furcht und Elend des III. Reiches: 24 Szenen. Berlin: Aufbau ("AuroraBücherei"), 1948.

Furcht und Elend des Dritten Reiches: Eine Auswahl. Edited by Hans Kaufmann. Berlin-Leipzig: Volk und Wissen, 1948.

Furcht und Elend des Dritten Reiches: 24 Szenen. In *Stücke* 6, vol. 1, *Stücke aus dem Exil*, 235–408. Frankfurt am Main: Suhrkamp, 1957.

Hundert Gedichte, 1918–1950. Berlin: Aufbau, 1958.

Brecht on Theatre. Edited and translated by John Willett. London: Methuen, 1964.

The Messingkauf Dialogues. Edited and translated by John Willett. London: Methuen, 1965.

Poems, 1913–1956. Edited by John Willett and Ralph Manheim, with the cooperation of Erich Fried. London: Methuen, 1978.

Plays: Two. Translated by John Willett. Introduction by Hugh Rorrison. London: Methuen, 1987.

Große kommentierte Berliner und Frankfurter Ausgabe. Edited by Werner Hecht, Jan Knopf, Werner Mittenzwei and Klaus-Detlef Müller. 30 volumes + *Registerband*. Berlin, Weimar: Aufbau and Frankfurt am Main: Suhrkamp, 1988–2000.

Letters, 1913–1956. Edited and with commentary and notes by John Willett. Translated by Ralph Manheim. London: Methuen, 1990.

Journals, 1934–1955. Edited by John Willett. Translated by Hugh Rorrison. London: Methuen, 1993.

Fear and Misery of the Third Reich. Edited and with introduction by John Willett and Tom Kuhn. Translated by John Willett. London: Methuen-A. & C. Black, 2002.

Brecht on Art and Politics. Edited by Tom Kuhn and Steve Giles. Translated by Laura Bradley et al. London: Methuen-A. & C. Black, 2003.

(ii) Other Primary Literature

Baumann, Hans. *Macht keinen Lärm: Gedichte.* Munich: Kösel & Pustet, 1933.

Borchardt, Hermann. *The Conspiracy of the Carpenters: Historical Accounting of a Ruling Class.* Translated by Barrows Mussey. Foreword by Franz Werfel. New York: Simon and Schuster, 1943.

Bredel, Willi. *Die Prüfung.* Prague: Malik, 1934.

———. *Der Spitzel und andere Erzählungen.* Moscow, Leningrad: Vegaar (Verlagsgenossenschaft ausländischer Arbeiter in der UdSSR), 1936.

Feuchtwanger, Lion. *Die Geschwister Oppenheim.* Amsterdam: Querido, 1933. [Later title: *Die Geschwister Oppermann*]

Goguel, Rudi. *Es war ein langer Weg: Ein Roman unserer Zeit.* Düsseldorf: Komet, 1947.

Kraus, Karl. *Die letzten Tage der Menschheit: Tragödie in fünf Akten mit Vorspiel und Epilog.* Vienna, Leipzig: Verlag "Die Fackel," 1919.

Liepmann, Heinz. *Das Vaterland: Ein Tatsachenroman aus dem heutigen Deutschland.* Amsterdam: Querido, 1933.

Mann, Heinrich. *Der Haß: Deutsche Zeitgeschichte.* Amsterdam: Querido, 1933.

———. *Mut.* Paris: Editions du 10. Mai, 1939.

Petersen, Jan [Hans Schwalm]. *Unsere Straße: Eine Chronik geschrieben im Herzen des faschistischen Deutschlands, 1933–34.* [Serialized in *Berner Tagwacht,* 1936]

Piscator, Erwin. *Das politische Theater.* Neubearbeitet von Felix Gasbarra. Vorwort von Wolfgang Drews. Reinbek bei Hamburg: Rowohlt, 1963.

Strindberg, August. *Werke.* Translated by Emil Schering. Part 1, vol. 12, *Kammerspiele.* Munich-Leipzig: Georg Müller, 1911.

Toller, Ernst. *Pastor Hall: A Play in Three Acts.* Translated by Stephen Spender and Hugh Hunt. London: John Lane The Bodley Head, 1938.

———. *Pastor Hall.* In *Gesammelte Werke,* edited by Wolfgang Frühwald and John M. Spalek. Vol. 3, *Politisches Theater und Dramen im Exil, 1927–1939,* 245–316. Munich: Hanser, 1978.

Wolf, Friedrich. *Das Trojanische Pferd: Ein Stück vom Kampf der Jugend in Deutschland.* Moscow: Vegaar (Verlagsgenossenschaft ausländischer Arbeiter in der UdSSR), 1934.

———. *Professor Mamlock.* Zurich: Oprecht & Helbling, 1935.

Other Works Consulted

Anon. [Otto Katz, Willi Münzenberg, et al.]. *Braunbuch über Reichstagsbrand und Hitler-Terror.* Basle: Universum-Verlag, 1933.

Anon. [Otto Katz, Willi Münzenberg, Bertolt Brecht, et al.]. *Braunbuch II. Dimitroff contra Goering: Enthüllungen über die wahren Brandstifter.* Paris: Carrefour, 1934.

Anon. [Willi Bredel]. *Als sozialdemokratischer Arbeiter im Konzentrationslager Papenburg.* Moscow, Leningrad: Vegaar (Verlagsgenossenschaft ausländischer Arbeiter in der UdSSR), 1935.

Anon. "Odnoaktnye p´esy Bertol´da Brechta" [One-Act Plays by Bertolt Brecht], *Internatsional´naya literatura* 8 (1938): 259.

Ayçoberry, Pierre. *The Social History of the Third Reich, 1933–1945.* Translated by Janet Lloyd. New York: The New Press, 1999.

Balfour, Michael. *Withstanding Hitler in Germany, 1933–45.* London: Routledge, 1988.

Barbon, Paola. *"Il signor B.B." Wege und Umwege der italienischen Brecht-Rezeption.* Bonn: Bouvier, 1987.

Bartov, Omer. *Hitler's Army: Soldiers, Nazis and War in the Third Reich.* Oxford: Oxford UP, 1991.

Bathrick, David R. "Moderne Kunst und Klassenkampf: Die Expressionismusdebatte in der Exilzeitschrift *Das Wort.*" In *Exil und innere Emigration*, edited by Reinhold Grimm and Jost Hermand, 89–109. Frankfurt am Main: Suhrkamp, 1973.

Bauer, Gerhard. "Lehren ohne Schüler: Brechts Schwierigkeiten beim Dichten gegen die Nationalsozialisten." In *Europäische Lehrdichtung: Festschrift für Walter Naumann*, edited by Hans Gerd Rötzler, et al., 262–79. Darmstadt: Wissenschaftliche Buchgesellschaft, 1981.

Bauland, Peter. *The Hooded Eagle: German Drama on the New York Stage.* Syracuse, NY: Syracuse UP, 1968.

Baumgart, Hans. *Der Kampf der sozialistischen deutschen Schriftsteller gegen den Faschismus, 1933–1935.* Berlin: Institut für Gesellschaftswissenschaft beim ZK der SED, 1962.

Baxandall, Lee. "Brecht in America." *The Drama Review* 12.1 (1967): 69–87.

Beetham, David, ed. *Marxists in Face of Fascism: Writings by Marxists on Fascism from the Inter-war Period.* Manchester: Manchester UP, 1983.

Beevor, Antony. *The Battle for Spain: The Spanish Civil War, 1936–1939.* London: Weidenfeld & Nicolson, 2006.

Behnken, Klaus, ed. *Deutschland-Berichte der Sozialdemokratischen Partei Deutschlands (Sopade), 1934–1940.* 7 vols. Frankfurt am Main: Zweitausendeins, 1980.

Benjamin, Walter. *Versuche über Brecht*. Edited by Rolf Tiedemann. Frankfurt am Main: Suhrkamp, 1981.

———. *Understanding Brecht*. Translated by Anna Bostock. London: Verso, 1998.

———. *The Work of Art in the Age of its Technological Reproducibility, and Other Writings on Media*. Edited by Michael W. Jennings, et al. Translated by Edmund Jephcott, et al. Cambridge, MA: The Belknap Press of Harvard UP, 2008.

Bentley, Eric. "The Real Story behind the Song 'The Peat Bog Soldiers.'" *Sing Out! The Folk Song Magazine*, September 1966 (16.4), 37–39.

———. *"The Private Life of the Master Race."* In *The Brecht Commentaries, 1943–1980*, 23–37. New York: Grove Press and London: Methuen, 1981.

Bergmann, Klaus B., and Rolf S. Schörken, eds. *Geschichte im Alltag — Alltag in der Geschichte*. Düsseldorf: Schwann, 1982.

Berlekamp, Brigitte, and Werner Röhr, eds. *Terror, Herrschaft und Alltag im Nationalsozialismus: Probleme einer Sozialgeschichte des deutschen Faschismus.* Münster: Westfälisches Dampfboot, 1995.

Bernecker, W. L. "Kapitalismus und Nationalsozialismus: Zum Problem der Unterstützung Hitlers durch die Wirtschaft." In *1933: Fünfzig Jahre danach. Die nationalsozialistische Machtergreifung in historischer Perspektive*, edited by Josef Becker, 49–88. Munich: E. Vögel, 1983.

Bessel, Richard, ed. *Life in the Third Reich*. Oxford: Oxford UP, 1987.

Beyerchen, Alan D. *Scientists under Hitler: Politics and the Physics Community in the Third Reich*. New Haven, CT, London: Yale UP, 1979.

Billinger, Karl. *Schutzhäftling Nr. 880*. Paris: Carrefour, 1935.

Bishop, Philip E. "Brecht, Hegel, Lacan: Brecht's Theory of Gest and the Problem of the Subject." *Studies in Twentieth-Century Literature* 10 (1985): 267–88.

Bleuel, Hans-Peter. *Strength through Joy*. London: Secker and Warburg, 1973.

Bloch, Ernst. *Erbschaft dieser Zeit*. Zurich: Oprecht & Helbling, 1935.

Bohnert, Christiane. *Brechts Lyrik im Kontext: Zyklen und Exil*. Königstein/Ts.: Athenäum, 1982.

Borgert, Wolfgang, and Michael Krieft. "Die Arbeit an den *Deutschland-Berichten*: Protokoll eines Gesprächs mit Friedrich Heine." In *Die "Grünen Berichte" der Sopade: Gedenkschrift für Erich Rinner*, edited by Werner Plum, 49–122. Bonn: Friedrich-Ebert-Stiftung, 1984.

Botz, Gerhard. "Methoden und Theorien der historischen Widerstandsforschung." In *Arbeiterbewegung — Faschismus — Nationalbewusstsein*, edited by Helmut Konrad and Wolfgang Neugebauer, 137–51. Vienna: Europa, 1983.

Brecht, Bertolt. *Die Bibliothek Bertolt Brechts: Ein kommentiertes Verzeichnis*. Bearbeitet von Erdmut Wizisla, Helgrid Streidt, and Heidrun Loeper. Frankfurt am Main: Suhrkamp, 2007.

Broszat, Martin. "Resistenz und Widerstand: Eine Zwischenbilanz des Forschungsprojekts." In *Bayern in der NS-Zeit*, edited by Martin Broszat, et al. Vol. 4, *Herrschaft und Gesellschaft im Konflikt*, Part C, 691–711. Munich: Oldenbourg, 1981.

———. "A Social and Historical Typology of the German Opposition to Hitler." In *Contending with Hitler: Varieties of German Resistance in the Third Reich*, edited by David Clay Large, 25–33. Cambridge: Cambridge UP, 1991.

Buck, Elmar. "Götterdämmerung allüberall: Der gewöhnliche und der interessant gemachte Faschismus." In *Literaturmagazin 9: Der neue Irrationalismus*, 179–207. Reinbek bei Hamburg: Rowohlt, 1978.

Burden, Hamilton T. *The Nuremberg Party Rallies, 1923–1939*. New York: Praeger, 1967.

Busch, Walter. *Bertolt Brecht: "Furcht und Elend des Dritten Reiches."* Frankfurt am Main: Diesterweg, 1982.

Claas, Herbert. *Die politische Ästhetik Bertolt Brechts vom "Baal" zum "Caesar."* Frankfurt am Main: Suhrkamp, 1977.

Claas, Herbert, and Wolfgang Fritz Haug, eds. *Brechts Tui-Kritik: Aufsätze, Rezensionen, Geschichten*. Berlin: Argument, 1976.

Clarke, Alan. "'They came to a country': German Theatre Practitioners in Exile in Great Britain, 1938–45." In *Theatre and Film in Exile: German Artists in Britain, 1933–1945*, edited by Günter Berghaus, 99–119. Oxford, New York: Berg, 1989.

Cohen, Robert. "Brechts *Furcht und Elend des III. Reiches* und der Status des Gestus." *The Brecht Yearbook* 24 (1999): 192–207.

Cook, Bruce. *Brecht in Exile*. New York: Holt, Rinehart and Winston, 1982.

Das Wort. Edited by Bertolt Brecht, Lion Feuchtwanger, and Willi Bredel. Moscow: Jourgaz, June 1936–March 1939.

"Das Wort": Bibliographie einer Zeitschrift. Berlin, Weimar: Aufbau, 1975.

"Das Wort": Registerband. Berlin: Rütten & Loening, 1968.

Davies, Peter. *"Das Wort."* In *The Modern Restoration: Re-thinking German Literary History, 1930–1960*, edited by Stephen Parker, Peter Davies, and Matthew Philpotts, 107–25. Berlin, New York: de Gruyter, 2004.

Demetz, Peter, ed. *Brecht: A Collection of Critical Essays*. Englewood Cliffs, NJ: Prentice-Hall, 1962.

Dickhut, Willi. *So war's damals. . .: Tatsachenbericht eines Solinger Arbeiters, 1926–1948*. Stuttgart: Neuer Weg, 1979.

Diewald-Kerkman, Gisela. *Politische Denunziation im NS-Regime oder die kleine Macht der "Volksgenossen."* Bonn: Dietz, 1995.

Dimitrov, Georgi. *For a United and Popular Front*. Sofia: Sofia Press, 1935.

————. *Die Volksfront zum Kampf gegen Faschismus und Krieg*. Strasbourg: Editions Prométhée, 1935.

————. *Ausgewählte Schriften in drei Bänden*. Berlin: Dietz, 1956–58.

————. *Gegen Faschismus und Krieg: Ausgewählte Reden und Aufsätze*. Leipzig: Reclam, 1982.

Domarus, Max, ed. *Hitler: Reden und Proklamationen, 1932–1945*. Vol. 1, *Triumph, 1932–1934*. Wiesbaden: Löwit, 1973.

Drachkovitch, Milorad M., and Branko Lazitch, eds. *The Comintern: Historical Highlights: Essays, Recollections, Documents*. [Hoover Institution]. New York: Praeger, 1966.

Dümling, Albrecht. *Laßt euch nicht verführen: Brecht und die Musik*. Munich: Kindler, 1985.

Eisler, Hanns. *Fragen Sie mehr über Brecht: Gespräche mit Hans Bunge*. Darmstadt-Neuwied: Luchterhand 1986.

Emmerich, Wolfgang. "'Massenfaschismus' und die Rolle des Ästhetischen: Faschismustheorie bei Ernst Bloch, Walter Benjamin, Bertolt Brecht." In *Antifaschistische Literatur: Programme, Autoren, Werke*, edited by Lutz Winkler. Vol. 1, 223–90. Kronberg/Ts.: Scriptor, 1977.

Engberg, Harald. *Brecht auf Fünen: Exil in Dänemark, 1933–1939*. Wuppertal: Peter Hammer, 1974.

Engels, Friedrich. (See under: Marx, Karl).

Ermolaev, Herman. *Soviet Literary Theories, 1917–1934: The Genesis of Socialist Realism*. Berkeley: California UP, 1963.

Erpenbeck, Fritz. *Lebendiges Theater: Aufsätze und Kritiken*. Berlin: Henschel, 1949.

Evans, Richard J. *The Coming of the Third Reich*. London: Allen Lane, 2003.

————. *The Third Reich in Power, 1933–1939*. London: Allen Lane, 2005.

————. *The Third Reich at War, 1939–1945*. London: Allen Lane, 2008.

Ewers, Hanns Heinz. *Horst Wessel: Ein deutsches Schicksal*. Stuttgart, Berlin: Cotta, 1932.

Fackler, Guido. *"Des Lagers Stimme": Musik im KZ. Alltag und Häftlingskultur in den Konzentrationslagern, 1933 bis 1936*. Bremen: Temmen, 2000.

Farquharson, John E. *The Plough and the Swastika: The NSDAP and Agriculture in Germany, 1928–1945*. London: Sage, 1976.

Fischbach, Fred. "Pour une nouvelle lecture de Brecht à la lumière de la musique de scène de Hanns Eisler." *Recherches Germaniques* 13 (1983): 137–66.

Fischer, Conan. *The German Communists and the Rise of Nazism*. New York: St. Martin's Press, 1991.

Fitzpatrick, Sheila, and Robert Gellately, eds. *Accusatory Practices: Denunciation in Modern European History, 1789–1989*. Chicago, London: U of Chicago P, 1997.

Focke, Harald, and Uwe Reimer. *Alltag unterm Hakenkreuz: Wie die Nazis das Leben der Deutschen veränderten.* Reinbek bei Hamburg: Rowohlt, 1989.

Frank, Hans. *Neues Deutsches Recht.* Munich: Franz Eher, 1936.

Fuegi, John. *Bertolt Brecht: Chaos according to Plan.* Cambridge: Cambridge UP, 1987.

———. *The Life and Lies of Bertolt Brecht.* London: HarperCollins, 1994.

Gamm, Hans-Jochen. *Der Flüsterwitz im Dritten Reich.* Munich: List, 1963.

Gehl, Jürgen. *Austria, Germany and the "Anschluß," 1931–1938.* Oxford: Oxford UP, 1963.

Geiger, Heinz. *Einführung in die deutsche Literatur des 20. Jahrhunderts.* Opladen: Westdeutscher Verlag, 1977.

Gellately, Robert. *The Gestapo and German Society: Enforcing Racial Policy, 1933–1945.* Oxford: Clarendon, 1990.

———. *Backing Hitler: Consent and Coercion in Nazi Germany.* Oxford: Oxford UP, 2001.

Gersch, Wolfgang. *Film bei Brecht: Bertolt Brechts praktische und theoretische Auseinandersetzung mit dem Film.* Munich: Hanser, 1975.

Gerstenberger, Heide. "Alltagsforschung und Faschismustheorie." In *Normalität oder Normalisierung? Geschichtswerkstätten und Faschismusanalyse,* edited by Heide Gerstenberger and Dorothea Schmidt, 35–49. Münster: Westfälisches Dampfboot, 1987.

Gerz, Raimund. *Bertolt Brecht und der Faschismus: In den Parabelstücken "Die Rundköpfe und die Spitzköpfe," "Der aufhaltsame Aufstieg des Arturo Ui" und "Turandot oder der Kongreß der Weißwäscher." Rekonstruktion einer Versuchsreihe.* Bonn: Bouvier, 1983.

Gilbert, Shirli. *Music in the Holocaust: Confronting Life in the Nazi Ghettos and Camps.* Oxford: Clarendon, 2005.

Goebbels, Joseph. *Vom Kaiserhof zur Reichskanzlei: Eine historische Darstellung in Tagebuchblättern (vom 1. Januar 1932 bis zum 1. Mai 1933).* Munich: Zentralverlag der NSDAP, 1934.

———. *Goebbels-Reden.* 2 vols. Edited by Helmut Heiber. Düsseldorf: Droste, 1971.

Goering, Hermann. *Reden und Aufsätze.* Edited by Erich Gritzbach. Munich: Zentralverlag der NSDAP, 1938.

Goldhahn, Johannes. *Das Parabelstück Bertolt Brechts als Beitrag zum Kampf gegen den deutschen Faschismus.* Rudolstadt: Greifen, 1961.

Gorelik, Mordecai. *New Theatres for Old.* New York: Samuel French, 1940.

———. "Brecht: 'I am the Einstein of the New Stage Form.'" *Theatre Arts* 41 (March 1957): 72–73 and 86–87.

Graml, Hermann, et al., eds. *The German Resistance to Hitler.* London: Batsford, 1970.

Gross, Babette. *Willi Münzenberg.* Stuttgart: Deutsche Verlags-Anstalt, 1967.

Gruchmann, Lothar. *Justiz im Dritten Reich, 1933–1940: Anpassung und Unterwerfung in der Ära Gürtner.* Munich: Oldenbourg, 1988.

Grunberger, Richard. *A Social History of the Third Reich.* Harmondsworth: Penguin, 1971.

Günther, Hans. "Erbschaft dieser Zeit?" *Internationale Literatur (Deutsche Blätter)* 6.3 (1936): 87–90.

Gyseghem, André. *Theatre in Soviet Russia.* London: Faber and Faber, 1943.

Hartung, Günter. "*Furcht und Elend des Dritten Reiches* als Satire." In *Erworbene Tradition: Studien zu Werken der sozialistischen deutschen Literatur,* edited by Günter Hartung, et al., 57–118. Berlin, Weimar: Aufbau, 1977.

Hay, Julius. "Put´ k realizmu" [The Path to Realism]. *Teatr* 2–3 (1939): 32–39.

Hecht, Werner, et al., eds. *Bertolt Brecht: Sein Leben und Werk.* Berlin: Volk und Wissen, 1971.

———, ed. *Brecht im Gespräch: Diskussionen, Dialoge, Interviews.* Frankfurt am Main: Suhrkamp, 1975.

Heiden, Konrad. *Geschichte des Nationalsozialismus: Die Karriere einer Idee.* Berlin: Rowohlt, 1932.

———. *Adolf Hitler: Das Zeitalter der Verantwortungslosigkeit. Eine Biographie.* Zurich: Europa, 1936.

Heinze, Helmut. *Brechts Ästhetik des Gestischen: Versuch einer Rekonstruktion.* Heidelberg: Carl Winter, 1992.

Herden, Werner. *Wege zur Volksfront: Schriftsteller im antifaschistischen Bündnis.* Berlin: Akademie, 1978.

Herf, Jeffrey. "German Communism's Master Narratives of Antifascism: Berlin-Moscow-East Berlin, 1928–1945." In *Divided Memory: The Nazi Past in the Two Germanys,* 13–39. Cambridge, MA, London: Harvard UP, 1997.

Herlinghaus, Hermann. *Slatan Dudow.* Berlin: Henschel, 1965.

Hermes, Richard. *Witz contra Nazi.* Hamburg: Morawe & Scheffelt, 1946.

Heyen, Franz Josef, ed. *Nationalsozialismus im Alltag: Quellen zur Geschichte des Nationalsozialismus vornehmlich im Raum Mainz-Koblenz-Trier.* Boppard: Boldt, 1967.

Hillach, Ansgar. "'Ästhetisierung des politischen Lebens': Benjamins faschismustheoretischer Ansatz — Eine Rekonstruktion." In *"Links hätte noch alles sich zu enträtseln. . .": Walter Benjamin im Kontext,* edited by Burkhardt Lindner, 127–67. Frankfurt am Main: Syndikat, 1978.

Hillenbrand, Karl Michael. *Underground Humour in Nazi Germany, 1933–1945.* London: Routledge, 1995.

Hiller, Robert L. "The Symbolism of *Gestus* in Brecht's Drama." In *Myth and Symbol: Critical Approaches and Applications,* edited by B. Slote, 89–99. Lincoln, London: Nebraska UP, 1963.

Hinrichs, Klaus [August Wittfogel]. *Staatliches Konzentrationslager VII: Eine "Erziehungsanstalt" im Dritten Reich.* London: Malik, 1936.

Hirsch, Werner. *Hinter Stacheldraht und Gitter: Erlebnisse und Erfahrungen in den Konzentrationslagern und Gefängnissen Hitlerdeutschlands.* Zurich, Paris: Mopr, 1934.

———. *Sozialdemokratische und kommunistische Arbeiter im Konzentrationslager.* Strasbourg: Prometheus, 1934.

Hitler, Adolf. *Mein Kampf.* Munich: Zentralverlag der NSDAP, 1938.

Hoffmann, Peter. *The History of the German Resistance, 1933–45.* Translated by Richard Barry. Cambridge, MA: MIT Press, 1977.

Holz, Arno. *Die Kunst: Ihr Wesen und ihre Gesetze.* Berlin: Issleib, 1891.

Hüfner, Agnes. *Brecht in Frankreich, 1930–1963: Verbreitung, Aufnahme, Wirkung.* Stuttgart: Metzler, 1968.

Huß-Michel, Angela. *Die Moskauer Zeitschriften "Internationale Literatur" und "Das Wort" während der Exil-Volksfront (1936–1939).* Frankfurt am Main: Peter Lang, 1987.

Hüttenberger, Peter. "Vorüberlegungen zum 'Widerstandsbegriff.'" In *Theorien in der Praxis des Historikers,* edited by Jürgen Kocka, 117–34. Göttingen: Vandenhoeck & Ruprecht, 1977.

Jarmatz, Klaus, et al. *Exil in der UdSSR.* Vol 1, *Kunst und Literatur im antifaschistischen Exil, 1933–1945.* Leipzig: Reclam, 1979.

Jaschke, Hans-Gerd. *Soziale Basis und soziale Funktion des Nationalsozialismus: Studien zur Bonapartismustheorie.* Opladen: Westdeutscher Verlag, 1982.

Kallis, Aristotle A., ed. *The Fascism Reader.* London: Routledge, 2003.

Kantorowicz, Alfred. "Deutsches Theater in Paris." *Die Neue Weltbühne* 52 (1938): 1649–51.

———. *Deutsches Tagebuch.* 2 vols. Munich: Kindler, 1959, 1961.

Kater, Michael H. *Doctors under Hitler.* Chapel Hill, London: North Carolina UP, 1989.

Kaufmann, Hans. *Bertolt Brecht: Geschichtsdrama und Parabelstück.* Berlin, Weimar: Aufbau, 1962.

Kershaw, Ian. *The Nazi Dictatorship: Problems and Perspectives of Interpretation.* Third edition. London: Edward Arnold, 1993.

Kirfel-Lenk, Thea. *Erwin Piscator im Exil in den USA, 1939–1951: Eine Darstellung seiner antifaschistischen Theaterarbeit am Dramatic Workshop der New School for Social Research.* Berlin: Henschel, 1984.

Kitchen, Martin. "The Third International and Fascism." In *Fascism,* 1–11. London, Basingstoke: Macmillan, 1976.

Klemperer, Klemens von. *German Resistance against Hitler: The Search for Allies Abroad, 1938–1945.* Oxford: Clarendon, 1992.

Knepler, Georg. "Was des Eislers ist . . ." *Beiträge zur Musikwissenschaft* 15 (1973): 29–48.

Knopf, Jan. *Bertolt Brecht: Ein kritischer Forschungsbericht. Fragwürdiges in der Brecht-Forschung.* Frankfurt am Main: Fischer-Athenäum, 1974.

———. *Brecht Handbuch: Theater: Eine Ästhetik des Widerspruchs.* Stuttgart: Metzler, 1980.

———. *Gelegentlich Poesie: Ein Essay über die Lyrik Bertolt Brechts.* Frankfurt am Main: Suhrkamp, 1996.

Koch, H. W. *In the Name of the Volk: Political Justice in Hitler's Germany.* New York: St Martin's, 1989.

Konrad, Hans. "Gescheiterte Autarkie." *Die Neue Weltbühne* 31 (October 1935): 1289–92.

Koonz, Claudia. *The Nazi Conscience.* Cambridge, MA: The Belknap Press of Harvard UP, 2002.

Kraushaar, L. *Deutsche Widerstandskämpfer, 1933–45.* Berlin: Dietz, 1970.

Kreft, Jürgen. "Realismusprobleme bei Brecht," http://kgg.german.or.kr/kzg/kzgtxt/68_13.pdf (accessed 26 February 2009).

Kreuzer, Helmut, and Karl-Wilhelm Schmidt, eds. *Dramaturgie in der DDR (1945–1990).* 2 vols. Heidelberg: Carl Winter, 1998.

Kuczynski, Jürgen. *Das Elend des deutschen Arbeiters unter dem Nationalsozialismus, dargestellt anhand der Jahresberichte der Gewerbeaufsichtsbeamten* [1938]. Reprinted in Jürgen Kuczynski, *Die Geschichte der Lage der Arbeiter unter dem Kapitalismus, 1933 bis 1945.* Vol. 6, 193–216. Berlin: Akademie, 1964.

Kugli, Ana, and Michael Opitz, eds. *Brecht Lexikon.* Stuttgart, Weimar: Metzler, 2006.

Kuhn, Tom. "The Politics of the Changeable Text: *Furcht und Elend des III. Reiches* and the New Brecht Edition." *Oxford German Studies* 18–19 (1989–90): 132–49.

———. "Under the Crooked Cross: Brecht's *Furcht und Elend des III. Reiches* at the BBC." In *"England? Aber wo liegt es?": Deutsche und österreichische Emigranten in Großbritannien, 1933–1945.* Edited by Charmian Brinson, et al., 181–91. London: University of London Institute of Germanic Studies and Munich: Iudicium, 1996.

Kühn, Volker. *"Deutschlands Erwachen": Kabarett unterm Hakenkreuz, 1933–1945.* 3 vols. Weinheim-Berlin: Quadriga, 1989.

Kulisiewicz, Aleksander. *Adresse: Sachsenhausen. Literarische Momentaufnahmen aus dem KZ.* Edited by Claudia Westermann. Translated by Bettina Eberspächer. Gerlingen: Bleicher, 1997.

Lammel, Inge, and Günter Hofmeyer, eds. *Lieder aus den faschistischen Konzentrationslagern.* Leipzig: Friedrich Hofmeister, 1962.

Langbein, Hermann. *". . . nicht wie die Schafe zur Schlachtbank": Widerstand in den nationalsozialistischen Konzentrationslagern.* Frankfurt am Main: Fischer, 1980.

Langhoff, Wolfgang. *Die Moorsoldaten: 13 Monate Konzentrationslager: Unpolitischer Tatsachenbericht.* Zurich: Schweizer Spiegel, 1935.

———. *Rubber Truncheon: Being an Account of Thirteen Months Spent in a Concentration Camp.* Translated by Lilo Linke. London: Constable, 1935.

Large, David Clay, ed. *Contending with Hitler: Varieties of German Resistance in the Third Reich.* Cambridge: Cambridge UP, 1991.

Lehmann, Hans-Thies, Marc Silberman and Renate Voris, eds. *The Other Brecht / Der andere Brecht.* (International Brecht Society) Madison, WI: Wisconsin UP, 1992.

Leppert-Fögen, Annette. *Die deklassierte Klasse: Studien zur Geschichte und Ideologie des Kleinbürgertums.* Frankfurt am Main: Suhrkamp, 1974.

Ley, Robert. *Soldaten der Arbeit.* Munich: Zentralverlag der NSDAP, 1938.

Liepmann, Heinz. "...*wird mit dem Tod bestraft.*" Zurich: Europa, 1935.

Lindner, Burkhardt. *Bertolt Brecht: "Der aufhaltsame Aufstieg des Arturo Ui."* Munich: Fink, 1982.

Loewe, H. C. "Gespräch mit Bert Brecht." *Der Arbeiter* (New York: Deutsche Sprachfaktion), 23 November 1935.

Loewy, Ernst, ed. *Exil: Literarische und politische Texte aus dem deutschen Exil, 1933–1945.* Stuttgart: Metzler, 1979.

Longerich, Peter. *"Davon haben wir nichts gewusst!" Die Deutschen und die Judenverfolgung, 1933–1945.* Munich: Siedler, 2006.

Löwenthal, Richard. "Widerstand im totalen Staat." In *Widerstand und Verweigerung in Deutschland, 1933, bis 1945,* edited by Richard Löwenthal and Patrick von der Mühlen, 11–24. Berlin: Dietz, 1982.

Lozowick, Yaacov. *Hitler's Bureaucrats: The Nazi Security Police and the Banality of Evil.* London, New York: Continuum, 2000.

Lucchesi, Joachim, and Ronald K. Shull. *Musik bei Brecht.* Frankfurt am Main: Suhrkamp, 1988.

Lüdtke, Alf, ed. *Alltagsgeschichte: Zur Rekonstruktion historischer Erfahrungen und Lebensweisen.* Frankfurt am Main, New York: Peter Lang, 1989.

———. "The "Honor of Labor": Industrial Workers and the Power of Symbols under National Socialism." In *Nazism and German Society, 1933–1945,* edited by David F. Crew, 67–109. London: Routledge, 1994.

Lukács, Georg. *Theorie des Romans.* Berlin: Cassirer, 1920.

———. "Reportage oder Gestaltung: Kritische Bemerkungen anläßlich eines Romans von Ottwalt." *Die Linkskurve* 7 (1932): 27–30 and *Die Linkskurve* 8 (1932): 26–31.

———. "Größe und Verfall des Expressionismus." *Internationale Literatur* 1 (1934): 153–73.

———. "Der Briefwechsel zwischen Schiller und Goethe." [1934]. In *Werke 7: Deutsche Literatur in zwei Jahrhunderten,* 89–124. Berlin, Neuwied: Luchterhand, 1964.

————. "Es geht um den Realismus." *Das Wort* 3 (June 1938): 112–38.

————. "Marx und das Problem des ideologischen Verfalls." *Internationale Literatur (Deutsche Blätter)* 7 (1938): 103–43.

————. *Essays über Realismus.* Berlin: Aufbau, 1948.

————. *Skizze einer Geschichte der neueren deutschen Literatur.* Berlin: Aufbau, 1952.

————. *Der historische Roman.* [Completed 1936–37]. Berlin: Aufbau, 1955.

————. *Die Zerstörung der Vernunft.* Berlin: Aufbau, 1954.

————. *Wie ist Deutschland zum Zentrum der reaktionären Ideologie geworden?* Budapest: Akademiai Kiadó, 1982.

Lunn, Eugene. *Marxism and Modernism: An Historical Study of Lukács, Brecht, Benjamin, and Adorno.* Berkeley, Los Angeles: California UP, 1982.

Lyon, James K. "Zur New Yorker Aufführung von Brechts *Furcht und Elend des Dritten Reiches.*" In *Deutsches Exildrama und Exiltheater,* edited by Wolfgang Elfe, et al., 67–76. Bern, Frankfurt am Main: Peter Lang, 1977.

————. *Bertolt Brecht's American Cicerone: With an Appendix containing the Complete Correspondence between Bertolt Brecht and Ferdinand Reyher.* Bonn: Bouvier, 1978.

————. *Bertolt Brecht in America.* Princeton, NJ: Princeton UP, 1980.

————. "Brecht's Sources for *Furcht und Elend des III. Reiches*: Heinrich Mann, Personal Friends, Newspaper Accounts," *New Essays on Brecht / Neue Versuche über Brecht.* Ed. Maarten van Dijk et al. *The Brecht Yearbook / Das Brecht-Jahrbuch* 26 (Toronto: The International Brecht Society, 2001): 295–305.

————. "*Furcht und Elend des III. Reiches.*" In *Brecht Handbuch,* edited by Jan Knopf. Vol. 1, *Stücke,* 339–57. Stuttgart, Weimar: Metzler, 2001.

Lyon, James K., and John B. Fuegi. "Bertolt Brecht." In *Deutsche Exilliteratur seit 1933.* Vol. 1, *Kalifornien.* Edited by John M. Spalek and Joseph Strelka, 268–98. Bern, Munich: Francke, 1976.

Macdonald, Giles. *1938: Hitler's Gamble.* London: Constable, 2009.

Mallmann, K.-M., and G. Paul. "Omniscient, Omnipotent, Omnipresent? Gestapo, Society and Resistance." In *Nazism and German Society, 1933–45,* edited by David Crew, 166–96. London: Routledge, 1994.

Marsch, Edgar. *Bertolt Brecht: Kommentar zum lyrischen Werk.* Munich: Winkler, 1974.

Marx, Karl. *Early Writings.* Introduced by Lucio Colletti. Translated by Rodney Livingstone and Gregor Benton. London: Penguin, 1992.

————. *A Contribution to the Critique of Political Economy.* Introduction by Maurice Dobb. London: Lawrence & Wishart, 1971.

Marx, Karl, and Friedrich Engels. *Manifesto of the Communist Party.* Moscow: Foreign Languages Publishing House, 1959.

————. *Werke.* 44 vols. Edited by Institut für Marxismus-Leninismus beim ZK der SED. Berlin: Deutz, 1956–90.

Mason, Timothy W. *Nazism, Fascism and the Working Class.* Cambridge: Cambridge UP, 1995.

Mayer, Hans. *Bertolt Brecht und die Tradition.* Pfullingen: Neske, 1961.

McDermott, Kevin, and Jeremy Agnew. *The Comintern: A History of International Communism from Lenin to Stalin.* London: Macmillan, 1996.

McKenzie, Kermit E. *Comintern and World Revolution, 1928–1943: The Shaping of Doctrine.* London, New York: Columbia UP, 1964.

McNally, Joanne. "'Die Moorsoldaten': From Circus-cum-Cabaret to International Anthem." In *Words, Texts, Images,* edited by Katrin Kohl and Ritchie Robertson, 215–30. Oxford: Peter Lang, 2002.

Mehringer, Hartmut. *Widerstand und Emigration: Das NS-Regime und seine Gegner.* Munich: DTV, 1997.

Mennemeier, Franz Norbert. "Bertolt Brechts Faschismustheorie und einige Folgen für die literarische Praxis." In *Literaturwissenschaft und Geschichtsphilosophie: Festschrift für Wilhelm Emrich,* edited by Helmut Arntzen, et al., 561–74. Berlin, New York: de Gruyter, 1975.

————. "Bertolt Brecht: *Furcht und Elend des Dritten Reiches.*" In *Modernes Deutsches Drama: Kritiken und Charakteristiken.* Vol. 2, *1933 bis zur Gegenwart,* 60–65. Munich: Fink, 1975.

Mennemeier, Franz Norbert, and Frithjof Trapp. "Zur deutschsprachigen Exildramatik." In *Handbuch des deutschen Dramas,* edited by Walter Hinck, 431–39. Düsseldorf: Bagel, 1980.

Merson, Allan. *Communist Resistance in Nazi Germany.* London: Lawrence & Wishart, 1985.

Middell, Eike, et al. *Kunst und Literatur im antifaschistischen Exil, 1933–1945.* Vol. 3, *Exil in den USA.* Leipzig: Reclam, 1979.

Mittenzwei, Werner. *Brechts Verhältnis zur Tradition.* Berlin: Akademie, 1972.

————. "Die Szenenfolge *Furcht und Elend des Dritten Reiches.*" In *Bertolt Brecht: Von der "Maßnahme" bis "Leben des Galilei,"* 193–218. Berlin, Weimar: Aufbau, 1973.

————, ed. *Dialog und Kontroverse mit Georg Lukács: Der Methodenstreit deutscher sozialistischer Schriftsteller.* Leipzig: Reclam, 1975.

————. "Die Verbreitung der Wahrheit: Langhoffs 'Die Moorsoldaten.'" In *Kunst und Literatur im antifaschistischen Exil, 1933–1945.* Vol. 2, *Exil in der Schweiz,* edited by Werner Mittenzwei, 162–66. Leipzig: Reclam, 1978.

————. *Das Leben des Bertolt Brecht oder Der Umgang mit den Welträtseln.* 2 vols. Frankfurt am Main: Suhrkamp, 1987.

Mosse, George L. *The Nationalization of the Masses: Political Symbolism and Mass Movements in Germany from the Napoleonic Wars through to the Third Reich.* Ithaca, NY, London: Cornell UP, 1975.

Mühlberger, Detlef, ed. *The Social Basis of European Fascist Movements.* London, New York, Sidney: Croom Helm, 1987.

Müller, Ingo. *Hitler's Justice: The Courts of the Third Reich.* Cambridge, MA: Harvard UP, 1991.

Müller. Klaus-Detlef. *Die Funktion der Geschichte im Werk Bertolt Brechts: Studien zum Verhältnis von Marxismus und Geschichte.* Tübingen: Niemeyer, 1967.

Münch, Alois. *Bertolt Brechts Faschismustheorie und ihre theatralische Konkretisierung in den "Rundköpfen und Spitzköpfen."* Frankfurt am Main: Peter Lang, 1982.

Münster, Arno. *Antifaschismus, Volksfront und Literatur.* Hamburg, Berlin: Verlag für das Studium der Arbeiterbewegung, 1977.

Münzenberg, Willi. *Propaganda als Waffe.* Paris: Carrefour, 1937.

Nicosia, Francis R., and Lawrence D. Stokes, eds. *Germans against Nazism: Nonconformity, Opposition and Resistance in the Third Reich.* New York, Oxford: Berg, 1990.

Noakes, J., and G. Pridham, eds. *Nazism: A Documentary Reader, 1919–1945.* Vol. 1: *The Rise to Power, 1919–1934.* Exeter: Exeter UP, 1998.

———, eds. *Nazism: A Documentary Reader, 1919–1945.* Vol. 2: *State, Economy and Society, 1933–1939.* Exeter: Exeter UP, 1997.

———, eds. *Nazism: A Documentary Reader, 1919–1945.* Vol. 3: *Foreign Policy, War and Racial Extermination.* Exeter: Exeter UP, 2001.

Noakes, Jeremy, ed. *Nazism: A Documentary Reader, 1919–1945.* Vol. 4: *The German Home Front in World War II.* Exeter: Exeter UP, 1998.

Olden, Rudolf. *Hitler der Eroberer.* Amsterdam: Malik, 1933.

Overy, R. J. *War and Economy in the Third Reich.* Oxford: Clarendon, 1994.

Patsch, Sylvia M. *Österreichische Schriftsteller im Exil in Großbritannien: Ein Kapitel vergessene österreichische Literatur.* Vienna, Munich: Christian Brandstätter, 1985.

Pausewang, Gudrun. *Erlaubter Humor im Nationalsozialismus (1933–1945).* Frankfurt am Main: Peter Lang, 2007.

Petersen, Jan [Hans Schwalm]. "Deutschland ist nicht Hitler." *Neue Deutsche Blätter* 2 (1934–35): 344–45.

———. "Verdacht: Aus dem Tagebuch eines Illegalen." *Internationale Literatur* 6.5 (1936): 27–32.

Peukert, Detlev J. K. *Die KPD im Widerstand: Verfolgung und Untergrundarbeit an Rhein und Ruhr, 1933–1945.* Wuppertal: Peter Hammer, 1980.

———. *Inside Nazi Germany: Conformity, Opposition and Racism in Everyday Life.* New Haven, CT: Yale UP, 1987.

Peukert, Detlev J. K., and Jürgen Reulecke, eds. *"Die Reihen fast geschlossen": Beiträge zur Geschichte des Alltags unterm Nationalsozialismus.* Wuppertal: Hammer, 1981.

Philpotts, Matthew. *The Margins of Dictatorship: Assent and Dissent in the Work of Günter Eich and Bertolt Brecht.* Oxford, Bern: Lang, 2003.

———. "Bertolt Brecht." In *The Modern Restoration: Re-thinking German Literary History, 1930–1960*, edited by Stephen Parker, Peter Davies, and Matthew Philpotts, 262–96. Berlin, New York: de Gruyter, 2004.

Pike, David. *German Writers in Soviet Exile, 1933 to 1945.* Chapel Hill: North Carolina UP, 1982.

———. *Lukács and Brecht.* Chapel Hill: North Carolina UP, 1985.

Pirker, Theo, ed. *Komintern und Faschismus: Dokumente zur Geschichte und Theorie des Faschismus.* Stuttgart: Deutsche Verlags-Anstalt, 1965.

Poddel, Peter. *Flüsterwitze aus Brauner Zeit.* Munich: Hornung, 1954.

Poulantzas, Nicos. *Fascism and Dictatorship: The Third International and the Problem of Fascism.* Translated by Judith White. London: NLB, 1974.

Reich, Bernhard. "Zur Methodik der antifaschistischen deutschen Dramatik." *Das Wort* 2 (July 1937): 63–72.

Ritchie, J. M. *German Literature under National Socialism.* London, Canberra: Croom Helm, 1983; Totowa, NJ: Barnes & Noble, 1983.

———. "Staging the War in German." *Forum for Modern Language Studies* 21.1 (1985): 84–96.

Rokotov, Timofei. "Malen'kie p'esy B. Brechta" [Short Plays by B. Brecht]. *Sovetskoe iskusstvo*, 7 August 1941.

Rosenhaft, Eve. *Beating the Fascists? The German Communists and Political Violence, 1929–1933.* Cambridge: Cambridge UP, 1983.

Rousset, David. *L'univers concentrationnaire.* Paris: Editions du Pavois, 1946.

Sändig, Reinhard. "Brecht und die Volksfront." *Weimarer Beiträge* 14.9 (1978): 70–98.

Schieder, Wolfgang, ed. *Faschismus als soziale Bewegung: Deutschland und Italien im Vergleich.* Hamburg: Hoffmann & Campe, 1976.

Schmädeke, Jürgen, and Peter Steinbach, eds. *Der Widerstand gegen den Nationalsozialismus: Die deutsche Gesellschaft und der Widerstand gegen Hitler.* Munich: Piper, 1985.

Schmeer, Karlheinz. *Die Regie des öffentlichen Lebens im Dritten Reich.* Munich: Pohl, 1956.

Schmiechen-Ackermann, Detlef. *Nationalsozialismus und Arbeitermilieus: Der nationalsozialistische Angriff auf die proletarischen Wohnquartiere und die Reaktion in den sozialistischen Vereinen.* Bonn: J. H. W. Dietz Nachfolger, 1998.

Schmitt, Hans-Jürgen, ed. *Die Expressionismusdebatte: Materialien zu einer marxistischen Realismuskonzeption.* Frankfurt am Main: Suhrkamp, 1975.

Schneider, Peter. "Literatur als Widerstand: Am Beispiel von Bert Brechts *Arturo Ui.*" In *Atempause: Versuch, meine Gedanken über Literatur und Kunst zu ordnen*, 111–26. Reinbek bei Hamburg: Rowohlt, 1977.

Schumacher, Ernst. "'Dann macht doch, was hilft!': Brechts *Furcht und Elend des Dritten Reiches* in den Münchner Kammerspielen." In *Brecht-Kritiken*, edited by Christa Neubert-Herwig, 215–18. Berlin: Henschel, 1977.

Schütz, Erhard, and Jochen Vogt. "Gestentafel des faschistischen Alltags." In *Einführung in die deutsche Literatur des 20. Jahrhunderts*. Vol. 2, 294–302. Opladen: Westdeutscher Verlag, 1978.

Schwarz, Minni, ed. *Lachen verboten: Flüsterwitze aus den Jahren 1938–1945*. 4 vols. Vienna: Im Weltweiten, 1947.

Seger, Gerhart H. *Oranienburg: Erster authentischer Bericht eines aus dem Konzentrationslager Geflüchteten*. Karlsbad: Graphia, 1934.

Sellin, Kurt, ed. *Vox populi — Die Hitlerei im Volksmund*. Heidelberg: Freiheit-Verlag, 1946.

Seydewitz, Max. *Civil Life in Wartime Germany: The Story of the Home Front*. New York: Viking, 1945.

Silberner, Edmund. *Kommunisten zur Judenfrage: Zur Geschichte von Theorie und Praxis des Kommunismus*. Opladen: Westdeutscher Verlag, 1983.

Silone, Ignazio. *Der Faschismus: Seine Entstehung und seine Entwicklung*. Zurich: Europa, 1934.

Stalin, J. V. *Works*. Vol. 2. *1907–1913*. London: Lawrence and Wishart, 1953.

———. *Works*. Vol. 13. *1930–1934*. London: Lawrence and Wishart, 1955.

Sternberg, Fritz. *Der Faschismus an der Macht*. Amsterdam: Contact, 1935.

Stolleis, Michael. *The Law under the Swastika*. Chicago, London: U of Chicago P, 1998.

Stollmann, Rainer. "Faschistische Politik als Gesamtkunstwerk: Tendenzen der Ästhetisierung des politischen Lebens im Nationalsozialismus." In *Die deutsche Literatur im Dritten Reich: Themen — Traditionen — Wirkungen*, edited by Horst Denkler and Karl Prümm, 83–101. Stuttgart: Reclam, 1976.

Stöver, Bernd. *Volksgemeinschaft im Dritten Reich: Die Konsensbereitschaft der Deutschen aus der Sicht sozialistischer Exilberichte*. Düsseldorf: Droste, 1993.

Swales, Martin. "Brecht and the Onslaught on Tragedy." In *The Text and its Context: Studies in Modern German Literature and Society*, edited by Nigel Harris and Joanne Sayner, 277–88. Oxford: Peter Lang, 2008.

Tauscher, Rolf. *Brechts Faschismuskritik in Prosaarbeiten und Gedichten der ersten Exiljahre*. (Brecht-Studien 5). Berlin: Brecht-Zentrum der DDR, 1981.

Thamer, Hans-Ulrich. "'Ästhetisierung der Politik': Die Nürnberger Reichsparteitage der NSDAP." In *Faszination und Gewalt: Zur politischen Ästhetik des Nationalsozialismus*, edited by Bernd Ogan and Wolfgang W. Weiß, 95–104. Nuremberg: W. Tümmels Verlag, 1992.

Toller, Ernst. "Unser Kampf um Deutschland." *Das Wort* 2 (March 1937): 46–53.

Trotzki, Leon. *Schriften über Deutschland.* 2 vols. Frankfurt am Main: Suhrkamp, 1971.

Turk, Horst. "Das Gestische Theater Bertolt Brechts." *Etudes Germaniques* 44 (1989): 38–53.

Vansittart, Sir Robert. *Black Record: Germans Past and Present.* London: Hamish, 1941.

Vetlesen, Arne Johan. *Evil and Human Agency: Understanding Collective Evildoing.* Cambridge: Cambridge UP, 2006.

Viertel, Berthold. *Schriften zum Theater.* Edited by Gert Heidenreich and Manfred Nöbel. Berlin: Henschel, 1970.

Vietrich, Wolfgang. "Auseinandersetzung mit faschistischer Wirklichkeit anhand von Bertolt Brechts Szenenmontage *Furcht und Elend des Dritten Reiches.*" *Politische Didaktik* (1978): 76–85.

Vinçon, Inge. *Die Einakter Bertolt Brechts.* Königstein/Ts: Anton Hain, 1980.

Vogel, Benedikt. *Fiktionskulisse: Poetik und Geschichte des Kabaretts.* Paderborn: Schöningh, 1993.

Voges, Michael. "Klassenkampf in der 'Betriebsgemeinschaft': Die *Deutschland-Berichte* der Sopade (1934–1940) als Quelle zum Widerstand der Industriearbeiter im Dritten Reich." *Archiv für Sozialgeschichte* 23 (1982): 329–83.

Völker, Klaus. "Brecht und Lukács: Analyse einer Meinungsverschiedenheit." *Kursbuch* 7 (1966): 80–101.

———. *Brecht-Chronik: Daten zu Leben und Werk.* Munich: Hanser, 1971.

———. *Brecht-Kommentar zum dramatischen Werk.* Munich: Winkler, 1983.

———. *Bertolt Brecht: Eine Biographie.* Munich: Hanser, 1976.

———. *"Ich verreise auf einige Zeit": Sadie Leviton. Schauspielerin, Emigrantin, Freundin von Helene Weigel und Bertolt Brecht.* Berlin: Transit, 1999.

Wächter, Hans-Christof. *Theater im Exil: Sozialgeschichte des deutschen Exiltheaters 1933–1945.* Munich: Hanser, 1973.

Wagner, Frank Dietrich. *Bertolt Brecht: Kritik des Faschismus.* Opladen: Westdeutscher Verlag, 1989.

Wagner, Peter. "Das Verhältnis von 'Fabel' und 'Grundgestus' in Bertolt Brechts Theorie des epischen Theaters." *Zeitschrift für deutsche Philologie* 89 (1970): 601–15.

Walter, Hans-Albert. *"Das Wort."* In *Deutsche Exilliteratur, 1933–1950,* edited by Hans-Albert Walter. Vol. 4, *Exilpresse,* 462–502. Stuttgart: Metzler, 1978.

Weiskopf, Franz Carl. *Die Stärkeren: Episoden aus dem unterirdischen Krieg.* Prague: Malik, 1934.

Wekwerth, Manfred, ed. *Schriften: Arbeit mit Brecht.* Berlin: Henschel, 1973.

White, John J. "Brecht and Semiotics: Semiotics and Brecht." In *Bertolt Brecht: Centenary Essays*, edited by Steve Giles and Rodney Livingstone, 89–108. Amsterdam, Atlanta, GA: Rodopi, 1998.

———. *Bertolt Brecht's Dramatic Theory*. Rochester, NY: Camden House, 2004.

———. "Unpacking Mother Courage's Wagon: A Peircean Approach to De-Familiarization in the Plays of Bertolt Brecht." In *C. S. Peirce & les études sémiotiques*, edited by Harri Veivo. *Recherches sémiotiques* 24 (2004): 133–52.

White, John J., and Ann White. "Mi-en-leh's Progeny: Some of Brecht's Early Theatrical Parables and their Political Contexts." In *The Text and its Context: Studies in Modern German Literature and Society*, edited by Nigel Harris and Joanne Sayner, 327–37. Oxford: Peter Lang, 2008.

Wilkinson, James D. *The Intellectual Resistance in Europe*. Cambridge, MA, London: Harvard UP, 1981.

Willett, John. *The Theatre of Bertolt Brecht: A Study from Eight Aspects*. London: Eyre Methuen, 1959.

Wirth, Andrzej. "Über die stereometrische Struktur der Brechtschen Stücke." *Sinn und Form: Zweites Sonderheft Bertolt Brecht*, 346–87. Berlin: Rütten & Loening, 1957.

Wizisla, Erdmut. "Unmögliche Schlußszene: Typoskript zu *Furcht und Elend des III. Reiches* entdeckt." *The Brecht Yearbook* 22 (1997): 1–6.

———. *Walter Benjamin and Bertolt Brecht: The Story of a Friendship*. Translated by Christine Shuttleworth. London: Libris, 2009.

Wolfenstein, Alfred. "Sie sind wenige — Ihr seid viel!" *Das Wort* 2 (June 1937): 63–65.

Wyss, Monika. *Brecht in der Kritik: Rezensionen aller Brecht-Uraufführungen sowie ausgewählter deutsch- und fremdsprachiger Premieren*. Munich: Kindler, 1977.

Zelnhefer, Siegfried. "Die Reichsparteitage der NSDAP." In *Faszination und Gewalt: Zur politischen Ästhetik des Nationalsozialismus*, edited by Bernd Ogan and Wolfgang W. Weiß, 79–94. Nuremberg: W. Tümmels Verlag, 1992.

Ziemer, Gregor Athalwin. *Education of Death: The Making of the Nazi*. London, New York: Oxford UP, 1941.

Index